EUROPEAN BROADCASTING LAW AND POLICY

European broadcasting policy has attracted attention from many disciplines because it has dual nature: cultural and commercial. This book offers a detailed treatment of European broadcasting law, set against an overview of policy in this area. In this respect the authors identify tensions within the EU polity as regards the appropriate level, purpose and mechanism of broadcast regulation. Key influences are problems of competence, the impact of changing technology and the consequences of increasing commercialisation. Furthermore, the focus of the analysis is on the practical implications of the legal framework on viewers, and the authors distinguish both between citizen and consumer and between the passive and active viewer. The underlying question is the extent to which those most in need of protection by regulation, given the purpose of broadcasting, are adequately protected.

JACKIE HARRISON is Professor of Public Communication at the University of Sheffield. Her three principal research interests are the study of news; European communication, information and audio-visual policy and regulation; and public service broadcasting and communication. She is an established author, and has undertaken many funded research projects for the television industry.

LORNA WOODS is Professor in Law at the University of Essex. She is known for her work in the fields of EC law and, particularly, media regulation and freedom of expression. She is co-author of a best-selling textbook in the field of EU law and has written a monograph on the free movement of goods and services.

EUROPEAN BROADCASTING LAW AND POLICY

JACKIE HARRISON AND LORNA WOODS

CAMBRIDGE
UNIVERSITY PRESS

CAMBRIDGE UNIVERSITY PRESS

Cambridge, New York, Melbourne, Madrid, Cape Town, Singapore, São Paulo, Delhi

Cambridge University Press
The Edinburgh Building, Cambridge CB2 8RU, UK

Published in the United States of America by Cambridge University Press, New York

www.cambridge.org
Information on this title: www.cambridge.org/9780521613309

First published 2007

Printed in the United Kingdom at the University Press, Cambridge

A catalogue record for this book is available from the British Library

ISBN 978-0-521-84897-8 hardback
ISBN 978-0-521-61330-9 paperback

CONTENTS

In view of the economic and cultural importance of the broadcasting sector in the EU and its Member States, the appearance of this study of European broadcasting law and policy is timely. The content and delivery of broadcast media such as television are of central importance both for the viewer and for society more generally. Watching television remains a very important leisure activity for most people. Clearly technological innovations such as the internet have combined with the emergence of digital television to produce an increasingly diverse set of 'offerings' for consumers, but although internet broadcasting remains for the most part in its infancy, at the same time the introduction of interactive services on digital TV has led to a narrowing of the divide between what is 'online' and what is 'TV'.

Bringing together expertise from the fields of legal and journalism studies, the two authors fill an important gap in the available literature by providing an analysis and critique of the role of the European Union institutions in regulating broadcast media. They draw an important distinction in terms of seeing the viewer both as consumer and as citizen, ensuring that their analysis is not solely market-based, but is also informed by the difficult considerations which surround the future of public service broadcasting, alongside commercially driven offerings.

Part I of the book sets the scene, identifying the general issues which have shaped broadcasting policy in the EU context over the past thirty years, and highlighting the differing provisions of EU law which apply to different aspects of broadcasting policy in the context of a single market, including the regulation of ownership, content and delivery. Part II looks in more detail at some specific questions such as ownership, the broadcasting of sport and advertising, which touch upon some of the most controversial issues facing regulators at the present time. In their analysis, the authors seek to reflect the difficulty of combining both an economic viewpoint and a cultural viewpoint in relation to the social, political and economic centrality of broadcasting. As they note, this is complicated by the factors which shape an EU-level response in the area of broadcasting such as the complex and incomplete nature of the EU's competences in the field, as well as the problems of regulating such a swiftly changing technological domain.

The authors argue that broadcasting is best understood as something which can contribute to social, political and cultural purposes. They find that current broadcasting regulation at EU level takes a multi-faceted approach to the role of broadcasting in relation to these purposes. Regarding viewers as citizens requires a different nature of regulatory thinking than does regarding them as consumers in a market-place. The citizen's domain is characterised by universal availability (even if in practice not all citizens take up what is on offer), whereas in the consumer domain private interest considerations of ownership and access dominate: the ability and willingness to pay is crucial. The authors perceive a shift in European broadcasting towards commercial overstatement and public service understatement, and they call for attention to be paid not merely to the creation of European champions capable of competing globally, but also to diversity of suppliers and content.

This work makes a stimulating contribution to the interaction of European law and broadcasting policy, and its careful and critical assessments and warnings are a most welcome contribution to the analysis of the current and future developments in the European Union's competence in broadcasting. Accordingly, we welcome this work's appearance in the series Cambridge Studies in European Law and Policy.

Laurence Gormley
Jo Shaw

PREFACE

The origins of this book lie in a discussion we had one summer about the broadcasting of sporting events, and the way in which access to such broadcasting rights was affecting the broadcasting sector. During the course of this discussion, we realised that similar themes were arising as arose in other contexts, such as the quota provisions in the Television without Frontiers Directive. Further, although there were some detailed treatments of the tensions within the EU polity as regards the appropriate level, purpose and mechanisms of broadcast regulation, there were no similar treatments of the substance of broadcasting law and policy at the EU level. Moreover, the existing discussions of the area seemed rather abstract; we considered that in looking at the substance of the rules, we should consider the practical implications from the perspective of those arguably most influenced by those rules, that is, the viewers. This has meant that, in addition to providing a detailed and accurate picture of the law (admittedly one of the objectives of this book), we would analyse that law and underlying policy to identify the extent to which the needs of viewers are protected.

One of the initial questions for us related to the scope of this book. As we point out, there is no one thing within the Union as a single broadcasting policy. Instead, the broadcasting sector is affected by a number of instruments: some, such as the Television without Frontiers Directive, are clearly aimed at regulating broadcasting, but others, such as the four freedoms and competition policy, have a more incidental effect. Where, then, to draw the line, as a complete treatment of all potential relevant areas would have resulted in an encyclopaedia rather than a book? The Television without Frontiers Directive was an obvious starting-point, but we then decided to include those aspects of law which would have an impact on the range of content available to viewers. To this end, we included a review of the infrastructure regulation, media mergers and the state-aid rules relating to public service broadcasting. A full treatment of the communications package and of competition rules and the broadcasting sector in general lies outside the scope of this book. Likewise, although television standards are central to the reception of television services, and copyright issues may also affect content, they too have not been covered. The law is up to date as of 31 July 2006. We have, however, included in an appendix the main issues arising from the revised text of the proposal as agreed by the Common Position of the Council, 24 May 2007. Although at the time of correcting proofs the European Parliament had yet to vote on the revised proposal, it was not envisaged that there would be major changes to the proposal.

This book is long overdue. We would therefore like to thank the commissioning editor and series editor for their patience. We would also like to thank the many friends and colleagues, too numerous to mention individually, who have helped us, directly or indirectly, in the writing of this book. Particular thanks must go, in no specific order, to Neil Sellors, Chris Marsden, Steve Anderman, Christian Twigg-Flesner, Roger Brownsword and Sheldon Leader. Finally, this book is in memory of Henry, who inadvertently was responsible for starting this project off.

Jackie Harrison
Lorna Woods
September 2006

CASE LIST

Before the European Courts:

Alphabetical

Adoui and Cornaille, 115-6/81 [1982] ECR 1665

Alpine Investments BV v. *Minister van Financien*, C-384/93, [1995] ECR I-1141

AltmarkTrans GmbH v. *Nahverkehrsgesellschaft Altmark GmbH*, C-280/00, [2003] nyr, judgment 24 July 2003

Amministrazione delle Finanze dello Stato v. *Simmenthal SpA* (Simmenthal II), 106/77, [1978] ECR 629

Arbeitsgemeinschaft Rundfunkanstalten (ARD) v. *PRO Sieben Media AG*, C-6/98, [1999] ECR I-7599

Binon, 243/83, [1985] ECR 2015

Bond van Adverteerders v. *Netherlands*, 352/85,[1988] ECR 2085

Bosman, see *URBSA* v. *Bosman*

Bouchereau, 30/77, [1977] ECR 1999

Carpenter v. *Secretary of State for the Home Dept.*, C-60/00, [2002] ECR I-6279

Cassati, 203/80, [1981] ECR 2595

Centros v. *Erhvervs-og Selskabsstyrelsen*, C-212/97 [1999] ECR I-1459

Comité Central d'Entreprise de la Société Anonyme Vittel v. *Commission*, T-12/93, [1995] ECR II-1247

Commission v. *Belgium*, C-11/95, [1996] ECR I-4115

Commission v. *Belgium* (Cable Access), C-211/91, [1992] ECR I-6756

Commission v. *Council* (Titanium Dioxide Case), C-300/89, [1991] ECR I-2867

Commission v. *Italy*, 173/73, [1974] ECR 709

Commission v. *Netherlands* (Mediawet), C-353/89, [1991] ECR I-4069

Commission v. *UK*, C-222/94, [1996] ECR I-4025

Corbeau, C-320/91, [1993] ECR I-2533

RTL v. *Niedersächsische Landesmedienanstalt für privaten Rundfunk*, C-245/01, [2003] nyr, judgment 23 October 2003

Rutili v. *Ministre de l'Interiori*, 36/75, [1975] ECR 1219

Sacchi, 155/73, [1974] ECR 409

Sociedada Independente de Comunicação SA v. *Commission*, T-46/97, [2000] ECR II-2125

Stichting Collective Antennevoorziening Gouda v. *Commissariat voor de media*, C-288/89, [1991] ECR I-4007

Sverige 1000 AB v. *Norwegian Government*, E-8/97, [1998] 3 CMLR 318

The Queen (on the application of Bidar) v. *London Borough of Ealing, Secretary of State for Education and Skills*, C-209/03, [2005] nyr, judgment 15 March 2005

TV10 SA v. *Commissariaat voor de Media*, C-23/93, [1994] ECR I-4795

United Brands Co and United Brands Continental BV v. *Commission*, 27/76, [1978] ECR 207

URBSA v. *Bosman*, C-415/93, [1995] ECR I4921

Van Duyn, 41/74, [1974] ECR 1337

Vereniging Veronica Omroep Organisatie v. *Commissariaat voor de Media*, C-148/91, [1993] ECR I-487

Vlaams Gewest v. *Commission*, T-214/95, [1997] ECR II-717

VT4 Limited v. *Vlaamse Gemeenschap*, C-56/96, [1997] ECR I-3843

Wachauf v. *Germany*, 5/88, [1989] ECR 2609

Walrave and Koch, 36/74, [1974] ECR 140

Wouters v. *NoVA*, C-309/99, [2002] ECR I-1577

Numerical

26/62, *NV Algemene Transport- en expeditie Onderneming Van Gend en Loos* v. *Nederlandse Administratie der Belastingen*, [1963] ECR 1

56 & 58/64, *Etablissements Consten SA & Grundig-Verkaufs-GmbH* v. *Commission*, [1966] ECR 299

6/72, *Europemballage Corporation and Continental Can Co. Inc.* v. *Commission*, [1973] ECR 215

155/73, *Sacchi*, [1974] ECR 409

173/73, *Commission* v. *Italy*, [1974] ECR 709

33/74, *JHM Van Binsbergen* v. *Bestuur van de Bedrijfsvereiging voor de Metaalnijverheid*, [1974] ECR 1299

36/74, *Walrave and Koch*, [1974] ECR 140

41/74, *Van Duyn*, [1974] ECR 1337

36/75, *Rutili* v. *Ministre de l'intérieur*, [1975] ECR 1219

European Court of Human Rights

Cases before the National Courts

R. v. *Independent Television Commission*, ex parte *TV Danmark 1 Ltd*
[2001] UKHL 42

Commission Decisions

ABC/Générale des Eaux/Canal+/WH Smith Commission Decision, Case
IV/M.110 OJ [1991] C 244.

Aerospatiale/Alenia/de Havilland Commission Decision, 91/619/EC, Case
IV/M53, OJ [1991] L 334/42.

AOL/Time Warner Commission Decision, 2001/718/EC, Case IV/M1845,
OJ [2001] L 268/28.

Apollo/JPMorgan/Primacom Commission Decision, Case COMP/
M.3355, 15 June 2004.

BBC Digital Curriculum Commission Decision, N 37/2003 OJ [2003] C
271/47.

BBC Licence Fee Commission Decision, Case NN 63/01 OJ [2003] C 23.

BBC News 24 Commission Decision NN 88/98 OJ [2000] C 78.

Belgium (French speaking community) Commission Decision, N 548/2001,
OJ [2002] C 150/7.

Bertelsmann/CLT Commission Decision, M.779, 7 October 1996.

Bertelsmann/Kirch/Premiere Commission Decision, Case IV/M.993 OJ
[1999] L 53/1.

BiB/Open Commission Decision, OJ [1999] L 312/1.

BSkyB/Kirch Pay TV Commission Decision, COMP/JV.37, 21 March 2000.

Bundesliga Commission Decision, COMP/C.2–37.214, 19 January 2005.

CECED Commission Decision, Case IV. F. 1/36-718 OJ [2000] 187/17.

CLT/Disney/SuperRTL Commission Decision, Case IV/M.566, 17 May,
1997.

CVC/SLEC Commission Decision, COMP/M.4066, unreported, 20
March 2006.

Denmark/TV2 Commission Decision, C2/2003 (ex NN 22/02) C(2004)
1814, final.

Deutsche Telecom/BetaResearch Commission Decision, OJ [1999] L 53/3.

EBU *Eurovision*, Commission Case IV/32.150 OJ [2000] L 151/18.

English Football Premier League (FAPL) Commission Decision, COMP/
38.173 and 38.453 C(2006)868 final.

English Football Premier League (FAPL) Commission Decision, COMP/
38.173 and 38.453 Article 19(3), OJ [2004] C 115/02.

Eurofix-Bauco, Commission Decision, OJ [1988] L 65/19.

Football World Cup Commission Decision, IV/36.888, OJ [2000] L 5/55.

France/SPF Commission Decision, C(2002) 2593 final, N 797/2001 OJ [2003] C 71/3.

French international news channel Commission Decision, N 54/2005 OJ [2005] C 256/25.

Funding for RTP Commission Decision, NN 31/2006 OJ [2006] C 222/4.

General Electric/Honeywell Commission Decision, COMP/M.2220.

Kinderkanal and Phoenix Commission Decision, NN 70/98 OJ [1999] C 238/03.

Microsoft Commission Decision, COMP/C-3/37.792, Commission Decision, C(2004) 900 final.

MSG Media Service Commission Decision, 94/922/EC, Case IV/M.469 OJ [1994] L 364/1.

NC/Canal Plus/CDPQ/Bank America Commission Decision, Case IV/M.1327, OJ [1999] C 233/21.

NewsCorp/Telepiu Commission Decision, COMP/M.2876 2 April 2003.

Ad hoc measures to Dutch public broadcasters and NOS and NOB, Commission Decision C2/04 (ex NN 170/03) OJ [2004] C 61/8.

Nordic Satellite Distribution Commission Decision, 96/177/EC, Case IV/M.490 OJ [1996] L 53/20.

Financing of the Portuguese Public Television, Commission Decision, NN 141/95 OJ [1997] C 67.

Funding for RTP, Commission Decision, NN 31/2006.

RTL/Veronica/Endemol Commission Decision, OJ [1996] L 134/32.

Screensport/EBU Commission Decision, Case IV/32.524 OJ [1991] L 63.

Société française de production Commission Decision, 97/238/EC OJ [1995] L 95/19.

Société française de production Commission Decision, 98/466/EC OJ [1998] L 205/68.

Telenor/Canal+/Canal Digital Commission Decision, COMP/C.2-38.287, 29 December 2003.

Telia/Telenor Commission Decision, Case IV/M.1439 OJ [2001] L 40/1.

TPS Commission Decision, 1999/242/EC, Case IV/36.237.

UEFA Commission Decision, COMP/C.2-37.398 OJ [2003] L 291/25.

UGC/Noos Commission Decision, COMP/M.3411, 17 May 2004.

Vivendio/Canal plus/Seagram Commission Decision, COMP/M.2050.

Vodafone/Vivendi/Canal+ Commission Decision, COMP/JV 48, 20th July 2002.

Legislation

European Legislation

Directives

Council Directive 2002/21/EC Framework Directive OJ [2002] L 108.
Council Directive 2002/20/EC Authorisation Directive OJ [2002] L 108.
Council Directive 2002/19/EC Access Directive OJ [2002] L 108.
Council Directive 2002/22/EC Universal Service Directive OJ [2002] L 108.
Council Directive 2002/58/EC Data Protection and Electronic Communications Directive, OJ [2002] L 108.
Council Decision 676/2002/EC Radio Spectrum Decision, OJ [2002] L 108.
Council Directive 89/552/EEC on the co-ordination of certain provisions laid down by law, regulation or administrative action in Member States concerning the pursuit of television broadcasting activities, OJ [1989] L298/23, as amended by Directive 97/36/EC OJ [1997] L 202/30.
Council Directive 90/387/EEC on the establishment of the internal market for telecommunications services through the implementation of open network provision, OJ [1990] L 192/1.

Decisions

Decision 276/1999 on the Safer Internet Action Plan OJ [1999] L 33/1
Decision 1151/2003 amending Decision 276/1999 OJ [2003] L 462/1

National Legislation

Communications Act 2003 (c. 21) (London: HMSO, 2003).

PART I

1

Introduction

The broadcasting sector in the European Union (the Union) is in a state of flux. Rapid technological development and increasing commercialisation have provided new challenges for regulators and policymakers, who seek to harness the potential of new technology to provide a regulatory environment that is for the good of everyone. Despite extensive consultation and reviews of the regulatory framework in the Union over the last decade or so, a failure to consider directly the broadcasting environment from the perspective of all viewers has created a regulatory framework in which a full range of broadcasting services is not universally provided. The underlying assumption of policymakers is that, in a properly functioning broadcasting environment, industry will thrive economically, develop new technology and new services and consequently cater for all viewers. The expectation is that the resulting environment will also create greater viewer choice and broadcasting will continue (somehow) to fulfil its public service remit, particularly its socio-cultural and democratic function. Yet, in so far as viewers are considered, it is as consumers of broadcast services and not as citizens. This approach, we argue, fails to represent the citizen viewer and neglects the valuable attributes of broadcasting that go beyond purely economic concerns.

The history of broadcasting in the Union began at national level with governments' various attempts either to monopolise or control it.[1] From the start, broadcasting has attracted a high degree of governmental involvement because of its perceived power to influence those who listened to radio or watched television. As television became established post-war,

[1] Television broadcasting was relatively slowly established in the Union, but by the end of the 1960s all member states of what was then the European Economic Community had at least one television station. The regulation of television built upon the structures established for radio, but because of the high costs of television production, spectrum scarcity and concerns about the political and ideological potential of television, member states deemed it necessary to establish public monopolies in order to ensure that the service worked for the national public good. See D. Krebber, *Europeanisation of Regulatory Television Policy: The Decision-making Process of the Television Without Frontiers Directive from 1989 and 1997* (Baden-Baden: Nomos Verlagsgesellschaft, 2002), p. 39.

public and private broadcasting emerged and audiences were regarded as either citizens in need of support or consumers in need of entertainment (sometimes both). Broadcasting policy is either regarded as something that operates in the interest of public service, operates in the interest of economic freedom or attempts to reconcile both. In essence, two arguments proceed in parallel: those based in non-economic concerns; and those based on economic concerns.

The Union's policy initiatives towards broadcasting were, and still are, regarded as a means to encourage and foster, depending on your point of view, national identity, a common Union cultural heritage or commercial freedom for a valuable Union-based market. National broadcasters were expected to reflect their respective national cultural heritages. Citizens were able to share in a minimal but 'common knowledge'.[2] The assumption that broadcasting has an impact, however ill-defined and insubstantial, forms the basis for the view that broadcasting should serve social, cultural and political purposes, beyond commercial objectives.[3] Parallel to these non-economic concerns was the issue of the evolving commercial identity of broadcasting, notably the introduction and expansion of the private sector, which began to coexist with public broadcasters. Of course, the philosophy of the two sectors is different. Private sector broadcasters do not necessarily have the public good as their primary purpose, whilst public sector broadcasters are often subject to public interest obligations. We will show how this bifurcated world constantly re-emerges in all aspects of Union broadcasting policy. Given the distinctions between the two types of broadcasting, and their respective interests, we are faced with the following problems: to what extent can we realistically expect private sector broadcasters to produce programming that serves non-economic purposes, therefore fulfilling the function of a public service broadcaster? Conversely, to what extent can we expect and do we want to expect public service broadcasters to provide commercial services? The answers to these questions need to be considered in the context of a highly competitive

---

[2] A. Graham, 'Broadcasting Policy in the Multimedia Age', in A. Graham, C. Kobaldt, S. Hogg, B. Robinson, D. Currie, M. Siner, G. Mather, J. Le Grand, B. New and I. Corfield (eds.), *Public Purposes in Broadcasting* (Luton: University of Luton Press, 1999), pp. 17–46, p. 19.

[3] These effects have generated what economists call externalities. Externalities arise 'once we suppose, as both common sense and research suggests (a) that television has some influence upon the lifestyles, habits, interests, etc, of those who watch it and (b) that these habits and interests have implications for those around us . . . even just the belief that television affects behaviour is sufficient for externalities to exist'; see Graham, 'Broadcasting Policy in the Multimedia Age', in Graham *et al.*, *Public Purposes in Broadcasting*, p. 26.

international environment. In short, the history of broadcasting in the Union centres on the interrelationship between commercial imperatives and a wide range of non-trade values.

Increased commercialisation, as a result of deregulation, liberalisation and privatisation policies; an increased number of players in the market, many of which are private sector entities; and more television channels, have together challenged existing assumptions about the Union's broadcasting environment and viewers' relationship to it, as well as the appropriate level and style of regulation. Economic pressures on broadcasters, driven by channel expansion, have led, across the Union, to increased competition for viewers. This has, in turn, had an impact on broadcasting content and formats, with successful formats and popular content tending to dominate programme schedules, arguably reducing choice and diversity of content available to viewers. Against this background, policymakers in the Union are under pressure to remove regulatory constraints from broadcasters in a commercialised environment so as to reduce their costs, which could also have an adverse impact on the quality and reach of content available to viewers.

The introduction of different distribution platforms and the subsequent growth of digital channels also have consequences for the level of access to content enjoyed by different viewers. Even if a diverse range of content were made available via this growth, the development of pay TV[4] means that some viewers cannot afford to access certain types of content, usually what is called premium content: film and sport. The trajectory towards pay TV is likely to continue and prove far-reaching, with television content increasingly being seen as a commodity that must, in one form or another, be paid for.[5] This is part of a more general trend in which content (however defined: entertainment, education or information) is seen, by transnational corporations, as a valuable commercial asset which may legitimately be restricted to those able and prepared to pay for it. At the same time, commercially driven technological developments are raising barriers to access to a diverse range of content and, increasingly, interactive television applications. This trend towards the reduction of free access is further exacerbated because it is no longer just films and sport that fuel pay TV, but the use of content archives, interactive dating,

---

[4] Pay TV refers to digital television services for which a viewer must pay a monthly subscription to a pay TV supplier.

[5] It is arguable that television was never really free, given the fact that public service broadcasters are often funded by licence fee or other form of tax. None the less they were free at point of access and the fee was not determined by reference to what one watches.

games and betting and, more recently, high-cost specially commissioned programmes and series.

While some viewers currently choose to remain in a passive linear, analogue, free-to-air environment, their freedom to do so will diminish and in some member states be short-lived. Across the Union, governments are preparing to stop transmitting analogue signals and to switch over to digital transmission. Although some digital television will be broadcast free to air, such as digital terrestrial television (DTT) in the UK (known as 'Freeview'), it is by no means certain that this will be the general pattern across the Union. Even if it were, free-to-air transmissions will increasingly introduce the viewer to newer technology, such as non-linear interactive television and the options to 'top up' their free-to-air viewing with subscriptions to further channels and services. Commercial services will certainly seek to benefit from anything that might be regarded as a meagre public service digital provision, as we have seen in the UK with top-up TV providers[6] doing so on the back of 'Freeview'.

These developments illustrate a trend in the Union broadcasting market, towards the commodification of information and the increasing digitalisation of content. Given this, two assumptions are prevalent. First, a consumerist approach is the best way to organise the television market. Secondly, free-to-air television is insufficient in either the amount of programming hours of particular types of programming, or in the variety of genres provided, and does not fully serve the preferences of viewers. These assumptions return us to the questions we raised earlier. Is the commercial sector sufficient for all purposes, or has the public sector a unique role to play? A policy environment that accepts the assumption about the necessity of a consumerist approach and the insufficiency of free-to-air television is likely to create a digital divide. This is nothing other than a payment divide, with basic subscription charges and additional service charges dividing up between them the content to which a viewer can have access. Against this background, regulation seeks to balance commercial interests and technical considerations[7] with the preferences of the viewer.

Our argument is straightforward. It is that, given the significance of broadcasting to the viewer and society, the viewing experience should be at the centre of policymaking, regulation and legislation. We are not

---

[6] See for example www.topuptv.com/

[7] There is some call for a distinction in regulation depending on whether the content accessed is broadcast traditionally or provided on demand. This push–pull distinction is very important in current regulation, indeed it could be said currently to define the way in which the viewer is perceived in regulatory terms.

suggesting that this should be the only concern, rather that it should be a central concern. The task of finding the 'right' balance is difficult and compounded by the fact that viewing experiences are diverse and the viewers' interests perceived to be in need of protection are not homogeneous. Regulation makes assumptions about the capacities of viewers to access and use technology and broadcasting services. We question the assumptions that geographical and financial barriers are not serious constraints to access and that the level of assumed competence of the viewer in using technology to create an individualised viewing experience. Within broadcasting policy, the viewer can be regarded as either a market-based consumer, or as a citizen with rights of access to certain content. Following on from this we propose that the viewing experience is shaped by whether regulation sees the viewer as a citizen or a consumer. This distinction remains central to our analysis of Union broadcasting policy. A secondary issue, linked to this distinction, is that of the expectations about how viewers engage with technology, which we refer to as the distinction between active viewing in a non-linear broadcasting environment, and passive viewing in a linear broadcasting environment (see table 1).

While we avoid engaging in audience psychology, it is nevertheless the case that the Union does seem to rely upon assumptions about how people will behave. These assumptions are not clearly elaborated; we analyse them in terms of the distinction between active and passive viewers (see table 1). For us the terms active and passive viewer make explicit what is often hidden within Union broadcasting thinking. Consequently they will be considered, in what follows, under our primary distinction, consumer viewers and citizen viewers and can be represented diagrammatically as shown overleaf.

In our opinion the viewing experience is quintessentially different when using the distinction between consumer and citizen. The consumer resides in the commercial domain. This is market-based and economically determined, viewers are individualistic, and viewers and broadcasters both regard content, in all forms, as capable of being purchased and owned. Information is not necessarily a public resource to be disseminated on behalf of the public good, but is private property to be exploited for financial gain. The citizen resides in the public domain and regards particular types of content as a social and civic asset. Such content should be available to all and enjoyed communally. Communication infrastructures are seen as adding to the cultural fabric of collective identity and belonging. The citizen requires that certain civic functions are

Table 1. *The scope of regulatory considerations regarding the viewing experience*

Commercial Domain	Viewing Experience	Public Service Domain
ACTIVE VIEWING EXPERIENCE (PPV, subscription, non-linear)	PERSONALISED SCHEDULES AND INTERACTIVE SERVICES	ACTIVE VIEWING EXPERIENCE (FTA, wide range of PSB services, non-linear)
CONSUMERS		CITIZENS
PASSIVE VIEWING EXPERIENCE (FTA, commercial, linear)	RELIANCE ON LINEAR SCHEDULING	PASSIVE VIEWING EXPERIENCE (FTA, limited range of PSB services, linear)
INDIVIDUALISTIC INFORMATION AS A COMMODITY		COMMUNAL INFORMATION SEEN AS PART OF PUBLIC SPHERE AND CULTURAL HERITAGE

Key to abbreviations in table, above:

PPV – pay-per-view
FTA – free-to-air
PSB – public service broadcasting

fulfilled by broadcasters and, most importantly, believes that such services should not be subject to payment barriers. Naturally enough, the absolute nature of this distinction is heuristic. Many of us are both consumer and citizen. Thus, although the two categories are easily characterised as distinct, we also recognise that that distinction is, in reality, fluid. Nevertheless, our analysis of broadcasting requires the distinction to be maintained so that we can achieve a degree of clarity over what Union policymakers and regulators mean when discussing and deciding broadcasting policy.

The distinction between citizens and consumers also relates to the nature of the content that should be available to satisfy their respective viewing preferences. As regards citizens, content reach reflects programming which supports particular social, civil and political values, and which tends to emphasise the positive role of broadcasting in supporting democratic activity and in fostering a public sphere. Thus, we would expect to see a wide spectrum of programming covering different subject-matters via a range of genres, importantly news, current affairs, documentaries, educational programmes and, it has been argued, sport.[8] Since the 'invention' of modern sport in the late nineteenth century, sport has been strongly associated with the inclusive and exclusive construction of identity and difference. Since the development of modern sport occurred at the same time as a wave of nation-building, it has also always been particularly associated with nationalism. As we will see in chapter 2, one of the roles ascribed to public service broadcasting (PSB) is that of fostering national identity and social cohesion. Accepting this, broadcast sport has an important part to play in building a citizen's sense of identity and belonging. The key aspect of citizens' programming is the fact that it is universally available and free to air.

Quite different from this is the content diet of the consumer. No content type (or genre) is, in principle, excluded from their diets, although particular groups of consumers tend to focus on a narrower range of programmes, reflecting pre-existing interests and consumption patterns. While the content range itself may appear to be wide, from guns to bikes to sport and so on, it is usually gathered around core interests. A caricature of this viewing type is that a consumer watches the same thing from different sources. This can be contrasted with a citizen who watches varied things from the same source.

The factors affecting the viewers' engagement with content, that is whether the experience is active or passive, comprise two categories: personal factors; and environmental factors. Personal factors relate to the viewers' own skills and abilities in navigating the choices available (media literacy) and mastering the technology needed to make those choices.[9] Environmental factors are those that arise from the broadcasting sector. Increased commercialisation has brought with it subscription and pay-per-view TV and some content types have become the virtually exclusive preserve of pay TV. To receive such content, a viewer needs to be able to pay for it and not everybody can afford to do so. Thus, a viewer might

---

[8] M. Roche and J. Harrison, 'Cultural Europeanisation through Regulation?: The case of media-sport in the EU', unpublished paper presented at the *International Association for Media and Communication Conference*, Media Sport Working Group, Barcelona, July 2002, p. 16.

[9] See Ofcom Special Report, *Consumer Engagement with Digital Communication Services*. An attitudinal segmentation model was developed to provide understanding of the way UK consumers engage with digital communication services. Five consumer segments were identified: enthusiasts, functionalists, economisers, abstainers and resisters. Available at www.ofcom/org.uk/research/cm/consumer_engagement/, p. 3.

have the personal capacity to be active, but be frustrated in so doing by environmental factors.

Consumers seeking an active viewing experience have to be able to pay for content and correspondingly arrange their viewing around a set of options that reflect their particular desired content reach and their willingness to pay. Such viewers assemble their own viewer package from a combination of free to air, subscription channels and pay per view, and construct their own particular programme schedule.[10] A caricature of such a consumer is that they are unconcerned that others cannot enjoy the same privileges and their viewing choices are based entirely on a selfish and individualised desire to maximise their own enjoyment. Their viewing choices could be characterised as being ones that could reinforce already held preferences and prejudices, and are located entirely in the commercial domain. Theoretically, such viewers may have a disregard for the social and cultural value of broadcasting and could choose endlessly to watch programming that is deemed to be 'unsuitable' or may be harmful.

Citizens who actively control their viewing experience will expect the content to be available to them, and from which they choose what to watch, to reflect the values and aspirations of their citizenship boundaries. This citizen seeking an active viewing experience assumes that not only are certain types of content available but also that access to that content is guaranteed. Such content is traditionally found, though today by no means exclusively, in free-to-air PSB, which is often supported by the state.[11] What is common to these two types of active viewing experience is that the viewers are media literate and able to locate the type of content they want. The bewildering world of multi-channels, different distribution networks and payment options is understood and,

[10] For this type of consumer, content can be chosen eclectically and may include a reality TV programme with programmes from a pay-per-view culture channel in the same package. Some programming which arguably serves elements of the public service remit (i.e. educates and informs the audience) is now only available on a pay-per-view or subscription basis. Channels, such as Artsworld shown in the UK, initially required an additional payment per month, but now is available as part of a bundle of other channels which are acquired when a subscription is paid. Television news is still protected and shown on a free-to-air basis (although the number of news sources available is restricted according to the type of technology the viewer purchases). In a multi-channel pay-TV environment the further privatisation of certain types of information seems inevitable. The area of greatest concern to date has been in relation to the privatisation of particular popular sporting events (see ch. 12).

[11] State support can take a variety of forms from cash subsidies, tax breaks, through to access to frequencies. State support does not necessarily imply a direct state control of content.

subject to overcoming any environmental constraints, is successfully navigated.

The phrase passive consumer requires clarification. What we mean by the phrase is the viewing experience of the traditional linear free-to-air commercial television viewer who was targeted by advertising and who, it was hoped, would respond by consuming what was advertised. The content range reflects a tendency towards entertainment rather than a diverse range of programming. This viewer is a so-called couch potato. What we do not mean are those consumers who wish to purchase a service but are constrained by environmental factors, for example, willingness and ability to pay, or reception difficulty. While clearly illustrating the difficulties created by considering television content to be purely a commodity, here the best one can say of such viewers is that they are rendered inactive, over-spend or are left frustrated in their viewing choices.

The passive citizen viewer also represents a more traditional figure. Instead of customised packages, citizen passivity is based on a linear viewing experience with content selected from a very limited range of channels, usually provided free to air, traditionally by PSB.[12] Essentially, the passive citizen viewer is in the hands of the scheduler, and consequently, the limited channel options represent a constructed viewer content reach. Obviously such limitations and constructions vary across the Union and for a variety of historical and political reasons. However, the point remains that passive citizens have traditionally relied on PSB content, but this is precisely the sort of content, with its formal scheduling, that is being undermined by multi-channel, niche broadcasting. The increasing commodification of information has also meant that the variety of content available for universal distribution is constantly being reduced, thus forcing citizen viewers into ever more commercial considerations. As such, this form of passivity is becoming scarcer.[13] In reality, such viewing looks irredentist, harking back to simpler times. The drift from this type of experience to a consumerist-driven environment is palpable and,

---

[12] The experience of Freeview in the UK is fascinating from this point of view. Initially offered as a free-to-air alternative to the pay TV channels provided by BSkyB, a subscription payment now allows for further channels to be added as top-ups, indicating that this type of viewing cannot escape from commercial options.

[13] The British public service broadcaster, the BBC, is restructuring its production and commissioning of content to allow '360-degree commissioning' of all content to be shown on all platforms. The BBC's vision is that, although linear channels have several more years of life (in the US, the prognosis for such channels is that they have only five more years of life), the future of broadcasting must be focused on on-demand media as audiences move to use other types of media platforms to access content (L. Rouse, 'The BBC's Vision Thing', Broadcast, 28 July 2006, 15).

without counter measures, inexorable. The issue of whether content is available in the public domain or the commercial domain ultimately decides the viewing experience.

In toto, table 1 deals with the parameters of possible viewing experience that exist in both the linear and non-linear broadcasting environment. These quadrants of viewing experience represent no more than idealised possibilities and, as such, are the extremes of viewing experiences which, we argue, any regulatory policy should take into account. We use these types of viewing experience throughout the book as the extent of the viewing options available to both the Union consumer and citizen. Our concern is that Union broadcasting regulation, informed by broadcasting policy, while claiming to take into account the needs of the viewers, does not clearly recognise the distinction between consumers and citizens, nor take into account the fact that, for some, the viewing experience is necessarily passive. Union broadcasting regulation tends towards a perception of the viewer that conflicts least with commercial interests, that is an active consumer, arguably under-protecting those most in need of regulatory intervention.[14] It is our view that regulators should remember passive citizens, who want to be able to watch a reasonably wide range of quality programmes without either having to pay for additional services and engage with new technology to find appropriate programming,[15] or being forced to settle for increasingly emiserated public service television supplied free-to-air.

It could, of course, be argued that increased deregulation, facilitating greater industry freedom, is not problematic, a view we reject for a number of linked reasons. In general terms, there may be no co-ordination of provision across different broadcasters serving a common area. In such a scenario each broadcaster makes its decisions in the light of its own interests and obligations, without necessarily incorporating any reference to the overall provision of broadcasting services across a particular area, and, clearly, without reference to the possible viewing experience of anyone other than active consumers.[16] Two things are wrong with this. First, that such content as is provided is exclusive of non-economic

---

[14] Similarities can be found with criticisms of consumer policy: see e.g. G. Howells and T. Wilhelmsson, *EC Consumer Law* (Aldershot: Ashgate, 1997), p. 18.

[15] Ofcom, *Digital Switchover: An Audit of Viewers' Priorities.* Ofcom notes that although switchover will pose relatively few challenges for some, other viewers may need help to ensure that they know what they need to do, when they need to do it and the options open to them (available on the Ofcom website), p. 1.

[16] While active consumers are in the most favoured position, they are still susceptible to Henry Ford's version of consumerism, namely, you can have any colour so long as it's black.

calculations as to its merit. Secondly, there is the risk that industry members congregate to provide services in the middle ground, whether this be a result of cartel-type thinking, playing it safe, satisfying advertisers' needs for a significant audience share or merely (and often) a lack of imagination. While consumers' interests in having choices which they can pay for are taken into account (though even here there are some imposed limits to choice), it is not the case that such interests necessarily coincide with those of citizens. Indeed, as we shall show, most arguments to the contrary fail to deal with concerns of universality, quality and diversity of content.

A reliance on the market may provide choice, but it is less clear about the substance of that choice and the persons to whom that choice is really available. Given the inherently majoritarian bias, or bias towards those who can pay, of a market-based model, the difference between a consumer-based model and that based on citizens' interests is that the former 'emphasizes the satisfaction of aggregated individual desires, the other improvement in quality of collective civic participation and information . . .'.[17] Individual choices aggregated do not necessarily lead to the best collective results, nor do they take into account the fact that not all will be able to afford to pay. Freedom of choice here is rendered a formal not a substantive freedom. As we shall see in chapter 7, there are specific problems relating to the way competition policy goals and broadcasting policy goals, especially goals focusing on issues such as freedom of speech, diversity and plurality, interrelate. Thus, any approach which only provides an increased level of formal freedom is only providing increased economic choices for those select groups who can afford to pay for the choices they wish to make. This 'cash limit' will, given the finite resources of the content market, limit the scope of others to choose, either because they cannot match market prices or because they are unwilling to pay. In either case, limits and restrictions to choice are set by price and not wider (cultural) concerns. Choices based on satisfying the preferences of those who are willing and able to pay also limits the choices of other groups, including future viewers who might have different preferences from contemporary viewers.

As we shall argue, the problems within the regulatory framework arise from a failure by policymakers to focus directly on the diversity of the viewing experience itself; to favour the active consumer and play down or ignore the particular difficulties faced by both the active and passive

---

[17] H. Shelanski, 'The Policy Limits of Markets: Antitrust Law as Mass Media Regulation', *Law and Economics Workshop*, University of California, Berkeley, Paper 7, 2003, p. 7.

citizen viewer. In particular, the Union's broadcasting policy and law have, in part, been a by-product of a range of factors, both direct and indirect, which have caused a drift towards a broadcasting framework which assumes that the viewing experience is active and takes place in the commercial domain. We identify three main factors which account for this drift: technological changes; increased commercialisation of the broadcasting sector; and the conflicting policies and competences within the Union. The first two originate from the general broadcasting environment, that is, they are external; the latter is clearly specific to the Union.

As regards the first external factor, the impact of technological change on the broadcasting environment and on the viewer is enormous and difficult to unravel, let alone anticipate. We have already suggested that technological change affects both the broadcasting environment and the viewer in dramatic ways. The issue here is the type of regulatory response to such change that is appropriate. The question is whether regulation can, or should, be replaced by technology itself and reliance on the viewers' use of that technology (for example, via V-chips, electronic programme guides (EPGs) and encryption technologies); or whether technological developments necessitate specific regulatory responses. The current policy drift is towards the former view and is one which favours the active viewer who is both media literate and a technophile.

The second external factor relates to the increased commercialisation of the broadcast environment. Here we see an interconnection between commercialisation and liberalisation of markets, and the increased number of channels and platforms consequent on technological developments. In this context, choice and the viewers' ability to access and manage choice are again crucial and reflect the Union's general view about consumer choice. It assumes apparent increased choice in the number of products is good, without there being any consideration of quality of the products, or the consumers' ability to access them. As well as exacerbating the passive/active distinction, this approach may also influence the diversity of programming available, which also has repercussions for the public domain. Another aspect of the commercialisation of the broadcasting sector manifests itself in the strength of the private sector, which increasingly constitutes large transnational conglomerates. These transnational companies have the financial resources to lobby political institutions and use the court system, bringing expensive litigation to challenge the actions both of member states and the Union institutions that do not suit the industry's commercial interests, with the result that the Union broadcasting world is forever subject to dispute over what is regarded by the industry as fair or unfair.

As for our third factor, within the Union, difficulties arise from the different fields of competence and the varying types of action the Union may take. Essentially, the problem with competence can be seen in two ways: first, the power struggle between member states and the Union; and secondly, the tension between trade and non-trade values. The stronger Union competence lies in the commercial context. Cultural policy, at least in its initial phase, was developed as exceptions to normal trade policy. Member states retain the power to determine their respective regulatory regimes, thus influencing the content available to the viewer, but they can only do so in so far as such regimes are compatible with the free-trade rules contained in the EC Treaty. The institutions, particularly the European Court of Justice (ECJ), have recognised that diversity, freedom of expression and the protection of culture are, in principle, worthy of protection, provided the measures to do so do not have a disproportion-ately adverse effect on trade. In sum, whereas member states might look to viewer protection, the Union seems to look to trade interests. The difficul-ties arising from this split are compounded by the fact that public service broadcasters, with their social, cultural and political remits, are national in nature. It is the private operators that have seen the opportunities of transnational broadcasting, even if it is just to evade national regulatory systems.[18] The Television without Frontiers Directive[19] (TWFD) has had the effect of supporting this type of behaviour, whilst providing limited support for social and cultural purposes in broadcasting. This may be seen as a result of the limitations on Union competence in the cultural field. In prioritising trade values, the system is geared towards content that satisfies the consumer rather than the citizen.

Our concerns for both the citizen and the consumer, as they are rep-resented in broadcasting policy regulation and law, will be addressed through these three factors, and their interrelationship with the view-ing experience in its different manifestations within the broadcasting environment. In chapter 2 we address the perceived value and functions

---

[18] This practice is sometimes called regulatory arbitrage or forum shopping: C. Marsden, 'Introduction: Information and Communications Technologies, Globalisation and Regu-lation', in C. Marsden (ed.), *Regulating the Global Information Society* (London: Routledge, 2000), pp. 19–21.

[19] Council Directive 89/552/EEC of 3 October on the co-ordination of certain provisions laid down by law, regulation or administrative action in member states concerning the pursuit of television broadcasting activities OJ [1989] L298/23, as amended by Directive 97/36/EC OJ [1997] L 202/30.

of broadcasting at a theoretical level. In chapter 3 we look in detail at the two external factors of technological change and the increased commercialisation of the broadcasting sector. In chapter 4 we look at the internal factor concerning conflicting policies and competences within the Union. Chapter 5 provides an overview and analysis of Union broadcasting policy, which is discussed, in accordance with our three themes established by the preceding chapters. Combined, these chapters form part 1 of the book and provide the analytic backdrop against which we look in more detail at particular aspects of the regulatory framework for broadcasting in part 2.

Given the significance of access issues to the distinction between consumers' and citizens' viewing requirements, we consider in chapter 6 the regulation of infrastructure under the Communications Package.[20] We then outline the decisions of the Commission and the European courts (ECJ and Court of First Instance) in relation to merger policy in chapter 7. These cases affect the power of member states to regulate their national broadcasting systems. With the vertically integrated nature of the international media environment, mergers potentially have an impact throughout the distribution chain, affecting both content and access to infrastructure. Not only may mergers limit plurality of content but they may also limit access to that content, adversely affecting the viewing experience. Chapters 8–12 consider the TWFD, looking first at negative regulation and then positive regulation. Even within the limitations imposed by negative regulation in TWFD there are weaknesses arising out of the patchwork regulatory approach and the principle of regulation by the member state of establishment (the 'home country' principle). The 'home country' principle allows a 'race to the bottom' in terms of regulatory standards (chapter 8), as broadcasters seek the lightest regulatory regime. In this sense, viewers might not be able to rely on the regulatory enforcement system in the country of reception. This tendency to require viewers to be self-reliant (or active) is reinforced by the tendency to self- or co-regulation, as well as other soft law measures, and the use of technology in place of law, especially in terms of controlling potentially harmful content. This may be the result of industry lobbying; certainly the need to take industry views into account in a changing technological environment

---

[20] Council Directive 2002/21/EC Framework Directive; Directive 2002/20/EC Authorisation Directive; Directive 2002/19/EC Access Directive; Directive 2002/22/EC Universal Service Directive and Directive 2002/58/EC Data Protection and Electronic Communications Directive OJ [2002] L 108. There is also a decision on Radio Spectrum: Decision 676/2002/EC OJ [2002] L 108.

can be seen in the context of the frequency of advertising rules (chapter 9). We consider content regulation (including the content of advertising) in two successive chapters, one dealing with negative rules (chapter 10), the second (chapter 11) dealing with positive obligations, notably quotas. A second type of positive rule is found in the listed-events chapter (chapter 12). One might anticipate that, whereas both citizenship- and consumer-based values require negative regulation to provide for their protection, citizenship values require additionally positive obligations to be imposed on broadcasters. The effectiveness of such positive obligations is questionable. Chapter 11 illustrates the difficulty of seeking to protect culture in a trade-based instrument. Additionally problems arise, particularly for the citizen, with the privatisation of certain types of information, such as sporting events (chapter 12). An alternative solution is to locate the obligation to provide universal access to appropriate content within the remit of PSB. In chapter 13 we examine state aid and the constraints placed upon member states and their ability to support public service broadcasting (PSB).

The book concludes with an assessment of the Union broadcasting policy including the recent review of the TWFD and, to a much lesser extent, the Communications Package. Although the review of TWFD, resulting in a draft second amending directive (DSAD), has provided the opportunity to consider the impact of technological development on the regulatory structure, it is our view that the TWFD review is in some respects insufficient. As we suggest in the appendix dealing with the revised proposed for DSAD as agreed by the Common Position of the Council, there have been no substantial improvements in this regard. Crucially, the proposed directive fails to consider the cultural values of broadcasting, and how diversity and pluralism might be protected, despite considering these issues during the review process. In so doing, it overlooks the needs of those whom broadcast regulation might be expected to protect, namely the citizen viewer.

2

The value and functions of the broadcast media: protecting the citizen viewer

Introduction

In chapter 1, we introduced a basic distinction between the consumer and the citizen, a distinction, we argued, which affects the nature of the viewing experience and the details of the relationship between broadcaster and viewer. We further contended that this distinction has implications for the range and type of content offered, as well as access to that content, and underpins the nature of regulatory concerns that the Union needs to address. Although broadcasting can be seen as a commercial activity and content regarded as a commodity, there are arguments about its functions and values beyond its many and varied commercial aspects that need to be considered. These arguments are to be found in discussions of the relationship broadcasting has to citizenship, or, in other words, the way broadcasting meets the needs of viewers as citizens.[1] In this chapter we explore the underlying theories about the value and functions of broadcasting which have underpinned regulatory rhetoric, particularly that which claims to be serving the public interest.

We begin this chapter with a discussion of these theories, after which we go on to explore our distinction between citizens and consumers in more depth. We then consider the impact that this distinction has, expressly or implicitly, on the concept of public interest. This is followed by a discussion of the issue of access to broadcast content in relationship to the needs of citizens. We conclude with a discussion of how the interests of the citizen viewer can be protected and how technological change, and developments in the broadcasting sector, particularly commercialisation, affect the viability of broadcasting's social, political and cultural functions. There are three aspects to our discussion. The first concerns the

---

[1] D. McQuail, *Media Performance: Mass Communication and the Public Interest* (London: Sage, 1992); W. Lippmann, *Public Opinion* (New York: Harcourt, 1922); P. Dahlgren, *Television and the Public Sphere* (London: Sage, 1995), all *passim*.

public sphere and its relationship not only to the media in general but also to public service broadcasting (PSB) and how this latter relationship may encourage active citizenship. The second aspect concerns the diversity and quality of services available to viewers and their universality. Both sets of concerns are associated with the third aspect of our discussion, traditional public service broadcasting, especially the way in which it is regarded as catering for the needs of passive and active citizen viewers.

Theories about the value and function of the broadcast media

Evaluation of the importance and value of the broadcast media in society is, in part, centred upon contested views about the active and passive nature of viewers and the function of the media. We shall deal with these in turn. As we have argued, different types of viewing experience can be identified (see chapter 1, table 1); however, early theories of the mass media tended to be based on an overall pessimistic perception of the gullibility of viewers. The approach has often been referred to as the magic-bullet theory or hypodermic model of the media. It assumes that the mass media are highly persuasive and have a direct effect on viewers. Research which has extensively tested if a causal link between media content and the behaviour of the viewer exists has generally produced results which are equivocal about the correlation between content and effect. This lack of 'proof' is due to the numerous other variables that must be taken into account when considering the effects of media content on viewing. Where research has demonstrated a link between viewing and behaviour, the methods used have been widely criticised.[2]

Despite uncertainty about any harm that the broadcast media may cause, claims about the power of television in particular still attract media, public and policymakers' interest. Sometimes (and along with other theories; see below) such interest underpins broadcasting regulation aimed at protecting the public, especially children, from particular types of broadcast content (e.g. Article 22 of the Television Without Frontiers Directive (TWFD);[3] see chapter 10). Still, direct policy interventions in response

---

[2] See, e.g., D. Gauntlett, *Moving Experiences: Understanding Television's Influence and Effects* (London: John Libbey, 1995), p. 1.

[3] Council Directive 89/552/EEC of 3 October on the co-ordination of certain provisions laid down by law, regulation or administrative action in member states concerning the pursuit of television broadcasting activities, OJ [1989] L298/23, as amended by Directive 97/36/EC OJ [1997] L 202/30.

to specifically perceived media effects are relatively rare,[4] and such action is often dismissed in academic circles as being an over-reaction, or as an attempt to turn the media into a scapegoat rather than examine wider circumstances.[5] Recently the power of the media to shape or mould messages in a way which is then integrated into the audience's viewing choices has become a central theme in the study of political communications, particularly where the media are seen to be responsible for engendering a lack of civic engagement and disenchantment with politics.[6] This so-called 'agenda setting' role of the media, that is not telling viewers how to think but what to think about, is still today regarded as significant.[7]

Some academic researchers have, however, exercised scepticism about theories based on what the media do to people, and have refocussed their research on the question of what do people do with the media?[8] Interest in this area is evident in current attempts to stimulate media literacy and to teach people how to operate new media technologies, choose what to watch and to filter out different types of content.[9] Critics of this 'optimistic' approach (optimistic because all you have to do is teach people how to) argue that this approach ignores the real constraints which viewers face in their everyday lives (for example, levels of educational achievement, socio-economic status, and a strong and powerful media industry dominating the encoding process and so on) which may limit the audience's

[4] In Britain the murder of 2-year-old Jamie Bulger by two 10-year-old boys in 1993 was initially believed to be a copycat killing resulting from one of the murderers having watched a video called *Child's Play Three*, although this assumption was later dismissed. The policy response was to produce a series of amendments to the Video Recordings Act in the belief that video films needed stricter ratings than cinema films as children were likely to have easier access to the former. See also the American attitude to screen violence at www.apa.org/pubinfo/violence.html and http://europa.eu.int/comm/avpolicy/regul/new_srv/workshop_children.pdf

[5] B. Gunter, 'Media Violence: Social Problem or Political Scapegoat?', *Inaugural Lecture* (Department of Journalism Studies: University of Sheffield, 1995), *passim*.

[6] See the critique of the so-called 'media malaise' approach in P. Norris, *A Virtuous Circle* (Cambridge: Cambridge University Press, 2000), p. 4.

[7] For an overview of the agenda-setting debate see, e.g., M. E. McCombs and D. L. Shaw, 'The Agenda-setting Function of Mass Media', *Public Opinion Quarterly*, 36 (1972), 176–87, *passim*; M. E. McCombs and D. L. Shaw, 'The Evolution of Agenda-Setting Research: Twenty-five Years in the Marketplace of Ideas', *Journal of Communication*, 43(2) (1993), 58–67, *passim*.

[8] J. Halloran, *The Effects of Television* (London: Panther, 1969), pp. 18–19.

[9] See Commission, *The Work Programme 2003–2004* which calls for proposals to implement media literacy where the changing media landscape, due to new technologies and media innovation, makes it necessary to teach children (and parents) to use the media effectively. V. Reding, SPEECH/03/400. Also see the British Communications Act 2003, Section 11, 'Duty to Promote Media Literacy'.

ability to manipulate and critically choose content, to interpret media messages and to filter out unwanted programming.[10] Today research into viewer engagement with the media reflects an ongoing debate between those who believe in the 'power of the media to shape people's knowledge, beliefs and attitudes'[11] and active audience theorists, who argue that viewers are capable of understanding and resisting media images. Political and public debate is increasingly influenced by both concerns: that is the power of the media both to influence viewers and also to engage them. Broadcasting policy aims to protect the viewer from content which may be harmful. At the same time policymakers assume that audiences can be active, in that some audiences are already media savvy and those that are not can easily become so. This latter assumption underpins the current advocacy and promotion of media literacy. This debate, however, is nothing new and with some variation is to be found in a media functionalist approach.

Media functionalism argues that the media have a direct influence on social change, both for positive and negative reasons. That is, it sees the media as both performing an integrative function but having the capacity to cause harm. The integrative function expressed, in their terms, is the media's promotion of social cohesion and solidarity. The risk of harm, again in their terms, is the dysfunctional aspect of the media, which is their capacity for dissidence and potential to contribute to the breakdown of agreed values, agreed social norms and accepted social patterns of behaviour. This approach, combined with a belief in media effects, is influential for policymakers and regulators, and provides them with two distinct spheres of concern, positive and negative. Today the negative sphere rather than the positive sphere has priority, but it is useful to look closely at them both because each has continuing relevance.

The negative or dysfunctional aspect of the media which attracts concern is that attributed to its possible narcotising effect, where the stream of information which emerges from the media is superficial and irrelevant and dulls viewers' cognitive skills, psychological insights and emotional reactions. Television is heavily criticised in academic circles in this respect, particularly when commercialisation and the dumbing down of content are linked together. This association has generated concerns for the need

---

[10] See, e.g., S. Hall, 'Coding and Encoding in the Television Discourse', in S. Hall, D. Hobson, A. Lowe and P. Willis (eds.), *Culture, Media, Language* (London: Hutchinson, 1980), pp. 197–208, *passim*.

[11] K. Williams, *Understanding Media Theory* (London: Arnold, 2002), p. 209.

for television to provide for a variety of programmes to ensure that the television diet does not only comprise entertainment programming or endless sport. Whether a viewer is passive or active, the risks are attendant to both. For the active viewer, their programme diet could in theory be purely based around a very narrow range of content pumped out across a wide range of channels. In parallel, passive citizens who relied on a varied diet of programmes provided by a few channels or a single public service broadcaster find that, in the face of the commodification of content and the decline in traditional PSB offerings, an ever diminishing range of programming is available.

Two arguments have been advanced on the positive aspect of the media. First, although it does not sound very positive, it was argued that the media perform a surveillance function. That is, where they are seen to be providing a continuous stream of information about the world, which can help viewers to assess risk and danger and to participate in society.[12] Problematically, for the advocates of this argument, it must also be recognised that the media can also provide information which is poorly contextualised, or badly explained, resulting in unnecessary levels of viewer anxiety or media scares.[13]

The second positive argument seems to have carried more weight with policymakers. Media functionalists argued that the media can, and do, enforce or transmit desirable social norms and values (usually associated with liberal democracies), such as respect, freedom, equality and order. Here, it is argued that the media promote such ideas and values by bringing to society's attention the consequences of so-called deviant or illegal behaviour. Moral, political and social boundaries can therefore be established by the media and can, in turn, be subsequently reinforced through regulatory requirements: for example, the requirement to show certain types of programming that reflect national life and culture. Sometimes the media over-emphasise the nature of so-called deviant behaviour, where a condition, episode, person or group of persons are defined as threatening and are presented in a stereotypical fashion,[14] again with

---

[12] See P. Shoemaker and A. Cohen, *News Around the World* (New York: Routledge, 2006), for a discussion of the links that have been made between social behaviours such as surveillance and the mass media, pp. 12–13, 16–18 and 303–5.

[13] For a general discussion of these themes, see McQuail, *McQuail's Mass Communication Theory* (London: Sage, 2005), p. 97.

[14] The most oft-cited case of this occurred in Britain in 1964, when the media reported that the gathering of Mods and Rockers on the beaches in the south-east of England signalled a breakdown in social order. See S. Cohen, *Folk Devils and Moral Panics* (Oxford: Blackwell, 1973), who described the coverage of this new youth culture as a 'moral panic', *passim*.

the effect of reinforcing boundaries. Other scholars have focussed on the media's ability to influence society through their broadcasting of particular social norms and values, which themselves may have the power to mobilise people to participate in social change. In this vein, other analysts have argued that the media also have the ability to transmit cultural values, passing on crucial information about society's history, cultural heritage and identity. Here the media act as agents of socialisation.[15] These arguments have provided some insight, albeit at a descriptive level, into how broadcasting might work at a macro level and in so doing they provided some justification for PSB by emphasising broadcasting's non-commercial importance, potential political and social power and relevance.

Opposing all of the above approaches are the Marxist-influenced critical theorists of the media. Here ideology and conflict are the keys to understanding the media. To understand how the media work you have to question their power base and structure; their influence both directly through their programmes and indirectly through their ideological narrowness. Ultimately their criticism focusses on two aspects: first, the way the media justified certain forms of politics and economic activities; and secondly, the way the media trivialised the world by lacking, or diminishing the role of, any critical, cultural or moral quality in their broadcast content. Critical theorists remain concerned about the reduction of diversity and plurality of media content and services as a consequence of the structure of ownership and control and the operation of global media enterprises. Some of the more interesting critical theorists have noted the tensions inherent in competing public-interest claims made by a range of actors involved in broadcasting.

Originally, critical approaches tended to explain the relationship between capitalist ownership and media content in relation to the concentration of economic power, arguing that 'that power, the men – owners and controllers – in whose hands it lies enjoy a massive preponderance in society'.[16] More recently, researchers have concentrated on the 'impersonal economic determinants of the marketplace',[17] which can have an

---

[15] Socialisation is the process whereby the individual is converted into the person and is an inter-disciplinary term used to explore human development. Sociologists use the term to concentrate on the effects of social institutions such as the family, school and the media on the individual. See K. Dabziger, *Socialization* (London: Harmondsworth, 1971), *passim*.

[16] R. Miliband, *The State in Capitalist Society: The Analysis of the Western System of Power* (London: Quartet Books, 1973), p. 237.

[17] S. Cottle (ed.), *Media Organization and Production* (London: Sage, 2003), p. 9.

impact both on the content available and the accessibility of that content. For these critics, the way that owners gain commercial control over sectors of the media industry through concentration, vertical and horizontal integration and competitive activity is problematic. This is because, they argue, the primary rationale for such owners is to achieve shareholder value through increased profits and dividends, which means that they must maximize audience ratings to sell to advertisers, as well as seek to create other revenue streams through the expansion of other services, rather than focussing on citizen viewers' wider interests. The viewer is regarded as a consumer of those products advertised or services sold, and in addition the viewer is also 'sold' by the broadcaster to advertisers. In this way viewers are commodified as a media product. The concerns relating to this process of commodification of viewers in the broadcasting market underpin regulation of advertising, particularly its frequency (see chapter 9).

Research from the perspective of assessing the effects of the impersonal economic forces within the broadcasting market place also focus on the argument that powerful economic interests tend to exclude voices which do not have economic power or resources, usually minority groups, thereby, it is argued, reducing plurality of access and diversity of representation.[18] As table 1 in chapter 1 indicates, the responses of viewers to lack of choice differ depending on their circumstances, but it is easy to imagine that if plurality of access and diversity of representation are overtaken by sheer economic calculation, then the broadcast content and programme range becomes correspondingly narrow.

Although critical theorists accused both effects and functionalist theories of possessing a 'fundamental theoretical vacuity',[19] some of the underlying assumptions in those theories can be found in regulatory concerns. Ideas that 'in many ways mass media contribute (by their "effects") to this or that "positive" (functional) or "negative" (dysfunctional) outcome for "society"'[20] remain important and are subject to ongoing research into the mass media. Both effects analysis and the assessment of the positive and negative functions of broadcasting provide a basis for the media to

---

[18] G. Murdock and P. Golding, 'For a Political Economy of Communications', in R. Miliband and J. Saville (eds.), *The Socialist Register* (London: Merlin Press, 1973), pp. 205–34.

[19] A key problem has been in defining 'function' and it is not 'obvious which media activity is functional (or dysfunctional) to the stable operation of society. Nor is it clear for whom it is helpful and how.' See Williams, *Understanding Media Theory*, p. 49.

[20] McQuail, *McQuail's Reader*, p. 7.

be taken seriously by regulators and policymakers when considering the regulation to be undertaken in the public interest.[21]

Citizens and consumers

Although it is beyond the scope of this book to explore the contested nature of citizenship and to assess the enormous amount of literature on the subject,[22] the idea of the citizen viewer is central to our arguments. We agree with Lewis that 'the citizen is one way of imagining a link between the state and the individual'.[23] Correspondingly, we believe that citizens' viewing choices reflect the nature of that linkage. Equally, we recognise that, if broadcasting provides the content which meets citizens' needs and interests, then in theory citizens' viewing should reinforce their citizenship, with its attendant rights, responsibilities and obligations. Such content is typically found (though by no means exclusively) in broadcasting which is underpinned by positive regulatory requirements that place specific obligations on broadcasters. This type of content tends to be expensive to produce and is increasingly being compromised due to increased competition, deregulatory policies and the diminution of public service broadcasters' funding, in some cases accompanied by a narrowing of their remit.

Alongside the various aspects of their citizenship, there are other activities through which people engage with the media, the most important of which, from our point of view, is being a consumer. Where citizenship has a higher level of significance (referring to intangibles like identity and belonging), being a consumer implies a concrete, economic activity that is defined and de-limited by the structure, workings and efficiency of the market. To confuse the citizen with the consumer is to mix two very different things of unequal standing. However, it is important to note that consumer power has become increasingly evident as consumers

---

[21] T. Gibbons, *Media Regulation*, 2nd edn (London: Sweet and Maxwell, 1998), p. 2.

[22] See, e.g., T. H. Marshall, *Class, Citizenship and Social Development* (Greenwood: Westport, 1973), *passim*; M. Roche, *Rethinking Citizenship* (Cambridge: Polity Press, 1992), *passim*; C. Closa, 'The Concept of Citizenship in the Treaty on European Union', *Common Market Law Review*, 29 (1992), 1137–70; H. U. J. d'Olivera, 'Union Citizenship: Pie in the Sky?', in A. Rosas and E. Anatola (eds.), *A Citizen's Europe* (London: Sage, 1995), pp. 58–84; K. Faulks, *Citizenship in Modern Britain* (Edinburgh: Edinburgh University Press, 1998), *passim*.

[23] G. Lewis, 'Citizenship', in G. Hughes (ed.), *Imagining Welfare Futures* (London: Routledge/ Open University Press, 1998), pp. 103–50.

accrue greater amounts of money and are seen to demand more choice. As consumers become better informed shoppers, consumer rights are more regularly and strongly expressed. Whether these strengths are evenly distributed among all consumers is unlikely; and our model (in table 1, chapter 1) assumes differences in spending capacity between different consumers.

The politicisation of consumption in certain areas appears to make it more difficult to claim that citizenship is about identity and belonging, while consumption is merely about shopping and a matter of occasional activity. In other words, we need to recognise that discerning and politicised consumers exist alongside consumers who merely consume for pleasure, or for want of anything better to do. As we discuss later, the idea of consumption for pleasure can be linked to broader and more difficult questions about programme quality, for example in the case where consumption requires products or services which seek to entertain. While entertainment programmes are not necessarily poor quality, they are usually used by the television broadcasting sector to attract audiences. Large audiences are, obviously, seen as revenue-generating, either via increased subscriptions or enabling the broadcaster to charge higher prices for advertising. Today targeting large audiences to stimulate mass consumption is more and more associated with lowest common denominator populist programming, which predominantly seeks to titillate and excite the audience. In short, the nature and value of broadcast content is measured in terms of its economic value, rather than its social and cultural value. In principle, this makes viewers, in their role as consumers, actors in an exchange commission and nothing else.

Broadcasting and the public interest

Although the term 'public interest' has been used in relation to the entire range of media, what actually constitutes the public interest has been notoriously difficult to define. Scholars not only 'disagree on the definition of the public interest, they also disagree about what they are trying to define: a goal, a process, or a myth'.[24] Held noted difficulties in definition which she described as 'assertions of confusion', but she also argued that 'the concept is indispensable'.[25] Providing a simple definition of public

---

[24] F. Sorauf, 'The Conceptual Muddle', in C. J. Friedrich (ed.), *The Public Interest* (New York: Atherton Press, 1962), p. 186.

[25] V. Held, *The Public Interest and Individual Interests* (New York: Basic Books, 1970), p. 2 and pp. 203–28.

interest has not proved to be impossible, but problematically definitions themselves generally contain frequently contested value judgements.

Held's consideration of theories of public interest led her to identify three approaches to determining its meaning. These approaches illustrate the differences arising between individual interests and the public interest. First, preponderance theories hold that the public interest must not be in conflict with 'a *preponderance* or *sum* of individual interests'.[26] Preponderance can be related to amounts of power a group of individuals holds, or be based on the votes of a majority of individuals. Secondly, common interest theories hold that the public interest is met when there is unanimity and agreement among all members of a polity. The agreement of a common interest is synonymous with the public interest. While the possibility of conflicting individual interests is recognised, they do not constitute or contribute to the public interest. Both the preponderance and common interest theories adopt a 'majoritarian' approach to the public interest, which could be equated with 'giving the public what it wants'. The 'majority of consumers in the media market'[27] have their desires met, but it is at the expense of other groups. Such an approach ignores minority or dissenting voices. Here we can see the important role that PSB has traditionally played in providing content that caters for both minority and majority needs. The third theory identified by Held refers to 'unitary conceptions', which are determined in accordance with one dominant value or viewpoint. This approach does not allow for dissent from individual interests and 'what is a valid judgement for one is a valid judgement for all and consistent with the public interest'.[28] Such an approach to the public interest results in paternalism. McQuail argues that any attempt to chart a middle way between the free-market majoritarian approaches and the paternalist unitary approach is usually undertaken via 'ad hoc judicial determinations of what is or is not in the public interest in a given case'.[29] This latter approach would still leave us with the problem of having constantly to consider a range of competing public-interest claims. Indeed, as we shall see in chapters 4 and 5, law-making is not the sole preserve of political institutions, even if the judiciary claims just to be applying or interpreting existing legal rules.

As we can see from the above three definitions of public interest, the constituent elements identified as referring to the public interest are often

---

[26] Held, *The Public Interest*, p. 42.
[27] McQuail, *McQuail's Communication Theory*, p. 143.
[28] Held, *The Public Interest*, p. 45.
[29] McQuail, *McQuail's Communication Theory*, p. 143.

mutually inconsistent, and are often applied inconsistently to different media. In short, public-interest rationales and objectives for the media and their regulatory control start from different bases and give rise to a range of competing claims. Any justification of regulatory intervention should, logically, be able to be judged by reference to the objectives that it sets for itself and that it needs to meet. Yet it remains difficult to measure regulatory success because of the many tensions and contradictions inherent in defining the public interest. In short, regulatory starting-points vary. A clear understanding of what constitutes public interest in the broadcast media has been further complicated by the growing strength of the media industry and media professionals' interests.[30] In chapters 5 and 6, for example, we note the difficulties inherent in the development of a regulatory framework which seeks to include industry needs. The inclusion of a variety of viewpoints and needs within the regulatory conspectus has led to increased conflict over the values or norms of public interest in broadcasting. These values and norms traditionally associated with PSB (and referred to as serving the public good) are challenged by the needs of the broadcasting industry and advertisers and the perceived desires of consumers (often as articulated by broadcasters). The accommodation of industry voices in the policymaking process, and the unclear definition of public interest, has meant that the gulf between the viewing experiences of consumers and citizens has become wider and not, as the orthodox policy approach would have us believe, converging.[31]

Although the idea of serving the public interest is not exclusively synonymous with PSB, serving the public interest (where public interest relates to social and cultural concerns and a desire to preserve and enhance the foundations of liberal democracy) has its most concrete manifestation in the form of PSB in the Western European broadcasting tradition. Commercial broadcasters and public service broadcasters may both have a range of different levels of PSB obligations to fulfil and therefore serve the public interest in different ways. Commercial broadcasters generally apply consumerist logic to their programming, arguing that consumer preferences and demand determine what content is shown. They further argue that a consumerist approach to content provides consumers with a wide range of choice simply because there are different types of

[30] E. O. Eriksen and J. E. Fossum, 'Democracy through Strong Publics in the European Union?', *Journal of Common Market Studies*, 40(3) (2002), 401–24, p. 404.
[31] See, e.g., the use by Ofcom of the term 'citizen-consumer'.

consumers who want different things. The problem with this (as we have suggested in chapter 1) is that there is little or no evidence to suggest that the market, left to its own devices, will either identify diverse wants or provide true diversity of choice. It is more likely that successful programme formats (i.e. those that attract large audiences) will be copied in abundance, giving the illusion of choice, but in reality restricting that choice to a narrower range of programme types. In contrast, public service broadcasters work more closely within an ethos of social obligation, whereby choice for viewers is not simply based on consumer demand, but upon their ability to make a choice from a wide range of diverse programming required to fulfil the more complex requirement of their status as citizens.

In addition to competing public-interest claims, it is notable that social priorities also change over time; what is seen as being in the public interest today may not be tomorrow, if those priorities change. Consequently, the term 'public interest' can only be 'captured' temporarily and its application is constantly subject to reinterpretation. The normative functions of broadcasting that address public-interest concerns outside the economic sphere should be understood in the following context. A regulatory structure that attempts to balance a range of interests, commercial wants and technological change with viewers' desires must not only accommodate consumer interests to achieve a particular content reach but also ensure citizens have rights of access to certain content. Seen like this, the broadcasting environment is still left with the problem that the contested nature of public interest reduces a regulatory structure's effectiveness as a means to justify protection of certain aspects of broadcasting. Viewers' interests may be less well articulated than those of the industry, and the protection of particular externalities which have been linked to the role of the media in the public sphere may be seen to be of less importance, or more difficult to protect, than economic interests.

The broadcast media and the public sphere

Availability of broadcast material may be seen as contributing to an open and informative public sphere. The public sphere has been envisaged as a notional space between civil society and the state,[32] and provides an arena where public debate can take place and public opinion can

---

[32] J. B. Thompson, *Ideology and Modern Culture: Critical Social Theory in the Era of Mass Communication* (Cambridge: Cambridge University Press, 1992), p. 111.

develop. A rather limited view of the public sphere is to see it as a means of delivering information to citizens in order to allow them to contribute to the formation of public opinion and through it to acquire political influence. From this perspective, the public sphere is a means by which citizens can observe competing political groups, lobby and make informed voting decisions. Also, the public sphere, it is said, lets politicians know that they are being scrutinised. In complex contemporary societies, one of the most important elements of the public sphere is the mass media; either, it is argued, because they function as the fourth estate, or because they provide a constant flow of information. It is these views which give rise to the idea, often articulated by the courts in freedom-of-expression cases, that the media in general are the watchdogs of society.

A more complex view of the public sphere is generally seen to be that represented by Habermas and his understanding of the bourgeois public sphere[33] which can be described as a deliberative space rather than just an information forum.[34] Habermas's influential work on the public sphere identifies its origins in Europe in the eighteenth and nineteenth centuries. It arose out of the needs and interests of a commercial middle class and was formed in the growing number of coffee shops which became places to meet and discuss and debate business and contemporary concerns. The bourgeois public sphere is not, however, an aspirational ideal: its constitution and membership was male, middle class and exclusive. Habermas did not consider the possibility that alternative public spheres may arise in different forums, an omission that has attracted criticism and comment.[35] Further, Habermas also attracted criticism from historians who questioned his understanding of coffee-house culture. The idea of a bourgeois public sphere, however, is useful from the point of view that

---

[33] J. Habermas, *Structural Transformation of the Public Sphere* (Cambridge: Polity Press, 1989); for discussions of his work, see also C. Calhoun (ed.), *Habermas and the Public Sphere* (Cambridge, Mass.: MIT Press, 1992); W. Outhwaite (ed.), *The Habermas Reader* (Cambridge: Polity Press, 1996). The bourgeois public sphere initially developed in the realm of literature, later encompassing political issues and ideas; see Thompson, *Ideology and Modern Culture*, p. 111.

[34] The ideas and principles encompassed by the public sphere have been described as constituting a discursive forum through which individuals (conceived as a public of citizens) could contribute via rational–critical debate or reasoned and informed argument: see Thompson, *Ideology and Modern Culture*, p. 112.

[35] See, e.g., J. Curran, 'Mass Mass Media and Democracy: A Reappraisal', in J. Curran and M. Gurevitch (eds.), *Mass Media and Society* (London: Edward Arnold, 2000), pp. 82–117; Thompson, *Ideology and Modern Culture*, pp. 112–21.

it describes a certain kind of communicative rationality. This is the idea of communication which can occur without the exercise of coercion or manipulation, allowing for mutual understanding between individuals and groups in society to be reached. For Habermas, the media play, and have played, a vital part in providing the information from which such discussions can spring.

Habermas also addresses the way in which the public sphere(s) have changed in modern societies. He takes an essentially negative view of the contemporary media, arguing that the bourgeois public sphere of communicative rationality has collapsed, or has evolved and become dominated by a trivial mass media and the shallow politics of democratic popularism. From this perspective, the mass media became inextricably linked to the private worlds of money and commerce, limiting their ability to provide the material or the forum to facilitate public debate. The effects of media concentration and content commodification (and, indeed, we might add commodification of the audience) have, for Habermas, led to a 'refeudalisation' of the public sphere. Here, the growth of corporate capitalism has transformed the media into commercial operations which prioritised making profit for owners rather than providing information for readers and, by analogy, viewers. This process created a pseudo public sphere within which the public behaved as consumers, rather than discursive citizens engaged in rational–critical debate. In many European countries, regulation which has sought to balance the need for freedom of expression alongside further levels of social responsibility led to the establishment of a public service broadcaster; an action which challenges Habermas's pessimism and the inevitable refeudalisation of the public sphere. None the less, as we discuss in chapter 5, PSB supported by the state is under attack in the Union and, as we have already suggested, policy-makers are constantly conflating the viewing requirements of consumers and citizens.

PSB and the public sphere

The abolition of spectrum scarcity in a multi-channel era has, it is said, reduced the need for political intervention in broadcasting markets (see chapter 3). Consequently, the philosophical foundation and subsequent rationale for PSB have been increasingly questioned in the last two decades. Attacks come from a variety of critics, who perceive publicly funded, public service broadcasters to be financially privileged and causing a distortion in the broadcasting market place (see chapter 13). Often PSB providers are accused of wasting privileged resources, being dominated by particular elitist or establishment values and, consequently, of failing to meet their most vital goal, namely to serve all viewers.[36]

PSB has proved to be notoriously difficult to define, but discussions about it tend to refer to an agreed set of goals, albeit abstract goals.[37] Despite broad agreement about what PSB should entail, 'there has never been a generally accepted "theory" of PSB',[38] just national variants which have different operational scope and remits. In the UK, Ofcom noted that 'the problem with the term "public service broadcasting" is that it has at least four different meanings: good television; worthy television; television that would not exist without some form of public intervention; and the institutions that broadcast this type of television'.[39]

Recognising the definitional difficulties associated with PSB, Born and Prosser[40] provide a very useful survey[41] of the different ways PSB has been defined in contemporary sociological and policy studies. What their

---

[36] R. Collins, *From Satellite to Single Market: New Communication Technology and European Public Service Television* (London: Routledge, 1998), p. 10.

[37] There has been broad agreement at national and European level about the nature of these values which have been articulated in various compendia of PSB values prepared by both media professionals and academics: see, e.g., The Broadcasting Research Unit, *The Public Service Idea in British Broadcasting: Main Principles* (Luton: John Libbey, 1985), pp. 25–32; The Report of the European Broadcasting Union's (EBU) Perez Group, *Conclusions of the TV Programme Committee's Group of Experts on the Future of Public Service Broadcasting* (EBU: Mimeo 1983), p. 4; and, more recently, G. F. Lowe and T. Hujanen, *Broadcasting and Convergence: New Articulations of the Public Service Remit* (Göteborg: Nordicom, 2003), passim.

[38] McQuail, *McQuail's Mass Communication Theory*, p. 156.

[39] Ofcom, *Review of Public Service Television Broadcasting: Phase 1*, sect. 24, www.ofcom. org.uk/consultations/past/psb/psb/psb.pdf?a = 87101.

[40] G. Born and T. Prosser, 'Culture and Consumerism: Citizenship, Public Service Broadcasting and the BBC's Fair Trading Obligations', *The Modern Law Review*, 64(5) (2003), 657–87.

[41] Born and Prosser, 'Culture and Consumerism', p. 670, examine among others, the following well-known attempts to identify core PSB values or principles: Broadcasting Research Unit, *The Public Service Idea*; S. Barnett and D. Docherty, 'Purity or Pragmatism? Principles of Public Service Broadcasting', in J. Blumler and T. Nossiter (eds.), *Broadcasting Finance in Transition* (New York: Oxford University Press, 1991), pp. 3–7; Council of Europe, *The Media in a Democratic Society: Draft Resolutions and Draft Political Declaration* (1994); R. Collins and J. Purnell, *Commerce, Competition and Governance: The Future of the BBC* (London: Institute for Public Policy Research, 1995); The Tongue Report, appended to the European Parliament, *Resolution on The Role of Public Service Television in the Multi-Media Society*, 19 September, A4-0243/96; R. Woldt, *Perspectives of Public Service Television in Europe* (Düsseldorf: European Institute for the Media, 1998).

survey reveals is that there is a general consensus on which core values are embodied in PSB. In brief, these core values can be summarised as:

provision of services free to air (or affordable to the majority of people); universal access; universality of genres; provision of high-quality programmes in all genres; showing the capacity for innovation, creative risk-taking, pluralism, originality, distinctiveness and for challenging viewers; a mission to inform, educate and entertain, enriching the lives of the audience; programming that supports social integration and cohesion, reflecting and maintaining national identity and culture; provision of programming for regional, cultural, linguistic and social minorities; provision of independent, impartial and authoritative news and factual programming, drawing upon a plurality of opinions to provide support for an informed citizenry; complementing other public service provision and those with a purely commercial remit to enrich the broadcasting ecology and to limit advertising.

Born and Prosser go on to distil these PSB values into three core values: citizenship, universality and quality.[42] From these core values, it is easy to see how the requirements of the citizen viewer coincide with the core values of PSB, indeed PSB is supposed to facilitate the development of a critical rational public sphere in which citizenship can gain its political expression. The civic dimension to PSB is everything.

The relationship between citizenship and the media can be explored in terms of social responsibility and the role of the broadcast media in the public sphere. Universality and quality of service are ultimately required in order to facilitate the viewer's ability to access content and, possibly, to participate in the public sphere. Born and Prosser identify three types of universality.[43] They refer to the first as *technical, social and geographical universality*, where an infrastructure is provided which allows all citizens who so wish to receive broadcast signals for all free-to-air public services, regardless of where they live or their socio-economic status. The interests referred to in this category of universality are defined from the perspective of the viewer. They are not directly influenced by the needs of broadcasters (including platform operators and content providers). A second type of universality relates to the *range of programming (social and cultural universality)* that is provided. Here programming should cater for and reflect the tastes and interests of all citizens. The third type of universality

---

[42] Born and Prosser, 'Culture and Consumerism', p. 671.   [43] *Ibid.*, pp. 675–8.

encompasses the idea of *universality of genre*, whereby a mixed range of programming is provided that educates and informs citizens, as well as entertaining them. While agreeing in principle with these three types of PSB universality, the PSB world is more complicated. PSB obligations are not confined simply to publicly funded broadcasters. Thus, we need to look at these three types of universality in the setting of the modern and varied European broadcasting environment.

The first type of universality to consider is that of technical access. Today a modern communications infrastructure now allows would-be viewers to choose from a range of platforms (terrestrial, cable and satellite) and a wide range of additional services. Prior to the development of different types of broadcasting platforms, purchasing a television set, or paying a licence fee (or equivalent) were generally the only threshold to access. Crossing these barriers was a relatively simple affair and the subsequently received free-to-air analogue services had extensive viewer reach. Today access to services is controlled by technical barriers, the ability to receive cable or digital terrestrial signals, understanding how things work, differential pricing structures and channel options and the bundling of services (what might be called the 'triple whammy' of television, phone and internet service all from the same provider).

From both a social and individual point of view, two important questions arise as a result of developing technologies and their barriers to use. First, is the growth of new types of information technology likely to fulfil its potential for granting greater access to information? Secondly, is there a potential for information poverty and social exclusion? The development of digital technology in particular has increased the range of services potentially available, but to access any such services viewers will need new and constantly updated equipment. In addition to any costs for acquiring this equipment (though note that there have been significant subsidies in relation to set-top boxes/decoders),[44] viewers often have to pay additional subscription fees to access premium content such as sport (see chapter 12) and box-office films. In this environment, there is the risk that viewers can be excluded by both technical barriers and cost. Alternatively, they may feel frustrated by having to pay for both equipment and content, some of which they may well feel should be provided free (an example is

---

[44] In a survey of digital terrestrial television (DTT), it seems that in general the aim of lower cost set-top boxes has been met, though this might not be sufficient to ensure successful DTT take-up: Analysis Ltd, *Public Policy Treatment of Digital Terrestrial Television in Communications Markets, Final Report for Commission* (2005), pp. 5–6.

the reaction of the 'refuseniks' to having to pay for digital decoders when the analogue signal is switched off).

The packaging and pricing of content reflects the commodification of information. It is this which underpins the way access to content is managed, and ultimately controlled. Access to the decoder and associated software, both by viewers and providers of content, is necessary to broadcast and receive programming, thus giving control over who uses the technology to the body that owns or controls it. Questions of access to services point to an area where the separately regulated fields of infrastructure and content coincide and the decoder and software form a third element[45] in the distribution of content that can be seen as enabling and enhancing that distribution, or as a barrier to viewing which must in some way be overcome.[46] As we shall see in chapter 6, Union policy in this area has favoured the use of industry-developed standards and, at the moment, the different national markets have developed on the basis of proprietary standards, protected by intellectual property rights. This development risks the exclusion or marginalisation of certain content, depending on the relationships between various content providers and the platform operators. As noted earlier, the problems in this area are compounded by the fact that, with increased choice, viewers need to be guided through the range of services available, and information needs to be interpreted for them clearly, accurately and concisely. This is the function of the electronic programme guides (EPGs). EPGs can, however, be designed to favour the interests of certain content providers, usually the EPG operator and group companies. Furthermore, the position which a channel acquires on an EPG is crucial for attracting audiences,[47] meaning that some content providers are again likely to be marginalised.

---

[45] L. Lessig, *The Future of Ideas: The Fate of the Commons in a Connected World* (London: Random House, 2001), p. 23; see also Y. Benkler, 'From Consumers to Users: Shifting the Deeper Structures of Regulation', *Fed. Comm L.J.* 52 (1999), 561, pp. 562–3.

[46] This third layer can also be seen in digital rights management systems (DRM). An analysis of DRM lies outside the scope of this book, but it should be noted that DRM, although designed to protect copyright, can be criticised for an overbroad protection of the copyright holders' rights and be thus detrimental to the viewing experience (i.e. limiting access and use) and to competition. For examples of the problems in the broadcasting sphere, see, e.g., EBU, *Comments on the Public Consultation on the EC Commission's Discussion Paper on the Application of Article 82 of the EU Treaty to Exclusionary Abuses* (2006) DAj/HR, p. 3.

[47] In the Ofcom *Statement on Code on Electronic Programme Guides* (2004), Channel 4 is cited as having commissioned research with the BBC that suggests that viewers correlated higher positions on an EPG with higher programme quality, p. 19.

The development of digital television has raised further issues concerning technical universality, which go beyond the problems caused by subscription services (pay TV). The introduction of digital technology and the proposed switch-off of analogue transmission mean that even publicly funded public service broadcasters are restricting access to some of their services to those who have digital technology. The question of switch-over from analogue to digital may leave those viewers who cannot, or will not, adopt digital technology without even basic services. Analogue switch-off will free up the broadcasting spectrum, and may improve service provision to the majority of viewers. Issues relating to technical universality are significant because, while technical access is a prerequisite for any other form of universality, it is unclear at the moment how far the technical universality identified by Born and Prosser[48] will be protected in the contemporary broadcasting environment.

Born and Prosser's second (and to some extent third) category of universality entails provision of a certain range of programming. Social and cultural universality enhances citizen participation through the provision of a broad range of information, which encourages their activity in the public sphere. Media pluralism gives minorities the opportunity to express their views in a larger society, a practice which, as well as respecting those groups' rights to freedom of expression, should, in theory, reduce social confusion and, possibly, conflict because it increases the chances of understanding between different cultural groups. A diverse range of voices also adds to the general richness and variety of cultural and social life. It may open the way for social and cultural change, as new or marginal voices express opinions which challenge the status quo. In the broadcasting sector, diversity of programme provision and voices within those programmes can be achieved by internal pluralism, where a broad range of views and issues are expressed within one channel. Public service broadcasters usually have a remit to provide such a range of programme genres within one mass audience channel, as a way of serving all tastes and interests and protecting the needs of the passive viewer. In contrast, a regulatory system can aim to achieve external pluralism where diversity in practice is spread across a range of channels, some of which are broadcast via conditional access technology only. This form of external pluralism returns us to the above problems of access. It also runs the risk of generating what is known as audience fragmentation; where channels show only one type of programme, for example film channels, comedy channels, news channels, sports channels and so on. Here viewers divide

---

[48] Born and Prosser, 'Culture and Consumerism', pp. 675–8.

their time between many different channels rather than obtaining their viewing requirements from a limited number of channels which show a variety of programmes or genres.

Even were media pluralism to be achieved externally, true diversity of choice would be met only if something for everyone was available free-to-air. Furthermore, diversity of representation would require that the programming available truly represented different views and voices in society. Even more unlikely, but required for a truly pluralistic broadcasting and information environment, different individuals in society should, in principle, have free access to a transmission system through which they could broadcast their views and opinions. Such expectations are, however, utopian. As we note in chapter 1, even where measures are taken to allow wider access, plurality of ownership alone may not guarantee a diversity of perspectives. The media often imitate each other, especially if a particularly successful way of attracting viewers is discovered – as evidenced by the growth of reality tv programmes in recent years.[49]

Born and Prossers' third category, that of quality, has been notoriously difficult to define. It raises questions about what actually constitutes excellence or standards in programming and, furthermore, who gets to say so. Born and Prosser see the problem in recent debates about what constitutes quality in broadcasting as being the lack of willingness to adjudicate between different views, with both consumer preferences and producers' views being used as indicators of programme quality.[50] The problem about who should decide standards in broadcasting is not new, and the contemporary debate still covers old ground with the same set of protagonists: viewers and professionals. If broadcasters are allowed to take a major part in setting standards of quality, then the idea of broadcasting as a service to viewers is undermined, when the tastes of the programme makers do not coincide with those of the viewers for whom they seek to provide programmes. Allowing viewer preferences to influence decisions about broadcast content, however, means that rather than working to a set of so-called objective standards (imposed upon the viewing public by a public service broadcaster or regulatory body), content standards will become relative to people's tastes. Often a programme's success (and implicitly its 'quality') is measured in terms of how popular it is. Anthony Smith eloquently summed up the problem in 1973, when he noted that when broadcasting 'finds a level of taste at which it can successfully aggregate

---

[49] I. Hargreaves, *Journalism: Truth or Dare* (Oxford: Oxford University Press, 2003), p. 161.

[50] Born and Prosser, 'Culture and Consumerism', pp. 679–81. Also see G. Mulgan, 'Television's Holy Grail: Seven Types of Quality', in G. Mulgan (ed.), *The Question of Quality* (London: BFI, 1990), pp. 4–32.

its audience, it becomes culturally valueless; when it occupies a higher ground in a spirit of dedicated intellectual exclusiveness, it fails in its purpose of serving the entire society'.[51]

For those concerned about standards in relation to taste, decency and morality, the development of a wider range of programming has often meant that many established boundaries have been challenged. Often broadcasters use in their defence their desire to exercise creative freedom, whereas more critical analysts may see the provision of certain types of popular, but ground-breaking, programmes, such as reality TV formats, as being more about chasing ratings than widening the quality of choice. The pursuit of populism as a way of providing 'more' choice in the commercial broadcast sector tends to be based upon immediate success and popularity. The successful format is then copied and adapted, ultimately providing more programmes, but reducing diversity of quality programming available and, in the process, pandering to the tyranny of the majority. As the role of public service broadcasters is to assist in broadening and developing the public's taste, through provision of programming which the commercial sector would not necessarily provide, they are faced with a dilemma: how to provide challenging quality programming without alienating the audience. This dilemma links to questions about citizens' rights to receive information and what they can and should expect to be provided by public service broadcasters.

The question of what should be provided by a public service broadcaster has been addressed in economic terms by Graham, who argues that broadcasting with a public purpose has a particular characteristic, namely it is a 'merit' good.[52] These are goods, or more properly speaking in this case, services, which are regarded by governments as economically desirable, politically meaningful, socially significant or culturally valuable, and risk being undervalued by consumers in their normal market activities. Free consumer choice or sovereignty is no guarantee of the purchase of a merit good and as such is regarded as an inappropriate way of determining their distribution. Consequently, consumers should be encouraged or compelled to consume merit goods. Usually this involves governments in either providing the merit good directly, or subsidising its purchase. Thus, merit goods, such as public education or public health systems, are managed according to specific criteria to ensure that access is

[51] A. Smith, *The Shadow in the Cave* (London: Allen & Unwin, 1973), p. 24.
[52] A. Graham, 'Broadcasting Policy in the Multimedia Age', in A. Graham, C. Kobaldt, S. Hogg, B. Robinson, D. Currie, M. Siner, G. Mather, J. Le Grand, B. New and I. Corfield, (eds.), *Public Purposes in Broadcasting* (Luton: University of Luton Press, 1999), p. 27.

offered to all. As consumers tend to buy fewer merit goods than is in their own long-term interests, either through lack of desire or lack or means, managed public provision of certain goods and services has put pressure on citizens to support these services. Graham argues that without positive public service provision in the broadcasting system, there is a real danger that 'merit' programming would not be provided.[53] The original vision for PSB envisaged by the first BBC Director-General, Lord Reith, could exist only in a non-commercial environment, where programming was designed to benefit the viewers rather than maximise profits. In the twenty-first century the problem of defining a role for PSB and public service broadcasters is exacerbated by technological changes (see chapter 3), changes in viewer behaviour and expectations and the lack of an unequivocal political and social will required to protect those values associated with citizenship, universality and quality in broadcasting.

Programming which panders to consumer preferences has attracted criticism, as it is associated with a reduction in quality and standards. An undue emphasis by broadcasters on providing popular programming has been associated with a lack of innovation, degradation of production standards, technical standards and an overall reduction in educational programming in favour of greater amounts of entertainment. The problem is that popular programmes are popular and their success is judged in terms of high ratings figures rather than the intrinsic quality and value of a programme to society. Unfortunately, the requirement for PSB to become popular has led to a tendency for such broadcasters to enter the 'ratings race'. How far public subsidies, for example the licence fee, should be used to produce reality TV is very much a hotly contested and acrimonious debate. For some, like Blumler, these developments may have an impact on the extent to which the 'vulnerable values'[54] of PSB can continue to be protected.

[53] Graham et al., Public Purposes, p. 27.
[54] The term 'vulnerable values' was coined by Emeritus Professor Jay Blumler (see J. Blumler (ed.), Television and the Public Interest: Vulnerable Values in West European Broadcasting (London: Sage in association with the Broadcasting Standards Council, 1992)). He used the term in direct reference to the principles of the public service tradition which in the British context are generally taken to be the eight principles identified by the Broadcasting Research Unit (BRU), The Public Service Idea, pp. 25–32. The PSB values identified by the BRU were: geographic universality; universality of appeal; cater for disadvantaged minorities; foster national identity and community; be distanced from vested interests, in particular the government of the day; one main broadcaster to be funded via a licence fee directly funded by the corpus of users; encourage competition in good programming rather than competition for numbers; liberate rather than restrict programme makers. See also B. Franklin (ed.), British Television Policy: A Reader (London: Routledge, 2001), p. 21.

Conclusions

Policy decisions and regulatory structures in the broadcast sector have recognised that broadcasting requires special levels of responsibility to be imposed upon it. The obligations placed on broadcasting are, in part, a cautious reaction to a variety of theories about its power, likely impact on viewers and the belief in the importance of serving the public interest, via a free flow of information, which may contribute towards the functioning of a public sphere. We have seen that there are a number of different theoretical approaches taken in the analysis of the role of broadcasting and the way it operates. Despite their differences, some common themes seem to emerge. In particular, there is a reasonable amount of scepticism about the ability of the commercial sector to meet the needs of citizens. We share this scepticism, and regard it as a healthy place to stand and judge the purpose and significance of broadcasting regulation.

The high expectations which many have of the ability of broadcasting to meet specific public interest goals is expressed most clearly in a range of PSB obligations. While expectations about what public-service values entail have engendered common agreement,[55] problems remain about how to define abstract criteria such as public interest, citizenship, universality and quality, and to find the best way in which these may be exercised, measured and evaluated in a multi-channel broadcasting environment. Problematically, public-service values are eulogised within a broadcasting environment which prioritises consumer sovereignty[56] above meeting the needs of citizens.

---

[55] See the normative values identified by The Perez Group in 1983; the Broadcasting Research Unit in 1985; the Liège Conference on 'Vulnerable Values in Multichannel Television Systems' in 1990; Blumler in 1992 and the list referred to by Born and Prosser, 'Culture and Consumerism', p. 670.

[56] Gibbons, *Regulating the Media*, p. 302.

3

Regulation and the viewer in a changing broadcasting environment

Introduction

The dual nature of broadcasting as a cultural phenomenon and a commercial product causes difficulties for policymakers and regulators seeking to reconcile the conflicting interests that arise. The history of broadcasting and its regulation in the Union illustrates a variety of responses to these difficulties. There have been changes in the broadcasting sector, both in the increasingly commercial nature of the market structure and in technology. A central question is the extent to which these changes necessitate different regulatory approaches or, indeed, minimise the need to rely on traditional regulation to achieve policy goals. Two external factors, technological change and commercialisation (identified in chapter 1), are interlinked with different perceptions held by policymakers, regulators and, probably, broadcasters as to what the viewing experience should constitute, and consequently the viewer's needs, in an international information society. The interrelationship of technological change, commercialisation and these perceptions raises questions about the appropriate level and type of regulation needed. In this context, there is a tension between the needs of the consumer and the citizen, as well as in their different dispositions towards new technology.

To identify the extent to which regulatory responses are first, technologically determined, and secondly, influenced by industry claims, we will consider briefly the historical development of broadcasting and previous regulatory responses to earlier technological innovations. Following on from the analysis in chapter 2, we discuss these responses in the light of the historical social and moral concerns about broadcasting. In particular, we consider the specific arguments traditionally used to justify the regulation of broadcasting, whether as a public service or a commercial activity, and discuss different perceptions of the nature of the viewing experience and the needs of the viewer identified in chapter 1 in the light of these arguments. Whereas chapter 2 considered the value of broadcasting at a theoretical level, this chapter focuses on specific problems and regulatory responses. We then consider in more detail the significance of recent technological changes, such as digitalisation and convergence, on the broadcasting environment, its regulatory structures and perceptions held about the viewing experience.

Historical overview of the development of broadcasting

The first part of the history of broadcasting could be said to belong to the inventors who were probably unaware of the cultural, political and social phenomenon they were about to unleash. The first broadcast of music and speech is attributed to an American, Fessenden, in 1906, and crystal sets tuned in by their 'cat's whisker' became increasingly popular in Britain after the First World War. Although the Marconi Company began broadcasting in Britain in 1920, permission to transmit was withdrawn by the Post Office until 1922, when it granted a licence to broadcast to Marconi's 2LO, a commercial operator. The Wireless Telegraphy Act 1904 had stated that all wireless receivers and transmitters had to be licensed by the Post Office and gave the Post Office the scope to determine the terms of the licences.[1] The Post Office was concerned to avoid having to arbitrate between different commercial interests arising from the number of applications to broadcast, but also wanted to ensure that the airwaves were controlled. The solution, adopted in the UK in the 1920s to prevent a possible cacophony of transmissions, was to form one large private organisation, the British Broadcasting Company, from a consortium of radio companies. Issues relating to the need to control, and consequently to regulate, which came into play at this time were underpinned by assumptions about the nature of broadcasting, particularly its value, function and possible impact on the viewer (see chapter 2 and below). Here, and in spite of the fact that broadcasting technology originally developed from private innovation, the market-driven approach was abandoned in favour of a state-organised monopoly. The position changed again when the means adopted to control broadcasting and support the values attributed to it

---

[1] Issuing licences was the responsibility of the Postmaster-General of the Post Office. As noted by P. Scannell and D. Cardiff, *A Social History of British Broadcasting: Volume One 1922–1939* (London: Basil Blackwell, 1991), p. 384, 'the Post Office was regarded in this country and by governments as a sort of second rate Department, as no more than a stepping-stone to higher things'. The lack of expertise in the Post Office in the 1920s meant that the Post Office had little 'will or ability to exercise authority over the content of broadcasting with any clarity or consistency'.

was the formation of the British Broadcasting Corporation (BBC). The BBC was set up by Royal Charter on 1 January 1927, no longer a private company, and was licensed to provide public service broadcasting (PSB). The BBC was to hold a monopoly of radio broadcasting in the UK until the Sound Broadcasting Act legalised commercial radio in 1972. It also held a monopoly in television broadcasting when that was introduced as a generally available service,[2] until the 1954 Television Act was passed. It was this piece of legislation that provided the basis for the development of commercial television in the UK. The early phases of broadcasting in the UK can be characterised as a move from private to public sector, and from the possibility of numerous providers to a monopoly. Monopoly state providers were to become a characteristic of the national broadcasting systems within the Union during the mid part of the twentieth century.

In the 1920s experimenters were already working on a way to transmit visual images, even though early radio was only just beginning to be used by the public. The possibility of this new technology was understood and appreciated by only a few engineers and technophiles, a situation which has repeated itself with ever-changing communication technology, for example, the early adopters of mobile phones, video recorders, satellite, cable and, recently, digital television. Despite early public ambivalence towards many of these technologies, they have been gradually accepted to the point where most are a ubiquitous part of everyday life. Regardless of their ubiquity, there will always be those who are unable to 'programme their video recorder'. None the less, throughout the last century our ability to communicate has been influenced by technology, institutional development as well as an 'amplified human propensity to do so'.[3] The perceived need to control or monitor such technological and commercial developments has been a major factor in shaping the different regulatory responses to broadcasting.

Early regulatory responses to social, cultural and moral concerns

The current Union regulatory framework is under review. As part of this review, various interested bodies have identified their own concerns and claimed that these necessitate particular regulatory responses. To be able

---

[2] Television Limited was formed in the UK in 1925 and in 1926 the Post Office gave it an experimental television licence.

[3] M. Tracey, *The Decline and Fall of Public Service Broadcasting* (Oxford: Oxford University Press, 1998), p. 4.

to assess such claims relating to the contemporary broadcasting market, it is useful to revisit the anxieties which accompanied the invention of the first universal broadcast technology and the ways in which these were dealt with. The first of these was the radio, or wireless.

Although the development of wireless was a competitive international process, the institutions which were to use the new technologies to transmit content were national, and reflected national cultural and social concerns of the time.[4] In the 1920s the first wireless transmissions were viewed as a failure because broadcasting to a number of people at the same time, where more than one person could listen in to a communication between sender and receiver, was seen to be unnecessary (the idea of point to multi-point broadcasting was anathema). The military was concerned because frivolous messages blocked the airwaves. The press was concerned that readership of newspapers would decline. Actors and performers were afraid that audiences to theatres would dwindle. Some feared that children would lose the ability to read and become more adept at aural interpretation. Apocryphal tales were told about how it was important to open windows to allow the radio signal to leave the room. Fear about technology and its consequences (whether for business, health, psychological or social reasons) is not new. It may be that in the years to come, concerns about mobile phones and other communications technologies may seem similarly naïve. Although some of the health concerns may seem far-fetched, commercial concerns will always be raised when new technologies (and services) threaten established ones, often with good reason. Anxiety about technology has always existed, but it is not universally experienced or easily addressed. Regulators have increasingly had to make decisions about the level of anxiety and lack of engagement with technology by members of the public, that is, passive viewers, who we have argued need to be recognised and protected by broadcasting policy.[5]

Leaving the market to its own devices is not without practical problems. For example, in the USA the wireless companies were originally fully

---

[4] Scannell and Cardiff, *A Social History of British Broadcasting*, p. 7.

[5] See Ofcom Special Report, *Consumer Engagement with Digital Communication Services*. An attitudinal segmentation model was developed to provide understanding of the way UK consumers engage with digital communication services. Five consumer segments were identified: enthusiasts, functionalists, economisers, abstainers and resisters. Available at www.ofcom/org.uk/research/cm/consumer_engagement/ p. 3 and Ofcom, *Digital Switchover: An Audit of Viewers' Priorities*. Ofcom notes that although switch-over will pose relatively few challenges for some, other viewers may need help to ensure that they know what they need to do, when they need to do it and the options open to them (available on the Ofcom website), p. 1.

incorporated into an open business system with no government control. American radio stations were allowed to grow in number and to sell advertising from 1922, firmly establishing broadcasting as an industry. By 1924 there were over 500 wireless stations in the USA and the broadcasting boom had resulted in chaos in the airwaves with interference and overlapping of signals alongside frequent interruptions from advertisements. These developments raised problems of content and co-ordination.[6] The policy choice in the UK, and in other European countries, to introduce a monopoly broadcaster can be seen, in part, as a response to this problem. The need to co-ordinate potentially overlapping radio transmissions remains an issue to this day, as Union policymakers consider the possibility of spectrum trading, which could move the Union's regulation of such matters closer to the American position (see chapter 6).

Also of concern to early European policymakers were issues involving the moral, political and social content of the programmes that were broadcast. The formulation and subsequent evolution of British broadcasting policy at least began from the premiss that this powerful new medium exhibited both potential and risk.[7] Responding to both these concerns, in the UK it was decided that the BBC, a monopoly, licence-fee funded organisation would be charged with a social responsibility and a public purpose,[8] and was in theory to remain free of government control.[9] From such a start, it was hoped that the BBC would both raise intellectual and cultural standards and avoid becoming a neonate ministry of propaganda. It was the former that was to prove contentious. The nature of broadcasting content, and how best to control or manage it, is always contested and, as we saw in chapter 2, some theorists have suggested that broadcasting content influences, or even affects, 'susceptible' people. These fears seem

---

[6] Currently, the approach within the Union has been to require the licensing of spectrum use whether on an individual or general basis. In the light of technological progress which, according to the Commission, is progressively reducing the risk of interference, individual licences are no longer necessary, save in exceptional circumstances. Commission, *Staff Working Document on the Review of the EU Regulatory Framework for Electronic Communications Networks and Services* SEC (2006)816, p. 12. As we shall see in chapter 6, the Union is currently considering the possibility of introducing spectrum trading.

[7] D. Krebber, *Europeanisation of Regulatory Television Policy: The Decision-making Process of the Television Without Frontiers Directive from 1989 and 1997* (Baden-Baden: Nomos Verlagsgesellschaft, 2002), p. 9.

[8] J. Le Grand and B. New, 'Broadcasting and Public Purposes in the New Millennium', in A. Graham, C. Kobaldt, S. Hogg, B. Robinson, D. Currie, M. Siner, G. Mather, J. Le Grand, B. New and I. Corfield (eds.), *Public Purposes in Broadcasting* (University of Luton Press: Luton, 1999), p. 113.

[9] A. Crisell, *Understanding Radio* (London: Methuen, 1986), p. 18.

to have underpinned national and Union regulation from the start, with
the result that part of the regulators' repertoire has always been aimed at
ensuring that television images do no harm and do not contribute to the
breakdown of social order or cultural decline.[10] These fears have generated arguments about the images that do, or do not, harm viewers. Today
there is still disagreement (see chapter 2) about the impact on the audience and society of screen violence, bad language or immoral content, as
is evidenced by the ongoing debates in effects research.[11]

Alongside fears about the negative effects of broadcasting were more
optimistic assessments of the value of broadcasting. European broadcasting systems have also been developed according to the belief that television
has an important positive role to play in a liberal democracy and in the
development of a public sphere (see chapter 2). In nineteenth-century
Britain, Burke and Carlyle saw the independent press as a Fourth Estate,
but with increasing commercialisation throughout the twentieth century
the British press, in particular, became tainted by the partisan and bellicose
views and interests of its owners.[12] Consequently, in Britain in the 1920s
a medium free from commercial interests (a licence-fee funded public
service broadcaster) was seen to be the best means to protect freedom of
expression and to counter the sensationalism of the press. An additional
task for the BBC was to introduce, or re-introduce, the public to certain
national symbols of public life and public ceremonies or, in other words,
the symbols and icons of a British identity and common culture. In a
multicultural, multi-channel era, these tasks may seem somewhat quaint
and incongruous.

All of the above concerns indicate that there are different starting-points
for regulation, different assumptions within regulation and different reasons by which regulation can be justified or undertaken. Indeed, Feintuck
identifies four conflicting rationales for regulation of the broadcasting
sector:[13] first, effective communication; secondly, diversity, both practical

---

[10] See, e.g., Articles 22 and 22a of the Television without Frontiers Directive (TWFD), Council Directive 89/552/EEC on the co-ordination of certain provisions laid down by law,
regulation or administrative action in member states concerning the pursuit of television
broadcasting activities, OJ [1989] L298/23, as amended by Directive 97/36/EC OJ [1997]
L 202/30.

[11] See, e.g., D. Gauntlett, *Moving Experiences: Understanding Television's Influence and Effects*
(London: John Libbey, 1995), *passim*; W. J. Potter, *On Media Violence* (London: Sage,
1999), p. 1.

[12] Scannell and Cardiff, *A Social History of British Broadcasting*, p. 12.

[13] M. Feintuck, *Media Regulation, Public Interest and the Law* (Edinburgh: Edinburgh University Press, 1999), p. 43.

and cultural; thirdly, economic justifications; and fourthly, public service.[14] Effective communication requires regulation of the spectrum to
ensure access to it is not dominated by only a few broadcasters, or, in
an era of spectrum scarcity, overwhelmed by too many. Secondly, diversity refers to the number of broadcasters operating in a system and is
linked by policymakers and analysts to plurality of supply (see chapters 2
and 7), although it is recognised that a plurality of suppliers is no guarantee of real diversity of content or freedom of expression. Thirdly, economic justifications for regulation stress the benefits that arise from an
efficiently operating market, although there is considerable debate over
what actually makes the market efficient, interference or freedom. Regulation here is usually undertaken to counterbalance threats to the broadcast
media, which can occur with the formation of private cartels or oligopolies
which constrain the free flow of information and engage in abusive business practices in the sector. According to this approach, intervention is
required only where there are examples of market failure which must
be corrected in order to ensure the proper functioning of the market.
As noted in chapter 2, failure is perceived to be particularly likely when
the sector concerned provides 'merit goods'[15] or 'public goods'.[16] A purely
economic approach to regulation has been subject to many criticisms, due
to its fundamentally utilitarian nature and the way in which it reinforces
existing inequalities.[17] Finally, the public service rationale for regulation
can be seen in two ways – economically and politically. From an economic
perspective, public service extends the economic argument into considerations of what should be undertaken to either protect or promote those
things which are regarded as desirable, but which, for whatever reasons,
the market will not supply, or, if it does so, will charge a price. Charging
for such services then produces subsequent problems of access. This view
sees public service as a response to market failure and the problem of
providing merit goods. From a political perspective public service as a
political choice is based in ideas about what a state should provide for

---

[14] Ogus seems to suggest that the justification for regulation can be broken down into two
groups: social welfare regulation; and economic regulation, but that both are introduced in
response to market failure: A. Ogus, *Regulation: Legal Form and Economic Theory* (Oxford:
Clarendon Press, 1994), pp. 4–5.

[15] Graham, 'Broadcasting Policy in the Multimedia Age', in Graham *et al.*, *Public Purposes*,
p. 27.

[16] Feintuck, *Media Regulation*, p. 47.

[17] M. Kelman, 'Legal Economists and Normative Social Theory', from *A Guide to Critical
Legal Studies* (Cambridge, Mass.: Harvard University Press, 1987) cited by Feintuck, *The
Public Interest*, p. 7.

its citizens. Somewhat unfashionably, we have concerns about the economic perspective being applied to public service, because we believe in this case it limits the scope of PSB to providing only those services which the market will not provide (see chapter 13).

Approaches to regulation

As broadcasting 'lies at the crossroads of many forces'[18] and is seen as something which may variously have an economic, social, cultural, moral, intellectual or even a political purpose, it is unsurprising to note that policies creating the broadcasting systems were 'creatures of the moment'.[19] Although we have seen historical variation in regulatory approaches and precise broadcasting models varied in different European countries, the overall general structures which from time to time emerged were very similar.[20] Public service broadcasting organisations appeared across Europe (and in many other parts of the world), and each was regarded as being a vital communicator in existing or newly developing liberal democratic systems. Governments across Europe intervened in the broadcasting sector, the technology for which had been created through private entrepreneurship. They first created state monopolies and then disbanded them. Essentially, both these moves were political choices. Certainly, they were not a technology-driven necessity.

In a strict sense, regulation was not involved in the context of state monopolies. Regulation is the control by public power of private actors;[21] such monopolies form part of the apparatus of the state. This point is illustrated by the fact that the independent regulatory authority in the UK was introduced only with the arrival of commercial television. This does not, of course, mean that the BBC was not subject to particular obligations, as it had to meet the terms of its licence and charter. With the increasing power of private-sector operators, the dismantling of state monopolies, the ascendancy of neo-liberal economics and its corresponding belief in 'small government', the position is changing yet again. Gibbons identifies the interplay between the introduction of commercialisation and the need for regulation to ensure media pluralism, a debate which can be found occurring across Europe.[22]

---

[18] Tracey, *The Decline and Fall of Public Service Broadcasting*, p. 19.   [19] *Ibid.*, p. 19.

[20] Krebber, *Europeanisation of Regulatory Television Policy*, p. 39.

[21] Note that, increasingly, private bodies are exercising public functions and it is arguable that they also should be included within a concept of regulation: M. Feintuck, *The Public Interest in Regulation* (Oxford: Oxford University Press, 2004), p. 6.

[22] T. Gibbons, 'Pluralism, Guidance and the New Media', in C. Marsden (ed.), *Regulating the Global Information Society* (London: Routledge, 2000), p. 307.

In the Union there has been a trend towards liberalisation, where less regulation is regarded as desirable (see chapter 4). It is, however, questionable what is meant by less regulation: whether quantitatively there are fewer rules; whether any regulatory system is less onerous in terms of the qualitative standards to be met; or, as we shall see below, whether qualitative standards should be set and implemented by bodies other than state bodies. As part of this 'deregulatory tendency', there has been a move away from sector specific regulation which seeks to control industry actors' actions in advance, to an approach which relies on the market to provide public interest objectives. Competition law, which operates generally, is used to correct specific market failures after they have occurred. This is a move, in principle, from *ex ante* regulation to *ex post* regulation. Given the nature of the broadcasting sector, this seems to be more difficult to apply in practice than in theory, and some commentators have suggested that in the communications sector there has been some blurring of the boundaries between different approaches to regulation.

Within the broadcasting sector, however, sector specific *ex ante* regulation, such as that found in the Television without Frontiers Directive (TWFD)[23] remains. Conversely, within the communication networks industries a more competition-based, *ex post* approach has been introduced (see chapters 6 and 7). The nature and scope of television regulation contained in the TWFD is currently in the process of revision, a revision which has become necessary due to debates concerning the approach to regulation generally, changes in technology and the consequent changing relationship between viewer and broadcaster. Overall, though, there is a general trend towards co-regulation and self-regulation, as well as more informal forms of governance, such as the agreement of policy guidelines, reflected within the broadcasting sphere. As the *Communication on the Community's Audiovisual Policy in the Digital Age* suggested, regulators should take into account the degree of user choice and control over content in determining the appropriate level and/or type of regulation (see chapters 4 and 5).[24] Even so, the broadcasting sector still remains characterised by a significant level of government control via independent

---

[23] Council Directive 89/552/EEC of 3 October on the co-ordination of certain provisions laid down by law, regulation or administrative action in member states concerning the pursuit of television broadcasting activities OJ [1989] L298/23, as amended by Directive 97/36/EC OJ [1997] L 202/30.

[24] Commission, *Communication on Principles and Guidelines for the Community's Audiovisual Policy in the Digital Age*, COM (1999)657 final. See more recently Commission, *Paper for Focus Group: Regulation of Audiovisual Content*, September 2004, p. 2.

bodies, which have the function of determining standards of behaviour and supervising compliance with those standards.

There are many different mechanisms for regulation: notification; licensing; individual licences; restrictions on ownership; content requirements. These place both positive obligations as well as negative obligations on broadcasters. This level of state involvement is traditional top-down regulation in which the state is seeking to channel and control behaviour directly. The opposite end of the regulatory scale to top-down regulation is self-regulation, in which standards are set by those who are subject to them. Compliance is not enforced by any state sanction. Between these two ends of the regulatory scale are, of course, a variety of other different models involving varying levels of influence and control by both state bodies and those involved in the regulated sector. This variety can be described as co-regulation. Co-regulation occurs where both the public and private sector are involved, although the precise nature and limits of a co-regulatory structure are unclear.[25] Co-regulation can be seen as desirable because of its consensual nature. Further, in terms of the protection of fundamental interests such as human rights, the underlying threat of state action is seen as appropriate, or even necessary in terms of states' responsibilities under international law. Arguably, co-regulation contains the advantages of both regulation and self-regulation. As it evolves across the Union, it is to be hoped that it does not contain the weaknesses of both.

Co-regulation, and to some extent self-regulation, are seen as potentially more efficient forms of regulation because both utilise industry involvement in the standards-setting process. If the broadcasting industry is involved in this process, they become part of it and are, in theory, more likely to comply, as they subscribe to the standards that they themselves have helped to set. Additionally, industry involvement means that the standards that are set are practical and attainable, although, as we will see in chapter 6, this does create problems. There are concerns that the standard-setting process may be used by the industry to favour their commercial position.[26] At the very least, there is a concern that industry

---

[25] For a recent discussion of the meaning of co-regulation and its role in 'solving' some of the challenges facing traditional approaches to regulation see, e.g., Hans Bredow Institut, *Study on Co-regulatory Measures in the Media Sector, Interim Report, Study for the European Commission*, Directorate Information Society 19 May 2005, pp. 1–22, available: http://europa.eu.int/comm/avpolicy/stat/2005/coregul/coregul-interim-report.pdf

[26] European Parliament, *Report on the Application of Articles 4 and 5 of Directive 89/552/EEC, as amended by Directive 97/36/EC for the period 2001–2002* (2004/2236(INI)), A6-0202/2005 (The Weber Report), p. 13.

members would be reluctant to set standards at a high level. There is also a question of principle, in that it is not always clear whose voices are being represented in this process and how standards are determined. It is particularly questionable the extent to which the voice of the viewer, particularly the citizen, is adequately heard in such a process.

The role of industry bodies may have a further impact in that technology itself can limit the choices or the freedom of action of other industry actors and the viewer. In this sense, technology constitutes a form of regulation. As Lessig argued in the context of the internet:

> [i]f the regulator wants to induce a certain behaviour, she need not threaten or cajole, to inspire the change. She need only change the code – the software that defines the terms upon which the individual gains access to the system . . .
>
> Code is an efficient means of regulation. But its perfection makes it something different. One obeys these laws as code not because one should; one obeys these laws as code because one can do nothing else. There is no choice about whether to yield to the demand for a password; one complies if one wants to enter the system. In the well implemented system, there is no civil disobedience. Law as code is a start to the perfect technology of justice.[27]

This argument can be used in the context of a smart card and set-top box, just as much as in the context of a computer and access to internet sites (see chapters 6 and 10). Although regulation by technology may be effective, there are concerns in that the standards incorporated are those chosen by private actors (often acting in their own commercial interests), rather than those set by government in the public interest.[28] As we suggest below, there are also questions about whether the technology ends up controlling the viewer rather than the other way round, and if the viewer's choice in practice is actually reduced or removed.

---

[27] L. Lessig, 'The Zones of Cyberspace', *Stanford LR* 48 (1996) 1403–11, p. 1408.

[28] For a discussion of some of the problems of relying on private actors to enforce government policy, see, e.g., J. Boyle, 'Foucault in Cyberspace: Surveillance, Sovereignty and Hardwired Censors', *University of Cincinnati LR* 66 (1997) 177. Discussing the use of the V-chip in the United States, he comments, at p. 202, 'The V-chip seems to be merely a neutral facilitator of parental choice. The various acts of coercion involved the government making the television company insert the thing into the machine, the public private board choosing which ratings criteria will be available for parents to use simply disappear into the background. Finally, the distributed privatized nature of the system promises that it might actually work; though admittedly, state administration of the television system poses fewer headaches than state administration of the Internet.'

Impact of digitalisation and convergence
on the regulatory environment

The impact of technology on Union broadcasting policy is not new. The original genesis for the *TWF Green Paper*[29] resulting in the TWFD was the impact of the inherently transnational nature of satellite broadcasting on a national regulatory structure (see discussion on jurisdiction in chapter 8). Underpinning current broadcasting policymaking are assumptions about the inevitable power of convergence and the 'determining effect of technology', especially digitalisation.[30] Neither the precise meaning of digitalisation or convergence nor their impact is clear cut. With this in mind, we now go on to discuss each of these in turn.

Digitalisation relies upon a common format or binary language, plus the compression of signals, allowing the volume of information which is transmitted to be increased enormously. This development has had an impact on the regulation of content. There are three linked points: abundance/scarcity; convergence; and interactivity. The first point refers to the fact that in the terrestrial analogue era there were a limited number of frequencies available for television broadcasting. This scarcity, as we suggested earlier, was used to justify regulation.[31] In a digital era, scarcity seems to be replaced by abundance. Whereas analogue transmission converts images and sound into electric signals which are converted back to images and sound by receiver equipment, digital transmission uses the binary language of computers, namely ones and zeros. In analogue transmission, the whole of each individual frame of film or video is transmitted, meaning that, in order to broadcast the image, each complete frame must be redrawn on the screen. Using digital technology, only the changes from frame to frame are transmitted, allowing more information to be sent using the same amount of bandwidth. Digital data can also be compressed at the point at which it is sent and then decompressed via a set-top box. This reduces further the amount of information it is necessary to transmit. Given this effectiveness, arguments for regulation

---

[29] Commission, *Television without Frontiers: Green Paper on the Establishment of the Common Market for Broadcasting*, COM (1984) 300 final.

[30] S. Clegg, A. Hudson and J. Steel, 'The Emperor's New Clothes: Globalisation and e-Learning in Higher Education', *British Journal of Sociology of Education*, 24(1) (2003), 49–53, p. 50.

[31] E. Barendt, *Broadcasting Law* (Oxford: Clarendon Press, 1993), p. 4 cites the *Peacock Committee Report on Financing the BBC*, Cmnd 9824 (1986) as a classic discussion of the reasons for regulation.

based on spectrum scarcity have been undermined, though not entirely removed.[32]

Secondly, convergence means the distinctions between telecommunications and broadcasting increasingly become redundant. Digitalisation enables technologies to converge, though the precise meaning of this term is disputed (see below). The convergence of communication technology[33] means that the same content can now be distributed over different networks, and questions arise about the justification for treating content differently purely by virtue of the communication network used (see chapter 5). This argument can be characterised as one based on the principle of technological neutrality. For example, the development of Internet protocol television (IPTV), or television-ready personal computers, provides new viewing contexts for viewers, but raises questions about how best to regulate that content across different platforms and delivery systems.

The third aspect of digitalisation is interactivity. Digital television signals can be easily integrated with other digital signals, making interactive programming possible, and potentially changing the relationship which is established between the sender and receiver of signals. The relationship between the sender (broadcaster) and receiver (viewer) of signals can be characterised in three broad ways. First, the most basic interactive relationship comprises a stand-alone information service, where the viewer can access information via a text-type service available through an interactive menu, similar to the existing Teletext service. Secondly, an enhanced programming service allows the viewer to get more information on an item featured during a broadcast programme. Pictures and text are transmitted simultaneously through a single channel and viewers can select different combinations of these to be displayed on their screen using a remote control (for example, access to sports statistics, use of a different camera angle or access to a choice of mini screens).

---

[32] See, e.g., concerns expressed by the European Broadcasting Union in the context of the proposed introduction of spectrum trading, European Broadcasting Union, *EBU Contribution to the European Commission's Call for Input on the Forthcoming Review of the EU Regulatory Framework for Electronic Communications and Services*, 30 January 2006, p. 2. www.ebu.ch/CMSimages/en/leg_pp_telecom_package_310106_tcm6-42308.pdf

[33] Commission, *Green Paper on the Convergence of the Telecommunications, Media and Information Technology Sectors, and the Implications for Regulation. Towards an Information Society Approach*, COM (1997) 623; Commission, *Public Consultation on the Convergence Green Paper: Communication to the European Parliament, the Council, the Economic and Social Committee and the Committee of the Regions*, COM (1999)108.

Finally, transactional services allow the viewer to interact with the television in order to vote, bank, gamble, play games or shop. The platform provider can control the range of sites and the quality and type of service provided, via a 'walled garden'. In theory, unrestricted access to the internet via broadband connections to a television may be allowed. Internet protocol television enables the same functions and services to be accessed through the technologies used for computer networks.

The availability of content over different platforms, and different content being available on the same platform, are two examples of different forms of convergence: technical convergence and service convergence, respectively. It is unsurprising, then, that 'convergence' does not have a settled meaning. The general description usually just covers technological convergence where different and previously discrete economic sectors of electronic media and telecommunications converge. It can also mean that previously distinct areas in services, markets and ownership converge.[34] The term has also been used in different ways to justify various types of policy action. In the British context the impetus for the *Communications White Paper* in 2000, which led eventually to the creation of the 'super-regulator', Ofcom, was the promise of convergence brought about by digitalisation and the need for a converged regulatory structure. In this example, New Labour discourse disconnected 'convergence' from its technical meaning and associated it with the liberalisation process. Convergence in this case was used as a means to justify deregulation, the removal of restriction on ownership and privatisation. In so doing, the UK Labour Party has been seen to use the 'discourse of convergence as a neo-liberal Trojan Horse'.[35] In other words, the policy adopted was a political choice, based on a political interpretation of the meaning and significance of technological change; it was certainly not the only possible response.

In the late 1990s in both the Union and national context, the need was recognised to harness the changes in relationships which would occur between different actors in the media sector: audiences and

---

[34] W. Sauter, 'The Role of European Economic Law in the Information Society: Balancing Private Freedoms and Public Interests in the Context of Convergence between Telecommunications, Media and Information Technology', in P. Nihoul (ed.), *Telecommunications and Broadcasting Networks under EC Law: The Protection Afforded to Consumers and Undertakings in the Information Society* (Köln: Bundesanzeiger, 2000), pp. 286–309.

[35] T. Sampson and J. Lugo, 'The Discourse of Convergence: A Neo-liberal Trojan horse', in G. F. Lowe and T. Hujanen, *Broadcasting and Convergence: New Articulations of the Public Service Remit* (Goteborg: Nordicom, 2003), pp. 83–92, p. 83.

producers, broadcasters and narrowcasters. Convergence of technology has not resulted in single electronic devices replacing existing platforms, as might have earlier been thought. Rather, convergence has given rise to a range of new platforms through which digitised information can be distributed and marketed. These developments have raised challenges for sector specific regulation and national regulators as to how best to harness the potential of these new economic and technical opportunities, how to regulate partially converging sectors and how to protect the special nature of broadcasting.[36] The *Convergence Green Paper* identified the divergence in views about the inevitability of convergence as falling between two main camps, the maximalists and the minimalists.[37] The maximalists perceived current regulatory structures as inadequate, as all networks would be able to deliver services to any platform, and because much regulation retained a national focus which would be inappropriate in an international services market. The minimalists argued that convergence would have less impact than that envisaged by the maximalists, and held that broadcasting policy should actively promote social, cultural and ethical values, regardless of which particular technology was used for delivering services. As such, minimalists preferred two sets of rules, one for economic aspects and another for service content, as in existing broadcasting policy, in order to guarantee efficiency and quality. As we will see in chapter 5, despite the divergent views about the likely impact of convergence, its potential benefits have become a central theme in European integration, becoming closely linked to the information society[38] project.

Although the development of new technologies and new services may seem positive from the perspective of the viewer, problems arise at a number of levels. Convergence of services to one platform may mean that the viewer can access differently regulated services in the same way. Since the same technology is used, the viewer may not be aware of the different levels of regulation applicable to the content they receive. Further, at its most basic level, digital television requires equipment capable of decoding

---

[36] E.g., the number of people who listen to the radio via digital television is growing. Rajar figures show that 28.8 percent of all adults have at some time listened to radio using their television set as at June 2004, almost half the number that have access to digital television. This practice raises issues for the nature of radio and the amount of information that can be placed on a television screen. www.ofcom.org.uk/research/industry_market_research/m_i_index/cm/overview/rmd/2_1/?a = 87101.

[37] Commission, *Green Paper on Convergence*, p. 2.

[38] Sauter, 'The Role of European Economic Law', pp. 286–309.

the signal. This equipment will become essential when analogue switch-off occurs. The viewer will be required to acquire more equipment, which will have cost implications. Even for the viewer of digital television, there are problems of access because of the different platforms and the encoded nature of pay TV (see chapters 1 and 6).

As we pointed out in chapter 1, as channel numbers expand it becomes more difficult for the viewer to choose from a bewildering array of programmes. Digital delivery systems allow the viewer to browse the channel line-up using an on-screen electronic programme guide (EPG). The EPG allows the viewer to look at lists of programmes showing on all channels at the same time and allows the viewer to customise viewing. This activity, coupled with new personal video recorders (PVRs), and recording technology such as Tivo or Sky$^+$, which record programmes directly onto a hard drive, enables the viewer to be relatively free of the constraints of scheduling. Although a certain level of time-shifting has been possible since video was introduced in the 1980s, recent technological possibilities introduce a new level of personalisation into the viewing process. The new technologies allow a far greater amount of information to be recorded and easily stored. It is in conjunction with the EPG that the greatest change in relationship between viewer and content can be seen. The new technologies allow a systematic categorisation of programmes which direct the viewer to types of programme in which the viewer has already expressed an interest, via 'favourites'. This type of system reinforces existing viewer preferences and could restrict the variety of programming chosen. Two issues arise. First, the viewer can effectively become isolated, if he or she so chooses, from major national televised events, rendering the attempts to establish and foster collective viewing of events more difficult. It arguably devolves decision-making about choice of programmes to technical devices, which may bring its own problems (see chapter 10). Secondly, devices such as Tivo or Sky$^+$ allow the viewer to fast-forward through advertisements. The industry argues that this is a new development, leaving the advertising sector in search of new ways to target the television audience. In fact, although Tivo and Sky$^+$ may facilitate technological control over the viewing of advertisements, it is not a new practice. Fast-forwarding through the adverts is a commonplace activity, as those who have recorded programmes on video or DVD well know. Correspondingly, the claim for a particular regulatory response, lifting the prohibition on product placement, to ameliorate the problems caused to advertisers and broadcasters by viewers being able to avoid advertisements via the use of technology, deserves much closer scrutiny.

Successful lobbying by the advertising and broadcasting industries on this point may have repercussions for editorial integrity of programmes, which may, in turn, have adverse consequences for the viewing experience (see chapter 9).

Regulation and the viewing experience

Many of the traditional justifications for broadcast regulation focus on the role of broadcasting in creating an informed citizenry. These justifications underpinned both positive and negative regulation. 'Good' information was to be protected and provided; 'bad' information prohibited. Implicit in this approach is a perception held by policymakers and, as a consequence, regulators, of the role of the viewer in choosing what to watch (see table 1, chapter 1). The underlying assumption was that the viewer simply receives any information that is provided. Therefore, in order to serve the interests of the citizen, the content must necessarily be of a different type from that which serves consumer interests (see chapter 2). With technological change and increased commercialisation, viewers appear to have more choice of viewing material, with the result that it also appears as if the viewing experience itself has changed. Certainly this is the view of industry participants and some regulators. Commercial broadcasters are more and more likely to see viewers as consumers rather than as citizens, and regulatory interests have to some extent followed this trend. For example, some obligations within the Communications Act 2003 in the UK are explicitly addressed to consumers. There are very few references, by contrast, to the requirements of citizens.

In fact, the viewing experience is changing in ways which may have an impact on viewers' ability either to be active citizens or to become more discerning consumers. Viewers are often now seen to be less passive, or at least are given the opportunity to be more active. The idea of the empowered viewer, however, overlooks a prior concern in that it makes certain assumptions about the capacity of each individual viewer to make choices, and even assumes that they have access to complete information on which to base their choices. It does not cater for the needs of those viewers from more vulnerable groups, such as children, some elderly people, the mentally incapacitated, those viewers who find new technology confusing, viewers who are too poor to afford digital equipment, those viewers who would rather have things chosen for them, those who share reception technology, such as aerials, and even those who are too busy to engage with new technology and services available. Some of these

problems have been identified in consumer protection law more generally.[39] Within Union law, although measures to protect the consumer are
permitted, these are limited to those measures that are necessary to protect
the interests of the reasonably well-informed consumer, arguably leading
to inadequate levels of protection for those who do not meet this relatively
high threshold.[40]

In part, the possibility of customising the viewing experience arises
from an increased number of channels, which in theory offer greater
choice, as well as PVRs and other navigation devices. Concomitant to this
is the way interactivity is changing the viewing experience. Whereas before
producers and publishers have controlled the content and delivery, digital
technology in theory can enable end users to change and manipulate the
information they receive, or to provide it themselves. Examples of user-
generated content range from that found in traditional programming,
such as letters (or SMS/MMS messages and emails) from viewers read
out in the studio to viewers sending in video clips from mobile phones,
whether of an event of national significance or of themselves doing something stupid. Such content can also be found on broadcaster-maintained
websites, such as the BBC's Video Nation.[41] All of these developments
have the potential to transform the consumers' or citizens' relationship
with broadcasting from a traditionally passive and linear one to an increasingly interactive and non-linear one. This transformation leads to a whole
new set of negotiated relationships with the suppliers of information and
its receivers, and could require a new set of regulatory requirements.
Whilst there may be arguments based on consumer choice and freedom
of expression for lighter regulation, there are other consequences, such as

---

[39] S. Weatherill, *EC Consumer Law and Policy* (London and New York: Longman, 1997).

[40] See, e.g., Case C-210/96 *Gut Springenheide and Rudolf Tusky* v. *Oberkreisdirektor des Kreises Steinfurt-Amt für Lebensmittelüberwachung* [1998] ECR I-4657, para. 31; Case C-220/98 *Estée Lauder Cosmetics GmbH & Co OHG* v. *Lancaster Group GmbH* [2000] ECR I-117, para. 27. These cases are based on the notion of the average consumer; the European Court of Justice (ECJ) refers to vulnerable consumers only rarely, although the Advocates-General have occasionally identified a difference between a casual consumer and an average one. The extent to which this is problematic is open to debate as the ECJ, when assessing the average consumer, takes into account the consumers at which the product was targeted. Vulnerability will then be taken into account at the level of deciding what an average consumer in the particular target group is. This approach does not defend the position of vulnerable consumers by comparison with the average consumer for whichever group is in issue.

[41] www.bbc.co.uk/videonation/takepart/index.shtml.

the unforeseen invasion of privacy,[42] which may militate towards more stringent regulation.

Here the terms 'linear' and 'non-linear' are used to differentiate between traditional and interactive services.[43] Linear broadcasting is underpinned by editorial responsibility to determine what is shown and when. Non-linear broadcasting places the responsibility of what is viewed and when with the viewer or consumer. Such non-linear services, like video on demand (VOD) and other interactive services, allow the consumer to choose the broadcast content they wish to see at any time, on any delivery platform, thereby changing the nature of the relationship between the viewer or consumer and the content supplier. The distinction between the two types of services is crucial when it comes to decisions about control of broadcast content and who is responsible for it, as the continuing development of non-linear broadcast services could render editorial intervention by the programme maker redundant.

Interactive digital television has the potential to offer one-stop shop convenience to the consumer, allowing individuals to personalise and customise their viewing experience free from formal scheduling constraints, and to pay extra for particular goods and services. Consequently, digital television is constituted from a mixture of commercial relationships between television, telephony, utilities, Internet and on-line services. Notwithstanding the convenience for the consumer of customisation and personalisation of the viewing experience, views about the potential of digitalisation are very mixed. Concerns are rooted in the problems of information overload, trivialisation of information[44] and the development of an access divide,[45] consumer apathy about new digital initiatives, and the privatization of information, all of which can

---

[42] The broadcasters are encouraging members of the public to send in their own pictures and videos. A victim of a tragedy recorded by a member of the public, however, may well object to having his or her image broadcast. Equally, if a person uploads video or photographs to a website, notwithstanding any policy on the part of the broadcaster, it will effectively be impossible to withdraw that information as it may already have been copied via other people accessing the site.

[43] Note the draft second amending directive (DSAD) introduces definitions based on the linear and non-linear distinction: Commission, Proposal for a Directive Amending Directive 89/552/EEC, COM (2005) 646 final, 2005/0260 (COD), SEC (2005) 1625 and 1626.

[44] N. Postman, *Amusing Ourselves to Death* (London: Methuen, 1985), *passim*.

[45] H. Schiller, *Information Inequality* (New York, Routledge, 1996), *passim*; J. Curran and J. Seaton, *Power without Responsibility* (London: Routledge, 2003), p. 259; S. Barnett, 'New Media, Old Problems: New Technology and the Political Process', *European Journal of Communication*, 12(2) (1997), 193–218, p. 204.

result in a 'lack of choice for technologically deprived viewers'[46] (see chapter 6).

In contrast to the pessimistic views above, digitalisation is seen by some policymakers as having tremendous potential to enable citizens and businesses together to derive maximum benefit from the so-called knowledge economy.[47] Paradoxically, this enthusiasm for new digital technologies is both underpinned by an economic rationale and optimism that digitalisation can encourage and foster an empowered and engaged citizenry.[48]

Conclusion

This chapter has explored some of the historical and technological developments of the television broadcasting sector. In so doing, we have identified the responses of policymakers at a general level in reaction to these developments. Different attitudes towards the viewing experience influence the shape of regulatory responses. What is significant for us is the fact that these regulatory responses, although arguably tailored to cope with the changing technological and commercial environment, are nothing other than economic or political choices and are not in themselves inevitable or determined by consistent understandings of the broadcasting sector. None the less, as our discussion of the policy responses to digitalisation and convergence suggests, new technologies pose both opportunities and risks. Our concern is that the former are exaggerated and are promoted over the consequences of the latter, thereby stimulating the expanding commercial environment which sees viewers as consumers who are free to choose from the range of broadcasting options now available. This approach relies upon an over-simplification of the nature of the viewing experience, and persistently underplays the potential cultural value and importance of broadcasting content.

[46] M. Wells, 'BBC Defends Digital Ratings as MP Criticises "Bribery"', *Guardian*, 8 January 2003, p. 2.

[47] In particular, see the current i2010 strategic action plan launched by the Commission on 1 June 2005. i2010 follows on from the eEurope 2005 plan and focuses on information technologies that the Commission considers to be crucial in the overall Union objective of increasing innovation and jobs. The approach the Commission has chosen to take is focused on the convergence of content and infrastructure industries. Of particular interest is the potential which arises from the development of digital technology, the mobile Internet and third-generation mobile telephony, digital television and radio and nanotechnologies. In the framework of i2010 the Commission has issued a proposal for revising the TWFD.

[48] See Commission, *Communication on an information and communication strategy for the European Union*, COM(2002)350 final.

As we noted in the above analysis of digital technological change, the role of the viewer has moved beyond that of passive subject; the viewer is now sometimes an actor, or part of the regulatory control mechanism (for example, see the discussion regarding the V-chip in chapter 10). Problematically, the technology used might not be neutral in its operation (see EPGs discussed above and in chapter 6). We believe that current policy does not adequately take account of the difference between citizens and consumers, or of viewers' differing dispositions towards technology, particularly interactive technology, which exacerbates the divide between passive and active viewing.

Our concern is that the term 'empowerment', often used by policymakers, conceals certain problems of access and choice; limited by personal and external factors and by the deceptions within technology itself. It may appear that the viewer has greater choice and responsibility in 'pulling', selecting and controlling the material that is viewed. Choice could be delimited by both the phenomenon of a constantly unchanging content range and the particular way it is packaged. This assumption about choice also fails to recognise that the technology may act as a censorship device. Although viewers may select the general parameters of the type of material they want to view, the technology operates to make choices about the material that is excluded at a programme by programme level. There is a further concern that viewers may simply revert to relying on another mechanism (i.e. here the technology) to make decisions for them, thus negating the potential for personal or individual intervention in and control of the viewing experience. In chapter 10 we question the value of current media literacy initiatives. In other words, if we expect to make real choices, the quality of information needed on which to base those choices is crucial. This becomes critical in the context of advisories (see chapter 10), and for electronic programme guides (EPGs) (see chapter 6). The picture is complex, but as we shall see in the next two chapters, made more so within the Union which has its own problems with reconciling the tensions between cultural and commercial objectives.

4

Union competence

Introduction

Broadcasting policy lies across a number of fault lines within the terrain of the Union relating to its purposes and its powers. Broadcast policymaking has occurred within the developing framework of the Union in which, over time, we have seen expanding Union competence accompanied by changing relationships with member states. This relationship is not just a power struggle between different levels and institutions of government. It also has an impact on the value ascribed to different types of policy areas, depending on whether an area is seen primarily as Union competence, or a field falling mainly within the preserve of the member state. Difficulties also arise out of the different types of competence awarded to the Union itself, which result in tension between these areas of competence, and affect the types of measure that can be taken at Union level.

This chapter delineates the nature of the Union as a body of attributed competence, as well as considering its relationship with the constituent member states. It is important to note that this chapter does not consider political or policy processes; rather, it identifies the legal framework within which political and judicial actors operate and the consequent law-based limitations on their respective freedom of action. We commence with a brief introduction to the Union and the principles upon which it operates. We then consider judicial harmonisation, which is the application of treaty freedoms and competition policy, as it limits the scope of member states to regulate in many areas. The limitations to enacting positive harmonising measures, that is, the acts of the political institutions to produce Union level legislation, are discussed. A final section considers the types of action that the Union might take in a given policy area, before concluding remarks identify some general points about the coherence of Union judicial and political law-making.

Development and expansion of the European Union

The European Union was originally formed by the Treaty of Rome (EC Treaty) and was at that point called the European Economic Community (the Community). The Maastricht Treaty (TEU) introduced the idea of the European Union (the Union), of which the Community now constitutes part. Essentially we are concerned in this book with policy fields which fall within the scope of the Community, although for ease of reference we shall refer, save where absolutely necessary, to Union law. The Union has grown in size and scope through its complex and overlapping treaties.[1] One attribute has not changed: the Union is a body with conferred powers. It can act only within the terms of its constituent treaties. None the less, over the decades the Union's ability to act in a variety of areas of public policy has increased, extending beyond the commercial, into the social, the cultural and even into the area of European citizenship. The desire to build a peaceful and prosperous Europe that would benefit from trade agreements meant that the original EC Treaty had a mainly economic focus,[2] although this relatively limited remit and purpose did not last, as the expanding list of objectives in Article 2 EC illustrates.[3]

Despite the functional expansion of the Union, its central focus remained the creation of a common market. To achieve this end, the EC Treaty provided for the free movement of goods, services, people and capital (the four freedoms). In the context of broadcasting, it is the free movement of services that is the most relevant.[4] Article 49 provides that 'restrictions on freedom to provide services' are to 'be prohibited in respect of nationals of member States who are established in a State of the Community other than that of the person for whom the services are intended'. Additionally Articles 81 and 82 prohibit anti-competitive agreements and the abuse of a dominant position, respectively, so as to prevent the

---

[1] The 1997 Single European Act, the 1992 Maastricht Treaty (entered into force in 1993), the 1997 Amsterdam Treaty (entered into force in 1999), the 2001 Nice Treaty (entered into force in 2003) and in the 2004 Constitutional Treaty (subject to ratification by each of the member states). If it comes into force, the Constitutional Treaty will replace the existing structure.

[2] Even in its original format, the EC Treaty had a social focus, aiming, e.g., to improve living conditions.

[3] For a brief discussion of Union policy competences, see E. Bomberg and A. Stubb, *The European Union: How Does it Work?* (Oxford: Oxford University Press, 2003), pp. 116–18. For a more law-focused overview of the expansion of Community competence up to the Treaty of Nice see, e.g., D. Wyatt, 'The Growing Competence of the European Community', *E.B.L. Rev* 16(3) (2005), 483–88, *passim*.

[4] Case 155/73 *Sacchi* [1974] ECR 409.

distortion of competition in the common market. These provisions constitute the central planks of Union competition policy and are principally aimed at private actors, although member states are precluded from putting laws in place which effectively require anti-competitive behaviour by private actors. State action in distorting the market is also constrained by the EC Treaty, in the main by the state-aid provisions, Articles 87 *et seq*. All these provisions can affect state monopolies in services, including those providing public service broadcasting.[5]

The effectiveness of these provisions has been increased by a number of doctrines enunciated by the European Court of Justice (ECJ), notably the doctrine of supremacy.[6] Supremacy means that, in the event of a conflict between Community law and that of a member state, Community law takes priority.[7] From the perspective of the Union, the conflicting national law is 'disapplied' without need for action by the relevant member state's legislature.[8] This doctrine arguably creates a European market without there necessarily being a corresponding European regulatory space. The exceptions to the freedom to provide services, which to a certain extent return competence to the individual member states, are thus significant. It is these exceptions that, in the absence of Union legislative action, allow member states a certain regulatory space, albeit subject to review within the European legal order. Although the treaties operate to define the scope of Union action, they effectively determine the permitted scope of member-state action, too.

Although the four freedoms go some way to ensuring an internal market, on their own they might be insufficient, or take inadequate account of other policy interests. The original EC Treaty recognised this. It was, after all, a *traité cadre*, that is a framework treaty which was intended to be supplemented by further rules enacted by institutions set up for this purpose. It is here that we see the effect of the Union being a creature of limited competence: such rules can only be made where the treaty grants the relevant institutions the power to act, in accordance with the

---

[5] Case C-260/89 *Elliniki Radiophonia Tileorassi AE (ERT)* v. *Dimotiki Etairia Pliroforissis (DEP) and Sotirios Kouvelas* [1991] ECR I-2925.

[6] For a review of the relationship between member states and the Union in the light of the Constitutional Treaty, see, e.g., A. Dashwood, 'The Relationship between the Member States and the European Union/European Community', *CML Rev* 41(2) (2004), 355–81.

[7] Case 26/62 *NV Algemene Transport- en expeditie Onderneming Van Gend en Loos* v. *Nederlandse Administratie der Belastingen* [1963] ECR 1, principle recognised in the Constitution at Article I-6.

[8] Case 106/77 *Amministrazione delle Finanze dello Stato* v. *Simmenthal SpA* (Simmenthal II) [1978] ECR 629.

procedure specified in the particular provision. Originally, in addition to some sector-specific provisions, there were two main general provisions on which the institutions could rely to enact legislation: Article 94 EC and Article 308 EC. Both provisions required unanimity in Council and required that the European Parliament be consulted for their enactment. Article 94 provided for measures in relation to the common market, Article 308 related to situations where the Community had tasks, but no powers. Both could be seen as general fall-back provisions, that is, where sector-specific provisions did not apply. During the early years of the Union, these provisions were, somewhat infamously, interpreted broadly. In addition to these two provisions, there are specific provisions relating to liberalisation of the services sector, enabling the enactment of directives for the co-ordination of national laws.[9] Where the Union has acted, member states are, as we have seen, limited in their freedom of action by the operation of the doctrine of supremacy. Their policy and legislative choices must respect Union law.

Legislative progress was slow because of the requirement for unanimity between the member states in Council. The result was Article 95, introduced in 1987 by the Single European Act (SEA), which provides for measures 'which have as their object the establishment and functioning of the internal market' by way of harmonisation (sometimes called approximation) of national laws. Crucially, for the enactment of such measures, qualified majority voting (QMV) was permitted in Council.[10] With the possibility that member states might be outvoted, it seems that the issue of competence became more pressing. In this context, the contested notion of subsidiarity[11] is central both in terms of illustrating the difficulties and providing a partial solution.

Subsidiarity is a mechanism whereby the question of which level of government should act on a given policy question is addressed. Subsidiarity arises only where both member states and the Union have a claim to act;

---

[9] Article 47(2), which originally required unanimity in Council but which now refers to qualified majority voting (QMV) (see below).

[10] QMV is a system of voting in which the different member states are ascribed a certain number of votes depending broadly on their respective sizes. At the time of its introduction, QMV meant that approximately 70 per cent of the total votes available was required to pass a measure by contrast to the unanimity requirement often seen in international law. With successive enlargements, the issue of the weighting of the votes has become contentious as 'large' member states sought to prevent the dilution of their voting power: more member states meant that it would be easier for a coalition of (smaller) states to outvote the others. QMV now involves a double majority in terms of votes and of population.

[11] Article 5 EC.

it then imposes a test of comparative efficiency which could, in theory, imply either an upward or downward movement of regulatory competence in a given case. Further, subsidiarity also imposes tests of necessity and proportionality on any proposed action. Although the principles of subsidiarity, in general, may seem non-contentious, their application in a given case could well be less clear cut. This depends in part on whose view of efficiency, necessity and proportionality is taken, and bearing in mind the aims of any proposed action. It has been suggested that, in practice, subsidiarity operates at a political level rather than being used in a legal context to limit Union action.[12] Subsidiarity might, therefore, operate to affect the scope or form of Union action proposed by the Commission,[13] an assessment supported by the move towards more informal mechanisms of co-ordination not involving formal law-making, discussed further below.[14]

It should be noted that harmonising legislation is not the only form of action that the Union may take. Indeed, with functional expansion, we see a number of new policy areas being introduced, but in some of which the power to legislate is limited. Notably this affects Article 151,[15] introduced by the TEU, which specified that the Community should

> contribute to the flowering of the cultures of the Member States, while respecting their national and regional diversity; at the same time to bring the common cultural heritage to the fore.

Although the power to harmonise national law is also excluded by this provision, the Union is encouraged to take this policy area into account when developing other policies. While the Union does not have legislative competence in the area of culture, it still has some competence in this and other flanking policy areas such as sport. The requirement to take flanking policies into account also illustrates the fact that it is not possible

---

[12] Although a number of cases have been brought challenging Community action on the basis of subsidiarity, the European courts have refrained from basing any judgment on this principle.

[13] G. Howells and T. Wilhelmsson, *European Consumer Law* (Aldershot: Ashgate, 1997), pp. 9 and 304.

[14] S. Weatherill, 'Why Harmonise', in T. Tridimas and P. Nebbia (eds.), *European Union Law for the Twenty-First Century: Rethinking the New Legal Order* (Oxford: Hart Publishing, 2004), vol. 2, p. 18.

[15] Contrast the position of consumer protection policy and environmental policy, in which Community action is envisaged so as to ensure a high level of protection: Articles 6, 95(2), 152. See further below.

to draw bright lines between the different policy areas. It is consequently not possible clearly to delimit the boundaries of Union competence. The relationship between flanking policies, such as culture, and the common market can be problematic, as we shall see below, and in the context of broadcasting, in chapter 5.

Judicial harmonisation

The ECJ has played a crucial role in the development of the Union. Not only did it introduce the doctrine of supremacy of Community law and that of direct effect[16] but in the early years, in particular, it took an expansive view of Community competence. Consequently the ECJ has confirmed its jurisdiction over areas that might not have been thought to be included in the original economic scope of the EC Treaty. Although broadcasting is an industrial sector, its status as a 'cultural' industry seemed to indicate that it fell outside the scope of the EC Treaty, as the area of culture was a domain in which the original version of the EC Treaty did not give the Union competence to act. The ECJ held that the cultural nature of broadcasting did not take it outside the scope of the EC Treaty. Thus, television broadcasts have been treated by the ECJ as tradable services,[17] subject to rules on free movement between member states (Article 49 EC).[18]

The EC Treaty itself envisages some grounds of derogation from the freedom to provide services: these are contained in Article 46 EC. Article 46 identifies a limited set of reasons justifying member states' action contrary to Article 49: public policy, public security and public health. Over time the ECJ has developed a further group of justifications, which have no basis in the EC Treaty, sometimes referred to as a rule of reason[19] or overriding interests. These are grounds of general public interest and are a category of justifications that are potentially limitless, although neither

---

[16] The doctrine of direct effect refers to the principle that certain rights under Community law may apply directly to the Union citizen, regardless of whether they have been enacted in national law: see Case 26/62 *Van Gend en Loos*.

[17] Case 155/73 *Sacchi*; Case 52/79 *Procureur du Roi* v. *Debauve* [1980] ECR 833; Case 352/85 *Bond van Adverteerders* v. *Netherlands* [1988] ECR 2085.

[18] This distinction may have significance more generally, as the debate about the quotas provisions illustrates: see chapter 11. On the current status of the audio-visual sector within GATS, see F. Smith and L. Woods, 'The GATS and Audiovisual Sector', *Comms L* 9(1) (2004), 15–21.

[19] Note that this is different from the 'rule of reason' found in American anti-trust law and disputed in relation to Articles 81 and 82: see chapter 7.

they nor Article 46 can justify member states' action for economic reasons. The crucial difference between the two categories is that a member state can only seek to rely on the judge-made justifications if the national law does not discriminate between national products and those originating from other member states.

What also became clear was that the use of derogation from Article 49 does not constitute the reversion of a particular policy area to the member states' exclusive competence.[20] Instead, although the right to determine which non-trade issues require protection and the level at which they should be protected in principle remains within the sphere of the member states, the mechanisms which member states use to achieve those ends is subject to review on the basis of their compatibility with the EC Treaty by the Court. In this assessment the proportionality of the measure is crucial.[21] Proportionality requires three things: that the national measure must be appropriate to achieve its goal; there must be no other, less intrusive, equally effective measure available; and the measure must be proportionate to its aim. The *Sacchi* judgment[22] does not, therefore, necessarily indicate that the Union at this stage had cultural competence. Rather, the member states' competence in this area was being constrained by the Union's general trade powers. Although the Union had no positive cultural competence at that time, it can be seen as developing a form of negative policy by defining the limits of what is acceptable in national regulation, whether by reference to the free movement of services, or the competition or state-aid provisions. The scope of this policy is discussed in chapter 5.

Of particular concern in regard to the scope of Article 49, and therefore the boundary of acceptable member states' action, was the question of whether Article 49 should apply to any of the following types of national rule: directly discriminatory measures alone; measures which, although equal in form, operate to disadvantage non-national services; or even those measures which operate equally but still make life more difficult for traders. Crucially, the ECJ would not look at the national system in isolation, but the national system in the context of the common market. Rules between member states could vary and this in itself could create barriers to the cross-border provision of services. The issue of whether rules in

---

[20] L. Gormley, *Prohibiting Restrictions on Trade within the EEC* (North Holland: Elsevier Science Publishers B.V., 1985), pp. 123–221.

[21] See Case 352/85 *Bond van Adverteerders*, Case C-353/89 *Commission* v. *Netherlands* (Mediawet) [1991] ECR I-4069.

[22] Case 155/73 *Sacchi.*

this context should be caught by Article 49 was not initially certain. In *Sacchi* the Court took a narrow view of the type of discrimination that would trigger Article 49. At this point, rules which did not directly discriminate against services from other member states would be acceptable. This position changed, not only in the context of broadcasting services but in relation to Article 49 in general, altering the balance between the trade interests protected by Union law and other interests protected by national law.

Once a national measure has triggered the application of Article 49, it will be struck down unless it can be justified. The burden of showing justification will fall to the member state and, consequently, the national policy in issue will be subject to judicial scrutiny at the Union level. This step in relation to broadcasting came in *Bond van Adverteerders*,[23] although the principles in the case had a more general application. It is in this case that we see the ECJ first expressing the point that national rules regulating the media should be viewed as restrictions on the freedom to provide services, albeit restrictions that are capable of justification.[24] This is a move from a test which looks for discrimination to trigger the application of Article 49, to a test which focuses on whether a restriction to trade exists. This test is broader, meaning non-discriminatory rules might be caught by Article 49. Member states' action became more likely to be subject to review, and the focus of discussion within the context of the EC Treaty became that of justifying regulation. Indeed, the position with regard to services now is that a hindrance to the cross-border exercise of the right, even if that hindrance is indirect, will trigger Article 49.[25]

It is trite but true to say that the effect of the ECJ's approach as regards the permitted scope of member states' actions has been deregulatory, whether through the application of Article 49 or, less commonly, the competition provisions. In the context of broadcasting, we see the move from a highly regulated industry, characterised by state monopoly in many member states, to one in which private companies compete; that is, the tendency to deregulation and liberalisation, and to privatisation and

---

[23] Case 352/85 *Bond van Adverteerders*.

[24] Contrast the approach in Case 52/79 *Debauve*, para. 13.

[25] For an early discussion of the development of the case law, see G. Marenco, 'The Notion of Restriction on the Freedom of Establishment and the Provision of Services in the Case-Law of the Court', *Yearbook of European Law* 11 (1991), 111–50. More recently, note Case C-60/00 *Carpenter* v. *Secretary of State for the Home Department* [2002] ECR I-6279, which concerned the impact of a wife's deportation on her husband's business activities. The ECJ talked in terms of the exercise of a fundamental right, rather than considering the issue of market access.

corporatisation.[26] The focus has been on the national markets and on their impact on the internal market. Neither consumers nor citizens are considered directly, although there is an implicit policy position here, that more choice is generally a good thing, and that this will benefit consumers. It is, however, questionable whether a policy based on choice, with regulation focusing on the provision of information to aid that choice, is ultimately beneficial from the point of view of the citizen. It has been noted in the context of consumer policy, that 'the consumers who would need the information most, that is the poor and uneducated consumers, seem to have the least possibilities of using it'.[27] This does not take into account the lack of real alternatives, especially for those without money. In relation to our table in chapter 1, such an approach does not take into account the needs of passive viewers, who may not have the capacity to access or assess such information, and is likely to frustrate those viewers who wish to access services but cannot afford to do so.

Competition policy

As cases such as *Sacchi* and the later decision in *ERT*[28] make clear, the need for justification of national regimes must be considered not just in relation to the four freedoms but also in the light of the competition rules. Questions about autonomy of policy areas and competing policy goals may arise in this context also. National regimes can put, for example, a monopoly service provider in a position where its business activities are going to be scrutinised closely because of its strength in the marketplace and because of its impact on undertakings in other member states. Further, the broadly defined concept of 'undertaking' can also cover governmental actions, through public bodies because the status of a body is not relevant for the application of competition law. From the perspective of broadcasting policy concerns, competition law may have an important role to play even when we are considering the actions of the private sector and not the interrelationship between competition policy and national broadcasting regulatory regimes. The media sector is one in which there

---

[26] Liberalisation can be seen as the introduction of competition to monopoly or near monopoly markets, whereas deregulation can be viewed as a reorientation of regulatory policy to increase corporate freedom. Privatisation can be distinguished from corporatisation in that the former can be considered the sale of public assets; the latter is the process of encouraging the public sector to act like the private sector. See, e.g., G. Murdoch and P. Golding, 'Corporate Ambitions and Communication Trends in the UK and Europe', *Journal of Media Economics* 12(2) (1999), 117–32, pp. 118–19.

[27] Howells and Wilhelmsson, *Consumer Law*, p. 313.   [28] Case C-260/89 *ERT*.

has been a significant amount of consolidation of media holdings and joint ventures, some of which are seen to have a significant, adverse effect on diversity of suppliers and content.

Article 81 precludes restrictive agreements between independent undertakings, whether the undertakings have a vertical[29] or horizontal[30] relationship. Agreements falling foul of the prohibition in Article 81 will be automatically void (Article 81(2)), unless they fall within the cumulative, four-point exemption in Article 81(3). Article 81(3) requires that the agreement must lead to an improvement in the production or distribution of goods, or the promotion of technical or economic progress; consumers must receive a fair share of the resulting benefit; the restrictions contained in the agreement must be indispensable to the achievement of the benefits; and the agreement as a whole must not lead to the substantial elimination of competition.

The scope of the Union's power to intervene, in the form of the Commission, in the operation of (member states') markets is determined by reference to Article 81. In a similar vein to the approach to Article 49, the constituent elements of the Article 81(1) prohibition have been interpreted broadly. The ECJ has interpreted the terms 'agreement' and 'undertakings' widely. An effect on trade, which effectively constitutes the boundary between the competence of the member states to act in competition matters and that of the Union, is easily found. A key element in whether an agreement falls foul of Article 81 is whether there is an adverse impact on competition. The distortion of competition is analysed by reference to the market, determined by reference to the product provided (product market) and the geographic area over which it is supplied (geographic market). Essentially, we are asking if there are any acceptable substitutes for a product within a given area,[31] which will act as an effective constraint on the competitive behaviour of the parties on the market.

Substitutability can be analysed in terms of supply-side substitutability or demand-side substitutability. Although undertakings might be

---

[29] That is, they operate at different points in the distribution chain; see, e.g., Cases 56 and 58/64 *Etablissements Consten SA & Grundig-Verkaufs-Gmbh* v. *Commission* [1966] ECR 299.

[30] Operators active at the same level in the economy.

[31] See, e.g., Case 6/72 *Europemballage Corporation and Continental Can Co. Inc.* v. *Commission* [1973] ECR 215, para. 32; Case 85/76 *Hoffmann-La Roche & Co AG* v. *Commission* [1976] ECR 461, para. 28; Case 27/76 *United Brands Co and United Brands Continental BV* v. *Commission* [1978] ECR 207, paras. 11 and 44.

constrained by supply-side substitutability,[32] the Commission's approach is to focus on demand-side substitutability,[33] namely consumer preference. On this basis, the question is whether consumers can switch products immediately and whether substitutes are available. This assessment is primarily made now by using the 'small but significant non-transitory increase in price' (SSNIP) test. If a price rise would cause customers to purchase a different product, or the same product from a different area, to such an extent that the price rise is unprofitable, the alternative products, or the same products from a different area, form part of the same market. We can see that there is also a geographic element to this test. The same product might be found in two (or more) geographic areas: in determining the extent of these areas, a number of factors might be relevant to assessment, such as transport costs, the nature of the product as well as differing national regulations.[34]

The Commission has been criticised for delineating too narrow product markets and for not following economic principles sufficiently when assessing corporate behaviour. In particular, the Commission has challenged agreements which have had the effect of partitioning the common market, even if there are no adverse consequences if the agreement is assessed from an economic perspective. The extent to which non-economic concerns are, or should be, taken into account in the assessment of Article 81, particularly Article 81(3), has been a matter of some debate. This has particular relevance for broadcasting policy as it should also incorporate the needs of cultural policy, or recognise the special nature of sporting events. The Court of First Instance (CFI) has held that the primary considerations which the Commission should take into account must be competition related,[35] though some other considerations have

---

[32] It is sometimes difficult to distinguish between supply-side substitutability, where a manufacturer can easily switch its production to another product in the same product market, and potential competition. The Commission suggests that the question is time-scale: if production can be switched in the short term without significant cost or risk, that the new product will be in the same product market. If a producer could only enter the market in the longer term and after incurring costs, that producer's presence will be relevant for determining market power, but not the relevant market. See Commission, *Notice on Market Definition*, OJ [1997] C 372/5, paras. 20–3.

[33] The ECJ has emphasised that both aspects must be taken into account: see, e.g., Case 6/72 *Continental Can*.

[34] *Ibid.*, paras. 28 *et seq.*

[35] Case T-12/93 *Comité Central d'Entreprise de la Société Anonyme Vittel* v. *Commission* [1995] ECR II-1247. See also impact of the modernisation of competition law enforcement according to which the Commission has issued guidelines to national authorities on the interpretation of Article 81(3), in which economic considerations are emphasised:

been noted, albeit tangentially. Indeed, a number of Commission decisions seem to have been motivated by other considerations: in addition to the creation of the internal market, the Commission has paid regard to industrial policy goals.[36] As the Commission's Annual Report for 1996 said,

> Competition policy has both a Commission policy in its own right and an integral part of a large number of Union policies and with them seeks to achieve the Community objectives set out in Article 2 of the Treaty.[37]

In practice, these varied considerations may mean that tensions exist between potentially competing objectives of competition law and other goals. The creation of the internal market, for example, might require intervention when competition policy might not. Further, the relative weight to be ascribed to the different policy goals is not clear, and becomes more complex as increasing numbers of fundamental principles, such as the guarantee of freedom of expression,[38] start to fill in the Union's constitutional framework. None the less, the Commission seems to be moving towards adopting a more economic-based approach, as can be seen in guidance on the determination of the relevant product market[39] and the guidance given to national authorities on the application of Article 81(3).[40] Whether such a stringent economic line will be followed in all cases by the European courts is another question, as is the level of protection awarded to non-trade values. As regards public services, it may be that they will be sufficiently protected by Articles 16 and 86(2) EC (see below), although we have some doubts about this (see chapter 13).

Article 82 deals with dominant undertakings, including state monopolies, to prevent them weakening still further the competitive conditions

---

Commission, *Guidelines on the application of Article 81(3) of the Treaty*, OJ [2004] C 101/97. This guidance is discussed below.

[36] In *Aerospatiale/Alenia/de Havilland*, Commission Decision 91/619/EC, Case IV/M53, [1991] OJ L 334/42, however, the Commission prohibited the merger where the objective was to create a 'European champion'.

[37] Commission, *XXVIth Annual Report on European Competition Policy* (1996). See more recently, Commission, *XXXIInd Report on Competition Policy* (2002), which states 'one of the main purposes of European Competition Policy is to promote the interests of consumers, that is, to ensure that consumers benefit from the wealth generated by the European economy . . . the Commission thus takes the interest of the consumers into account in all aspects of its competition policy', p. 12.

[38] The recitals to the Merger Regulation specify that fundamental principles are to be respected.

[39] Commission, *Notice on Market Definition.*

[40] Commission, *Guidelines on the application of Article 81(3)*, OJ [2004] C101/97.

on the relevant market. The concept of the market, both product market and geographical market, is central to a finding of a breach of Article 82, as dominance does not exist in the abstract but in the context of a market. Similar analytical techniques are used to define the market in relation to Article 82 as are used in relation to Article 81 (and in the Merger Regulation, see chapter 7). Article 82 prevents the abuse, not the existence, of a dominant position. It also provides a list of practices which indicate such abuse, although this list is not exhaustive. In the context of broadcasting, it is exclusionary behaviour, such as refusal to supply, which is most relevant (see chapter 6). In terms of its objectives, we suggest there are similarities between Article 82 and the Merger Regulation, which aims to prevent a significant lessening of competition in the market. Subject to the narrow grounds set out in Article 86(2), which protect undertakings providing 'services of general economic interest' (SGEIs), less technically known as public services, there is no express exception to Article 82. The role of Article 86(2) in providing space for member states' policies regarding the provision of public services is therefore significant, as it is in relation to the provision of state aid.

Article 86(2) specifies that undertakings entrusted with the provision of an SGEI are subject to the competition rules 'in so far as the application of such rules does not obstruct the performance, in law or in fact, of the particular tasks assigned to them'. This 'exception' is still subject to the proviso that '[t]he development of trade must not be affected to such an extent as would be contrary to the interests of the Community'. In the same manner as Article 16 EC, which re-emphasises the member states' competence in the area of providing public services, Article 86(2) carries a somewhat mixed message. It is an exception to the competition rules, but subject to the interest of the development of trade at Union level. The interests of the citizen at national level, often protected through a legislative process, may therefore be overridden by commercial interests at the Union level determined by bureaucrats in the Commission, subject to the review of the European courts. This may give rise to concerns both about its democratic nature and as regards the coherence and autonomy of policy in flanking areas and the scope of policy freedom left to member states.

The relationship between the common market and other relevant values in the EC Treaty

So far we have seen that the ECJ has adopted an expansive view of the circumstances in which Article 49 will apply, and thus an expansive field of application for a trade-based approach. Even within the public sector, competition policy has limited member states' involvement. There are two sets of factors that should be taken into account against this background. First, the scope of the four freedoms and competition policy has meant that many areas fall within Union competence. Secondly, the use of the derogating provisions (whether Article 46, 81(3) or 86(2)) can be seen as a form of negative policy development in the areas so affected, but it must be questioned the extent to which such policies can be considered as autonomous and/or coherent. Any policy developed in this way is based on individual cases brought within the context of the member states' various legal systems, and judged by reference to a trade-based system of values. These factors arise from the relationship between the member states and the Union. There are issues within the Union legal order itself, too.

The Union has changed in scope and focus since its inception. It has been an ongoing development that has challenged and changed the types of values and objectives that are being protected and recognised. As the successive treaty amendments have introduced into the Union's legal order wider values which are non-economic, such as citizenship and a concern to respect national and European cultural values, potential areas of tension between the different objectives of the Union itself have arisen.[41] These expanded aims of the Union have affected the ECJ's reasoning, as can be illustrated by the ECJ's approach in cases involving the free movement of workers, in which citizenship has been used to protect the rights of Union migrants and, incidentally, constrain the freedom of member states.[42]

Citizenship has not had an effect outside the case law on free movement of individuals. One can argue that this is self-evidently right: goods are not citizens and it can hardly be argued that an individual has a citizenship right to acquire products specifically from abroad. Services (such as public service broadcasting (PSB), public health, education) cause difficulty, however, if we argue that individuals have a citizenship right to access services that relate to their status as citizens. This has relevance here given the fact that many Union institutions have accepted the link

---

[41] L. Woods, *Free Movement of Goods and Services in the European Community* (Aldershot: Ashgate, 2004), p. 8.

[42] See, e.g., case C-184/99 *Grzelczyck* [2001] ECR I-6193 and case C-209/03 *The Queen (on the application of Biidar) v. London Borough of Ealing, Secretary of State for Education and Skills*, judgment 15 March 2005.

between broadcasting and citizenship, particularly in relation to PSB.[43] A cynic might argue that the use of citizenship arguments in other circumstances has been at the expense of the member states' freedom of action, and is therefore a vehicle for expanding Union competence.[44] By contrast, interpreting the scope of Article 49 in the light of citizenship values might operate so as to protect member states' ability to regulate in the interests of pluralism, promote democracy or counter the threats posed by exploitative commercialisation. Such interpretations might limit Union competence, however, as a greater range of member-state action could fall outside the scope of Article 49 in the first place, and therefore not be subject to review in accordance with internal market values. Such an interpretation is unlikely to find favour with the ECJ. None the less, it seems a little surprising that citizenship has not been considered more directly when derogation from Article 49 has been in issue. This may be because the connection between citizenship, notably European citizenship protected by Article 18 EC, and national broadcasting systems is, in reality, slim.

There is a more obvious connection between broadcasting and cultural concerns, covered by Article 151. As noted, culture should be taken into account in other areas of policy. In a case against Belgium,[45] however, the ECJ rejected the argument that the general prohibition in Article 49 should be interpreted in the light of Article 151 EC. In the Constitutional Treaty, Article I-3 provides, under the heading 'Union's objectives', that '[t]he Union shall respect its rich cultural and linguistic diversity, and shall ensure that Europe's cultural heritage is safeguarded and enhanced'. Whether this sort of obligation would change the ECJ's interpretation of one of the four freedoms is highly questionable, especially where, by contrast with other policy areas, such as the protection of the environment and consumer protection, a high level of protection of culture is not required on the part of the Union.[46] Given the doubts over the likelihood

---

[43] See, e.g., European Parliament, *Resolution on the Role of the Media*, OJ [1985] C288/113 and further chapter 13.

[44] This sort of argument has been used before, in relation to the development of human rights protection within the Union. See famously the discussion between J. Coppell and O'Neill, 'The European Court: Taking Rights Seriously?', *CML Rev* 29 (1992), 669; and the response by J. Weiler and Lockhart, '"Taking Rights Seriously" Seriously: The European Court and its Fundamental Rights Jurisprudence', *CML Rev* 32 (1995), 51–94 and 579–627.

[45] Case C-11/95 *Commission v. Belgium* [1996] ECR I-4115.

[46] For a discussion of the impact of amendments to the EC Treaty on the interpretation of the freedom to provide services, see Woods, *Free Movement of Goods and Services*, pp. 298–9.

of the Constitutional Treaty coming into force, the question of the impact of the Union's cultural objectives on other policies is moot.

Positive harmonisation

Although reliance on general treaty provisions, especially in the light of an expansive approach to the scope of the freedom to provide services on the part of the ECJ, might prove effective in terms of the creation of the internal market, there are problems with relying solely on this mechanism. As noted earlier, judicial (or negative) harmonisation is deregulatory, removing national rules. Not only might total deregulation be undesirable in policy terms but reliance on judicial harmonisation is, as suggested above, piecemeal. It also has the effect of transferring decision-making, not only from the national to European level[47] but also from political actors to the judiciary. This could have an effect on policy coherence (see chapter 5), as well as our ability to hold policymakers responsible for their choices. There is a concern that the state-based regulatory order may be replaced with an irresponsible market-place. Against this background, the advantages of enacting legislation at the Union level seem clear (though the issue of responsibility for those choices might not become much more certain).[48] The matter is not quite that simple. Quite apart from the difficulties of getting the necessary level of agreement, which would seem, despite QMV, more problematic in an enlarged and increasingly diverse Union, there are issues relating to the fields in which the Union should take action and the nature of that action.

We have seen that the SEA introduced an 'easier' legislative procedure, Article 95. The consequence of this development seems to have been greater member-state sensitivity to competence, as well as a European Parliament which seemed keen to flex its legislative muscles following the introduction of the co-decision procedure.[49] We can see examples of these

---

[47] Arguably under the preliminary rulings procedure (Article 234 EC), the national judiciary have a role, too, in making the reference to the ECJ. None the less, they are bound by the ECJ's interpretation of Union law, which of course takes priority over the national law.

[48] There has been criticism of the difficulty of individual national parliaments holding the Council as a whole to account, as each member state can call to account only one of its members; additionally, there remains the possibility for a national government to avoid responsibility by 'blaming' the Union activities on the other member states.

[49] Initially, the European Parliament was a consultative assembly only, decision-making lying entirely in the hands of the Council. With the various treaty amendments, the powers of the European Parliament have increased in this context: co-decision effectively gives the European Parliament a joint say in the form of legislation enacted in that it has what

problems in the broadcasting field. For example, the introduction of the
Television without Frontiers Directive (TWFD)[50] was contentious, with
some of the member states arguing that, because of its cultural focus,
the Union did not have competence to act. The subsequent attempt to
enact a media mergers regulation also came to nothing, as a result of infighting between the various directorates in the Commission, and a lack
of a clear treaty base.[51] The point is whether a particular proposal can
be tied in to the need to ensure the establishment or functioning of the
internal market, or, in a similar vein, whether the cross-border provision
of services is made easier.[52] A corollary is the degree to which the substance
of the proposed measure is to be dictated by this internal market logic.
There are two, linked, questions. Is there a treaty base for action; and, if
so, which is the appropriate base?

These questions were the subject of a number of (relatively) recent
cases concerning the attempts of the Union to prohibit the advertising
of tobacco products due to concerns about public health.[53] Indeed, it
was the public-health concerns that made the subject so difficult, because
although the Union now has public health competence, it is a supporting
form of competence, and harmonisation was expressly precluded.[54] The
case concerned a challenge by Germany, which had been outvoted in the
political process, to the legality of the Tobacco Advertising Directive[55]
which had been enacted on the basis of what are now Articles 95, 47(2)

amounts to a veto over Community legislation made using this procedure. The various
treaties have expanded the number of policy areas which use this procedure; should the
Constitution come into force, the co-decision procedure will be renamed the 'ordinary
legislative procedure', reflecting the fact that its use should be the norm rather than the
exception.

[50] Television without Frontiers Directive (TWFD), Council Directive 89/552/EEC of 3 October 1989 on the co-ordination of certain provisions laid down by law, regulation or administrative action in member states concerning the pursuit of television broadcasting activities OJ [1989] L 298/23, as amended by Directive 97/36/ EC of the European Parliament
and of the Council of 30 June 1997.

[51] On the attempts of the Union to regulate in this area, see A. Harcourt, 'Regulation of
European Media Markets; Approaches of the European Court of Justice and the Com-
mission's Merger Task Force', *UtLR* 9(6) (1998), 276–91, p. 288; and R. Craufurd Smith,
'Rethinking European Union Competence in the Field of Media Ownership: The Internal
Market, Fundamental Rights and European Citizenship', *E.L. Rev.* 29(5) (2004), 652–72,
p. 663 *et seq.*

[52] Article 47(2) EC.

[53] Case C-376/98 *Germany* v. *Parliament and Council* (Tobacco Advertising Directive) [2000]
ECR I-8419.

[54] Article 152(4) EC.

[55] Directive 98/43 on the approximation of the laws, regulations and administrative provisions of the member states relating to the advertising and sponsorship of tobacco products,
OJ [1998] L 213/9.

and 55.[56] The ECJ here followed its previous case law: where market-making is incidental to the main purpose of the measure, the market-making provisions cannot be relied on. Thus, the test is whether the measure 'actually contributes to eliminating obstacles' to free movement and 'to removing distortions of competition'.[57] In its reasoning, the ECJ suggested that distortions of competition should not be theoretical but appreciable, although it did accept that future barriers to trade could justify action under Article 95. Disparities between the national legal systems of the member states would, without anything more, be insufficient.[58] There is, therefore, a difference between the trigger for Article 49, and negative harmonisation, and the scope of Article 95, justifying positive harmonisation. The former is wider than the latter.

The Union does not have a general regulatory competence. None the less, the ECJ was keen to emphasise that, although the aims of Article 95 may be to liberalise the market, this does not mean that the Union is precluded from taking any regulatory action whatsoever. Indeed the ECJ distinguished the situation in the Tobacco Advertising Directive from the advertising rules in the TWFD which preclude tobacco advertising on television. Those rules facilitated the free movement of services by providing a base level of protection in that area.

In the *Tobacco Advertising* case, the applicant government also argued that, as the directive's principal concern was the protection of public health, the appropriate treaty base should have been Article 152, which specifically deals with public health and, as noted, at Article 152(4), which precludes harmonisation. According to the applicant, the use of Article 95 was an attempt to subvert the proper division of competence. Although the ECJ agreed that Article 95 should not be abused, equally the prohibition on advertising did not mean that public health could not inform harmonisation measures. Indeed, public health requirements may legitimately form part of the Union's other policies, including market-making, as recognised by Article 152(1) EC.[59] Similarly, cultural policy should also

---

[56] At the time the directive was enacted, these provisions were numbered Articles 110a, 57(2) and 66, respectively.

[57] Case C-376/98 *Tobacco Advertising Directive Case*, para. 95.

[58] Contrast the *Titanium Dioxide Case*, Case C-300/89 *Commission v. Council* [1991] ECR I-2867, in which the differences had a direct impact on production costs; in *Tobacco Advertising Directive*, although the rules might affect advertising agencies, those effects were too indirect. See, more recently, the *Biotechnological Inventions Case*, Case C-377/98 *Netherlands v. Parliament and Council* [2001] ECR I-7079, para. 18.

[59] Case C-376/98 *Tobacco Advertising Directive case*, paras. 78 and 88; see also Case C-77/98 *Biotechnological Inventions*, para. 28; Case C-491/01 *R. v. Secretary of State for Health*, ex parte *British American Tobacco, et al.* [2002] ECR I-11453, para. 62.

be taken into account where relevant: the decisions upon which the media programmes are based have as their treaty base the industrial policy provisions, but with additional express reference to Article 151 EC. There are two ways to view the development of flanking policies. The first way is that it balances the needs of unrestricted market freedoms with other policy choices. Potentially, this minimises the risk of policy one-sidedness,[60] that is unfettered market freedoms (or the market without the state), within the Union legal order. The second way is that it may be that other policies are constrained by the circumstances in which internal market policy may now operate. Similar points may be made in relation to the provision of services, as the case of the TWFD illustrates.

A further argument could be used to support the contention that the Union has competence; that is, viewing the market from the perspective of the viewer (or the recipient of the information-society service). As has been noted in the context of consumer policy, consumers are more likely to use services or buy goods originating from other member states when they have confidence in the level, quantity and type of information about the product and in the system of protection should things go awry. Presumably, this would give the Union an interest in regulating, as can indeed be seen in the context of e-commerce. Here the Union potentially has the advantage of focusing the legislative framework, at least at a basic level, on the interests of consumers or, possibly, citizens. This sort of reasoning has not, however, been generally used.

Different models of harmonisation (or co-ordination and approximation) are possible which allow the member states different degrees of freedom. Harmonisation does not require uniformity. Nor does it make any assumptions about the quality, substantively speaking, of the harmonising legislation. In assessing this quality, we question whether the Union is about removing barriers to trade or whether it contains some element of a 'social Europe';[61] especially since some policy areas, such as protection of the environment and consumer protection, hypothesise a high base level of protection.[62] The different answers to this question lead to different conceptions (between member states and between the Union institutions) about the level of action needed at the Union level,

---

[60] A. Von Bogdandy and J. Bast, 'The European Union's Vertical Order of Competences: the current law and proposals for its reform', *CML Rev* 39 (2002), 227, p. 245.

[61] S. Weatherill, *EC Consumer Law and Policy* (London and New York: Longman, 1997), pp. 2–3; Howells and Wilhelmsson, *Consumer Law*, p. 305.

[62] See Article 95(3) EC, Article 6 EC. Cultural policy envisages no particular level of protection.

and in this way links to debates about the treaty base. Two issues though are pre-eminent: one relating to the degree of flexibility, the other relating to the degree of regulatory intervention. While these two issues can be paired in practice, as we now go on to do below, they are not indissolubly linked.

As regards freedom of action, we can characterise two main models: first, that which attempts to create a level playing-field and which therefore allows little room for manœuvre; and, secondly, that which is based on regulatory competition. This second model imposes a minimum European standard but allows member states individually to set higher standards. Goods or services originating from other member states which meet the required minimum (according to the state of origin) must be allowed to flow freely through the Union, even if those products do not meet the regulatory requirements in the host member state. This principle is sometimes referred to as the country of origin principle. Proponents of this regulatory competition model often see the level playing-field model as linked to a more interventionist policy. For example, the inclusion in the original EC Treaty of the provisions requiring equal treatment of men and women was based on the argument that enterprises in those member states that had adopted the equal treatment principle would be at a competitive disadvantage compared into those undertakings located in a member state which imposed no such policy. The level playing-field approach is criticised for not allowing regulatory competition and innovation; and 'as a suppression of competitive and cultural diversity'.[63] On this reasoning, companies should be allowed to base themselves wherever they choose, taking into account factors such as the favourability of the domestic regime. Accordingly, mutual recognition and market access are central, since without them diversity creates barriers.

There are criticisms of the regulatory competition, or minimum harmonisation, approach. It assumes that it is possible and acceptable to equate competition between undertakings with competition between regimes. Also, it leads to regulatory arbitrage[64] (see chapter 8 for a discussion of forum shopping in the broadcasting context) and, in a commercialised environment, a likelihood that most companies will choose to locate themselves in the least-demanding member state, leading to a downward pressure on standards. Even the existence of Union standards

---

[63] Weatherill, 'Why harmonise?', p. 11.

[64] C. Marsden, 'Introduction: Information and Communications Technologies, Globalisation and Regulation', in C. Marsden (ed.), *Regulating the Global Information Society* (London: Routledge, 2000), pp. 19–21.

may affect member state domestic initiatives, potentially acting as a brake on such activities.[65] This clearly has the potential to affect the regulatory environment or, more crucially, the standards of the product received even in a member state which seeks to espouse higher standards. Whilst this argument focusses on member states and industry players, it should not be forgotten that standards would have an impact on the experience of consumption.

Types of Union action

As suggested above, the issues affecting European governance do have consequences for the nature and degree of broadcasting regulation, as well as affecting questions as to who has responsibility for policymaking and its enforcement. Even the nature of the European measures which are enacted as a result of policymaking initiatives illustrate the fact that responsibility for implementation of Union law is not just a question for the Union. Directives, for example, are, in theory, framework pieces of legislation which specify the ends to be achieved, but leave member states to achieve those goals within their respective legal systems. Member states' authorities are responsible for enforcing these rules. Furthermore, in some directives, specific roles and obligations are envisaged at Union law level for national regulatory authorities (NRAs) and they thus play a crucial role in the European regulatory structure (see chapter 6). As we shall see in chapter 7, the modernisation of Union competition, which introduced the possibility of national authorities making decisions under Article 81(3) (hitherto the preserve of the Commission), has likewise resulted in greater involvement for the national competition authorities and courts. The degree, however, to which such co-operation allows real discretion in policy-making is open to question. In this sense, there is a distinction between decentralisation of enforcement and subsidiarity; the application of Article 81(3), for example, is subject to detailed guidance by the Commission in the interests of a uniform application of the provision across the Union. The involvement of NRAs does, however, raise questions not only about who has the power to regulate but also about who should be responsible for any policies and their failures.[66]

---

[65] Howells and Wilhelmsson, *Consumer Law*, p. 388.
[66] S. Weatherill discusses the arrangements in the Treaty for reviewing the Union's exercise of its powers: 'Better Competence Monitoring', *EL Rev* 30(1) (2005), 23–41.

We have noted that subsidiarity concerns not just the issue of which level of government should be responsible for law-making in a given area but the proportionality of those laws. This, potentially, indicates a tendency towards less formal regulatory intervention; what might be termed 'soft law'. Soft law is a broad, ill-defined and possibly misused term and it is not always clear whether it refers to policies which supplement the law or whether it may be used as a replacement for the law. In general, soft law comprises instruments that are not legally binding, although three distinct types can be identified. First, soft law could include types of act envisaged in the treaties, such as recommendations and opinions.[67] Secondly, the institutions, notably the Commission, have developed other forms of instrument not listed in the treaties, such as guidance as to how it will interpret provisions.[68] Thirdly, and more problematically still, are the opinions of various sorts of advisory committees within the Union structure. Increasingly, harmonising legislation will delegate technical issues to specialist committees, contributing to the view that decision-making within the Union structure is technocratic. Also, although one might suggest that some of these committees allow the appropriate use of expertise,[69] there are equally concerns about their democratic accountability and legitimacy, as well as concerns that some groups, at least, are dominated by industry interests.[70] Although efficient, the use of soft law is contentious as, in most cases, it bypasses formal democratic procedures and the ability of the courts to exercise judicial oversight is limited.

The Commission *White Paper on Governance* takes the theme of limited governmental intervention further, suggesting a limited role for traditional top-down regulation and favouring other forms of regulatory models.[71] The 1997 *Green Paper on Convergence*[72] had indicated that a minimal approach to regulation in a converging communications

---

[67] Article 249 EC.

[68] See, e.g., Commission, *Notice on Market Definition*, Commission, *Guidelines on the Assessment of Horizontal Mergers and the Council Regulation on the Control of Concentrations between Undertakings* OJ [2004] C 31/3 (chapter 7); Commission, *Interpretative Communication on Certain Aspects of the Provisions on Televised Advertising in the "Television without Frontiers" Directive* C (2004) 1450, 23.03.2004, OJ [2004] C 102/2 (ch. 9).

[69] W. Sauter and E. Vos, 'Harmonisation under Community Law: The Comitology Issue', in *Lawmaking in the European Union* (The Hague: Kluwer Law International, 1998), p. 180.

[70] See, e.g., in the infrastructure sector, S. Kaitatzi-Whitlock, 'The Privatising of Conditional Access Control' *Communications and Strategies*, 25 (1997), 91.

[71] Commission, *European Governance: A White Paper*, COM(2001) 428 final.

[72] Commission, *Green Paper on the Convergence of the Telecommunications, Media and Information Technology Sectors, and the Implications for Regulation. Towards an Information Society Approach* COM(1997)623, ch. V.

environment was necessary. Its principles, in the communications sector, are in line with the general approach taken to regulation claimed by the Union. It follows that regulation is expected to be based on clearly defined policy objectives; be the minimum necessary to meet those objectives; further enhance legal certainty in a dynamic market; and aim to be technologically neutral and be enforced as closely as possible to the activities being regulated. In line with this, graded regulatory models, such as co-regulation[73] or regulated self-regulation, through a state-run regulatory framework, or other forms of self-regulation, or self-monitoring by end-users[74] are being considered as possibly more appropriate ways for setting social, cultural and political standards in broadcasting.[75] They have also been considered in the context of the second review of the TWFD.[76] Here, a link between a less-than-certain competence for Union action and a desire for less statutory regulatory types can be discerned.

With the development of co-operation procedures within the Union, a more formal recognition of different means of developing standards has developed. The move towards soft governance in the Union was initiated in March 2000 and reaffirmed in the conclusions of the Lisbon Council Summit (European Council 2002) when the European Council formally established its Open Method of Co-ordination (OMC). OMC is a method of policymaking which allows for the agreement of policy guidelines through exchanges of information on best practice, benchmarking, monitoring, target-setting and peer review.[77] Such an approach

---

[73] In accordance with Art. 27 of the TWFD member states shall 'bring into force the laws, regulations and administrative provisions necessary to comply with this Directive'. This opens the possibility to install co-regulation. However, co-regulatory models are already applied in the present framework, especially with respect to the application of rules on advertising and the protection of minors. In the *Fourth Report on the Application of the TWFD* the Commission states that 'where this mechanism fails to produce the expected results, the Commission reserves the right to submit a classic legislative proposal to the legislator'.

[74] See the report study commissioned by the EC: D. Keller and S. G. Verhulst, 'Parental Control in a Converged Communications Environment: Self-regulation, Technical Devices and Meta-information', *DVB Parental Control Report* (Oxford: University of Oxford, 2000). The study sought to differentiate between technical devices designed for analogue broadcasting and those suitable for a digital age.

[75] See A. Scheuer and P. Strothmann, *Media Supervision on the Threshold of the 21st Century: What are the Requirements of Broadcasting, Telecommunications and Concentration Regulation?* (Strasbourg: European Audiovisual Observatory, 2001), p. 3.

[76] Commission, *Proposal for a Directive of the European Parliament and of the Council amending Council Directive 89/552/EEC*, COM(2005)646 final, p. 9.

[77] A. Harcourt, *The European Union and the Regulation of Media Markets* (Manchester: Manchester University Press, 2005), p. 15.

potentially allows discretion on best practice to be exercised by national regulatory bodies, which retain policymaking competence (albeit within the Union framework). Controversially, OMC also allows the Council to bypass the democratic structures of the European Parliament, increasing concerns about democratic deficit in policymaking. It may also signal a greater Union deference or sensitivity to competence issues.

In sum, the types of measure favoured by the Union institutions seem to reflect the larger constitutional concerns and developments. Thus, the move to soft law and to different types of regulatory structure can be seen as deregulation in the sense that it is a move away from traditional command and control structures. They are being used as a solution in the context of areas in which competence is seen as problematic. We can see the use of OMC as a way of respecting, if not harnessing, the diversity of approaches within the Union. Further, the use of other actors in the governance process could be criticised as a sop to subsidiarity concerns. Worryingly, as we shall see in specific policy areas within the broadcasting field (chapter 5), it could be the case that such action at the Union level is worse than nothing. The involvement of interested parties directly in standard-setting processes raises questions about the representative nature of the resulting standards. There is a general concern that there are imbalances of power through the strong lobbying of industry groups, as well as their involvement (directly or indirectly) on various committees. It is not clear how the voice of the citizen, or even that of the consumer, is to be heard in this process. There is also the possibility that Union action constrains national initiatives, resulting in neither the national nor supranational level of government taking full responsibility for policy initiatives, blurring the boundary of responsibility and contributing to the impression of a democratic deficit. Whilst the purpose of this chapter is not directly to analyse the accountability of the Union institutions, it has raised the issue of the accountability and transparency of decision-making and whether the citizens' interests will necessarily receive adequate attention in the light of industry lobbying.

Conclusion

This chapter has focussed on general themes affecting law and policymaking within the Union which, although expressed generally, will have an impact on specific areas of policy, such as broadcasting policy. In general terms, we can see that the original free market or economic focus of the Union has had an impact on the level and type of regulatory measures used. There has been a trend towards the private sector as both a preferred model and a preferred actor within the Union. Deregulation, privatisation, liberalisation and the use of private companies all characterise the Union. Equally, there is an assumption that choice is good and will provide benefits, presumably for all. This is a flawed assumption. Despite this, it should be noted that the Union is not an entirely commercially driven entity, and there are provisions which militate towards greater provision of public service and greater levels of consumer (and citizen) protection. None the less, it remains true to say that these are not currently given the consideration they deserve. In so far as the institutions do act, they seem, somewhat ironically, to be limited by provisions designed to protect the diversity of member states and, crucially, their competence. It is not surprising that Union harmonising policy, based as it must be on internal market considerations, sometimes lacks coherence.

5

European broadcasting policy

Introduction

In chapter 1 we outlined a range of different viewing experiences divided between those of the consumer and the citizen. Our concern is that the difference between the citizen and the consumer, and their varied needs, has not been specifically addressed by either the Union institutions, or the member states in the context of broadcasting policy. Consequently, our concern is that those viewers most in need of regulatory protection are neglected by broadcasting policymakers. Unless the Union institutions make a conscious attempt to promote and protect the requirements of citizen viewers, we believe that broadcasting policy will continue to drift towards deregulation and focus on an aggregated notion of the viewer who is a consumer, both informed and active. We argue that this drift is the result of the influence of three factors we identified in chapter 1. These factors are rapid technological change, the increasingly commercialised broadcasting sector and the consequences of the Union's limited competence in the social, cultural and educational aspects of broadcasting. In this chapter we now analyse the impact of these three factors on Union broadcasting policy. We take these in a reverse order, so as to provide an analysis of the development of Union broadcasting policy historically and the issues relating to competence which have delimited the scope and scale of regulation which has emerged. The increased commercialisation of the broadcasting market and the impact of technological change are then assessed within this context.

Brief overview of broadcasting policy in the Union

We have shown in chapter 4 that there is no specific provision dealing with broadcasting policy within the EC Treaty. Indeed, although we refer to broadcasting policy throughout this book, the power of the Union to act in this area is not based on a single article but can be found in a range of provisions. Broadcasting issues were thus initially dealt with as a matter falling within the free movement of services,[1] or within the competition provisions,[2] and cultural, educational and political concerns were dealt with as exceptions to the trade rules. The European Parliament's 1982 Hahn *Report on Radio and Television Broadcasting*[3] is often regarded as the beginning of the development of a positive Union broadcasting policy, as it championed the link between information supply by the broadcasting sector and European integration at the level of individuals. The view held was that European integration was unlikely to be achieved if the broadcasting media continued to be controlled at the national level.

The European Parliament attempted to initiate debate about the significance of pluralism, protection of diversity of opinion and the need to protect these values in the new environment that was becoming dominated by commercialisation.[4] Such a view signalled a particular policy strand which was focused on the democratic, integrative and cultural potential of broadcasting.[5] The Union's political institutions realised that there was a need to engage citizens within the political process. Discussions about the amelioration of the perceived 'democratic deficit', the creation of a 'people's Europe' and a need to strengthen the sense of Union identity inevitably led to questions about the most effective ways that information about the Union could be successfully communicated to citizens.[6] Similarly, the broadcast media were perceived to be able to enhance the citizen's sense of belonging to the Union. None the less, at this stage there were no Union powers in this context (European citizenship only being introduced in 1994 with the TEU); the discussions by the institutions, particularly those of the European Parliament, were no more than that, discussions.

In 1984 the Commission's *Television without Frontiers Green Paper*[7] re-emphasised the relationship between European integration and television.[8] It argued that satellite technologies were 'a cultural challenge' and

---

[1] Article 49 EC.   [2] Articles 81, 82 and 86 EC.

[3] Parliament, *Report on Radio and Television Broadcasting in the European Community* (The Hahn Report, 1982), Document 1–1013/81.

[4] Parliament, *Resolution on Broadcast Communication in the European Community: The Threat to Diversity of Opinion Posed by the Commercialisation of New Media* OJ [1984] C 117/198–201.

[5] Commission, *Communication on Principles and Guidelines for the Community's Audiovisual Policy in the Digital Age*, COM(1999) 108, 1 December 1999.

[6] Parliament, *Resolution on Radio and Television Broadcasting the European Community*.

[7] Commission, *Television without Frontiers: Green Paper on the Establishment of the Common Market for Broadcasting*, COM (1984) 300 final.

[8] Commission, *TWF Green Paper*, p. 20.

that the Union should 'place them within the context of a broad plan for the future of Europe not based on economic precepts alone'.[9] In this, it seems wider in its concerns than merely responding to the negative harmonisation of the European Court of Justice (ECJ). Its broad-based approach addressed the need for political freedom, including freedom of information, opinion and expression.[10] It linked these political freedoms to the desirability of cross-frontier broadcasting.[11] The *Green Paper* and the consequent draft directive[12] addressed cultural interests to a greater degree than the directive which emerged as the Television without Frontiers Directive (TWFD)[13] in 1989.[14]

In addition to the TWFD, Union attempts to regulate content can be seen in the *Human Dignity Green Paper and Recommendation*,[15] which was recently reviewed. The *Human Dignity Green Paper and Recommendation* is an example of the institutions relying on soft law to develop further agreement on areas affected by the Union legislation, but which did not directly fall within its legislative competence. The Union has also taken other non-legislative action, arguably representing a much more interventionist approach to the media sector. It has provided financial support to the broadcasting and film industry through a variety of MEDIA[16] programmes, the first of which was launched by the Commission's DG X

---

[9] *Ibid.*, p. 37.

[10] E.g., European Convention on Human Rights, 10(1); Universal Declaration of Human Rights; International Convention on Civil and Political Rights Art 19(1) and (2) and the Final Act of the Conference on Security and Cooperation in Europe (CSCE). See Commission, *TWF Green Paper*, p. 39.

[11] 'Recognising the need for restrictions set down in Article 10(2) which are necessary in a democratic society, in the interests of national security, territorial integrity or public safety, for the prevention of disorder or crime, for the protection of health or morals, for the protection of the reputation or rights of others, for preventing the disclosure of information received in confidence or for maintaining the authority and impartiality of the judiciary', Commission, *TWF Green Paper*, p. 40.

[12] Commission, *Television and the Audio-visual Sector: Towards a European Policy*, European File 14/86 (Luxembourg: Office for Official Publications of the European Communities, 1986).

[13] Council Directive 89/552/EEC of 3 October on the co-ordination of certain provisions laid down by law, regulation or administrative action in member states concerning the pursuit of television broadcasting activities OJ [1989] L298/23, as amended by Directive 97/36/EC OJ [1997] L 202/30.

[14] R. Collins, *Broadcasting and Audio-Visual Policy in the European Single Market* (London: John Libbey, 1994), p. 67. See also R. Negrine and S. Papathanassopoulos, *The Internationalisation of Television* (London: Pinter, 1990), p. 76.

[15] Commission, *Green Paper on the Protection of Minors and Human Dignity in Audiovisual and Information Services*, COM (1996) 483, final.

[16] 'MEDIA' refers to Mesures pour Encourager le Développement de l'Industrie Audiovisuelle.

(now DG Education and Culture) in 1988. Some argued that the single European market created by the TWFD would lead to a domination of English-language programming in the Union. MEDIA 92 was therefore established to promote the production and dissemination of audiovisual works throughout the Union and to protect cultural diversity. The original MEDIA programme was renewed and continues to this day, and for much the same reasons. Despite criticisms about inadequate funding,[17] the MEDIA programmes have been considered to be quite successful, though whether this assessment takes place from a cultural or industrial policy perspective is debatable.

In the 1990s a series of reviews and high-level meetings was held to try to assess the impact new technologies would have on the primary goals of broadcasting policy.[18] The TWFD was reviewed in the light of the changing technological environment, but it was apparent that not all issues had been adequately addressed. The nature and type of regulation that could best meet policy goals, and the relationship between broadcast content and its means of delivery (infrastructure) were discussed.[19] The Union had already taken some action with regard to certain aspects of infrastructure regulation. It tried to create common European technical standards regarding broadcasting transmission formats but with limited success, as industry players involved in standard-setting delayed and ultimately frustrated the process. By contrast, the liberalising approach taken to the telecommunications sector was perceived as successful, with a competitive environment being introduced in most sectors of the telecommunications market. With the introduction of liberalisation in the infrastructure markets, the open-network provision directives[20] were amended so as

---

[17] See David Graham and Associates Limited, *Study on the Impact of Measures Concerning the Promotion and the Distribution and Production of TV Programmes* (Community and National, 2005), provided for under Article 25(a) of the Television without Frontiers Directive, available http://europa.eu.int/comm/avpolicy/stat/studi_en.htm#3.

[18] Commission Communication, *Principles and Guidelines for the Community's Audiovisual Policy in the Digital Age*, COM (1999) 657 final, pp. 8–9.

[19] Commission, *Green Paper on the Convergence of the Telecommunications, Media and Information Technology Sectors, and the Implications for Regulation. Towards an Information Society Approach* COM (1997) 623; The European Audiovisual Conference, co-organised by the Commission and the British Presidency of the Union, in Birmingham in April 1998 (available at http://europa.eu.int/eac/bg-intro_en.html) and a High Level Group on audiovisual policy chaired by Commissioner Marcelino Oreja in 1997 which was published in a report entitled *The Digital Age: Report of the High Level Group on Audiovisual Policy*, Office for Official Publications of the European Communities, Luxembourg (ISBN 92-828-4690-3).

[20] Directive 90/387/EEC on the establishment of the internal market for telecommunications services through the implementation of open network provision OJ [1990] L 192/1.

to impose certain *ex ante* obligations on operators designated as having significant market power. These obligations were to be implemented in national law by the national regulatory authority, which had little discretion as to how the obligations were to be applied. An approach based on non-discrimination and the use of market power continues in the current communications framework, although the Communications Package[21] is currently under review as part of the i2010 initiative to create a 'single European information space'.

The *Communications Review*[22] outlined five general principles for regulatory action in a digital communications environment which militated towards a lesser degree of intervention in the market. The earlier *Green Paper on Convergence*[23] had argued that lighter touch regulation in a converging communications environment was necessary. None the less, the *Communications Review* accepted that television might have to continue to be treated differently, though the TWFD appeared outdated. This concern for the special attributes of broadcasting is reflected in the more or less contemporaneous Protocol on Public Service Broadcasting annexed to the Amsterdam Treaty, in response to a number of challenges by commercial operators to national public service broadcasting (PSB) systems under competition law.

The current review of the TWFD was, in the main, triggered by digital convergence.[24] The political institutions were aware, even at the time of the first revision of the TWFD, that some matters had been left unresolved, arguably on the basis of the developing nature of the technology and markets. The current review became linked to the i2010 project which re-emphasised the necessity of adopting an integrated approach to both information society (including transmission mechanisms) and audiovisual media policies in the Union. Concurrently with the review process a number of studies were commissioned by the Commission on the implementation of the current TWFD and, significantly, on co-regulation in the

[21] Directive 2002/21/EC Framework Directive; Directive 2002/20/EC Authorisation Directive; Directive 2002/19/EC Access Directive; Directive 2002/22/EC Universal Service Directive: Directive 2002/58/EC Data Protection and Electronic Communications Directive; Decision on Radio Spectrum: Decision 676/2002/EC OJ [2002] L 108.

[22] Commission Communication, *Towards a New Framework for Electronic Communications Infrastructure and Associated Services: the 1999 Communications Review*, COM (1999) 539 final.

[23] Commission, *Green Paper on Convergence of the Telecommunications*, ch. V.

[24] In a report adopted in 2003, the European Parliament expressed its support for a revision of the scope of TWFD with the definition of audiovisual content to be expanded to take account of media convergence (see Parliament, *Report on Television without Frontiers*, A5-0251/2003, also referred to as the Perry Report, PE 312.581/DEF).

media sector in the member states. A series of Issues Papers, published by the Commission in July 2005, outlined the areas under consultation: access to events of major importance to society; promotion of cultural diversity and of competitiveness of the European programme industry; protection of general interests in television advertising, sponsorship, teleshopping and self-promotion; protection of minors and public order and the right to reply; and short extracts of events together with other elements not covered by the TWFD. A proposal for a draft second amending directive (DSAD) has recently been published by the Commission following the consultation.[25] This is now the subject of further public debate as the institutions consider the proposal. As part of the ongoing review of communications in the light of the Lisbon Agenda and the i2010 initiative, the Communications Package is now also under review. Central to this review is the extent to which market principles can be extended and whether spectrum trading should be permitted. A change in the approach to these issues would be likely to have an impact on the broadcasting environment. Given the relatively early stage in the review process, it is not possible to comment in detail on its ultimate form, although we do return to it briefly in the concluding chapter.

Competence, coherence and autonomy of broadcasting policy

To state that there has been a single European broadcasting policy is to oversimplify the matter. The wide range of provisions and approaches to broadcasting policy arises from the lack of a specific treaty base for broadcasting. This leads us to question the extent to which there is a coherent broadcasting policy, or whether it is simply a collection of responses to other considerations, such as freedom to provide services and competition policy. Furthermore, the extent to which measures such as the introduction of citizenship and cultural competence[26] have had any significant impact on the scale and scope of broadcasting policy and the regulatory structure and system which has emerged also requires consideration. It is doubtful whether the limited competence of the Union in the broadcasting field, where broadcasting is seen as a cultural service, means that the resulting Union broadcasting policy can ever be autonomous from the underlying trade-based treaty provisions,

---

[25] Commission, *Proposal for a Directive amending Directive 89/552/EEC*, COM (2005) 646 final, 2005/0260 (COD), SEC (2005) 1625 and 1626.

[26] Article 151 EC. See also Article 87(3), but note prior existence of Article 30 EC.

whether these be the four freedoms or competition policy, which will have an impact on the content of broadcasting policy. This issue is explored below, looking first at jurisprudence of the ECJ, focusing mainly on the case law on negative harmonisation (rather than competition law), and then at positive harmonisation and other acts of the political institutions.

The first case on broadcasting to come before the ECJ was *Sacchi*, which concerned the acceptability of the Italian broadcasting regime which established a state monopoly broadcaster.[27] In this case the ECJ provided a definition of broadcasting in accordance with the EC Treaty, namely that broadcasting could be understood as a service (see chapter 4). Subsequent cases gave a broad understanding to this concept,[28] so both pay TV and free-to-air television were caught within Article 49.[29] In recognising the legitimacy of the monopoly status of broadcasters granted by the state, the ECJ in *Sacchi* endorsed 'dualism' as a principle of broadcasting policy:[30] broadcasting services exist for the purpose of remuneration; but also to fulfil social and democratic functions. Through this definition, the ECJ established which national rules would be acceptable under Article 49, thereby determining the scope of possible member-state action and indirectly creating space for content regulation. The size of this space can be examined through a discussion of several cases.

Sacchi had left a number of questions unresolved, or rather opened up the possibility of new questions. It is unsurprising that further cases to clarify the extent to which member states were free to regulate television were referred to the ECJ. Since the principal broadcasting regime is not set at Union level, but instead set by individual member states at the national level, what was (and still is) measured by the ECJ was the compatibility of those regimes with the EC Treaty. *Debauve*[31] concerned the Belgian broadcasting system, which prohibited the broadcasting of advertisements, even for channels retransmitting by cable television broadcasts from other member states and which had been authorised in those member states. The ECJ accepted the Belgian government's arguments based on the need to protect the general interest.

---

[27] Case 155/73 *Sacchi* [1974] ECR 409.

[28] See, e.g., L. Woods, *Free Movement of Goods and Services within the European Community* (Aldershot: Ashgate, 2004), pp. 168–74.

[29] Case 352/85 *Bond van Adverteerders* v. *Netherlands* [1988] ECR 2085.

[30] D. Ward, *The European Union Democratic Deficit and the Public Sphere* (Oxford: IOS Press, 2004), p. 55.

[31] Case 52/79 *Procureur du Roi* v. *Debauve* [1980] ECR 833.

What is significant, both in terms of the development of the services' jurisprudence as a coherent body of law and in terms of the EC's balancing of trade and non-trade concerns in the audiovisual sector, is that the ECJ not only emphasised the special nature of broadcasting but saw it as a factor affecting the interpretation of whether there was a restriction on the freedom to provide services in the first place. Member states' concerns here operated to limit, or at least to shape, the scope of Union competence, whilst still themselves having to comply with treaty rules.[32] This view of what constituted discrimination or a restriction for the purposes of Article 49 would change, altering the balance between the trade and other interests.

Bond van Adverteerders concerned Dutch rules which limited advertising over cable networks. The rules were intended to establish and maintain a pluralistic, non-commercial broadcasting system. The exclusive right to broadcast advertising was granted to a state body, which used the money generated to subsidise both the broadcast media and the press in the interests of pluralism, and to ensure that the different sectors of Dutch society were represented in the media. In this case, the rules were found to be a restriction of the freedom granted by Article 49 and were not justified. Although the national measures aimed to achieve laudable goals, acceptable in principle under Union law, they were disproportionate to their aim. As we shall see below, the issue of proportionality is crucial in the balancing of trade and non-trade concerns.

Following *Bond van Adverteerders*, the focus of discussion within the context of the EC Treaty became one of justifying regulation. Although the Union had no positive cultural competence at that time, it can be seen in *Bond van Adverteerders* and subsequent cases as developing a form of negative policy, by defining the limits of what is acceptable in national regulation by reference to the free movement of services. A similar process can be seen in the competition field, particularly where state monopolies were involved, and, subsequently, in that of state aid. Although the ECJ had accepted that broadcasting regulation might be in the public interest, the scope of any exception based on cultural considerations in the broadcasting field was not really elaborated until the '*Mediawet*' cases.[33] These

---

[32] The operation of a derogation is not to reserve to a member state an exclusive area of competence. L. Gormley, *Prohibiting Restrictions on Trade within the EEC* (North Holland: Elsevier Science Publishers B.V., 1985), p. 124.

[33] Case C-288/89 *Stichting Collective Antennevoorziening Gouda* v. *Commissariat voor de media* [1991] ECR I-4007; Case C-353/89 *Commission* v. *Netherlands* (Mediawet) [1991] ECR I-4069.

cases consist of a preliminary reference and an action by the Commission, but both actions challenged the same national rules. The rules in issue concerned the Dutch rules which had been amended since the case of *Bond van Adverteerders*. None the less, the exclusive right to sell advertising time on television was granted to the same body as before and the broadcasting of advertising on private channels remained limited. The same policy objectives were in view. In its final analysis, the ECJ concluded the Dutch rules were too far-reaching and therefore disproportionate; some rules were viewed as having an economic aim. Although the ECJ has found some national broadcasting rules to be acceptable (such as in the case of *TV10*, which was based on different reasoning, discussed in chapter 8), in many instances it has taken a similar approach to national rules, that is finding them disproportionate.[34]

Mediawet, in principle, accepted the cultural policies as falling within the rule of reason, which can be relied on only in relation to non-discriminatory national rules. At the level of broadcasting regulation, this is significant as the express treaty derogation, which has been interpreted narrowly,[35] would not include such rules. Public policy is the most likely of the three categories of derogation listed in Article 46 (see chapter 4) to encompass the regulation of broadcasting. The test commonly used to assess the acceptability of national measures on this basis is that the measure is necessary to counter 'a genuine and sufficiently serious threat to public policy'.[36] The threat must affect one of the fundamental interests of society.[37] Case law is silent as to what might be viewed by the ECJ as being such fundamental interests. Even were one to accept that the democratic functions of the broadcast media constitute fundamental interests of society, in particular the interests of citizens, the requirement that the threat be genuine and serious suggests a high level of immediacy between the regulated action and the adverse consequence for society. Although one might have sympathy with the views of theorists who recognise the important role that the broadcast media play in society (chapter 2), in this regard

[34] Case C-211/91 *Commission* v. *Belgium* (Cable Access) [1992] ECR I- 6757; Case C-11/95 *Commission* v. *Belgium* [1996] ECR I–4115.
[35] Case 36/75 *Rutili* v. *Ministre de l'Interiori* [1975] ECR 1219, para. 27; Case 41/74 *Van Duyn* [1974] ECR 1337, para. 18.
[36] Case 36/75 *Rutili*, para. 28.
[37] Case 30/77 *Bouchereau* [1977] ECR 1999, applied Joined Cases 115 and 116/81 *Adoui and Cornaille* [1982] ECR 1665, para. 8. Additionally, the Commission suggested that Article 46 EC must be read in the light of Article 10(2) of the ECHR and that therefore only issues identified in that provision Court fall within Article 46. The Court of Human Rights in Strasbourg has not taken this approach.

it is far from clear that the operation of a less regulated or commercial media system would satisfy this element of the Article 46 jurisprudence. Unfortunately, as we have seen in chapter 4, the boundaries between discriminatory and non-discriminatory rules are not clear,[38] adding an extra element of uncertainty, and potential incoherence, in this area.

The ECJ's reasoning in *Mediawet* opens up a number of questions about the values that the ECJ accepted needed protection and the mechanisms whereby they may be protected. The Dutch argument was based on cultural policy but, in accepting this point, it is not clear whether the ECJ was concerned with culture in a high-brow or popular sense, or the issue of cultural diversity *per se*. If it were the latter, what would cultural diversity mean in the context of the ECJ's jurisprudence? The phrase is ambiguous and could refer either to a wide range of 'quality' programmes where different views are represented; or, to a diversity of programme suppliers. The question of what constitutes cultural diversity in programming is complex, relating to other questions about the public-service role of broadcasting, the provision of a broad range of information and the stimulation of activity in the public sphere (see chapter 2). The ECJ did not address these issues, leaving us with a very sketchy understanding of cultural diversity and cultural policy. The ECJ's judgment is open to the interpretation that what the Court means by cultural diversity in *Mediawet* is actually an attempt to open member states' broadcasting markets up to non-national products. On this reasoning, the cultural diversity argument serves internal market ends. Certainly, the Commission in its TWF *Green Paper*[39] made the same link.

The reasoning in the *Mediawet* judgments is, in many respects, ambiguous. On the one hand, we can see a specific reference to the 'cultural tasks' of the system, such as managing a sound library, keeping film archives and managing orchestras and choirs.[40] Further, the ECJ seemed to accept that the maintenance of programme quality itself could be an object of cultural policy. On the other hand, the ECJ did not accept that culture is linked to a particular state, namely that broadcasters cannot be under an obligation to have 'all or some of their programmes produced by a Dutch undertaking'.[41] The ECJ referred specifically to Article 10 of the European

---

[38] See, e.g., Case C-17/00 *François De Coster* v. *Collège des bourgmestre et échevins de Watermael-Boitsfort*, [2001] ECR I-9445.

[39] Commission, *TWF Green Paper*, p. 46.   [40] Case C-353/89 *Mediawet*, para. 29.

[41] Case C-353/89 *Mediawet*, para. 31. Note, however, the European programme quotas are permissible under the TWFD and, in many member states, in practice this turns into a national requirement.

Convention on Human Rights (ECHR), almost turning the issue into a question of freedom of expression and of equality of access.[42] The matter has not been clarified by subsequent rulings, as the ECJ has seemed to accept that diversity and culture are separate issues without clarifying what culture means.[43] Although respect for diversity of cultures is now inbuilt into the Union,[44] the shaping of the four freedoms by member-states' cultural policies, subject to a rule of non-discrimination, as seen in *Debauve*, is clearly at an end.[45] Further, the ECJ does not have a consistent concept as to what is required by cultural diversity, or even the public-interest goals protected by media regulation. Although a court can only ever respond to the cases brought before it, the ECJ's response to the broadcasting cases in this regard is unnecessarily incomplete in its analysis of the scope of public interest.

Given the potential deregulatory impact of judicial harmonisation on the national broadcasting regulatory systems, the need for political action at the Union level became more apparent. The divergences in broadcasting regulation throughout the Union continued to cause difficulties, as member states approached broadcasting regulation in different ways. Broadcasters could consequently avoid the regulatory regime in a particular member state by establishing in another and relying on Article 49 to be allowed to broadcast to the first member state. There was limited protection against such 'abuse' of Union law.[46] Some action at the Union level was deemed to be necessary to safeguard standards.[47] The development of satellite television, with its inherently cross-border broadcasting

---

[42] On the issue of the link between freedom of expression and culture, see arguments about the application of Article 81 in Case 243/83 *Binon* [1985] ECR 2015, albeit a case that did not concern broadcasting.

[43] Case C-11/95 *Commission* v. *Belgium*.

[44] This point will be re-emphasised by Article I-3 of the Treaty establishing a Constitution for Europe should it come into force.

[45] For a discussion of the impact of amendments to the EC Treaty generally on the interpretation of the freedom to provide services, see Woods, *Free Movement of Goods and Services*, pp. 298–9.

[46] See Case 33/74 *JHM Van Binsbergen* v. *Bestuur van de Bedrijfsvereiging voor de Metaalnijverheid* [1974] ECR 1299, para. 13; Case C-148/91 *Vereniging Veronica Omroep Organisatie* v. *Commissariaat voor de Media* [1993] ECR I-487; C-23/93 *TV10 SA* v. *Commissariaat voor de Media* [1994] ECR I-4795, discussed further in chapter 6. See also discussion in L. Woods and J. Scholes, 'Broadcasting: The Creation of a European Culture or the Limits of the Internal Market?', *Yearbook of European Law* 17 (1997), 47–, pp. 56–8.

[47] Parliament, *Hahn Report*, raised concerns about unlimited competition as a result of satellite broadcasting and recognised that standards and arrangements must be made for advertising by those broadcasters, pp. 7 and 17.

capacity,[48] made the discussion of the issues more pressing. The *TWFD Green Paper* sought to set out a legal framework for Union action in the broadcasting sector, and to encourage a common market in broadcasting services.

The matter was, however, contentious. The member states were not in agreement about the level and scope of action to be taken.[49] The Netherlands, for example, argued against the TWFD, on the basis that it would introduce the Convention on Transfrontier Television (CTT) (which had been agreed within the framework of the Council of Europe and which the Dutch government had not ratified) by the back door.[50] In addition, the European Parliament had different concerns from the Commission and the ECJ regarding the values to be protected in the broadcasting sector. Tensions between the different camps not only delayed the adoption of the TWFD but were also reflected in the inherent contradictions found within its terms.

As we have seen in chapter 4, the TWFD rests on an internal market treaty base (Article 47(2)). Those that challenged the TWFD were, in part, concerned about whether it was possible to base the TWFD on this provision, given the non-trade values protected by some of its provisions. The debate about the proper base, if any, for the TWFD to some extent continues. It has been argued that, given the Union now has flanking cultural competence, Article 151 should have been used for action in the cultural field. Problematically, Article 151 excludes the possibility of harmonising legislation in the cultural sphere. This fact is used by some as support for the argument that the TWFD in its entirety, or the quotas provisions, should not have been enacted. Article 151 post-dates the enactment of TWFD, however, and it is debatable whether a subsequent treaty amendment can invalidate a Union measure in this way.

In any event, the argument overlooks the fact that Article 151 is not the only possible base for Union action, nor is cultural policy even the primary

---

[48] Satellite footprints do not follow national boundaries, although the international agreements on the use of satellites have tried to strengthen control over regulation along national lines. WARC 77 tried to create national satellite services but this attempt was defeated by the introduction of the high powered DBS technology.

[49] R. Collins, 'Unity in Diversity? The European Single Market in Broadcasting and the Audio-visual, 1982–92', *Journal of Common Market Studies*, 32(1) (1994), 89–102, p. 95.

[50] The Dutch may well have had a point here. Despite one case against the UK in which the ECJ dismissed arguments based on the CTT, discussed ch. 7, the ECJ has held that the CTT and its explanatory memorandum may be used in the interpretation of the TWFD: Joined cases C-320-94, C-328/94, C-329/94, C-337/94, C-338/94 and C-339/94 *RTL and Others* [1996] ECR I–6471, para. 33.

justification for its action. As the *TWF Green Paper*[51] noted, the aim of the TWFD was to eradicate barriers to trade in broadcasting services arising from the member states' differing system of broadcast regulation, which had had a particular impact on advertising rules. The TWFD clearly, as its recitals emphasise, has an internal-market concern. Given that the relevant Union act should be based on the main or predominant legal basis,[52] it appears that the predominant aim of the TWFD was to facilitate inter-state trade. Using the internal market in service provision is therefore acceptable. The impact this assessment has on the type of provisions that might be properly included within its scope, or on the interpretation of the TWFD in general, is less clear, as we shall see when we consider the case law on the interpretation of the advertising frequency rules (see chapter 9). Here we can see that broadcasting policy cannot claim to be autonomous from its trade-orientated treaty base.

The ECJ's approach in *Debauve* caused the Commission to be worried that many national rules that might constitute restrictions to cross-border service provision would remain untouched by the four freedoms. The market in broadcasting services would, therefore, probably remain divided along national lines. Equally, the infrastructure market remained fragmented, due to the adoption of different technical standards across the member states. Many equipment manufacturers were concerned about the impact of this fragmentation on their ability to develop global products in the face of competition, particularly from the manufacturers from the Far East. Similar concerns about the global markets arose in the content field also; this time, content was flooding in from the United States of America, threatening European content production as well as its cultural distinctiveness. For the Commission, harmonisation was vital to create European markets to support European producers.[53] Thus harmonisation might be seen in both cases as supporting industrial policy goals. Although it could be argued that such a policy protects viewer interests, in maintaining sources of broadcast content that reflects individual member-states' cultures, the interests of industrial policy and viewer protection are not necessarily coterminous. It is doubtful whether, in the event of a conflict, viewer protection or protection of industry interests would take priority. In addition to our doubts as to whether this policy

---

[51] Commission, *TWF Green Paper*, p. 18.

[52] Case C-491/01 *R. v. Secretary of State for Health*, ex parte *British American Tobacco (Investments) Ltd and Imperial Tobacco Ltd, supported by Japan Tobacco Inc. and JT International SA* [2002] ECR I-11453, para. 94.

[53] Commission, *TWF Green Paper*, pp. 152–3.

really protects viewers' interests *vis à vis* content, we are sceptical as to the appropriateness of claims made by industry players about the need for support for the development of European-based global standards in the context of the equipment market. The connection between the interests of the viewer and the availability of specifically European terminal equipment is not clear. Some advantages may accrue to the more adventurous consumer who is able to access products from other member states when there are common interface standards, but these are far from general benefits.

Further problems for policymakers arose from the fact that the TWFD sought not only to manage differences between the member states and their cultural policies but also to introduce some form of pan-European cultural policy, albeit viewed from the perspective of competition and free-movement concerns. This seems a double step forward from the negative policy identified through judicial harmonisation; not only is there the beginnings of a positive cultural policy within the Union but that policy considers culture at the Union level rather than at the national level. Subsequent treaty revision has sought to curb this tendency; the Union has a supporting role regarding culture and harmonisation in this field is expressly excluded.[54] As noted in chapter 4, although these provisions clarify the competence for the Union in this field, at the same time they restrict the type of action it can take, limiting it to supporting actions. In principle, the idea of joint competence is not necessarily problematic, but the way co-operation is managed in practice may lead to lack of coherence in policy. We have seen this in relation to the discussion of the scope of the cultural exception from the freedom to provide services. It can also be identified in the approach to media mergers (see chapter 7).

The cultural-competence provision states that culture should be taken into account in other policy areas. These areas tend to have an economic focus. Notably, competition law aims to ensure that a competitive environment between market operators exists. As a corollary, it is hoped that a wide spectrum of views and opinions will exist in media markets. While policy has focused on the removal of the distortions to competition in broadcast services, the Union has not been successful in introducing a market-correcting measure (a media merger regulation) that would provide specific rules for the audiovisual sector to ensure media pluralism and diversity. Indeed, Union merger policy is, to some extent, undermined by the needs of Union industrial policy, which seeks to create

---

[54] Article 151(4) EC.

'European giants' in all sectors; this may operate to support trans-European media conglomerates (see chapter 7). Cultural policy objectives are therefore intermingled with other concerns, making it hard to speak of an autonomous policy area.

The attempt to produce a media merger regulation was abandoned when, in addition to conflicts between the directorates-general as to the focus of the proposed measure, the Commission failed to achieve a compromise between the member states and the European Parliament about ownership levels.[55] The proposed legislation was subject to particular scrutiny because, again, there were concerns about the Union's competence to take action to protect pluralism directly. Failure of the Union to achieve consensus on media merger legislation has led Papathanassopoulos[56] to argue that the Union will continue to be 'powerless to regulate the issue of concentration, apart from scrutinising mergers and acquisitions'. Indeed, the lack of any type of pluralism directive has meant that the Commission's attempts to regulate pluralism by the use of merger regulation and competition provisions leaves matters of internal pluralism (the diversity of content shown on any one channel) to the member states. A patchwork of rules continues to exist across the Union, which leads to variable levels of protection of the viewers' interests in regard to the diversity of content available to them. Indeed the prevailing assumption seems to be that, with more channels on offer, including the possibility of cross-border broadcasts, there is less need for regulation to ensure a wide diet of programming. The weaknesses in this argument are discussed in chapter 3.

Objections to Union measures which encroach on areas of member states' regulatory activity is symptomatic of the general problem of competence creep in the Union and the tension that exists in many policy areas between centralisation and local autonomy (subsidiarity). In the area of broadcasting, the lack of a specific treaty base for broadcasting has meant that, where areas of competence are particularly strained, more informal measures have been adopted. In the context of the *Human Dignity Green Paper and Recommendation*, we can see the institutions relying on soft law, such as recommendations[57] to develop further agreement on areas affected by Union legislation, but not formally within the

---

[55] S. Papathanassopoulos, *European Television in the Digital Age* (Cambridge: Polity Press, 2000), p. 113.

[56] *Ibid.*, p. 115.

[57] A recommendation is listed in Article 249 EC as one of the acts of the Union but it is not legally binding.

legislation's scope. The 1998 Council Recommendation[58] was aimed at achieving protection of minors and human dignity through the promotion of national frameworks, which were designed to provide a comparable and effective level of Internet and broadcasting regulation. The Commission's *Green Paper on the Protection of Minors and Human Dignity* pointed to a number of areas in which public-interest issues are dealt with either specifically or incidentally in a number of policy initiatives.[59] The *Green Paper* also identified a series of questions for debate on issues which the Commission considered as being central to its consideration of the future policy actions and relevant to its review of the TWFD. This included the type of regulatory approach that should be adopted; and the extent to which control mechanisms can, or should be, harmonised or standardised across the Union. It aimed to take into account the diverse range of cultures and values and the fact that in cultural matters the Union's role is limited.

These concerns are reflected in DSAD, in which the desirability and effectiveness of co-regulatory measures are highlighted.[60] Given the study of co-regulatory measures in the media, it could be suggested that their appropriateness has been thoroughly investigated and shown. This conclusion is open to doubt, since the publication of DSAD pre-dated the publication of the final phase of the report and, as the report noted, there are questions in some member states as to the democratic legitimacy of

---

[58] Council, *Recommendation on the Development of the Competitiveness of the European Audiovisual and Information Services Industry by promoting National Frameworks aimed at Achieving a Comparable and Effective Level of Protection of Minors and Human Dignity*, 98/561/EC OJ [1998] L 270/48, p. 3.

[59] Commission, *Green Paper on the Protection of Minors and Human Dignity in Audiovisual and Information Services*, COM(96)483, 1996, final. The introductory section, p. 1, stated that 'the Commission Communication on Services of General Interest in Europe contains a section on broadcasting in which it is pointed out that general interest considerations in this field basically concern the content of broadcasts and are linked to moral and democratic values, such as pluralism, information ethics and protection of the individual. Intellectual property is covered in the Green Paper on Copyright and Neighbouring Rights in the Information Society. The Commercial Communications Green Paper covers *inter alia* public interest issues in relation to advertising and sponsorship. A Directive has been adopted on the protection of individuals with regard to the processing of personal data. The Television Without Frontiers Directive, which is in the process of being revised, provides coordinated Community rules in a number of fields, including the protection of minors. The proposed Directive on Regulatory Transparency in the Internal Market for Information Society Services will facilitate Community coordination of future regulatory activity and the pursuit of public interest objectives that are worthy of protection.'

[60] Article 3(3) DSAD.

such measures. It may be that the Commission here is responding to different perspectives in the various member states as to the appropriate level of regulation to be adopted.

An alternative approach to the use of a recommendation can be seen in the MEDIA programmes, which are legally constituted via a Council decision. They aim to protect similar values through the provision of funding rather than through regulation. Despite their cultural purposes, they have an industrial policy legal base, again illustrating the lack of policy autonomy. These culturally protectionist measures are also evidence of a political compromise between market or policy interventionists and market or policy liberals.

This section has provided an overview of the scope of both the negative and positive policy developments in the broadcasting sector within the Union. The ECJ, although it has recognised in principle that concerns such as pluralism in the media, freedom of expression and cultural diversity are in the public interest, has not adequately developed these terms. The scope of these terms is uncertain. One could argue that the ECJ has tended to accept member states' assessment as to the proper scope of the public interest in broadcasting regulation, so that the ECJ's lack of clarity is less significant. None the less, problems arise from the deregulatory impulse introduced into the case law by the application of the doctrine of proportionality. Although it would be unfair to characterise the policy here as disregarding non-commercial aspects of the broadcasting sector, many aspects of policy are driven by internal market, competition and industrial policy considerations alone, or with scant regard for anything else. In one respect this is unremarkable, linking back to the limited nature of the Union's competence in cultural matters.

The limited competence of the Union may have disadvantages. Reliance on the various internal market treaty bases for Union action may open any proposals for action to hostile debate and limit the scope of any action that could be taken. Consequently, there is a risk that policymakers, in an attempt to avoid controversy and challenges to their competence, put forward or agree proposals that are unlikely to rile powerful lobby groups, or, in an attempt to secure agreement among groups with different views, include possibilities for more 'flexible' forms of law-making. The possible result of this is that policy in general and in the broadcasting sector does not address problems that are probably best dealt with by the Union. An example can be seen in the failure of the Union to agree the media mergers regulation.

Increasing commercialisation

The TWFD is often seen to be a factor in the increasing commercialisation of the Union's broadcasting market, as it allowed broadcasters to avoid national regulatory controls aimed at achieving the public interest goals of broadcasting. Deregulation and liberalisation of broadcasting was, however, already being undertaken in many member states. Further, as state monopolies were broken up, commercial channels were encouraged[61] and grew in number, facilitated also by changes in technology. Significantly, challenges to state broadcasters were made under free-movement and competition provisions, not just by the Commission but by commercial broadcasters. This was a factor in the privatisation and corporatisation process across the Union. As we have seen, the ECJ's approach undermined the protection accorded to PSB in the Union. The development of cable and satellite technology, which allowed for the existence of a greater number of channels, increased the trend towards competition and commercialisation of the sector.

The use of Union law to challenge a national monopoly can be seen in ERT.[62] ERT was a non-profit making public broadcaster which was controlled and supervised by the Greek state and had a monopoly in broadcasting from Greece and in retransmission of signals within Greece from elsewhere. DEP, which sought to retransmit broadcasts originating from sources other than ERT, argued that the relevant provisions were contrary to the Greek constitution, Article 10 ECHR (freedom of expression) and Articles 49 and 81 *et seq*. While there is nothing in the EC Treaty which prevents broadcasting from being entrusted to a state monopoly, the way that monopoly is organised must not infringe the treaty rules.[63] The ECJ noted that, as ERT had been granted a statutory monopoly, it would have a dominant position within the sense of Article 82 EC. The ECJ, under the terms of Article 86(1), argued that ERT's monopoly on retransmission of broadcasts from other member states could constitute discrimination against broadcasters based in other member states, as the national broadcaster could favour the broadcasting of its own national programmes. Such an action would be detrimental to programming from other member states, unless it could be justified on public-interest grounds. Here, the ECJ has defined broadcasting in relation to competition provisions, which

---

[61] Ward, *The European Union Democratic Deficit*, p. 56.
[62] Case C-260/89 *Elliniki Radiophonia Tileorassi AE (ERT) v. Dimotiki Etairia Pliroforissis (DEP) and Sotirios Kouvelas* [1991] ECR 1-2925.
[63] Article 86(1) EC.

in this case did not accommodate either freedom-of-expression or public-interest defences. The impetus is towards a multiplicity of providers, rather than accepting state monopolies, whether a public service broadcaster or not.

The Union institutions have recognised PSB as an important national institution. The Amsterdam PSB Protocol recognises, for example, both the importance of PSB and the fact that PSB lies within member-state competence. Member states, therefore, are left to define the scope and scale of PSB, but this must be done with reference to the competition and state-aid provisions. Consequently, any endorsement of PSB as a force for social or democratic good is evaluated against an economic assessment of how it affects broadcasting and telecommunications market activity. In an increasingly competitive international broadcasting environment, an economic argument against support for public service broadcasters across the Union is being strengthened. A series of challenges from commercial broadcasters about unfair trading based on the state support for PSB have sought to challenge the position of public service broadcasters across the Union (see chapter 13). As the rationale for state control of the spectrum has weakened (see chapter 2), so, too, has the philosophical justification for the privileged position accorded to state-aided broadcasting. Here we see competence issues being reinforced by changes in the market-place and in assumptions about the respective roles of private sector and public sector. Privatisation and commercialisation intertwine to limit the role of the state in the provision of broadcasting services, consequently changing the way broadcasting itself is perceived, as commodity rather than a public good.

The commodification of broadcasting is part of a trend which accepts the commodification of information more generally. Information becomes the private property of corporations; within the broadcasting sphere, this can be seen in the way premium content is treated. The rights to sporting events have become very valuable, as broadcasters use them to attract subscription revenue. The social and cultural aspects of sporting events so televised are ignored in the pursuit of these revenues. The excessive control of rights to content has been both threatened and facilitated by the development of digital technology. Whilst digital formats make it easier for the viewer to copy content, copyright owners have developed digital rights management systems (DRM) that limit the ability to copy, and control the devices on which such content can be viewed. Not only does this have the potential to limit viewers' enjoyment of content but it may threaten competition between infrastructure providers (see chapter 6).

None the less, Union policy in the form of the Directive on Copyright in the Digital Age[64] is to support DRM.

Greater commercialisation within the broadcasting sector has also brought competitive and financial advantages to commercial broadcasters and to member states. Many member states have sought to liberalise their markets in order to allow larger national broadcasting organisations to develop which can compete in an international market. The task of protecting cultural diversity within the European broadcasting industry, the protection of media pluralism through the provision of PSB[65] and the control of media concentration can easily be compromised by member states' desire to build competitive national broadcasting markets.[66] Combined with the lack of Union competence in this area this creates a climate which favours the increased commercialisation of the sector and defers to the increasing power of media conglomerates that is emerging. The interests of citizens are under threat in the increasingly commercialised and competitive broadcasting sector which is developing across the Union.

It is possible that viewers' interests will be further compromised in a system where lobbying by the industrial sector seeks to promote and safeguard each sector's own industry interests. The impact of industry lobbying can be seen at two levels. First, in many member states, the commercial sector (and sometimes the public service sector) has been encouraged to develop strategies that will improve its success in international markets. Here, what are regarded as unnecessary regulations, which, it is said, will stifle enterprise and ability to compete, may well be removed. Secondly, the industry lobby is powerful at the Union level, especially so since extensive consultation periods give the opportunity for non-political actors to have a voice. Consultations also tend to favour industry interest because of the resources industry players can mobilise during the time they are allotted to make their case. The determination of the advertising lobby to relax advertising rules in the review of the TWFD

---

[64] Directive 2001/29/EC of the European Parliament and of the Council of 22 May 2001 on the harmonisation of certain aspects of copyright and related rights in the information society, OJ [2001] L 167/10.

[65] See the specific Protocol on the system of public service broadcasting in the member states appended to the Amsterdam Treaty. The Protocol emphasises the importance of PSB for individual member states and states that the determination of the proper scope of PSB should lie with the member states; the Commission, by contrast, in its interpretation of the Protocol suggests that it has the power to review the scope of PSB in the interest of the common good and, in particular, in the light of competition policy.

[66] Commission, *Green Paper on Services of General Interest*, COM (2003), 270 final noted that the protection of media pluralism is primarily a task for the member states, sec. 74, p. 22.

is a case in point (see chapter 9). Furthermore, consultation exercises on interoperability have favoured industry views (see chapter 6). Additionally, many of the specialist committees involved in standards setting and policy development are dominated by those who have industry interests. A notable example was the membership of the Bangemann Committee in the convergence review. Finally, the move towards co-regulation and self-regulation, which may be influenced by competence concerns, also allows industry voices a greater degree of control about the standards with which they comply. To sum up, the Union is becoming increasingly subject to the way the industry perceives itself as a combination of self-regulator, policy consultant and economic powerhouse, all of which ensure that positive intervention in the interests of the non-economic role of broadcasting has been increasingly challenged.

Technology

One of the main triggers for the introduction of TWFD was the introduction of satellite broadcasting, particularly the direct-to-home (DTH) broadcasts. The introduction of new transmission platforms, first cable and then satellite, increased the number of channels possible. The increased capacity raised questions about the necessity for positive content regulation to ensure diversity of content. Technology was here used by industry and political institutions to shape policy and regulation, and justify those changes. The challenge to content regulation was reinforced with the introduction of digital technology and the perceived convergence of the communications industries and technology.

The debate about convergence began in the early 1990s. The Bangemann Report took up the idea with some enthusiasm, seeing convergence as an opportunity to create an information society and regulation as a barrier to its achievement. The market-driven revolution and a light-touch regulatory regime for all forms of communication envisaged by Bangemann has since been replaced by more sober considerations of the speed, scope and scale of convergence. Whereas the Bangemann Report had been published by the Information Society Directorate General (DG), the 1997 *Green Paper on Convergence* involved broadcasting policymakers from DG Education and Culture and different policy concerns are evident. The 1997 document endorsed media consolidation in a converging communications environment, recognising that economies of scale were to be achieved through media alliances and that measures were necessary to remove barriers to convergence. In addition, the *Convergence Green*

Paper took into consideration concerns ranging beyond the scope and interests of the Bangemann Report. The *Convergence Green Paper* recognised the continued need for sector-specific regulation to protect different values associated with telecommunications, broadcasting and the Internet.

The original *Convergence Green Paper* identified five principles for the future regulatory environment of a converged communications sector, which essentially focused on light-touch regulation (see chapter 4). In this approach, we can see similarities to the underlying principles suggested for broadcasting regulation in a contemporaneous policy document.[67] Whilst there was little resistance to light-touch regulation for the Internet and telecommunications, the input of DG Education and Culture was significant in that it highlighted the special nature of broadcasting content. The recognition that public-interest concerns should form part of a converging communications environment led to an evolutionary rather than a revolutionary approach to convergence in regulatory terms. A graduated, step-by-step approach to reform of the regulatory regime has emerged, and is one which continues to separate content from infrastructure and which recognises the different nature and value of content delivered by different delivery platforms.

This so-called technologically neutral approach builds on existing structures. A horizontal, technologically neutral, minimum regulatory approach has been taken in relation to infrastructure to encourage competition in the supply chain and to keep access open to networks and to prevent bottle-necks. Here the same regulatory framework, the Communications Package, is applied to all channels of delivery, ranging from telecommunications, cable, satellite and so on. In this way, the Union has sought to address the problem of any discrimination which might arise in relation to the mechanism of delivery and mirrors approaches taken to the interpretation of TWFD and the earlier case law on services.

In addition, a vertical approach has been taken for sector-specific issues relating to control and regulation of content. Here regulation is gradated according to the nature of content being supplied, ranging from Internet content through to broadcast content, in particular to the type of content where the public interest concerns are high.[68] This seems inconsistent with the much-vaunted technological neutrality principle found

---

[67] Commission, *Communication on Principles and Guidelines for the Community's Audiovisual Policy in the Digital Age*, COM (1999), 657 final.

[68] Commission, *The Convergence of the Telecommunications*; Commission, *Audiovisual Policy in the Digital Age*.

underpinning the early convergence documents. As we shall see in later chapters, questions arise as to whether the ECJ (and the Commission) is technologically neutral in regard to the essential facilities doctrine (see chapter 6) and in its approach to competition between different platforms (see chapter 7). Furthermore, although a common approach to carriage has emerged, it remains uncertain the degree to which the two issues of infrastructure and content can really be separated. As we shall see, in not fully dealing this issue, the institutions arguably failed to give priority to the needs of citizens, particularly the passive viewer, both in terms of right to access the infrastructure and the actual range of content made available.

Technological change and the perceived importance of convergence have had a significant influence on communications policy and the review of the TWFD seems also to have been driven by technological consider-ations. In December 2005 the Commission published DSAD which was based on an extensive consultation process.[69] Crucially, DSAD seems to change the scope of the TWFD by extending a basic tier of obligations to all media services and maintains the more stringent regime for broad-casting. According to the explanatory memorandum attached to DSAD, the aim was to ensure a technologically neutral approach to ensure a level playing-field. With a graduated approach, however, it is hard to see that technological neutrality is being upheld. Although DSAD does not distinguish between television platforms, it does distinguish between point-to-multipoint services and point-to-point services. Thus, DSAD distinguishes between services based on the nature of the service, rather than the platform used. This is a somewhat fine distinction as the nature of the service, essentially based on the push/pull distinction, is depen-dent on the technology available. In any event, the distinction seems to be based on concern for new market participants and their needs, rather than directly considering the viewer. None the less, it might be argued that DSAD recognises some common themes about the impact of media services on the viewer, and in particular the need to protect the vulnerable (passive) viewer, as well as society in general, from harmful content.[70]

In some respects the proposed extension of the TWFD in DSAD might seem to remove the need for a discussion of the boundary between, for

---

[69] Commission, *Proposal for a Second Amending Directive.*
[70] Contrast, e.g., Recital 28, which emphasises the impact of viewer control, with Recital 29, which recognises the impact of the media on formation of opinions.

example, video on demand (VOD) and near video on demand (NVOD). The current approach distinguishes between VOD and NVOD, with VOD classed as information-society services. VOD is delivered on demand on a one-to-one basis and therefore is not classified as broadcasting services. In contrast, NVOD is delivered on a one-to-many-basis and is classed as broadcast content. Given that exactly the same content may be delivered by both mechanisms, this distinction seems to have missed the point of sector-specific regulation. At one level, all the changes do is move the inquiry from determining the boundary of the TWFD to an internal inquiry as to which set of rules applies to a given service. The difficulties with determining the boundary between TWFD and information-society services look set to remain. They could be problematic, as VOD services increase and a lower level of protection is accorded to viewers for some content that they have been used to receiving as heavily regulated broadcast content. These issues, and the scope of TWFD in relation to the meaning of broadcasting, are discussed further in chapter 8 and in the appendix.

One final point concerns the approach of DSAD to types of regulation. Lighter touch is premised on two assumptions; first, positive regulation becomes unnecessary in an era of choice; and secondly, the need for negative regulation is minimised by the existence of technology, such as V-chips, encryption devices and other content-filtering mechanisms. Although the V-chip has not yet been introduced within the Union, studies commissioned which consider a technology/regulation symbiosis form part of the backdrop to DSAD. There are problems with these two assumptions. First, the choice argument assumes not only the viewers' willingness and ability to pay but also their ability to manage information and, crucially, navigation systems such as EPGs. It also does not address the impact of consumerist choices facilitated and reinforced via such technology on the broadcasting environment. In our view, Union policy can here be seen as committing errors of omission by not considering these problems. The second assumption introduces the possibility of regulation, even softer versions of regulation, being replaced by a reliance on technology and viewers' technological know-how. This effectively assumes that viewers are active, and changes the relationship between viewer, regulator and broadcaster. Here Union policy is based on the assumption that viewers (in particular, parents) will be willing to act as regulators of content for themselves and for their children, when, in practice, they may not choose or care to do so for a variety of reasons.

Conclusion

Three central and interlinked factors are evident from this overview, even if they do not constitute the only factors which may influence policy outcomes. The factors are: Union competence, increasing commercialisation of the broadcasting sector and technological change. Union policy has become more concrete through a move from negative harmonisation to positive measures such as the TWFD and, more broadly, the Communications Package. Even beyond legislative measures, we can see formal interventions such as the MEDIA programme. This does not mean, however, that broadcasting policy is autonomous. Not only are different treaty bases in issue, which allow different scope for action, but, given the Union's limited competence in the area of broadcasting seen as a cultural service, treaty bases have been used which have a different objective from that of broadcasting policy. This means that broadcasting policy is intertwined inevitably with other goals, such as the creation of the internal market, competition policy and industrial policy. It is also clear that policymakers are aware of the needs of citizen viewers and the values of broadcasting. Equally, we can see that the trade-based focus of broadcasting policy is becoming increasingly apparent and has a disproportionate impact on the type of regulation and the range of non-commercial interests being taken into account. Similarly, the sensitive nature of broadcasting suggests that member states are particularly keen to protect their own domain and thus we see, in borderline areas of Union competence (negative content regulation), the Union institutions relying on soft-law measures to negotiate agreement on these issues. The move to soft law has not just been a response to competence issues but also reflects a changing environment in which commercial factors and technological change operate to challenge and to undermine existing regulatory structures. Co-regulation, self-regulation and even a reliance on technology itself are becoming more popular options to ensure content standards (whether negative or positive) are met. This is part of a drift to a more commercialised environment, in which viewers are treated by industry and regulators as consumers rather than citizens. Equally, the increasing preference for technological solutions to regulatory questions assumes that viewers are active. The focus in initiatives, such as i2010, is to re-emphasise the need for light regulation for the development of information-society services, suggesting these trends will continue in an era of increasing convergence. These developments, however, do not, in our view, adequately protect viewers when regarded as citizens rather than consumers.

PART II

6

Access

Introduction

Any discussion about the need for content regulation presupposes that viewers are able to receive that content. Access to content depends on access to infrastructure and transmission/reception technologies; a fact we have noted in our discussion of the environmental factors affecting the viewing experience (chapter 1).[1] Although reception equipment is required to be able to view any form of television, with the advent of cable and satellite transmission technologies we see the introduction of conditional access systems (CAS), enabling pay TV. CAS creates the tollgate, allowing access to programming for only those who pay. In this, we see technology playing a part in the commodification and the commercialisation of the broadcasting environment.

The Union response to the policy challenges relating to access to content has combined two types of regulation. *Ex ante* sector-specific regulation, which seeks to attain public interest objectives and safeguard the position of the citizen (rather than the viewer as a consumer); and *ex post*, which is a general competition-based approach focusing on the operation of the market. Implicitly, a market-based approach is linked to a conception of communication as private property rather than a public resource. Combined with these, and further complicating matters, is the issue of infrastructure standards adopted by the Union, which is reliant on industry involvement. This is an approach that is replete with problems arising from the interplay of Union and member-state competence, the impact of commercialisation and the clash between industry interests and viewer needs. In all this, the approach the Union has taken to access has been

---

[1] See, e.g., W. H. Dutton, *Society on the Line: Information Politics in the Digital Age* (Oxford: Oxford University Press, 1999), pp. 4–5, who argues that information communication technologies (ICTs) shape access to information, people, services and technologies. These four dimensions are all concerned with what he refers to as 'tele-access'. For Dutton, the power and importance of ICTs lie not only in creating greater access to information but also in creating the opportunity for users 'to have more control over access, and over the terms of access', p. 11.

affected, if not driven, by technological developments and particularly the perceived impact of technical convergence. This mixture shows that it is unlikely that all viewers have been considered, particularly those who do not have the money to gain access to CAS or disposition to interact with CAS and content navigation systems.

The purpose of this chapter is to clarify the relationship between the infrastructure regulation and content provision. We then discuss the application of general competition law provisions before going on to consider the provisions in the Communications Package.[2] We assess the extent to which the infrastructure rules adequately protect the public interest aspect of broadcasting, through the rules on access to networks. We shall also consider the impact of these rules on electronic programme guides ('EPGs'), which straddle the boundary between transmission services and content, and illustrate weaknesses in the 'horizontal' approach to regulation proposed as a consequence of technological convergence. These issues essentially concern the relationship between content suppliers and the transmission companies, while recognising the role EPGs play in enabling viewers to choose the content they wish to watch.[3] The final part of the chapter is concerned with the position of citizens, especially with regard to PSB content, and an assessment of the Universal Service Directive (USD), specifically the 'must-carry' provisions.

One caveat must be issued. We shall not, given the book's focus on broadcasting, trace the development of the Communications Package from its liberalisation and open network provision ('ONP'), nor shall we deal with other infrastructure-related issues, such as the development of common standards for pictures (such as high definition television (HDTV)).[4] Our primary concern in this chapter is related to viewing possibilities that relate to current policy initiatives which affect access to content, and therefore the viewing experience.

---

[2] Directive 2002/21/EC Framework Directive; Directive 2002/20/EC Authorisation Directive; Directive 2002/19/EC Access Directive; Directive 2002/22/EC Universal Service Directive and Directive 2002/58/EC Data Protection and Electronic Communications Directive OJ [2002] L 108. There is also a decision on Radio Spectrum: Decision 676/2002/EC OJ [2002] L 108.

[3] As de Streel suggests, these can be viewed as wholesale markets: A. de Streel, 'The Protection of the European Citizen in a Competitive E-Society: The New E.U. Universal Service Directive', *Journal of Network Industries*, 4(2) (2003), 189, p. 193; the position as regards the viewers concerns the retail market. This characterisation moves away from the traditional view of services as not having wholesale markets.

[4] The requirement to broadcast wide-screen television is now found in the Access Directive in Article 4(2); see also Recitals 4 and 8.

The importance of access to infrastructure

We have suggested in chapter 2 that universality of service is significant in satisfying the needs of viewers, and, in chapter 1, that access issues affect the viewing experience both of citizens and consumers, in some instances constituting a constraining factor on the viewers' content reach. This issue and the need to ensure universality of service have been with us since the emergence of television services. From the beginning, and operating at a national level, common standards were developed. These nationally based analogue standards were not common to all European states. In general, viewers with a single receiver could receive only the limited number of channels available nationally.

The issues of access, transmission standards and interoperability gained new significance with the introduction of digital technology and pay TV services. Simple interoperability with a single universal receiver has become less likely. Different platforms have typically used different standards, reflecting the different transmission networks' respective physical characteristics. When other transmission networks are considered, for example, 3G mobile and the Internet, common standards seem further away than ever, despite the use of the same digital language and the pace of technological convergence. As further digital services emerge, these issues of access become more important and more of a problem.

Whilst new services raise new opportunities, problems arise for both viewer and broadcaster. To receive digital signals, viewers need a decoder, whether integrated into the television, or in the form of a set-top box (STB). The decoder is essentially a stripped-down computer, comprising elements of hardware and software, all of which may be protected by intellectual property rights, often owned by one company. The software element enables the content aspect of broadcasting to talk to the hardware element, so as to allow individuals to view the content. As a result of technological developments, a choice emerges. One possibility, each content provider produces its own software and hardware (i.e. the STB), which would be undesirable from the viewers' perspective. Viewers would be forced into either limiting the content available to them by reference to the decoder chosen[5] or having to buy more than one set of reception equipment.

[5] This is a variant of the 'walled garden' theory already expressed in some of the Commission's decisions in respect of multimedia mergers: see *AOL/Time Warner*, Commission Decision 2001/718/EC, Case IV/M1845, OJ [2001] L 268/28, discussed ch. 7 and *Vizzavi Vivendi/Canal plus/Seagram*, Commission Decision, Case COMP/M.2050.

The only alternative to this position is that one set of intellectual property rights becomes an industry standard. Were this to occur, the problem then becomes that, unless the technology supporting the chosen standard is available to all, one company might be able to control the selection of content across a particular platform.[6] Such control potentially risks denying access to some, or giving access on less favourable terms to some content providers in preference to others. Effectively, this would create a conditional access supplier who would 'own' the viewing household and determine the 'rules' by which viewers access content. Such a supplier could therefore make choices for viewers about the content available or affect, in a way that might not be visible, the conditions in which viewers make such choices. Thus, even were other service providers to have access to that household, their relationship would be likely to become indirect, occurring through the prism of the conditional access supplier's relationship with the viewer.[7] This state of affairs would be problematic from the perspective of ensuring diversity of suppliers and protecting viewers' interests.

The inherently limited number of transmission networks puts a certain power in the hands of those distribution companies regarding what programming is seen and by whom.[8] This simple fact has become of greater relevance with increasing commercialisation of the media and the tendency of the media companies towards vertical integration

---

[6] Although some aspects of the code might be unprotected under the Software Directive, Council Directive 91/250/EEC of 14 May 1991 on the legal protection of computer programs OJ [1991] L 122/42, as amended by Directive 93/98/EEC, this would apply only to small elements of the code. The Copyright Directive, Directive 2001/29/EC of the European Parliament and of the Council of 22 May 2001 on the harmonisation of certain aspects of copyright and related rights in the information society OJ [2001] L 167/10, provides for certain limited circumstances in which software writers can disassemble the code so as to write programs that will be interoperable with that program: see Article 6 Copyright Directive.

[7] This issue is seen in the telecommunications market, too, where the provider with control over the subscriber line, i.e. the line between the house and the first telecommunications network switch, has the primary relationship with the subscriber, even if other services (e.g. long-distance phone calls) are provided by other suppliers. See, e.g., P. Larouche, *Competition Law and Regulation in European Telecommunications* (Oxford: Hart Publishing, 2000), pp. 324–5.

[8] H. Galperin and F. Bar, 'The Regulation of Interactive Television in the United States and the European Union', *Fed. Comm L.J.* 55 (2002) 61. Effectively, each different transmission network has a monopoly within its geographic area. The extent to which the different platforms are in competition with each other is debatable. See further the approach taken within the telecommunications package, discussed below.

(see chapter 7).[9] From the perspective of the consumer, it might be possible to integrate decoders in respect of different standards into one STB or television. Although this would not solve diversity of supply issues, it does at least provide the 'one-stop box' solution. Whether it is practical in terms of cost, at least in the short term, is doubtful.

For the content provider, especially public service content providers, the issue of 'simulcasting' (i.e. broadcasting the same content across different platforms), so as to ensure that all viewers have access to their programming irrespective of reception technology, arises. The risk of the fragmentation of viewers across different platforms raises the question of whether all will have access to the same programmes, or at least the same quality and variety of programming. This question strikes at the heart of PSB principles (see chapter 2).

The discussion so far has concentrated on one single aspect of the link between infrastructure and content; the issue of access and transmission in a traditional linear broadcasting context. The relationship between infrastructure and content becomes even more complex with the introduction of digital television and interactivity. Here it should be noted that access may not be limited to the right to broadcast content that is traditional in format, but also the provision of enhanced services (see chapter 3 for a discussion of the different levels and types of interactive services available via digital television). The role of the EPG is also significant here. How a programme is described and where it is located on the EPG may affect viewer choice, either because the programme seems unattractive or because it is not easy to access.[10] EPGs may be part of the transmission technology, but they clearly have an impact on choice of content, as well as containing content themselves. With this in mind, what we have is not a new world of expanded viewer choice, but viewers, especially passive

---

[9] On the global media market, see OECD *Media Mergers* DAFFE/COMP (2003) 16. In respect of the European situation and the problems raised by media consolidation, see P. Bruck et al., *Report on Transnational Media Concentrations in Europe* (Strasbourg: Council of Europe, 2004).

[10] Galperin and Bar, 'Interactive Television' state '. . . the EPG is expected to become to the broadcasting industry what Web portals have become to the Internet: powerful tools to direct traffic and obtain advertising revenues', p. 77. For an example of this in practice, see the row between the BBC and BSkyB in which Sky responded to the BBC's intention to move to a different satellite by threatening to move the BBC to the bottom of the programme guide, among teleshopping and porn channels. The regulator was called in but the parties came to an agreement between themselves before the adjudication was due to be made: O. Gibson, 'BBC and BSkyB Settle Satellite Dispute', *The Guardian*, 13 June 2003.

viewers, limited in their choices by their access to appropriate technology. The boundary assumed between content and transmission which has driven the review of regulation, may in fact oversimplify the issue of access to content in a number of ways.

Competition law and essential facilities

Given the potential stranglehold, via access technologies and subscription or pay TV services, which media conglomerates, especially those that are vertically integrated, could have over the supply of content, we need to consider the mechanisms that exist to control their behaviour and assess the extent to which those mechanisms effectively protect viewers' interests. Of the general competition law provisions in the EC Treaty (see chapter 4), the most appropriate in this context seems to be Article 82. For example, a company with significant market power which limits, or strictly controls, access by content providers to its transmission network could fall within the prohibition on the abuse of a dominant position contrary to Article 82 EC. Should Article 82 apply, a company's freedom to behave entirely as it wished is constrained. In this context, Article 82 could operate so as to ensure that competing companies have access to the dominant company's CAS. The consequence for the viewing experience is that, in theory, a greater range of content suppliers will be available to viewers, albeit in a commercialised environment.

To fall within the prohibition in Article 82, a company must both be dominant and abuse that dominance. The ECJ has defined dominance as being the ability of an undertaking to act independently of its competitors, customers and consumers, and thus prevent effective competition.[11] In finding dominance, the Commission and the European Courts have reference to a number of factors, notably market share, though it has been argued that such an approach is problematic in the new economy.[12] Dominance is assessed by reference to the market,[13] the definition of which is discussed further in chapter 4. The two-stage test has been seen

---

[11] Case 85/76 *Hoffmann-La Roche & Co AG* v. *Commission* [1979] ECR 461, paras. 38–9. The determination by the Commission of the existence of dominance has been criticised, especially by economists, on the basis that the Commission has found dominance where the undertaking in question, in fact, has little market power.

[12] C. Ahlborn, D. Evans and A. Padilla, 'Competition Policy in the New Economy: Is Competition Law up to the Challenge?', *European Competition Law Review* [2001] 156–67, p. 162.

[13] Case 6/72 *Europemballage Corp and Continental Can Co Inc* v. *Commission* [1973] ECR 215, para. 32.

as problematic, as the answer to the question of whether an undertaking has dominance is to some extent dependent on the definition of the market (see also chapter 7).

Assuming dominance exists,[14] we now consider abuse. Article 82 lists a number of possible types of abuse. In the context of access, an operator which controls technology to which other operators need access to distribute their services may abuse that fact, particularly by a refusal to supply. The central question is whether such an operator would be obliged to contract with operators with which it had no wish to allow access to its facilities, or to supply information needed for interoperability.[15] The matter is particularly problematic when one company uses its control over technology, or intellectual property rights, to gain market power in another market. In the broadcasting sector, which is vertically integrated, this could occur when distribution companies use their power over distribution mechanisms to move into the content market.[16]

The essential facilities doctrine, which originated in the United States, goes some way to require a dominant company to contract with other operators, thus limiting the dominant company's freedom of contractual relationships. The European Court of Justice (ECJ) seems to have accepted a similar principle, based on the dominant company's special responsibility towards the competitive process in the market in which it is dominant. The ECJ thus expects a dominant company to behave in a manner which may not be in that company's best interests and, in particular, not to refuse to contract where the company has control over an essential facility. Because of this interference with basic property rights, the Union form of the doctrine seems to have been interpreted very narrowly.

In *Oscar Bronner* v. *Mediaprint*,[17] the ECJ laid down four conditions which have to be satisfied for a competitor to claim access to a dominant company's facilities: (1) the refusal to grant access is likely to eliminate all competition; (2) the refusal is incapable of being objectively justified; (3) access to the service is essential for the carrying out of the requesting

---

[14] The relationship between abuse and dominance has also been problematic; in some instances it has been argued that an undertaking must be dominant, as otherwise it could not have behaved in the way it did: Case 27/76 *United Brands* v. *Commission* [1978] ECR 207, para 121; *Eurofix-Bauco*, Commission Decision OJ [1988] L 65/19, Recital 71.

[15] See Commission, *Discussion Paper on the Application of Article 82 EC* (2006), point 9.2.3.

[16] The reverse problem is also possible where premium content is in issue, though it is debatable whether premium content can be viewed as an essential facility. On premium content, see further ch. 12.

[17] Case C-7/97 *Oscar Bronner* v. *Mediaprint* [1998] ECR I-7791.

person's business; and (4) there are no actual or potential substitutes for the service. The ECJ has adopted a similar approach in respect of intellectual property rights as it did for physical infrastructure.[18] In *Bronner*, the case concerned a home delivery service for newspapers; the ECJ determined that this was not essential for the selling of newspapers, though it may have been desirable. Problematically for a content provider seeking access to broadcasting capacity, even where it is not possible to replicate any of the platforms, it is arguable that the content provider does not have the right to choose the distribution platform of its choice. Thus, when there is capacity on another network a particular network such as a satellite network is unlikely to be viewed as an essential facility.

There are two main problems. First, this form of technological neutrality in the application of competition law does not pay adequate attention to the fact that the different platforms do not truly compete, given that viewers are unlikely to have more than one STB. Of course, the fact that different platforms are likely to be viewed as constituting separate product markets may contribute towards the determination of dominance in the first place (chapter 7). Secondly, in any event, even were the essential facilities doctrine argument to be successful, competition rules, with the exception of the merger rules,[19] tend to operate *ex post*; they do not prevent damage to the market and, as a corollary, to the consumer/viewer. It may be that competition policy is insufficient to protect media pluralism (see further chapter 7), a point which is recognised in the recitals to the Access Directive.[20]

The general structure of the Communications Package

The main aim of the Communications Package, which comprises a Framework Directive and four issue specific directives: the Access and

[18] Case C-241/91P *RTE* v. *Commission* (Magill) [1995] ECR I-743; Case C-418/01 *IMS Health GmbH & Co KG* v. *NDC Health GmbH & Co KG*, judgment 29 April 2004. For a discussion of refusal to deal and the different approaches to tangible and intellectual property, see, e.g., C. Ritter, 'Refusal to Deal and Essential Facilities: Does Intellectual Property Require Special Deference Compared to Tangible Property?', *World Competition* 28(3) (2005), 181–98.

[19] For a discussion of the early decisions on mergers in the pay TV field from the perspective of ensuring access, see N. Helberger, A. Scheuer and P. Strothmann, 'Non-discriminatory Access to Digital Access Control Services', *Iris Plus* 2 (2001); T. Gibbons , 'Control over Technical Bottlenecks: A Case for Media Ownership Law?', in *Regulating Access to Digital Television* IRIS Special (Strasbourg: European Audiovisual Observatory 2004), pp. 60–3.

[20] Recital 10, Access Directive.

Interconnection Directive, the Authorisation Directive, the Universal Service Directive (USD) and the Data Protection Directive, was the further liberalisation of the electronic communications sector.[21] Additionally, the new regulatory framework, introducing the Communications Package, sought the simplification and harmonisation of the conditions required for would-be participants to enter a national market. In general, its approach was to rely to a greater extent on the operation of the market, as constrained by general competition policy. Although also aimed at the eradication of long and complex licensing procedures for telecommunications operators, which were still found in some member states, the package was also aimed at introducing a converged approach to regulation, as it dealt not only with telecommunications operators, but also with some elements of information technology and broadcasting. The regulatory framework is expressed to cover 'the regulation of electronic communication services, electronic communications networks, associated facilities, and associated services'.[22] It was thus based on the principle elaborated in the *Convergence Green Paper* and *Communications Review*[23] that infrastructure should be regulated in the same way, irrespective of how the content is carried. A corollary is that direct content regulation lay outside the scope of the package.

The approach taken in the Communications Package can be seen as a form of convergence[24] between two main policy strands within the Union: internal market harmonisation (most of the directives are expressed to be harmonising directives based on Article 95); and competition policy. The assumption underpinning the package is that there will be a greater reliance on general competition law rather than sector-specific regulation. Certain key terms, such as significant market power (SMP), are borrowed from competition decisions. It has been suggested that using competition-based terms to trigger sector-specific regulation signals a hybridisation of regulatory approaches in this context.

---

[21] Note that the Framework Directive does not cover telecommunications terminal equipment, which is still regulated by Directive 88/301/EEC on competition in the markets in telecommunications equipment OJ [1988] L 131/73 as amended by Directive 94/46/EC OJ [1994] L 268/15 and Directive 1999/5/EC on radio equipment and telecommunications terminal equipment and the mutual recognition of their conformity OJ [1999] L 91/10.

[22] Framework Directive, Article 1(1).

[23] Commission, *Communication Towards a New Framework for Electronic Communications Infrastructure and Associated Services: The 1999 Communications Review* COM (1999) 539.

[24] A. F. Bavasso, 'Electronic Communications: A New Paradigm for European Regulation', *CMLRev* 41 (2004), 87–118, p. 94.

A significant role remains for national regulatory authorities (NRAs),[25] which are explicitly given a number of policy objectives: the promotion of competition, the internal market and citizens' interests. Significantly, Article 8(1) of the Framework Directive also provides that NRAs 'may contribute within their competencies to ensuring the implementation of policies aimed at the promotion of cultural and linguistic diversity, as well as media pluralism'. The main mechanism for the achievement of these goals is the imposition of *ex ante* obligations where competition policy is insufficient. Such obligations, in general terms, may be imposed on SMP operators, and the specific directives identify particular cases in which the NRAs may or must act. The NRAs have, therefore, a role in assessing when and on whom such obligations fall, though the extent of their discretion is not clear. In determining whether there is an operator on which *ex ante* obligations may be imposed, there is a three-stage test: the definition of the market (by the NRA on the basis of Commission guidelines and in the light of competition law: see chapters 4 and 7); the assessment of an operator's power on that market; and the imposition or withdrawal by the NRA of specific regulatory obligations. The directives contain a menu of such obligations from which the relevant NRA can select the most appropriate in the given circumstances. With the reliance on the activities of the NRAs, the regulatory system is to a certain extent decentralised, despite the 'Europeanising' tendency of harmonisation. As we shall see below, although NRAs may enjoy some freedom, they are still subject to Commission review, a factor which may emphasise the common European approach over a system in which individual member states, via the NRAs, retain some freedom of action.

Given the converged approach to regulation, the Authorisation Directive, which limits member states' ability to impose an individual licence based regime on operators, will apply to providers of networks for broadcast content, as well as telecommunication networks.[26] In broad terms, this means that they will be subject to a general licensing system, rather than the individual licences currently required.[27] Given the link between

---

[25] Co-operation between the Commission and the NRAs is organised through consultation and co-operation: Article 7 Framework Directive; note the role of the Communications Committee – the Commission has also established a European Regulators Group (ERG) for electronic networks and services: Decision 2002/627/EC – note recital 36.

[26] Note that the Authorisation Directive, which deals with the procedures for licensing electronic communications operators, does not deal with the licensing for broadcast content, although electronic communications networks for the provision of such content fall within the directive.

[27] Article 3(2) Authorisation Directive. Award of radio frequencies must be on objective, transparent, non-discriminatory and proportionate criteria: Article 9(1) Framework

networks and content,[28] the system does envisage that member states should be entitled to impose conditions on those providing such networks. An exhaustive list of such conditions is found in Annex A attached to the Authorisation Directive and includes must-carry obligations in compliance with the USD (discussed below), and restrictions in relation to illegal content in accordance with Union law (chapter 10).[29] Further, where an electronic communications network or services provider also provides content, the content aspect may also be subject to conditions.[30] We have here, therefore, an example of the Communications Package specifically taking into account content-based issues.

More significant for our discussion of the relationship between content and infrastructure/transmission is the Access Directive. It seeks to harmonise the rules for access and interconnection across all forms of publicly available communication networks. The terms 'access' and 'interconnection' deal with the relationship between the network operators and service providers, i.e. the wholesale level, rather than with the concerns of the 'end user'[31] or retail market: thus viewers and the viewing experience are not directly considered.[32] The basic assumption is that access and interconnection should be dealt with on a commercial basis, with parties free to contract with whom they choose.[33] The obligation is to negotiate, rather than necessarily to allow access to the infrastructure. There are exceptions. Article 8 permits the NRA to impose certain conditions on operators with SMP in particular markets. Specifically, where there is no sustainable competitive market at the retail level, or where it is in the end users' interests, an NRA may impose obligations to meet reasonable

Directive; see also Recital 12 of the Authorisation Directive. Member states are permitted to introduce criteria and procedures 'to grant rights of use of radio frequencies to providers of radio or television broadcast content services with a view to pursuing general interest objectives in conformity with Community law': Article 5(2) Authorisation Directive.

[28] The link between content licence and access to frequency can be seen in the way a number of member states have approached DTT and multiplex licences. See Analysys Ltd, 'Public Policy Treatment of Digital Terrestrial Television (DTT)', in *Communications Markets: Final Report for the European Commission*, p. 54.

[29] See also terms of TWFD, discussed in ch. 9, as well as content prohibited by the e-Commerce Directive: Directive 2000/31/EC OJ [2000] L 178.

[30] Recital 20, Authorisation Directive.

[31] The Framework Directive defines a 'user' as 'a legal entity or natural person using or requesting a publicly available electronic communications service', whilst a consumer is 'any natural person who uses or requests a publicly available electronic communications service for purposes which are outside his or her trade, business or profession'. In both cases, they are different from the subscriber to the service.

[32] Contrast Larouche's categorisation of access, which included consumer access: *European Telecommunications*, pp. 368–82.

[33] Recital 5, Access Directive.

requests for access to, and use of, specific network elements and associated facilities.[34] Obligations such as access to technical interfaces central to interoperability are specifically identified. The remedies specified in the Access Directive are thus behavioural rather than structural (except in rare cases). In this we see parallels to the approach being adopted under the Merger Regulation[35] (see chapter 7).

There are specific provisions regarding broadcasting: Article 5 permits NRAs to impose, to the extent that it is necessary to ensure accessibility for end users to broadcasting services, obligations on operators to provide access to certain application programme interfaces (APIs) and EPGs. The Access Directive also adopts the previous broadcasting specific regime found in the Standards Directive,[36] relating to CAS.[37] The central principle was that CAS operators were required to provide services to other broadcasters on 'fair, reasonable and non-discriminatory terms' (FRAND) and to license relevant intellectual property rights in the same way. Significantly, these obligations apply to operators irrespective of their market power, although Article 6(3) does envisage the possibility of non-SMP operators being subject to different (lighter) obligations. This possibility is subject to certain safeguards in relation to viewers and the operation of competition generally. It raises the question of whether this potential to lighten regulatory obligations on operators which do not have SMP illustrates an intention to remove sectoral regulation and increase the role for competition law.

It should be noted that access and interoperability are separate issues. Agreeing access will probably lead to interoperability (i.e. the CAS/API proprietor will make available the necessary information), but merely having interoperable hardware and software does not mean that a content provider has a right of access to a transmission network. The two issues are different: access is a commercial decision; interoperability is a technical matter. Considering access as a commercial decision reflects the trend, noted in chapter 1, towards the commodification of information and the consequent commercialisation of the viewing experience itself. This is a trend which runs contrary to the traditional assumption that services will be available free to air to everyone, and therefore with potential adverse consequences for passive viewers, either in terms of diversity of suppliers or ability to access content at all.

---

[34] Article 12, Access Directive.
[35] Regulation 139/2004 on the Control of Concentrations between Undertakings, OJ [2004] L 24/1 ('Merger Regulation').
[36] Directive 95/47/EC OJ [1995] L 281/51.   [37] Article 6, Access Directive.

The directives do not impose a single standard for CAS. Member states are merely under an obligation to 'encourage' industry to adopt an open standard and to encourage proprietors of APIs to make available all such information as is necessary to enable digital interactive television[38] to provide services in a fully functional form.[39] As Recital 31 to the Access Directive clarifies, this provision was included 'to ensure the free flow of information, media pluralism and cultural diversity'. Article 18(3) of the Framework Directive further specifies that the Commission should review the effect of leaving the matter to the member states. Under Article 17 of the Framework Directive, the Commission has the power to request that European standards be drawn up. In a response to a request by the European Parliament,[40] the Commission undertook[41] to include the European multi-media home platform (MHP) specification in the list of standards to be 'encouraged' by member states. The Commission, in preparing for the Article 18(3) review, undertook a number of studies and consultation procedures to identify the best way to ensure interoperability. Widespread adoption of the MHP standard would seem to be an obvious solution.[42] The Commission was of the view that the voluntary implementation of this standard by industry was the best way forward, despite the previous experience with standard setting in which industry involvement stymied agreement. Currently, however, the Commission has decided that the imposition of Union-wide standards is not justified[43] and that industry should be allowed further time to develop MHP.[44] This delay means that different proprietary standards become more and more entrenched in the market, with the result that the introduction of common standards is likely to occur at some cost to the viewer.

None the less, Annex I to the Access Directive requires that those holding intellectual property rights should not deter the inclusion of a common interface socket allowing connection to another CAS when licensing their own CAS to equipment manufacturers. The purpose is clearly to prevent

---

[38] Note that digital television does not require an API; further DTV transmission in Europe has been standardised by reference to ETSI standards.

[39] Article 18 Framework Directive.

[40] Parliament, *Resolution* A5-0435/2001 adopted 12 December 2001.

[41] Commission *Communication on Interoperability of Digital Interactive Television Services* [SEC (2004)1028] COM (2004) 541 final, p. 2.

[42] Parliament, Oral Question cited in Commission, *Communication on Interoperability*, p. 3.

[43] Commission, *Communication on Interoperability*, p. 7.

[44] Press Release IP/04/1012, 'Interactive TV: Commission Reiterates its Support for Open and Interoperable Standards, but Says Implementation Should Not be Made Legally Binding', 2 August 2004.

broadcasters from seeking to exclude other broadcasters from being able to access the viewer. This concern goes beyond the idea that a specific viewer might have to buy several decoders, or choose, when acquiring the equipment, which services he or she will be able to receive. It also envisages the possibility that a broadcaster might seek to tie-in all television/decoder manufacturers and effectively exclude other broadcasters from the market entirely.

By contrast, the USD includes interoperability requirements for digital consumer equipment.[45] Although these provisions initially might seem to focus on the interests of the viewer, it should be noted that plurality of programme supply may not be the only motive. Recital 31 also highlights the need to promote the take-up of digital services, i.e. there is a commercial interest also represented. Take-up of digital services is desirable for another reason; to allow the switch-off of analogue transmission. Although switch-off allows the relevant broadcasting frequencies to be re-allocated and used more efficiently,[46] it may risk the exclusion of some viewers from the digital world (see chapters 1 and 3).

The USD is aimed at protecting the rights of end users (which can perhaps be seen as 'retail access' or viewer access) and it contains specific provisions relating to broadcasting, the 'must-carry provisions'. These empower member states to protect PSB, ensuring that network operators do not exclude public service content in favour of their own programmes and services. Member states may do so only in very specific circumstances, set down in Article 31. It permits, but does not oblige, member states to impose 'must-carry' obligations for specified channels on transmission networks, 'where a significant number of end users of such networks use them as their principal means to receive radio and television broadcasts'.[47] It should be noted that the power of the member states is not limited to channels provided by public service broadcasters, but to specified channels broadcasting content in the public interest.[48] This is potentially broader than public service broadcasting (PSB), depending on the view taken of PSB obligations, and may include channels such as

---

[45] Article 24 and Recital 33, USD.
[46] Commission, *Communication on Accelerating the Transition from Analogue to Digital Broadcasting* COM (2005) 204 final (SEC (2005) 661), p. 3.
[47] Article 31(1), USD.
[48] The original Commission proposal limited the must carry obligations to PSB channels: T. Roukens, 'What are We Carrying across the EU These Days? Comments on the Interpretation and Practical Implementation of Article 31 of the Universal Service Directive', in *To Have or Not to Have Must-Carry Rules* (Strasbourg: European Audiovisual Observatory, 2005), IRIS Special, p. 8.

commercially provided educational or news programme channels. Member states do not have complete freedom in imposing such obligations. In addition to the requirements already noted, obligations 'shall only be imposed where they are necessary to meet clearly defined general interest objectives and shall be proportionate and transparent'.[49] Member states may specify remuneration to be paid to the network operator in respect of the carriage of 'must-carry' services, provided that such remuneration is applied in a transparent and proportionate manner. The USD does not say who should bear the cost of any such remuneration. In not dealing with content issues regarding 'must-carry' rules and leaving member states to decide the scope of any such obligations and remuneration, the USD can be seen as respecting the principle of subsidiarity and the fact that content regulation, TWFD notwithstanding, remains primarily a matter for the member states.[50]

Criticism of the general approach

Our major concern is the extent to which a move to an approach which seeks to limit sector-specific intervention is appropriate in the broadcasting market. Sector-specific regulation which is not based on competition-inspired principles protects non-market values. A move to a competition-based approach assumes that the market is the first provider of any service and that state intervention is only permissible when the market is inefficient or has failed (see chapter 3). The permissible scope of national broadcasting policy intervention is therefore limited to those occasions when the market is inefficient or fails. This approach to intervention is to allow the market to retain maximum freedom so that it might establish market-based efficiencies, which, in turn, generate fair prices and a wide range of choices. In so far as benefits of competition will trickle down to viewers, these are likely to be seen in economic terms. Non-economic issues, such as access to a diverse range of quality content, however, are less easily identified and quantified in a competition-based system, as we shall also see in chapter 7.

Further criticisms of the Communications Package concern the use of the SMP test and its relationship with competition law. At its most

---

[49] Article 31(1) USD.
[50] On subsidiarity and preserving national models of regulation, see van Velzen, *Report on the Commission Communication 'Towards a new Framework for Electronic Communications Infrastructure and Associated Services – The 1999 Communications Review'* (COM (1999) 539 – C5-0141/2000 – 2000/2085 (COS)).

general, the question must be whether this is an appropriate test to use in relation to sector-specific regulation. Competition law responds to specific situations, an identified agreement between undertakings, or a case of abuse of a dominant position on the market, in an *ex post* manner.[51] Competition law is about regulating a process on the assumption that a certain, desired, outcome will result. By contrast, sector-specific regulation not only imposes conditions on companies in advance, it operates in a general manner rather than in relation to specific cases. Cave and Crowther note that 'the Commission has been prepared to "negotiate" pro-competitive outcomes relying on a battery of *ex ante* interventions which are very much in the regulator's arsenal'.[52] Although the above view highlights similarities between the two systems of regulation in terms of the mechanisms used to solve the problems from a competition-based perspective, the individual nature of the response by companies is indicated by the word negotiate. From this we can then determine the general approach that is taken by the Commission, although it is not clear that the Commission's response to individual companies will be the same in all similar cases. It is arguable that this constitutes a crucial difference in the competition-based and sector-specific systems, which militates against an approach which uses tests from one type of system in another context.

Despite the fact that the Access Directive highlights the needs of the viewer in its recitals, its focus 'is on communications networks, associated facilities and services rather than content, and it appears to be simply assumed that making material available is sufficient to deliver pluralism'.[53] In any event, the emphasis is on viewers as users or consumers,[54] a commercial concept, rather than viewers as citizens; it is not clear whether in considering the plurality of the media there will be any qualitative assessment of the programming on offer in the light of public-interest goals, or whether mere consumer choice between different suppliers will suffice.

Access within the terms of the Access Directive does not include access by end users (whether consumers or otherwise); their interests are served incidentally. Article 5, however, by providing for end-to-end connectivity, allows an individual to choose content services independently of the

---

[51] Cave and Crowther suggest that informal guidance given by the Commission could be seen as *ex ante* involvement: M. Cave and P. Crowther, 'Preemptive Competition Policy Meets Regulatory Anti-trust', *ECLR* [2005] 481, pp. 488–9.

[52] Cave and Crowther, 'Pre-emptive Competition Policy', p. 489.

[53] Gibbons, 'Technical Bottlenecks', p. 63.   [54] Article 1 Framework Directive.

access provider, at least in theory.[55] But the aim of Article 5 is not concerned with diversity, but with the loss of consumer choice arising from a consumer being bound to one distributor. Article 5 accepts implicitly the economic argument that 'effective competition' will lead to diversity.[56] This secondary aspect to the promotion of diversity is reflected in the obligations imposed on the NRAs in the Communications Package. Whereas NRAs are obliged to promote competition, as indicated by the use of the word 'shall', they are under no such obligation as regards the promotion of diversity. They are merely permitted to promote diversity. This state of affairs may be explained by the scope of the Communications Package and by the principle of subsidiarity, which places the primary responsibility for content regulation on the member state. This means, however, that there is a weakness in the system of protection which implicitly suggests that the higher goal is that of competition rather than the attainment of diversity.

Significant Market Power (SMP)

Larouche noted that there has been a tendency to protect the broadcasting sector from the normal competition-based analysis by comparison with the telecommunications sector.[57] In any event, the competition law-based jurisprudence in relation to broadcasting is generally less well developed. These issues may have particular relevance for the NRAs as they seek to assess market power on particular product and geographical markets.[58] In the context of the USD and Access Directive, as well as the Communications Package in general, the definition of the product markets to determine whether SMP exists to trigger the possibility of imposing such obligations is crucial.[59] Whether the test incorporated is sufficient remains to be seen. It is harder to satisfy than the equivalent tests in the

[55] Note reasoning in *Vizzavi* case, which concerned a proposal to provide web-based services across a range of different platforms. The Commission was concerned that this might deter the development of alternative Internet portals. The parties gave a commitment to allow end users to change the default portal if they wanted to.

[56] See also Recital 27, Framework Directive.

[57] Larouche, *European Telecommunications*, pp. 336–7.

[58] For a discussion of defining markets in the context of competition law generally, see ch. 7.

[59] See Commission, *Recommendation on Relevant Markets*, discussed in A. de Streel, 'Market Definitions in the New European Regulatory Framework for Electronic Communications', *Info* 5(3) (2003), 27–47. On the markets relating to broadcasting, see p. 37. Note that different markets for the provision of CAS, as well as for services relating to EPGs and relating to the writing of applications compatible with APIs, were identified under general competition law: see Commission Decision, *BiB/Open* OJ [1999] L 312/1, at para. 30.

previous telecommunications regime and, in that respect, is deregulatory in its impact.

We also need to be aware that the test for SMP includes not just dominance by one company but also dominance by groups of companies, whether in a horizontal or vertical relationship. This issue is relevant for the broadcasting sector, which has become heavily integrated along vertical lines. There is some concern about the use of this test. Although it follows the approach based on the jurisprudence of the ECJ with regard to competition law generally, that case law has been contested. It is not entirely clear how and when joint dominance will be found. Such a lack of clarity will introduce further difficulties into the application of the SMP test. Additionally, it is arguable that the test does not take into account fully the vertically integrated nature of the broadcasting market and the possible effects of market power at one stage of the supply chain on other markets.[60] A particular concern arises with regard to the significance of content, especially premium content such as sport and films.[61] There may therefore be concerns as to the proper scope of obligations in terms of who is subject to them.

A further problem arises when we consider when the obligations are to be imposed. Although we are talking about *ex ante* obligations with regard to SMP operators, these obligations will only be imposed once the impact on the market has been assessed. It may well be that the obligations will, in fact, be imposed *ex post*, that is once the operator is shown to be dominant. Given the nature of the market and the speed with which markets in rapidly developing sectors can be foreclosed, it may be that operators with some market power may abuse their position without being dominant. The test may therefore be insufficient in terms of the companies caught. An alternative view is that the NRAs will be faced with the difficult assessment of determining when an operator will become dominant, so as to impose the relevant obligations in time. Given the criticisms of the Commission over its interventionist approach, noted in chapter 7, it may well be that there is a pressure towards being cautious in such circumstances, thus leaving the supply of services to the market as corrected by competition law.

---

[60] EBU, *Comments on the EU Commission's Proposals for Directives Regarding the Review of the Regulatory Framework for Communications* (2000).

[61] Note the approach of the competition authorities in this regard: *AOL/Time Warner*, Commission Decision 2001/718/EC, Case IV/M1845, OJ [2001] L 268/28, discussed ch. 7 and *Vodafone/Vivendi/Canal+* creating Vizzavi, an Internet portal, Commission decision COMP/jv 48, 20 July 2002.

As suggested earlier, there are problems with the assessment of market power in rapidly developing markets. Although some firms may have first-mover advantage and hold significant market power for a short period, it is argued that, because of the changes in technology, the firms are not dominant in competition terms because their market power is of short duration.[62] Certainly, the recitals to the Framework Directive highlight the fact that lack of effective competition must be durable to justify regulation, and that particular care seems to be required in respect of emerging markets, where new technologies are being deployed.[63] The problem is that, whilst such a company has market power, this may be complete and network effects may allow it to become entrenched. An example is when significant numbers of consumers buy a particular operator's STB and are therefore tied in to that provider. Even if control of the market changes hands to another company, it may not make any difference to the viewer, as the new dominant operator will be just as free to indulge in exclusionary behaviour as was its predecessor.

The above discussion has assumed that the nature of the markets on which dominance is to be assessed is clear. The general policy approach suggests that economic considerations are key to the determination of product markets.[64] It has, however, been noted that if competition policy approaches are respected, the NRAs may find themselves defining quite specific product markets (which will make a finding of dominance more likely) but which do not match the categories of markets set down in the Commission's *Guidance* or the Framework Directive.[65] There is a risk of considerable uncertainty about the determination of which operators will be found to have SMP and which should therefore be subject to *ex ante* obligations.

The definitions as regards broadcasting services are particularly problematic. The Commission *Recommendation on Relevant Product and Service Markets* for the purposes of the Communications Package identifies, as part of the wholesale markets, 'broadcasting transmission services' to deliver broadcast content to end users.[66] As a definition of a market this is not particularly helpful. Further, the recommendation itself notes that the

---

[62] Ahlborn *et al.*, 'New Economy', p. 162. See also the impact of this argument on the determination of whether a media merger is acceptable.

[63] Framework Directive, Recital 27.   [64] See, e.g., Access Directive, Recital 13.

[65] Analysys Ltd, *Report on DTT*, p. 78, pp. 83–6.

[66] Commission, *Recommendation on Relevant Product and Service Markets within the Electronic Communications Sector Susceptible to ex ante Regulation* (C (2003) 497) OJ [2003] L 114/45, Annex, para. 18.

individual NRAs have greater discretion regarding the analysis for CASs, in respect of obligations under Article 6(1) of the Access Directive. It is not clear whether this refers to the definition of the scope of the market itself, or to the analysis of competition therein. Nor does it explain how this element relates to the general group of broadcasting services identified within the broad phraseology of the recommendation. It should be noted that some have taken the view that the must-carry obligations in Article 31 USD will mean that there should not be access disputes in this context.[67]

The application of Article 5 of the Access Directive is not conditional on SMP, but rather when it is 'necessary to ensure accessibility for end users to digital radio and television broadcasting services specified by the member state'. This suggests that the main focus of the provisions is the needs of end users rather than the needs of the market. The needs of end users, however, may be different from those of citizens or even consumers, as the term 'end users' can include business interests (in this there is a similarity to the term 'consumer' as used in competition law). Article 5 is limited, in the context of broadcasting, to the services specified in the Annex to the directive, that is, APIs and EPGs. Other aspects of digital television may have an impact on the services available to viewers. For example, the return path in relation to interactive services; data on content; and memory caches and memory management systems in PVRs.[68] It is not currently possible to use Article 5 procedures in relation to these sorts of associated facilities. Any action in relation to these aspects of digital television would be limited to circumstances in which an operator had SMP. Furthermore, although the directives are expressed as technologically neutral, the language used in Annex I to the Access Directive appears to exclude new digital gateways from the scope of Article 5 and protection of rights of access is correspondingly limited.

Fair, Reasonable and Non-Discriminatory (FRAND)

In addition to identifying who is subject to these obligations, we need to understand the nature and scope of the obligation, an enquiry to which the meaning of FRAND is central. FRAND is not defined within the Communications Package, though certain provisions of the

---

[67] Roukens, 'What Are We Carrying Across The EU These Days?', p. 11.

[68] EBU, *Comments* p. 9; see also Galperin and Bar, 'Interactive Television' for examples of abuse in the US.

Access Directive do give some indication of what is meant by 'non-discriminatory'. Arguably, these provisions limit the possibility of EPG operators bundling a content provider's placement on the EPG with a requirement that it takes other services.[69] Other questions remain. In particular, are these terms to be assessed in the context of competing commercial undertakings; or should they take into account the fact that some broadcasters, at least, may be under specific obligations to fulfil societal goals? Whilst the answer to this question is not clear, that answer obviously has an impact on the viewing experience.

FRAND terms can still be expensive, an issue that Oftel in the UK recognised. Its approach[70] sought to restrict excessive profits, but still allowed platform providers to take into account levels of risk. This is particularly important given the rapid pace of technological development in the communications sphere and the need to introduce infrastructure, not just in terms of the service provider's network but also in terms of the individual's reception equipment. One particular problem relates to the costs of persuading viewers to acquire the necessary new technology. If subsidies are used, should the network operator be able to recover these, or a portion of them, via access charges? An important question is raised here, namely whether public service broadcasters can afford the market price, especially across a number of platforms. In its decision under general competition law in *Newscorp/Telepiu*,[71] the Commission required the platform operator to supply technical services 'at fair, transparent, non-discriminatory and cost-orientated conditions', thus limiting how much the operator could charge third-party content providers for the necessary service. This was not, however, aimed at the specific position of public service broadcasters.[72] The obligation in the directive is to negotiate; it is only SMP operators that might have the obligation to allow access.

In general terms, it is not clear how FRAND relates to content-based issues. The extent to which the FRAND terms address an absolute refusal to supply to any third parties is unclear, although this issue might be covered

---

[69] See Article 9(2) Access Directive; see commentary by A. Wichmann, 'Electronic Programme Guides – A Comparative Study of the Regulatory Approach adopted in the United Kingdom and Germany – Part 1', *C.T.L.R* 10(1) (2004), 16–23.

[70] Oftel, 'Ensuring Access on Fair Reasonable and Non-discriminatory Terms', 1999.

[71] *NewsCorp/Telepiu*, Commission Decision, Case COMP/M.2876, 2 April 2003.

[72] Although conditions were imposed on the merger, it has been questioned whether the conditions were far-reaching enough: A. Fikentscher and K. Merkel, 'Technical Bottlenecks and Public Service Broadcasting', *Regulating Access to Digital Television* (Strasbourg: European Audiovisual Observatory, 2004) IRIS Special, p. 103.

under general competition law via the essential facilities doctrine. Given the technical nature of the framework, it has been argued that the regime concerns bottlenecks related to transport and would not include content-based bottlenecks, such as exclusion on editorial grounds.[73] Questions have, however, been raised as to the grounds on which operators could refuse access. To what extent should one party be obliged to disseminate the views of another, when those views conflict on political, religious or even more general editorial grounds? This point raises difficult questions concerning conflicting rights to freedom of expression, a conflict which is perhaps not best dealt with in a competition-based analysis.[74]

Interoperability

The access requirement in Article 5 of the Access Directive is an improvement on its predecessor, the Advanced Television Standards Directive, in that the Access Directive does open up the possibility of EPGs being covered by access requirements. This provision is still limited to digital television, leaving pay TV on analogue systems unprotected. Also, despite the terms of Article 18 of the Framework Directive, the requirement does nothing to ensure interoperability.[75] Although interoperability does not guarantee access, and neither access nor interoperability provides any guarantees regarding the diversity and plurality of broadcast content, at least ensuring interoperability removes barriers to media (and content) pluralism. Rights to access EPGs are limited in a practical sense by lack of interoperability (see further below). Lack of interoperability makes the likelihood of a competitive market in EPG services, so reducing problems arising from dominance in this area, more distant.[76] There is a real risk that EPG services will continue to be provided by one dominant supplier (per platform). In this, an opportunity to support the aim of providing diversity of content supply has not been taken.

The Council of Europe Recommendation R(99) 1 specifically suggests that its signatory states adopt specific regulations dealing with CAS. It recommends that states introduce technical measures and standards to ensure interoperability. By contrast, under Union law, member

---

[73] N. Helberger and A. Springsteen, 'Summary of the Discussion', *Regulating Access to Digital Television* (Strasbourg: European Audiovisual Observatory, 2004) IRIS Special, p. 7.
[74] Helberger and Springsteen, 'Summary', p. 8.
[75] Helberger, Scheuer and Strothman, 'Non-discriminatory Access', p. 2 regarding Directive 95/47/EC on which the Access Directive is based *vis à vis* CAS.
[76] Helberger and Springsteen, 'Summary', p. 8.

states are limited in their freedom to impose national standards, as they may constitute a barrier to trade. The question of whether the Communications Package allows member states to make particular standards mandatory is affected by the scope of those directives (i.e. in principle, do the technical measures fall within electronic communications services or associated facilities?). This potential difficulty can be seen as an example of insufficient action at Union level, precluding member states' corrective action within the national sphere.

Looking at the interoperability provision, it is unclear what 'encourage' means within the terms of the Framework Directive. The Commission communication suggests that it does not mean 'to impose' standards. This implies a weak obligation, favouring industry-led standards rather than regulation. Such an approach prioritises the interests of the large conglomerates over the independent sector and the interests of viewers. Furthermore, the nature of the obligation on the member states is uncertain. It is unclear what level of action, if any, Article 18 of the Framework Directive requires them to take. The two paragraphs in Article 18 reflect the fact that there is a gap between European policy, which seeks to promote open standards in the interests of the common market, and reality, in that proprietary standards exist. The second paragraph of Article 18 is therefore aimed at limiting the content control that a proprietary API owner may have, by allowing other service providers to design services that function with the proprietary API. The weakness is compounded by the fact that there is no cut-off date by which open APIs, or a common standard, must be in place. The one firm date in the directive concerned the Commission's review under Article 18(3). This has already passed and the Commission clearly felt that its scope of action was inhibited by the fact that some member states had met the deadline for implementing the Communications package late.

In this context it should also be noted that the term 'interoperable', used for example in Articles 17 and 18 of the Framework Directive and Recital 31, is susceptible of a number of different meanings. There is a difference between including multiple interfaces in one type of hardware and making one interface open to many services. The Commission in its working paper distinguished between simple interoperability, which involves a single universal receiver, and multi-standard systems.[77] This latter concept is not really interoperability at all, but rather a proxy for it.[78]

---

[77] Commission, *Working Paper on Interactive Digital Television* SEC (2004) 346, p. 6.
[78] *Ibid.*

The distinction can be seen in the responses to the Commission's working paper on interoperability of digital interactive television. The commercial broadcasters suggested that interoperability has already been achieved; their view suggests that interoperability requires the availability of the same interactive services on different distribution platforms. This form of interoperability is based on technologies on the network, which allow the content to be moved from one system to another (including multiple authoring systems, which allow content to be generated for more than one API). On this basis, where there is demand, interactive services will become available across several platforms. Unsurprisingly, those who took this view of interoperability saw little benefit in the imposition of common standards. By contrast, those who supported the introduction of common standards took the simple view of interoperability.[79] The Commission, by declining to commit itself, is implicitly adopting the interoperability by proxy approach, rather than simple interoperability from the perspective of the viewer. The suggestion that there are greater threats to diversity of supply, such as vertically integrated media conglomerates, does not justify a failure to act here, especially when the market developments providing for consumer welfare are based on the functioning of a market which the Commission admits is flawed.

There is a difference between access regulation as found in the Access Directive, and a move towards open APIs. This raises uncertainty as to whether access regulation will be sufficient for more complex services, because it does not address re-authoring costs for use in conjunction with different APIs. Open/common standards have the advantage of being designed to serve the needs of the entire market rather than being designed to serve the needs of a particular broadcaster and its range of services/business model. Further, full and complete information about how the system operates will be available. For proprietary systems which are available for use by others, it is likely that only limited information will be made available. It would seem that requiring access to proprietary systems on its own is insufficient. Open standards seem more likely to be successful, although the obligations in the Framework Directive, or the will of the Commission, in this context seem to be weak. Allowing industry to develop its own standards might prove beneficial in terms of achieving a standard that is workable. Such an approach, however, has been crit-icised as being open to manipulation on the part of dominant market

[79] EBU, *Comments.*

players[80] and also constitutes the privatisation of standard-setting, which may not always operate in the interests of the viewer. A focus on open standards could also allow for a Union-wide standard to be developed. Although standard-setting might restrict innovation in some quarters, as the Commission has noted, given subsidiarity and the differences in the member states' markets, implementation of national standards across the Union is fragmented, which leaves the less economically well-developed member states dependent on the actions of the stronger member states.[81] None the less, given that there are significant numbers of proprietary APIs already on the market, forced migration to a common standard might have significant cost implications and it is unclear on whom the burden of that cost would fall. This problem is, however, endemic in a market with developing technology, as discussions about the possible change from the Union endorsed MPEG2 standard for STBs to the more efficient AVC standard illustrate.

Presentational aspects of EPGs

As presentational aspects of EPGs lie outside Article 5 of the Access Directive, so questions about how programmes are described and where they appear on the EPG (questions which exercised the BBC in relation to Sky) are not addressed by regulations. This allows the member states to make special provision, for example, in respect of the presentation of public service broadcasters, providing those rules comply with the basic principles of Union law, such as non-discrimination on grounds of nationality.[82] Whether member states would be permitted to require that, for example, national public service broadcasters should be given prominence, is questionable. Such a requirement could be considered as discriminatory as against other providers of broadcasting content which are based in other member states. A further weakness is, of course, that member states are not required to take any such action. Additionally, Article 5(1)(b) is of an optional character; again, although the possibility is there to protect access, it is not compulsory. There is thus no base level of protection. This is significant given the potential importance of the EPG for selecting content from the viewer's perspective.

---

[80] S. Kaitatzi-Whitlock, 'The Privatising of Conditional Access Control', *Communications and Strategies* 25 (1997), 91.
[81] Commission, *Working Paper*, p. 12.
[82] Article 5(3) requires that any conditions be non-discriminatory.

USD and must carry

The only measure in the Communications Package which is aimed at protecting viewers directly is the USD. This directive contains a 'must-carry' provision, which seeks to ensure that specified types of content are carried by certain operators. It can be seen, therefore, as forming part of a content universal service obligation, containing some rules relating to geographic coverage and to content. None the less, there are weaknesses in the protection awarded to viewers' interests. The difficulty lies in the underlying assumptions on which the entire regulatory framework is based, that is, the correction of market failures. Whilst this might provide some protection for consumers, citizens' needs seem to have been overlooked entirely. Citizens' interests are threatened by the view that must-carry obligations are a relic from the analogue era and that, with the development of digital services and the end of spectrum scarcity, there would be no need for such rules. The argument is based on the assumption that, in a world where content is scarce, popular content will be in demand and public service broadcasters (and others) will be able to access transmission networks, and therefore regulation to ensure they have access to transmission networks is unnecessary. Some have argued that such content providers should be under a must-offer obligation. This would avoid the danger that such content providers would only offer it to a limited number of transmission companies, giving those companies a competitive advantage.[83] This could be particularly problematic for new service providers. The assumption here is that a greater number of service providers is beneficial. It does not, however, look at the end result. Given our view of the public domain, we suggest that regulation should ensure that a certain minimum content service is available to the maximum audience, irrespective of geography, or ability to pay. As far as the citizenship-enhancing function of PSB or a Universal Service content package, the Communications Package is silent. It is also notable that the USD does not cover the possibility of must-offer obligations; presumably because these obligations might be thought to fall within the content end of television provision and be governed by either the TWFD or the general treaty rules.

---

[83] The significance of PSB and even free-to-air television is illustrated by the attempts of BSkyB to acquire ITV channels for its basic package, so as to improve its attractiveness to viewers. This desire is based on viewing popularity; once ITV's viewing figures started to drop, BSkyB became less enthusiastic and, conversely, ITV became more willing to contract with BSkyB: J. Doward, 'Sky Digital 'dumps' ITV', *The Observer*, 28 January 2001.

The strength of the must-carry obligation is, however, undermined by a vague reference to 'legitimate public policy considerations'.[84] Public policy is potentially a very broad concept, and arguably leaves significant discretion to the member states as to the policy considerations they wish to protect. Certainly, as we have seen in chapter 5, issues such as media pluralism, freedom of expression and cultural policy have been accepted as falling within legitimate public policy concerns.[85] Conversely, the phrase 'public policy' has also been interpreted very narrowly, in particular excluding economic concerns.[86] The problem in this particular regard is that the boundary between economic concerns and other public-interest considerations is sometimes hard to define, especially where the state is trying to ensure that the provision of a public service is economically viable.

The concern arises that a similarly limited view would be taken in the context of Article 31 USD. For example, the Flemish Community proposed introducing rules which imposed must-carry obligations in favour of all new commercial broadcasters. The idea was to give the new broadcasters time to develop market share and to establish themselves before having to negotiate on a commercial basis with the transmission companies. The measure was aimed at stimulating the development of innovative programmes in the region and to ensure that programming which would not otherwise have been aired received transmission time, contributing to the diversity of programming. The Commission disapproved of this measure, as it viewed it as economic rather than cultural.[87] The introduction of DTT may give rise to similar problems. An important question is that of whether supporting the introduction of DTT by giving broadcasters must-carry status on established networks, and therefore access to larger audiences, is an economic issue, a concern for effectiveness of spectrum use or a concern to ensure plurality and diversity.[88] In sum, although must-carry obligations are permitted, the circumstances in which they

---

[84] Recital 43, USD.

[85] Case C-288/89 *Collectieve Antennevoorziening Gouda* v. *Commissariaat voor de Media* [1991] ECR I-4007, paras. 22 and 23; Case C-353/89 *Commission* v. *Netherlands* [1991] ECR I-4069, paras. 29 and 30; Case C-148/91 *Veronica Omroep Organisatie* v. *Commissariaat voor de Media* [1993] ECR I-487, para. 9.

[86] Case C-17/92 *Distribuidores Cinematográficos* [1993] ECR I-2239, paras. 20 and 21; case C-211/91 *Commission* v. *Belgium* [1992] ECR I-6757, para. 9.

[87] P. Valcke 'The Future of Must-carry: From Must-carry to a Concept of Universal Service in the Info-communications Sector', in *To Have or Not to Have Must-carry Rules* (Strasbourg: European Audiovisual Observatory, 2005), IRIS Special, p. 33.

[88] On the different goals member states have attributed to the introduction of DTT, see Analysys, *Report on DTT*, p. 48.

may be imposed are constrained. We suggest that the conception of USD is limited, since it tries to make a rigid distinction between content and carriage. It tries to do this in a rapidly changing environment, one that cannot easily accommodate such a distinction.

Although the provisions are designed to be technology neutral and thus flexible, we need to consider whether the obligations, as specified, ensure universal coverage. Two problems are evident. The first problem arises because the division between content and transmission adopted in the Communications Package does not necessarily reflect the market. Whereas this analysis sees the market as divided in two, content and transmission, the market actually reflects a three-stage value chain: content providers in the sense of those who have editorial control; those who package the content into bundles and offer these to viewers; and the network operators who provide transmission capacity. Although a particular market player may perform more than one of these functions, the problem is that the must-carry obligation falls on the network provider. Presumably the must-carry content should be required to be included in a package for distribution. Although in some countries, such as the UK, a network provider is also the provider of content packages, in some member states, such as France, they are separate entities treated differently under national law.[89] The second problem is that member states may impose obligations on undertakings only where a significant proportion of end users use the relevant networks as their main means of receiving television and radio broadcasts. It is possible to envisage the situation where a small population group uses a means of transmission not normally used by the rest of the national group for reception of broadcasts. It is worrying if the consequence of the drafting of Article 31 is that such groups will be excluded from the protection of the must-carry obligations.

The must-carry provisions themselves identify the possibility of payment for carriage. Indeed, it seems that the Commission,[90] and even COCOM,[91] have assumed that payment might be required to make the member states' assessment of the necessity for the must-carry obligations proportional.[92] This overlooks two facts. The first is that, despite the

---

[89] Roukens, 'What Are We Carrying Across the EU These Days?', p. 8.

[90] Commission, *Working Document The 2003 Regulatory Framework for Electronic Communications – Implications for Broadcasting* (Doc. ONPCOM02-14), 14 June 2002; Commission, *Working Document 'Must Carry' Obligations under the 2003 Regulatory Framework for Electronic Communications Networks and Services*, 22 July 2002.

[91] Commission, *Working Document An Approach to Financing the Transport of 'Must-Carry' Channels, in relation to Article 31 of the Universal Service Directive*, COCOM03-38, 2 September 2003.

[92] Roukens, 'What Are We Carrying Across the EU These Days?', p. 13.

essentially one-directional nature of the access relationship in the broadcasting context, the network operator may itself benefit from carrying the content and might, indeed, expect to pay for that content rather than vice versa.[93] The second is that such an approach does not take into account the difficulties this might cause for PSB operators, who are under obligations to broadcast across multiple platforms, although some commentators have suggested that the issue of paying for transmission capacity might not fall to public service broadcasters alone.[94]

Review of Communications Package

The Communications Package has been perceived as successful.[95] None the less the Commission has commenced a review process to identify areas for change, propose reductions in administrative burdens and repeal out-of-date measures. The review is, at the time of writing, at a very early stage, none the less two main changes are likely to have an impact on the broadcasting sector: the changes to radio spectrum management; and the requirement, in the interests of the internal market, that must-carry obligations must be reviewed by specific deadlines.

The proposal regarding spectrum management is to continue to move away from individual radio spectrum licences to a market-based approach. The Commission envisages spectrum management operating on the principles of 'technology neutrality' and 'service neutrality'.[96] The former principle envisages that 'spectrum users would be free to use any type of radio network or access technology in a given spectrum band to provide a service'.[97] The latter principle envisages the provision of any service across a spectrum to which the service provider has access. The aim of these changes is to ensure a 'high level of fluidity of radio resources'[98]

---

[93] This seems to be the approach suggested by Eurostrategies, *Study on the Assessment of the Member States Measures Aimed at Fulfilling Certain General Interest Objectives Linked to Broadcasting, Imposed on Providers of Electronic Communications Networks and Services, in the Context of the New Regulatory Framework* (2003), http://ec.europa.eu/information_society/topic/telecoms/regulatory/studies/documents/finrep_18_march_2003.pdf. Note that Article 18(2) Framework Directive seems also to envisage remuneration for access to APIs.

[94] Roukens, 'What Are We Carrying Across the EU These Days?', p. 15.

[95] Commission, *Communication on the Review of the EU Regulatory Framework for Electronic Communications Networks and Services*, COM (2006)334 final, SEC (2006) 816 and 817, p. 6.

[96] Commission, *Staff Working Document on the Review of the EU Regulatory Framework for Electronic Communications Networks and Services*, SEC (2006) 816, COM (2006) 334 final, p. 13.

[97] *Ibid.*, p. 13.   [98] *Ibid.*, p. 14.

via the introduction of spectrum trading. The danger is that a service provider acquiring spectrum capacity might not provide the same type of service as the service provider selling the capacity on. Without any constraints, it might be more profitable for a television company to sell its spectrum rights to the provider of another service. In this example, it would not be possible to guarantee the same quality of content service continuing, or even the same type of service at all. To guard against this possibility, the Communication does suggest exceptions to achieve a number of legitimate general interest objectives, of which audiovisual policy, promotion of cultural and linguistic diversity and media pluralism are some. It remains to be seen what the precise level of protection allowed to these interests is.

The Commission expresses concern that the must-carry rules have not been reviewed sufficiently by the relevant NRAs. The implication is that in some member states must-carry obligations exist in excess of what the Commission views as necessary and proportionate. The Commission, in proposing that must-carry should be kept to a minimum, reflecting 'evolving market and technological developments',[99] seems to be suggesting that whilst must carry rules have not lost their purpose, they are certainly the exception rather than the norm. In both these proposals we can trace an internal market-driven approach that is deregulatory in effect. By requiring the exceptions for broadcasting policy to be limited to the minimum, it seems that citizens' concerns are not being accorded a high priority.

Conclusion

The adoption of the Communications Package signalled a move to a policy of letting the market decide in an era of privatisation, corporatisation and liberalisation. This may be appropriate in the context of the competitive telecommunications market. Given the emphasis on technical and regulatory convergence in the *Convergence Green Paper*, some aspects of broadcasting are also subsumed within the same approach. To us, though, it seems that this is far from adequate, as weaknesses in the market structure and the way commercial operators behave are not addressed. Further, the ability of viewers to access content is under-protected. Although the interests of the consumer get some mention in the recitals, they do not really form part of the 'top-level' rationale for the regulatory package. Specific problems arise from the hybridisation of competition law and

[99] *Ibid.*, p. 23.

traditional regulation, which suggests limited intervention in an *ex post* manner. It would also seem that common standards are required to ensure access to transmission facilities by the various content providers and, crucially, different types of viewer. The regulatory model selected, through a move from simple interoperability to interoperability by proxy, means viewer choice is, in practice, restricted to the content offered on one platform, or by one provider. This is a failure to regulate successfully by the Union, whilst precluding the member states from taking their own steps in this regard, a variant on the problem with competence that we typically see in the broadcasting sector. Finally, it must be questioned whether the approach to regulation, which, in the light of technological change, has been to separate content from infrastructure, undermines protection of quality and diversity of content. The boundary between content and infrastructure is not clear cut, and there are dangers that essential services, such as EPGs, fall between the regulatory systems, or are seen as adequately regulated as transmission technologies. Whilst it is claimed that the Communications Package takes important elements in content regulation into account, it does little more than play lip-service to the special needs of the broadcasting sector.

7

Media ownership: impact on access and content

Introduction

As chapter 6 has shown, the actions of private parties, particularly the big and powerful, may have an impact on the content available to viewers. Put briefly, limiting the range of different suppliers may adversely affect the range of content broadcast. Similar concerns about access, and the consequent impact on the range of content available, arise in the context of media mergers. These are particularly significant given the developments in the media market. Mergers and convergence of media corporations with each other and related corporations, throughout the 1990s and into the twenty-first century, have created vertically integrated media conglomerates and a greater concentration of ownership of media assets. According to Anup Shah (citing Bagdikian)[1] in 1983 50 corporations dominated most of each type of mass medium and the biggest media merger in history was valued at $340 million. In 1987 those 50 corporations had shrunk to 29, to 23 in 1990. By 1997 the 23 had reduced to 10 and included the $19 billion Disney–ABC deal, at the time the biggest media merger ever. In 2000 AOL Time Warner's $350 billion merged corporation was more than 1,000 times larger than the biggest deal of 1983. *The Nation* magazine in 2002 listed the top ten or 'big ten' media corporations as AOL Time Warner, Disney, General Electric, News Corporation, Viacom, Vivendi, Sony, Bertelsmann, AT&T and Liberty Media.[2] Each of these corporations is global in reach and vertically integrated. In essence they can be described as entertainment corporations which span distribution networks, technology products, content production (across all media and platforms), theme parks, toys, clothing manufacture, and retailing and the exploitation of content archives. They seek to maximise cross-selling and

---

[1] www.globalissues.org/HumanRights/Media/Corporations/ Owners.asp.
[2] www.thenation.com/special/bigten.html. Today's list would have to consider the inclusion of companies like Google and Microsoft, which are increasing their content reach and driving new ICT convergences, although how far they can be called entertainment companies is moot.

cross-promotional opportunities. Competition between the corporations is fierce and is centred on the aggressive pursuit of viewers. One aspect of this chase for audiences has been the explosion of media channels and services seeming to offer greater choice for viewers, but which only serves to disguise the fact that fewer corporations own more and more of those channels and services.

This chapter looks at the approach of the European Commission in its capacity as a competition authority and the European courts (European Court of Justice (ECJ) and Court of First Instance (CFI)) to identify the relationship between media specific issues and competition law and policy. One central question is whether the impact of mergers on the viewing experience is adequately taken into account, especially given the impact of media mergers on the diversity of suppliers and, crucially, on the diversity of content. In this assessment, two issues re-occur. First, are non-economic concerns, such as quality and diversity of content, appropriately or adequately taken into account in a competition-based assessment? This question is, in effect, a reformulation of the concern outlined in chapter 4 that, given the nature of the Union, the policy framework, whatever the area, seems not to be autonomous but trade-based, which in turn affects the values protected. In determining the extent to which this constitutes a problem, the specific nature of the broadcasting sector and the difficulties it raises for merger regulation need to be identified. Secondly, the interplay of different objectives within the Union has an impact on decisions in the competition sector. This issue illustrates tensions between a desire for more and newer types of service, and the need for 'good quality' services. Competition law may aim to provide diversity of suppliers and, as a corollary, choice, but it does not focus on the substance of that choice and the persons to whom these choices apply. This chapter identifies the extent to which viewers' interests are recognised, whether these are seen as citizens' or consumers' interests, or whether issues of competence and the focus on the market override their interests, especially those of the passive citizen viewer.

General problems in the media sector

Before we look at how the European Commission and the European courts have approached the question of diversity and media concentrations, we should note that there are problems which arise when taking a standard competition-law-based approach to cases in the broadcasting sector. These problems arise from the particular characteristics of the sector and the nature of competition law. In general terms, competition law is based on an economic perspective on the world, based on an assumption that companies will indulge in profit-maximising behaviour and that consumers make choices about what they want to buy on a rational basis, and assumes that they have full knowledge about products available. Central to this analysis is a rational transactional view of the world, based on willingness to pay a price. For us, two issues arise concerning the meaning of the term consumer and the best way to satisfy consumers' preferences.

First, the term consumer has, as we have discussed in chapters 1 and 2, a particular meaning which does not exactly coincide with the way in which the terms consumer and consumer welfare are used in competition law and policy. Indeed, the term, 'consumer' can be considered a problematic one, as in different areas of law it conveys different meanings. In our model (chapter 1) the consumer, whether active or passive, is one way of approaching the viewing experience and one which is contrasted with the viewing experience of a citizen. In our terms, the consumer is a viewer, that is, an individual within the broadcasting environment. The meaning of consumer in competition terms is different and, arguably, less well understood, especially in the context of reconciling the individual consumer in the market with consumer welfare in theory. Moreover, in competition law the term consumer is used to mean a generalised economic actor (not necessarily an individual), whose welfare refers to the levels of openness and efficiency achieved by the market and whose behaviour is reasonable, rational and informed. Whilst our model accepts consumption as a key attribute of the viewer as consumer, it focuses on the privatisation of the relationship with broadcast content and the commodification of that content, by contrast to the communal approach within the public sphere. There is no such juxtaposition in the competition model; all interests are reflected through the functioning of the market.

For us, the exclusion of citizens' interests from the term 'consumer' results in only a partial account of all the potential viewers in an audience. While a transactional view of the world has benefits, there are problems in determining the public interest by exclusive or excessive reference to only what the consumer wants, as it excludes citizens' interests. As we have noted in chapter 2, what the consumer would choose is not necessarily what is required for the creation of a well-functioning public sphere, the representation of minorities and other public interest considerations.[3]

---

[3] OECD, *Competition Policy Roundtables: Media Mergers*, 19 September 2003, DAFFE/COMP (2003) 16, p. 19, citing D. Gomery, 'The FCC's Newspaper-broadcast Cross-ownership

Furthermore, whereas citizenship implies some form of equality of rights and status, consumers have only a formal or abstract freedom limited and constrained by their respective economic power: an economic assessment of public interest is not necessarily a desirable one. There is a danger that it may serve to entrench the difference between rich and poor, and opens up the possibility of a digital divide.

Secondly, the view that 'consumer welfare' is best served by a competitive market tends to focus on the process (i.e. creation and maintenance of competition) and assumes that this will lead to desirable results which benefit the consumer. Such an approach aggregates the welfare of consumers into a general assessment of welfare, which does not reflect or represent the diversity of consumers, nor their different approaches to consumption. In relation to the consumption of broadcasting, this approach appears to ignore those consumers who are unable or unwilling (i.e. too poor to pay or insufficiently informed as to their choices) to participate in the consumption domain, and makes no concessions to their plight, in our terms passive viewers and those who are frustrated by external factors (see chapter 1). In broadcasting systems solely based upon willingness to pay, ideas about universality (chapter 2) and access are not required.

We have seen that the definition of the market (chapter 4) is key to any competition law assessment and is central to the application of the Merger Regulation which, as we shall see below, is triggered by a decrease in competition on a particular market. Defining markets in the broadcasting sector is problematic for a number of reasons.[4] In particular, the use of the small but significant non-transitory increase in price (SSNIP) test (see chapter 4) has given rise to particular problems for the broadcast media sector. Not only are there free-to-air stations to take into account but the sector is one that is characterised by rapid change and may involve markets, by virtue of the sector's vertically integrated nature, in which few transactions take place. Although the use of the SSNIP test is one which relies on the (assumed) behaviour of consumers, it is limited as it 'takes little if not no account of qualitative criteria such as strategic competition and innovation decisions, on the grounds of which a company may decide to compete not only on prices but also on services'.[5] For

Rules: An Analysis' (Washington DC: Economic Policy Institute, 2002), p. 2, available at: www.epinet.org/books/cross-ownership.pdf

[4] Economists view the broadcasting sector as a double-sided market: see, e.g., OECD, *Media Mergers*, p. 20.

[5] Bird and Bird, *Market Definition in the Media Sector – Comparative Legal Analysis – Study for the European Commission, DG Competition*, para. 26.

consumers interested in new services, an increase in price might not be the most relevant factor, especially as early adopters of new services and new technologies are notoriously price insensitive.

Furthermore, the definition of markets might vary depending on the perspective from which the market is defined: that of viewers; or that of advertisers. In the former situation, the broadcast content is the output. In the latter, an advertising-based analysis, programmes are not the output but the means by which viewers are attracted. Programmes are therefore viewed as production technologies. In this situation, 'viewers are not the relevant consumers; they are the product being sold to the advertisers'.[6] Consequently, a broadcaster might choose 'lowest common denominator' programming to appeal to a mass market in order to 'sell' the maximum number of viewers to an advertising market.[7]

The issue of substitutability which underpins the SSNIP test raises other questions. For example, can news provision on the radio or in the press be substituted for news provision on the television? From the advertisers' perspective there might be a great difference, especially as advertising revenue is generated by audience size. In general, it is difficult to say why different forms of programme are or are not substitutable for one another. Just as there are differences in genre, so there are differences across different media such as the press, television and radio.[8] There are also qualitative issues which range from reliability through to political preference in terms of, for example, news coverage. Looking at a specific television example, the British market, is 'The World' broadcast on BBC Four and produced by the World Service, which has a more global focus to the stories covered, substitutable for ITV's News at 10.30 p.m., for example, or even another version of the BBC news?[9] As this example illustrates, there are difficulties with assessing substitutability.

The broadcasting sector exhibits some features which reinforce the strength of operators with high market shares. There are high barriers

---

[6] H. Shelanski, 'The Policy Limits of Markets: Antitrust Law as Mass Media Regulation', *Law and Economics Workshop* (University of California: Berkeley, 2003), p. 22.

[7] Although one might suggest that there is a commercial decision to operate in a niche market, there is a likelihood that content available on such a market will not be cheap.

[8] OECD, *Media Mergers* notes at p. 32 that there seems to be some interrelationship between the pay TV and free-to-air television markets in that pay TV has developed more slowly in markets in which there are a large number of free-to-air channels. This reasoning seems to have played a part in the Commission's decision in *NewsCorp/Telepiu*, Commission Decision, COMP/M.2876, 2 April 2003.

[9] In the state aid decision concerning BBC News 24, discussed further in ch. 12, the Commission noted that a crucial distinction between the 24-hour news service provided by the BBC and Sky News was that the BBC carried no advertising.

to entry and, in many member states, significant regulatory constraints, including the prevalence of a universal service obligation. The need to have a broadcasting licence, of which there are usually a limited number, which, in respect of content services, has not been removed by the liberalisation of the transmission networks, restricts the number of market players at certain points in the distribution chain. As noted in the *Convergence Green Paper*,[10] content is central to broadcasting and, in particular, premium content (such as sport and films) is difficult to obtain as well as expensive, yet may be crucial to a company's success. Access to premium content may have a reinforcing effect; content providers will want access to the broadest audience and will therefore choose for preference the distribution system which has the widest audience base, usually those that are already established and with premium content at their disposal to attract viewers. This can make it difficult for new entrants to the market.[11] These difficulties are compounded where the existing operators are vertically integrated, which we have seen is increasingly the case.

An integrated content provider/broadcaster might be able either to deny a competitor access to an audience (via its stranglehold on a particular distribution network), or to deny it access to content. A vertically integrated company which supplied content could provide that content exclusively, or on better terms, to its own distribution operation than to competing distribution networks. Only consumers with access to that distribution technology would be able to access the content in issue. This can be especially problematic when we consider premium content, especially when the vertically integrated company has first-mover advantage in the market. Also, there is a concern that the range of content available on the platform would be limited, as a competitor's content, which could also be of better quality, has been excluded.

Furthermore, diversity of content is not necessarily well protected, if at all, by economic-based calculations within the merger and joint-venture contest as we can see with an illustration provided by the OECD report. It gives the example of two free-to-air stations merging.[12] Post-merger, the two channels intend to use to a greater degree the same programming. In economic terms, this might be seen as efficient by reducing programming

---

[10] Commission, *Green Paper on Convergence of the Telecommunications, Media and Information Technology Sectors and the Implications for Regulation* COM (1997) 623.

[11] D. Geradin, 'Access to Content by New Media Platforms: A Review of the Competition Law Problems', *ELRev* 30(1) (2005), 68–94.

[12] OECD, *Media Mergers*, p. 25.

costs. Equally, it could have an adverse impact as it reduces the scope and diversity of content.[13]

Overview of the Merger Regulation

The media sector has become increasingly characterised by transnational, vertically integrated conglomerates and, as we have suggested, mergers and joint ventures might adversely affect the viewing experience by limiting the content range available, or by charging monopoly prices. The continued consolidation of the media sector is controlled, in so far as it is controlled, at the Union level by the Merger Regulation[14] as well as by Article 81 and, to a lesser extent, Article 82.[15] It should be noted that historically neither Article 81 nor 82 was a particularly good fit for the problems raised by mergers, which led to the enactment of the Merger Regulation.[16] The Merger Regulation covers most mergers and joint ventures, the remaining joint ventures being assessed for compliance with Union law under Article 81 EC. Within the Merger Regulation, the Commission reviews mergers with a 'Community dimension'[17] according to a number of criteria set out in Article 2, discussed further below.

The assessment for the acceptability of mergers[18] within the Merger Regulation is based on a further test, which calls for the assessment of whether there is a 'substantial impediment to competition' (SIEC).[19] The

[13] See also the example given by Shelanski, 'The Policy Limits of Markets', pp. 17–18.

[14] Regulation 139/2004 of 20 January 2004 on the control of concentrations between undertakings (the Merger Regulation) OJ [2004] L24/1.

[15] Recital 27 Merger Regulation notes this point: specifying that 'the criteria of Article 81(1) and (3) of the Treaty should be applied to joint ventures performing, on a lasting basis, all the functions of autonomous economic entities, to the extent that their creation has as its consequence an appreciable restriction of competition between undertakings that remain independent'.

[16] See, e.g., Case 6/72 *Continental Can* [1973] ECR 215 in which it became apparent that Article 82 EC could only be used where a dominant position was strengthened rather than to prevent the emergence of a dominant position. Contrast the position under the Merger Regulation: Recital 26 specifies that 'a significant impediment to effective competition generally results from the creation or strengthening of a dominant position'.

[17] Those mergers not satisfying the Community dimension test may still be assessed under the relevant member state's own competition regime.

[18] Under Article 3(2) of the original merger regulation, there was a distinction between concentrative and co-operative joint ventures, co-operative joint ventures remaining under Article 81. There was a certain amount of confusion in this area and the 1997 amendment clarified the definitions. The most recent version of the Merger Regulation clarifies the scope of the types of agreement still further.

[19] For clarification of the notion of SIEC, see Recital 25, Merger Regulation, which provides that it extends 'beyond the concept of dominance, only to the anti-competitive effects

test is based on the identification of a market (product market and geo-graphical market) and an assessment of the relative market power of the players on that market. The concept of the market is clearly crucial in the assessment of whether a merger or joint venture is acceptable under Union law, whether it be assessed under the Merger Regulation or under Article 81. The Commission's recent *Horizontal Merger Guidelines*[20] refer on this issue to the 1997 *Notice on Market Definition*,[21] meaning similar principles used in cases under Articles 81 and 82 will apply to horizontal mergers.

If a merger or joint venture in principle falls within the scope of the Merger Regulation, there are still a number of factors which may result in the Commission finding the deal compatible with the common market. The most important of these 'defences' is that of increased efficiency, used to outweigh the Commission's concerns about the anti-competitive effect of the deal.[22] In such a case, the merger would not be found to impede effective competition significantly; that is, not fall within the scope of the Merger Regulation.[23] For such an argument to work, however, 'the efficiencies have to be of benefit to consumers, be merger-specific and be verifiable'.[24] The other major 'defence' referred to in the *Horizontal Merger Guidelines* is that of the 'failing-firm' defence. The logic behind this argument is that if the firm is failing, then the competitive structure of the market would deteriorate in any event; a merger in such circumstances would not bring about any anti-competitive effects.[25] Given the high-risk nature of the broadcasting market, this defence may be relevant to some media mergers.

of a concentration resulting from the non-coordinated behaviour of undertakings which would not have a dominant position on the market concerned'. See also Recital 26, Merger Regulation.

[20] Commission, *Guidelines on the Assessment of Horizontal Mergers and the Council Regulation on the Control of Concentrations between Undertakings* OJ [2004] C 31/3.

[21] Commission, *Notice on the Definition of the Relevant Market for the Purposes of Community Competition Law* OJ [1997] C 372.

[22] During the process of reforming the Merger Regulation the Commission in its 2002 *Report on Competition Policy* stated that 'a further object of the . . . proposal is to take greater account of the efficiencies that can result from mergers', p. 4. See also Commission, *Horizontal Mergers Guidelines*, para. 76.

[23] See also Recital 29, Merger Regulation.

[24] Commission, *Horizontal Mergers Guidelines*, para. 78.

[25] Commission, *Horizontal Mergers Guidelines*, at para. 90, identify a threefold test for the 'failing firm' defence to satisfy: (a) the allegedly failing firm would, in the near future, be forced out of the market; (b) there is no less anti-competitive alternative purchased the merger; and (c) in the absence of a merger, the assets of a failing firm would inevitably leave the market.

The Commission may have regard to other broader, non-economic goals when assessing mergers.[26] Article 2(1)(b), which identifies a number of other considerations such as 'the interests of the intermediate and ultimate consumers, and the development of technical and economic progress provided that it is to consumers' advantage and does not form an obstacle to competition', may indicate some flexibility in this regard.[27] Additionally, Recital 23 recognises that consideration should be given to the objectives set out in Article 2 of both the EC and EU Treaties. Article 2 EC sets out a broad list of the objectives which include 'a high level of ... social protection' as well as 'economic and social cohesion and solidarity among member states'.[28] It is also worth noting that in certain areas, such as the environment[29] and consumer protection, Union action should ensure a high level of protection. As we have noted in chapter 4, of particular relevance to the media sector is Article 151(4) EC, which requires the Community to take cultural aspects into account.[30]

The Commission has a number of choices when faced with a notified merger or joint venture. Where a case has been referred to the Commission

---

[26] Note the possible role of Article 86(2) in assessing the applicability of competition rules, discussed in, e.g., Joined Cases T-528, 542, 543 and 546/93 *EBU/Eurovision System* [1996] ECR II-649, para. 118. Article 86(2) is discussed further in the context of state aid, in ch. 12.

[27] Note, however, Craufurd Smith suggests that, in practice, the Commission has taken a narrow view of this provision: R. Craufurd Smith, 'Rethinking European Union Competence in the Field of Media Ownership: The Internal Market, Fundamental Rights and European Citizenship', *E.L. Rev.* (2004), 29(5), 652–72, p. 669.

[28] See, e.g., Case C-219/97 *Drijvende Bokken and Stichting pensioenfonds voor de Vervoeren Havenbedrijven* [1999] ECR I-6121, a case concerning a collective agreement to set up a single pension fund responsible for managing a supplementary pension fund for workers in which the ECJ referred to the objectives to be achieved by the Union in the 'social sphere'. In this case, the agreement was held not to infringe Article 81(1) in the first place rather than being justified under Article 81(3); the ECJ has referred to the inherent characteristics of the agreement which support public policy objectives in other contexts too, such as regards sporting clubs' arrangements. For a discussion, see R. Wesseling, 'The Rule of Reason and Competition Law: Various Rules, Various Reasons', in A. Schrauwen (ed.), *Rule of Reason: Rethinking another Classic of European Legal Doctrine* (Groningen: Europa Law Publishing, 2005), pp. 68–73.

[29] See, e.g., *CECED* Case IV.F.1/36.718 OJ [2000] L 187/47, which concerned an agreement between the manufacturers of washing machines to develop washing machines which were energy efficient.

[30] van de Gronden in 'Rule of Reason' suggests that '... in the near future it might successfully be argued that agreements, which the parties involved have concluded in order to realise goals in the fields of e.g. public health or culture, fall within the scope of Article 81(3) EC', pp. 90–1.

it makes a decision under Article 6: that the Merger Regulation does not apply (Article 6(1)(a)); that in principle the deal falls within the scope of the Merger Regulation but it does not raise serious doubts as to its compatibility with the common market (Article 6(1)(b), a non-opposition decision); or that a proposed deal does raise serious doubts (Article 6(1)(c)). In the last case, the Commission is required to initiate further investigations, resulting in a decision under Article 8. Following its investigations it may, under Article 8(1) Merger Regulation, declare the deal to be compatible with the common market. Here, the deal will go ahead in the form notified by the parties to the Commission. The Commission may declare the proposed deal to be incompatible with the common market (Article 8(3)). In such an instance, the deal should not go ahead. Where a deal which is incompatible with the common market has been implemented, the Commission can order the separation of the assets and/or the cessation of joint control and it may also impose a fine on the undertakings involved. One further course of action remains open to the Commission when investigating a notified merger or joint venture. Under Article 8(2) the Commission has the power to approve a merger or joint venture subject to conditions whereby the parties to the deal make commitments to modify their proposals so as to make them acceptable to the Commission. In mergers generally, the Commission prefers structural solutions over behavioural remedies. Behavioural remedies, since they are ongoing, would require medium- to long-term monitoring.[31] An example of the structural approach can be seen in the *AOL/Time Warner*[32] merger, in which the Commission approved the merger after the parties agreed to sever all links with the German media group Bertelsmann. Whether this is generally the position with media cases is debatable, as we shall discuss further below.[33]

Article 21(1) of the Merger Regulation provides that only the Commission has the authority to take action in respect of Community dimension mergers. Consequently, according to Article 21(3), no national law applies to such mergers, although Article 21(4) Merger Regulation allows for the

---

[31] Commission, *Notice on Remedies acceptable under Council Regulation 4064/89/EEC and under the Commission Regulation of 447/98/EC* OJ [2001] C 68/3.

[32] *AOL/Time Warner*, Commission Decision 2001/718/EC, Case IV/M1845, OJ [2001] L 268/28.

[33] Contrast the approach taken with the *BSkyB/Kirch Pay TV* joint venture discussed below. In OECD, *Media Mergers*, it was noted that competition authorities showed a penchant for behavioural remedies in cases where media mergers created or reinforced a gatekeeper power, p. 52.

protection of 'legitimate interests' by member states.[34] As Recital 19 of the Merger Regulation notes, member states are not precluded from taking appropriate action to protect legitimate interests other than those pursued by the Merger Regulation. Article 21(4) identifies three named legitimate interests: public security; plurality of the media; and prudential rules.[35] This is not an extension of member states' competence but recognition of their reserved powers in certain areas and the exercise of these powers is always subject to Union law.[36] Member states may therefore impose additional conditions on prohibited mergers; they cannot permit mergers that would be unacceptable under Union law. Any measures must comply with general Union law principles, notably non-discrimination and proportionality. Although recognition of the importance of the media is, in principle, a good thing, the exception supports the view that the free-market approach is the default position. Further, the existence of the plurality of the media 'exception' may be the reason that public-interest considerations have not received detailed consideration in merger cases.[37] By contrast, Article 21(4) has not been relied on in the context of media mergers, suggesting that member states seem content to leave the fight against transnational corporations to the Commission.

Cases in the media sector

In the light of the lack of regulation on media ownership at the Union level, there have been a significant number of cases which have come before the Commission in this sector, both under the Merger Regulation and Article 81 EC. We shall consider these cases to identify how the Commission decides if there is a problem in the first place and the extent to which countervailing considerations, such as media pluralism, may be taken into account. One of the central mechanisms by which the Commission

---

[34] This provision was found in Article 21(3) of the 'old' Merger Regulation. I. Nitsche, *Broadcasting in the European Union: The Role of Public Interest in Competition Analysis* (The Hague: T.M.C. Asser Press, 2001), p. 127, notes that member states did not make use of Article 21(3) of the old Merger Regulation, though they showed greater willingness to ask that a case be referred to national authorities as permitted by Article 9 Merger Regulation. The ECJ has now ruled on this provision. The first case was Case C-42/01 *Portuguese Republic* v. *Commission*, judgment 22 June 2004.

[35] Article 21(4)(3) does allow for a member state to argue that another national public interest object should fall within these provisions.

[36] Notes on Council Regulation (EEC) 4064/89 with a view to clarifying the scope of certain articles. See also ch. 4.

[37] Craufurd Smith, 'Rethinking European Union Competence', p. 669.

decides whether or not to approve a merger is that of looking at the parties' market power. Obviously, the broader the concept of a product market or of a geographic market, the more competing players there are likely to be, and therefore it is less likely that a particular merger will be viewed as anticompetitive.

From the cases decided in the media sector, it seems that the main distinction that the Commission and the courts have accepted is that between the retail distribution of pay TV and that of free-to-air television.[38] Although the idea of a total audience market might seem appealing at one level, the Commission has focussed on the different relationships involved: with free-to-air television, there is only an indirect relationship with the viewer and the role of advertising in funding commercial, free-to-air television is crucial. With pay TV, the broadcaster and the viewer have a direct relationship in which viewers' preferences have to be identified and met to persuade viewers into paying for a service when free-to-air television is available.[39] The market in this context is asymmetric and, although free-to-air television faces competition from pay TV, the two types of broadcasting are unlikely to be in direct competition.[40] Additionally, there are different conditions of competition, differences in the price of the services and of the characteristics of the services.[41] This is, then, a relatively narrow view of the product market, if we contrast it with a total television audience market. The Commission has been criticised for not linking its conclusion in law to economic arguments in this regard.

The case law is less clear cut when we consider the different types of transmission technology; the issue of whether there are separate markets for the different types of transmission technology has been influenced by the broadcasting environment in each of the member states.[42] In a number of decisions, the Commission has, however, emphasised the fact that, from the viewers' perspective, the different transmission technologies are not interchangeable because of the different set-top boxes (STB) required

---

[38] An exception can be found in *Kirch/Richemont/Telepiu* Case IV/M.140 OJ [1994] C 225/3. See Nitsche, *Broadcasting in the European Union*, p. 123.

[39] E. J. Carter, 'Market Definition in the Broadcasting Sector', *World Competition*, 24(1) (2001) 93–124, pp. 100–1.

[40] Carter, 'Market Definition', p. 99.

[41] *BSkyB/Kirch Pay TV*, Commission Decision, COMP/JV.37, 21 March 2000, para. 24.

[42] See *Apollo/JP Morgan/Primacom*, Commission Decision, COMP/M.3355, 15 June 2004, paras. 11 *et seq.* in respect of the German cable market; contrast *Telia/Telenor*, Commission Decision, Case IV/M.1439 OJ [2001] L 40/1, para. 278 in respect of the Nordic market. See Commission's *Explanatory Memorandum Recommendation on Relevant Product and Service Markets*, p. 37.

for reception of the various platforms and the switching costs involved in changing from one system to another (the lock-in effect).[43] In this context the technology-neutral approach seen in other aspects of media policy to ensure equality of opportunity between different platforms has not been applied. This approach re-emphasises the argument made in chapter 5 that the technology-neutral approach has its limitations when considering the interests of the viewer.

In contrast, there has been no distinction made between analogue and digital television,[44] the latter being a development of the former. The Commission has recognised that the situation in this regard may be complex, given that digital television may offer both pay TV and free-to-air television. As we suggested in chapter 1, there is a difference between the two types of broadcasting. The Commission has, however, contented itself with not excluding the possibility of making such a distinction from future market definitions.[45] From an economic point of view, this analysis might be preferable to that taken in respect of the different types of transmission technologies. The view is that an argument based on whether the buyer of the service would think that product capable of substitution by another would be preferable to one which relies on technological distinctions, especially given the rate of technological development. The adoption of such an argument would seem to give inadequate attention to the needs of the viewer, given the lock-in effect (discussed above and in chapter 6).

Even within the pay TV sector, the Commission has distinguished different markets, notably the difference between entertainment-based services and interactive television, with its more transactional nature. As regards the traditional content market, the Commission has, in some instances, recognised that there might be different markets even between different types of programming.[46] Crucially, from the viewers' perspective, the market for sporting rights is considered to constitute a product

---

[43] *MSG Media Service*, Commission Decision, 94/922/EC, Case IV/M.469 OJ [1994] L 364/1, para. 41.

[44] *Newscorp/Telepiù*, Commission Decision, COMP/M.2876 2 April 2003; *Telenor/ Canal+/Canal Digital*, Commission Decision, COMP/C.2–38.287, 29 December 2003, at para. 28; *UGC/Noos*, Commission Decision COMP/M.3411, 17 May 2004, paras. 13 *et seq.*

[45] *Bertelsmann/Kirch/Premiere*, Commission Decision, Case IV/M.993 OJ [1999] L 53/1 para. 18.

[46] In Case T-221/95 *Endemol v. Commission* [1999] ECR II-1299, an appeal against the Commission's decision in *RTL/Veronica/Endemol* OJ [1996] L 134/32, both the Commission and the CFI took the view that independent broadcasting productions constituted a separate product market from public service broadcasters' in-house productions because of the different conditions for production.

market in its own right.[47] Indeed, different sports may constitute their own sub-markets, which are not, from the viewers' perspective, substitutable for one another (see further chapter 12).[48] In the *Screensport* decision, the Commission emphasised that the viewers' interests were best served by being offered a range of (sports) channels from which they could make an informed choice.[49] The Commission's analysis adopts an approach based in the domain of consumption and favours the active viewer. It does not take into account the viewers' ability to pay for a range of channels, or their capacity to manage the choice available.

The Commission's approach, and that of the courts, assumes that a greater range of services in general terms will be a 'good' thing,[50] as we can see in *TPS*.[51] TPS was a digital pay TV channel set up through agreements between four French broadcasters, France Telecom and Suez Lyonnaise des Eaux. The joint venture itself did not infringe Article 81, as the creation of a competing channel to Canal+ and CanalSatellite was pro-competitive. Part of the agreement, however, gave TPS exclusive rights to certain content. In principle, these provisions were contrary to Article 81(1). None the less, the Commission accepted they were acceptable under Article 81(3)EC, as access to that content was essential to the success of TPS during the crucial start-up phase. The crucial point was that a new service was available, thereby, in theory, increasing the range of choice available and potentially leading to better subscription conditions. An argument which automatically equates more suppliers with increased choice is flawed, though, because it does not consider the quality or level of availability of the service. Nevertheless, such an argument still informs the analysis under Article 81(3) EC, in which market structure remains important. Ungerer emphasised that the Commission is concerned to ensure that new markets are not automatically the preserve of those operators which already have significant market power; the Commission

---

[47] See, e.g., *RTL/Veronica/Endemol.*

[48] *CVC/SLEC*, Commission Decision COMP/M.4066, unreported 20 March 2006, concerned the acquisition by a private equity investment firm of the Formula One Group, resulting in significant horizontal overlaps in the markets for television rights to major motor sports events in Italy and Spain. The Commission emphasised that Formula One and Moto GP are the closest substitutes in the broader relevant market, whilst leaving open the question of whether each constituted its own product market.

[49] *Screensport/EBU*, Commission Decision, Case IV/32.524, OJ [1993] L 179/23, para. 73.

[50] This would seem to tie in with the Commission's supposed ordoliberal approach: see below.

[51] *TPS*, Commission Decision 1999/242/EC, Case IV/36.237.

wants to see not just new services, but also more players in the media markets.[52]

Perhaps more significant from the perspective of pluralism and media ownership is the position of other premium-rate content, such as films. We have noted the problems consequent on the consolidation of the production of content and its distribution into a merged entity. This was an issue in both *AOL/Time Warner*,[53] which concerned a major Internet provider and two music publishers, and *Vivendi Universal*.[54] In *Vivendi Universal*, the notified deal would have resulted in a company with the world's second largest film library; the second largest library of television programming in the European Economic Area, as well as the largest music library. One of the parties to the merger, Canal+, was a leading pay TV operator in Europe and Vivendi had interests in Internet portals. The Commission noted that Canal+ was likely to end up with exclusive access to Universal's movie rights, premium content which is crucial in driving the success of pay TV. This raised a significant risk of market foreclosure in the pay TV market. Further, the music library together with the Internet activities also raised concerns about dominance of the Internet music supply market. The merger was permitted but on conditions which, in particular, limited Canal+ to only 50 per cent of Universal's film production, leaving the remaining 50 per cent to other operators in the broadcasting sector.

One of the big concerns regarding the information-technology sector is the rapid development of new digital technologies and services. This is significant as any assessment, particularly of market power, has to take into account the temporal nature of the market and the changing nature of the conditions on that market. A firm may be in a strong position only temporarily. It has been noted that a characteristic of 'new-economy' markets is competition for the market rather than within it. This means that the nature of the market is such that one operator may dominate, but only for a short period of time. It could be argued that consequently less action is required, since the market constantly rectifies itself against long-term dominance by one company. In its *Bertelsmann/Kirch/Premier*

---

[52] H. Ungerer, 'Competition in the Media Sector – How Long Can the Future be Delayed?', *Info* (2005) 7(5), 52–60.

[53] The Commission's definition of the market in this case has been criticised; in particular it is unclear whether from the demand side, that is the perspective of the consumer, the online music industry is different from buying music from high street outlets: see e.g. G. Monti, 'Article 82 and New Economy Markets', in C. Graham and F. Smith (eds.), *Competition, Regulation and the New Economy* (Oxford: Hart, 2004), pp. 25–6.

[54] *Vivendi/Canal plus/Seagram*, Commission Decision, COMP/M.2050.

decision, the Commission noted that the effect on the market would be a lasting one, involving, as it did, a number of media groups which already had extensive media holdings, reinforcing the need to control the joint venture.[55] The nature of the market was also taken into account in the *NewsCorp/Telepiu* case, in which the Commission, contrary to its previous policy, accepted a merger leading to a monopoly (branded Sky Italia) in the Italian DTH pay TV market. The Commission seemingly took into account the high costs involved in setting up such a business to accept that the market was, more or less, a natural monopoly. Significantly, the Commission imposed conditions particularly to ensure access to premium content so as not to preclude new entrants to the market. If we accept the principle that a company's behaviour will be affected by the threat of future competition, we can still ask whether this will have any real effect on the service delivered to the viewer. On an optimistic view, the company could seek to maintain viewer loyalty by continuing to innovate or provide cheap goods/services. Alternatively, a company could take pre-emptive action against future competition.[56] Such pre-emptive action is unlikely to be in the viewers' interest. In any event, it is questionable whether a change in market dominance from one company to another actually results in a change in services to viewers because they are still faced with little choice.

Further, as the Commission noted in its *Notice on Defining the Relevant Market*, in any given case it will consider the market against the background of single-market integration. It is questionable how strong a factor market integration is in the media sector, given the national nature of many of the broadcasting markets. The cases have tended to see the geographic market as the territory of the member state.[57] The effect of this is that issues of plurality of supply are considered national market by national market. As we shall suggest below, such an analysis neglects

---

[55] *Bertelsmann/Kirch/Premiere*, para. 100.

[56] Similar problems can be seen in the PC and software market, in which Microsoft was found to have abused its dominant position by various bundling and tying practices such as making the acquisition of the Windows operating system conditional on the acquisition of the Microsoft media player software. In its decision, the Commission imposed a €497,196, 304 fine as well as behavioural remedies requiring, *inter alia*, the provision of information required to allow interoperability of other programs with the Windows operating system and also an unbundled operating system. See *Microsoft*, Commission Decision COMP/C-3/37.792, Decision C(2004) 900 final. Microsoft is challenging the Commission's decision in Case T-201/04R *Microsoft v. Commission* and in Case T-313/05 *Microsoft v. Commission*, neither of which has been decided.

[57] *UGC/Noos*, para. 20.

overall diversity of supply within the Union, allowing the development of pan-European media conglomerates, and overlooks the position of minorities who live in more than one member state. It has been suggested that considering linguistic markets is another option.[58] Although linguistic factors are clearly significant, it should be noted that other cultural factors may also play a role. The existence of these other factors is likely to push the analysis towards a finding that the relevant geographic market is still that of the territory of a member state.[59] It has been suggested that new distribution technologies have enabled the consumer to seek products from a broader area, thus undermining the need for a geographic link between producer and consumer. Accepting this argument would mean that the relevant geographical market in a given case is likely to be broader and less likely to justify regulatory intervention. This argument emphasises supply-side considerations, that is, looking at the distribution chain, over those of the demand-side, that is, the viewers' perspective which will be linked to their own national cultures and languages.

Assessment of the approach of the Commission and the Courts

Both in respect of assessments under Article 81 and the Merger Regulation, the definition of the product market has been quite narrow. For example, the Commission has consistently distinguished pay and free-to-air television. This distinction has been criticised. Still more questions are raised by the distinction the Commission made within pay services of retail services and interactive services (such as banking) on the one hand, as opposed to entertainment-based services such as pay-per-view (PPV) and near video on demand (NVOD), on the other. Interestingly, the Commission did not consider other forms of interactive services, such as telephone banking, delivered via different mechanisms, when making its assessment in this area. The market definition could thus be seen as being artificially narrow. Both sets of market definitions indicate willingness on the part of the Commission to intervene; either in terms of reviewing what is going on, by preventing some media consolidation from taking place, or taking place subject to conditions. The imposition of conditions on mergers, 'regulation by the back door', will be discussed below.

---

[58] L. McCallen, 'EC Competition Law and Digital Television', *Competition Newsletter* (1 February 1999), 4–16, pp. 7–9.

[59] See *RTL/Veronica/Endemol*. In some cases the determination of a geographic market has been left open as it would not affect the outcome: e.g., *Kirch/Bertelsmann/Premiere*.

It has been suggested that the Commission has, in a number of cases, developed policy-driven reasoning, rather than relying on economics-based tests.[60] A policy-based approach can be seen in a number of cases,[61] notably *Bertelsmann/Kirch/Premiere*. There, the Commission expressed concern about technological progress being adversely affected should the merger be permitted.[62] Similar concerns were expressed in the linked merger between *Deutsche Telecom/BetaResearch*,[63] when the Commission discussed the risk that the d-box (a type of STB) developed by BetaResearch would become the digital standard and consequently all new operators would be dependent on BetaResearch's licensing policy.[64] The degree to which this is a primary or secondary motivation, especially given the terms of Article 2(1)(b) Merger Regulation, which specifically refers to the desirability of innovation, is a problem. As we shall see below, it may be that in the light of modernisation of competition law enforcement and a recent greater emphasis on economic considerations, decisions such as *Deutsche Telecom/BetaResearch* and *Bertelsmann/Kirch/Premiere* may become of historic interest only.[65] Whether they should be, given the importance of other considerations as recognised by the treaties, is far from certain.[66]

The Commission's approach to market definition has been criticised, both at a level of principle and as a matter of practical outcomes. It is questionable whether narrow market definitions which facilitate regulatory intervention by the Commission should be adopted when this is just

---

[60] Carter suggests that the Commission frequently departs from the quantitative tests in the Market Definition Notice because of the specific nature of the market in this sector: 'Market Definition', p. 96.

[61] *Nordic Satellite Distribution*, Commission Decision 96/177/EC, Case IV/M.490 OJ [1996] L 53/20, *MSG Media Services*. Ariño notes the significance of the vertical relationship in these cases: 'Competition Law and Pluralism' in European Digital Broadcasting: Addressing the Gaps', *Communications and Strategies* 54(2) (2004), 97–128, p. 109; C. Marsden, 'The European Digital Convergence Paradigm: From Structural Regulation to Behavioural Competition Law?' *Journal of Information Law and Technology* 3 (1997), p. 19. available at www2.warwick.ac.uk/fac/soc/law/elj/jilt/1997_3/marsden1/, last accessed 19 December 2005.

[62] *Kirch/Bertelsmann/Premiere*, paras. 119–22.

[63] *Deutsche Telecom/BetaResearch* OJ [1999] L 53/3, discussed in Commission, *28th Competition Report* (1998), paras. 96 and 141.

[64] The Commission seemingly took a similar approach in *AOL/Time Warner*: see Monti, 'New Economy Markets', p. 27.

[65] For a general discussion, see Odudu, 'A New Economic Approach to Article 81(1)', *ELRev* 27 (2002), p. 100; on Article 81(3) Bourgeois and Bock, 'Guidelines on the Application of Article 81(3) of the EC Treaty or How to Restrict a Restriction', *LIEI* 32(2) (2005), 111–21.

[66] M. Ariño, 'Competition Law and Pluralism', p. 103.

using competition policy as a means to achieve non-competition policy goals. One concern for those who favour a free-market approach is that this practice leads to inefficiency.

There are difficulties in second guessing the market as the Commission requires itself to do, especially given technological developments and the high-risk strategy consistently used by the broadcasting industry. These difficulties can be seen in the German pay TV example in which a deal between Bertelsmann, a publisher, a Kirch[67] group company and Deutsche Telekom was prohibited. The Commission took the view that the proposed joint venture, which would benefit from first-mover advantage, would seal off the German market, creating a dominant position for the joint venture in the services to be provided. The parties had a 'second try' at the joint venture in the *Bertelsmann/Kirch/Premiere* case. Despite the fact that the companies argued that DF1, the pay TV channel offered by Kirch, would not survive in the market and that there would therefore be no such pay TV service on the market at all (which in the event turned out to be the case), the Commission refused to let the deal proceed. The difficult question is whether it was better to stop the merger and end up with 'nothing', at least in the short term, than to allow these companies to establish a dominant position/first-mover advantage.[68] It has been suggested that the Commission's early reluctance to sacrifice current services in the long-term interests of plurality of supply has undergone some change.[69] Certainly, the Commission's decision in *NewsCorp/Telepiu* suggests a more pragmatic stance. It might be said that the Commission is, in cases such as these, faced with a choice between 'regulated' consolidation of the market in which the Commission imposes terms on the parties, and

---

[67] The Kirch media group is an example of a group which expanded its interests and holdings to a point where they ceased to be sustainable. The group began as Beta Film, which was established in 1959 by Leo Kirch. The company acted as a German distributor for US feature films. In the 1980s the Kirch media group became Germany's first national pay television network, beginning as a German distributor for US feature films. The group expanded its media holdings throughout the 1990s and in 2001 it purchased the rights for Formula 1 racing for US$1.54 billion and later the World Cup broadcasting rights. In mid 2002 Kirch went into receivership prior to declaration of bankruptcy by a number of its companies. In February 2002 its pay TV arm, Premiere, was reported as losing £1million per day and Kirch PayTV announced its insolvency, followed by its parent company KirchMedia and other units. The banks began dismantling the group. See www.ketupa.net/kirch1.htm for an overview of its numerous holdings prior to its collapse in 2002.

[68] See Nitsche, *Broadcasting in the European Union*, p. 121 and contrast the merger decision in *Newscorp/Telepiu*, in which something was held to be better than nothing.

[69] Ariño, 'Competition Law and Pluralism', pp. 110–11.

unregulated consolidation through market exit in which the remaining party is not controlled unless Article 82 comes into play.

The need to create strong European players in the broadcasting sector is a theme that runs through the Commission's communications in this area,[70] as indeed in many sectors. Here there is a concern that the opportunities provided by the digital age will benefit the large American conglomerates at the expense of Union companies. It has also been a factor in assessments under Article 81(3) EC. Thus, it seems that competition policy was encouraged by other policy factors to allow the development of large European companies in the media sector. Joint ventures such as that between Audiofina and Bertelsmann,[71] resulting in the formation of CLT Ufa, were considered acceptable, even though CLT Ufa became one of Europe's biggest broadcasters. The decision was strongly based on the fact that different geographic markets were discernible, and in competition terms, posing little threat. Similarly, the *BSkyB/Kirch* joint venture involved different national markets. Whether such a policy-based approach is desirable in economic terms has been questioned,[72] although it is not unique to the broadcasting sector. Significantly, it is hardly one that supports the development of a plurality of suppliers, diversity of content or the individuality of member states' cultures, all factors which may have a direct impact on the viewing experience. Cross-European giants might well result in homogeneous content across the Union, where, in order to secure maximum audiences, the content will be of the lowest common denominator.

We have already noted that one of the stated themes of the Commission's policy in the media sector is to encourage the development of new services, whether this means a greater number of existing types of service or the creation of new types of services.[73] Although limiting the influence

---

[70] See, e.g., Commission, *Communication on Audiovisual Policy*, COM (90) 78 final, Commission, *White Paper on Growth, Competitiveness and Employment: The challenges and ways forward into the 21st century*, COM (1993) 700 final, p. 63. See further ch. 5. Industrial policy considerations of this nature have been prevalent in other sectors, though they seem to be less commonly accepted now than in the 1990s.

[71] *Bertelsmann/CLT* Commission Decision, M.779, 7 October 1996. The only geographic market on which there was any significant overlap was in Germany in which there was a very competitive pay TV market.

[72] Nitsche, *Broadcasting in the European Union*, p. 128.

[73] See *Open/BiB*, Commission Decision, 15 September 1999, OJ [1999] L 312/1 in which the Commission accepted a joint venture between BSkyB, BT, Midland Bank and Matsusha Electric Europe was acceptable under Article 81(3) because of the new services that would be offered to consumers on digital interactive television services. Given the elimination of potential competition between BSkyB and BT, the Commission imposed conditions to

of a dominant player appears desirable, there is the question of whether audiences actually want 'more' services or 'newer services', rather than better quality services. Equally, it may be the case that a wide diversity of services is not economically viable; certainly this argument has been used to justify PSB (see chapter 13), as well as cases such as *NewsCorp/Telepiu.* A more general point is that competition law (whether we are looking here at assessments under the Merger Regulation or under Article 81(3)) has more difficulty with assessing dynamic or qualitative benefits than with those based on cost. In this there are similarities with the problems noted in the Bird and Bird Report concerning the reliance on the SSNIP test to determine media markets.[74]

The central issue is whether non-economic concerns should be taken into account as an exception to competition policy, for example under Article 81(3) and, if so, to what extent, or whether competition law itself should be interpreted by reference to overarching policy goals. This latter view suggests that competition policy is not autonomous or, if it is perceived as autonomous, that it is not the highest value in the Union legal order, being constrained by other values (such as the protection of human rights). The courts' approach here is likely to be cautious. In *Metropole*,[75] the CFI rejected an argument based on assessing the relevant agreement's positive effects on competition against its negative effects under Article 81(1) because that was the function of Article 81(3). This ruling must be distinguished from cases in which the Court has considered whether the restriction was inherent in the nature of the agreement.[76] The Court has applied the inherent restriction reasoning to agreements in which non-economic interests have played a significant role.[77] The scope of this rule, however, is not clear.[78] Neither of these approaches is exactly the same as requiring Article 81 or the Merger Regulation to be interpreted in the light of general treaty principles. Given the CFI's lack of enthusiasm in *Metropole,* and the lack of certainty surrounding the inherent restriction arguments, which can be seen as broadly parallel approaches, such an approach would not be certain of

---

ensure that there is competition from the cable networks; that third parties have sufficient access to Open's subsidised set-top boxes and to BSkyB's films and sports channels; and that set-top boxes other than Open's can be marketed. BT agreed not to expand its existing cable television interests in the UK and to divest its existing interests.

[74] Bird and Bird, *Market Definition in the Media Sector,* para. 26.
[75] *Metropole Television* (M6).
[76] Case C-309/99 *Wouters* v. *NOVA,* judgment 19 February 2002.
[77] Case C-309/99 *Wouters.*   [78] van de Gronden in 'Rule of Reason', p. 87.

gaining judicial favour. Certainly, we have not seen explicit reference to either Article 151(4) or freedom of expression as framing the extent of Article 81(1).

We have seen the difficulties with seeking to interpret Article 81(1) so as to allow non-economic factors to be taken into consideration at that point. Article 81(3) does open up such a possibility, but there are problems in its application at a number of levels. First, taking non-economic consider-ations into account suggests that, as an exception to competition policy, such considerations occur lower down any hierarchy of norms within a legal system. A further question relates to the identification of the interests we are protecting. End consumers are protected as a by-product of the competitive process[79] and, as we have noted, are thus protected in their capacity as economic actors, rather than as citizens. They are directly mentioned in Article 81(3) only as part of the fourfold criteria (see chap-ter 4) which must be satisfied to exempt an agreement which has fallen in principle within Article 81(1). The Merger Regulation, in Article 2(1)(b), also permits the possibility of taking consumer interests into account, although this factor does not seem to have been expressly discussed. It would seem likely that similar problems, in assuming that the viewer ben-efits from the operation of competition higher up the distribution chain, could occur in relation to the Merger Regulation as arise in the context of Article 81.

Although it is assumed that the end viewer will benefit from any deal falling within Article 81(3), the consumer protected by the terms of Article 81(3) is the direct consumer of the product defined in the prod-uct market. The direct consumer may not necessarily be the viewer. Many of the discussions of media policy and competition focus on the posi-tion of competitors to ensure their presence in the market, assuming that there will be a knock-on benefit for the end viewer, which is not proven.[80] Secondly, it is suggested that qualitative[81] features cannot be taken away down the value chain, because they are inherent in the product supplied. This is not necessarily true of the media sector: part of the quality in

---

[79] That the end view of competition is the protection of the end user is recognised in Recital 9, Regulation 1/2003; see also *Guidelines on Application of Article 81(3)* OJ [2004] C 101/97, para. 33.

[80] Bourgeois and Bock in 'Guidelines' suggest that the new Guidelines on Application of Article 81(3) abandon this assumption.

[81] The build standards and quality of a car, for example, remain the same throughout the distribution chain.

broadcasting lies in the way it is transmitted. We take for granted the transmission quality resulting in a certain standard of picture and sound quality but, with digitisation, it is now possible for the transmission to be manipulated so it contains extra information and features. This may be seen as changing the product, but can also be seen as a quality-of-service issue from the viewers' perspective. Similarly, the way programming is bundled and presented may change the nature of the product. Thus benefits at one end of the supply chain will not necessarily be passed on to the end viewer. In its assessments, the Commission has tended to assume that benefits will be passed on to the consumer, though not necessarily the end consumer (or viewer).

Furthermore, the concept of consumer does not equate to the general public. In some instances, for example when considering the environment, the Commission has attempted a broader view of consumer, equating that term to everyone within the Union. This, however, has been subject to criticism from a competition-policy perspective, particularly in an economics-based assessment of the impact of a deal on competition. Such criticism emphasises the point that there seems little room for 'public-interest' considerations, read from an economic perspective, within the text of Article 81.

The introduction of non-economic concerns, either as a factor interpreting the scope of Article 81(1) (discussed above), or in terms of Article 81(3) has not been consistently or well received. None the less, we can identify a number of cases in which non-economic concerns have been given express recognition. For example, in the relatively early *Screensport* decision, the Commission noted the need to provide coverage of minority sports as well as sports programmes with educational, cultural or humanitarian content.[82] This decision was overturned by the CFI, for whom these non-economic considerations were insufficiently connected with an economic analysis.[83] Subsequently, the Commission has followed the CFI's line. Indeed, even in cases in which non-economic considerations have been raised explicitly, the Commission also referred to other factors, such as consumer choice; non-economic considerations therefore seem incidental rather than central.[84] The Guidelines on Article 81(3) re-emphasise this aspect. Further, it seems that, pursuant to the terms of Merger Regulation Article 2(3), the competition factor prevails over other considerations; this point is implicit in the efficiencies argument noted

[82] *EBU/Eurovision System*, para. 62.   [83] *Metropole* (M6).
[84] Ariño, 'Competition Law and Pluralism', p. 108.

earlier. This means that if a merger creates or strengthens dominance, the Commission has to prohibit the merger, even if the effect of the merger is to create efficiencies such as technological or economic progress, despite the terms of Article 2(1)(b).[85]

Consequently, there is some dispute as to whether competition authorities should take into account issues such as media pluralism, in the context of either Article 81(1) or 81(3) and the Merger Regulation. As the Commission itself noted:

> Whilst the protection of media pluralism is primarily a task for the member states, it is for the Community to take due account of this objective within the framework of its policies.[86]

It is in any event questionable the degree to which competition operates to protect pluralism, or whether it does enough in this regard. The assumption seems to be that competition interests and pluralism interests coincide; an assumption that we dispute.[87] Conversely, there has been criticism of generalised statements about the importance of pluralism in these decisions, without any clarification.[88]

We have noted that there seems to have been a change in the Commission's approach. Rather than prohibiting mergers, it may now allow mergers subject to conditions, and these conditions tend to be behavioural rather than structural.[89] One example is found in *BSkyB/Kirch*, when the Commission cleared the merger, but subject to conditions relating to fair and non-discriminatory access to the d-box and consequently to the distribution mechanism for content providers. The condition is important as it seeks to ensure that third parties have access to the distribution mechanism and is significant given the parties' positions *vis à vis* content provision. Similarly, in *NC/Canal+/CDPQ/Bank America*, the Commission

---

[85] G. Monti, 'Article 81 EC and Public Policy', *CMLRev* 39(5) (2002), 1057–99, p. 1061, citing P. Camesasca, *European Merger Control: Getting the Efficiencies Right* (Oxford: Hart Publishing, 2000), pp. 40–6. Broadly speaking, an ordoliberal approach favours a diverse market-place rather than the concentration of wealth in the interests of efficiency. In the ordoliberal view, political freedom and economic freedom are intertwined. Too much economic power in the hands of one entity threatens individual political freedom and must therefore be constrained. The focus point then is not the market itself but the position of dominant players. Given the role of the media in society and its potential for influencing political opinion, the importance of constraining dominant voices would seem to be peculiarly relevant.

[86] Commission, *Green Paper on Services of General Interest* COM (2003) 270 final, p. 45.

[87] *MSG Media Services*; *RTL/Veronica/Endemol*; *Bertelsmann/Kirch/Premiere*.

[88] Nitsche, *Broadcasting in the European Union*, p. 121.

[89] OECD, *Media Mergers*, p. 305.

accepted the joint venture on the condition that Canal+ and Sogecable, a Spanish pay TV operator controlled by Canal+, undertook to promise non-discriminatory access to their distribution rights to any Spanish cable operator.[90] Yet another example can be found in *Newscorp/Telepiu*, when the Commission sought to ensure access to both content and infrastructure for competing undertakings. Similar points may also be made about the *Vivendi/Universal* merger.

This move to behavioural remedies is significant. Previously we have seen the Commission seeking to ensure multiple services in a market that is effectively insisting on platform competition at any cost. Whether this approach works is, as we have seen, contestable, and *NewsCorp/Telepiu* can be seen as indicating that the Commission has become aware of the difficulties. The cases identified in the previous paragraph suggest an alternative approach, one which focuses on ensuring access. This approach of trying to ensure fair, reasonable and non-discriminatory access has parallels with the approach to conditional access systems (CAS) taken under the Communications Package (see chapter 6). The terms in cases such as *Sogecable* on content obviously go further than the Communications Package, which is restricted, in terms of technology affected by fair, reasonable and non-discriminatory requirements, to CAS. In particular, it is notable that the obligations in *Sogecable* provide for a wholesale 'unbundled and non-exclusive' offer. This obligation is not as limited as a requirement to offer content on fair and non-discriminatory terms, because the Commission has imposed requirements as to how that content should be available to competitors. In this we can see links between competition policy initiatives and subsequent legislative initiatives.[91] Using a behavioural-remedies approach constitutes a form of regulation disguised as competition policy, which is compounded by the Commission's tendency to assume narrow market definitions so as to bring cases within its purview. This gives rise to concerns about the legitimacy and transparency of the approach and the expertise that DG Competition has for making assessments about non-economic public interest issues. De Streel noted that given this tendency, 'intervention in these cases is often more efficiently done by sector-specific regulation than merger remedies, which calls for an enhanced co-operation between the Commission and [national

[90] *NC/Canal Plus/CDPQ/Bank America*, Commission Decision, Case IV/M.1327, OJ [1999] C 233/21.
[91] Ariño suggests some other examples of links in 'Competition Law and Pluralism', pp. 114–15.

regulatory authorities]'.[92] Conversely, Levy suggested that action by DG Competition has prevented threats to pluralism that might not have been caught by a specific media merger regulation.[93] Whether or not we agree with the legitimacy of the Commission's involvement in media mergers, what is of central concern is the interests the Commission seeks to protect and the mechanisms by which it seeks to protect them. Our concern is that uncertainty in this regard could have an adverse impact on the quality of the decisions made, which, in turn, may have consequences for the viewing experience.

Conclusion

This chapter has outlined the approach of the Union competition authorities in the context of media mergers and sought to identify the difficulties facing them, especially as they seek to take into account both the specific characteristics of the broadcasting industry as an economic sector and, at the same time, give weight to its non-economic values, notably stimulating the production of a diverse range of content and information for the viewer. It is perhaps not surprising that, given that competition policy and broadcasting policy do not aim to achieve the same goals, there are sometimes tensions between the two. Where the Commission indirectly seeks to take into account non-economic goals that are not explicitly addressed by the legislation, the scope and weight of protection, as well as the mechanism by which such protection can be achieved, are uncertain. The case law is ambivalent, with the consequence that decisions do not form a consistent and coherent policy. On the one hand, we see that a high value is placed on economic considerations; on the other, the Commission has been criticised for manipulating tests so as to bring mergers and agreements within its purview. With the increasing tendency for the Commission to allow deals to proceed, but subject to behavioural conditions, the level of supervision by the Commission of the activities of media conglomerates has increased. Any assessment of these trends is affected by the assessor's viewpoint. For some, it is unacceptable that pure economic considerations are clouded by non-economic concerns; for others,

---

[92] A. de Streel, 'European Merger Policy in Electronic Communications Markets: Past Experience and Future Prospects', *The 30th Research Conference on Information, Communication and Internet Policy*, 28–30 September 2002, Virginia, p. 17, available at: http://tprc.org/papers/2002/99/EuropeMergerPolicy.pdf.

[93] D. Levy, *Europe's Digital Revolution: Broadcasting, Regulation, the EU and the Nation State* (London: Routledge, 1999), p. 98.

the Commission should take non-economic concerns into account, but there is debate as to how and to what extent it can do so. In the context of this debate, the position of the Commission is unenviable. The tools at its disposal are not designed to take citizens' interests directly into account. At best the wants of consumers are highlighted. As we have seen in chapter 6, considering the viewing experience through a consumer-based framework is likely to have consequences not only for the range of content available but also for the possibility of access to content.

As we suggest in chapter 10, the commercialisation of the broadcasting environment produces an environment in which information is viewed as a commodity rather than as a public good. It may be that the Commission has little choice, as the control of media transnational companies lies beyond the power of the individual member states, despite their competence in cultural matters. Given that the value of competition policy in the Union legal order is unlikely to be subordinated to other societal goals, at least in the near future, one solution would be to address the question directly by legislative action, despite the concerns of member states about the Union's competence (chapters 4 and 5). We believe that the Union has the competence to take action in respect of competition and internal market considerations (chapter 5). Our view is that it cannot be right that debates about competence, especially where Union competence is arguable, should prevent the enactment of a measure that is likely to prove the most effective in protecting diversity of suppliers and enabling access to content.

8

Jurisdiction, forum shopping and the 'race to the bottom'

Introduction

The underlying principle of the Television without Frontiers Directive[1] (TWFD) is that of a 'one-stop shop'; that is, where television services within the Union will be regulated only once. Jurisdiction is significant as it determines who is subject to regulation and by whom, thereby determining the level of regulation to which particular content services are subject. Given the inherently cross-border nature of satellite broadcasting, broadcasts from one member state are capable of reception in another. Content subject to the regulatory regime of one member state becomes available to viewers in another. This may be problematic if viewers are only used to the protection afforded by the regulatory framework in their own member state and do not know how to make judgments about all the content made available to them. The central question which arises in the context of the jurisdiction clause is whether individual member states should be permitted to continue to regulate all broadcasts capable of reception within their territory, or whether internal market considerations should take priority.

Convergence has raised further problems in that the boundaries between broadcasting and other forms of communication have blurred and, although there has been some degree of convergence in transmission regulation (chapter 6), there has not yet been convergence of content regulation between different types of service. Jurisdiction in relation to type of service seems to be becoming as problematic as the determination of which member state has the power to regulate a service in a particular case. Technical developments therefore make questions about jurisdiction more difficult in two senses: the geographical location of the regulator;

---

[1] Council Directive 89/552/EEC of 3 October on the co-ordination of certain provision laid down by law, regulation or administrative action in member states concerning the pursuit of television broadcasting activities OJ [1989] L 298/23, as amended by Directive 97/36/EC OJ [1997] L202/30.

and in terms of the appropriate legal regime within the relevant member state that should be applied.

The original version of the TWFD sought to address the issue of jurisdiction. The number of cases which arose on the interpretation of that provision suggests that this was not an entirely successful venture. The Amended Directive adopted the solution that the European Court of Justice (ECJ) developed. Yet, as we face a second revision process, the issue of jurisdiction has once again arisen. This chapter will trace the development of the jurisdiction clause and consider the impact on the viewing experience. In the light of this we shall assess the extent to which an appropriate balance between trade and non-trade issues has been found.

The original version of the Television Without Frontiers Directive

In its original version Article 2(1) provided:

> Each Member State shall ensure that all television broadcasts transmitted by broadcasters under its jurisdiction, or by broadcasters who, while not being under the jurisdiction of any Member State, make use of a frequency or a satellite capacity granted by, or a satellite up-link situated in, that Member State comply with the law applicable to broadcasts intended for the public in that Member State.

The provision envisages two possible situations: first, that where a member state would normally have jurisdiction; and secondly, one in which satellite frequencies and uplinks come into play. Looking first at the 'normal' situation, the approach was not helpful. In effect, the Union defined 'jurisdiction' by saying that those that have jurisdiction have jurisdiction. The definition did not help in defining who would normally have the jurisdiction to regulate broadcasts in a given situation. This is perhaps symptomatic of the different viewpoints held on this matter; one Advocate-General suggested that the use of such vague terminology was designed to cover the fact that there was no political agreement as to the approach to be taken.[2]

The Commission, however, thought the matter of jurisdiction was clear. In its original proposal, the draft directive proposed by the Commission included two defined terms not found in the TWFD as enacted: 'internal broadcasts', and 'cross-frontier broadcasts'. 'Internal broadcasts'

---

[2] Case C-222/94 *Commission* v. *UK* [1996] ECR I-4025, para. 46. The Advocate-General in his opinion in this case gives a thorough review of the possible interpretations of the jurisdiction clause.

were defined as the 'initial transmissions by public or private undertakings engaged in broadcasting on the territory of a Member State . . .' 'Cross-frontier broadcasts' concerned only those transmissions capable of reception by the public in another member state. These definitions indirectly addressed the issue of jurisdiction, and illustrate the Commission's approach in this matter. The term 'internal broadcast' assigned responsibility for regulation by reference to where the broadcasting body was established in the sense used in relation to the right of establishment contained in Article 43 EC. This principle of home-country regulation was reinforced by the inclusion in the definition of 'internal broadcasts' of the phrase 'including transmissions exclusively intended for reception in other Member States . . .'. On this approach, place of reception was irrelevant. This principle the Commission sought to re-emphasise in its explanatory memorandum and in its first *Report on the Application of Directive 89/552/EEC.*[3] As the Commission noted, the member state in which the broadcasting body was established would have jurisdiction 'irrespective of the destination of the broadcast'.[4]

Although the Commission might have been clear in its views on this point, there were other possible ways of viewing jurisdiction. The Convention on Transfrontier Television (CTT), enacted at approximately the same time, took a different approach, as the British government argued when the Commission brought action against it for faulty implementation of the TWFD.[5] The UK government had interpreted Article 2 TWFD to mean that jurisdiction to regulate content devolved to the state which controlled the radio frequency on which the television programme was broadcast, taking into account the intended recipients of the broadcast. The ECJ broadly agreed with the Commission and held that jurisdiction depended on 'establishment', although it should be noted that the ECJ seemed keen to distinguish between establishment in the usual treaty sense of the term, as defined in *Factortame*,[6] and establishment in the specific context of broadcasting. The test for establishment is usually taken to be 'the actual pursuit of an economic activity through a fixed establishment in another Member State for an indefinite period'.[7] The ECJ

---

[3] Commission, *Report on the Application of Directive 89/552/EEC and a Proposal for a European Parliament and Council Directive amending Council Directive 89/552/EEC* (COM (95) 86 final), p. 27.
[4] Commission, *Explanatory Memorandum*, para. 101.
[5] Case C-222/94 *Commission v. UK.*
[6] Case C-221/89 *Factortame and Others* [1991] ECR I-3905.
[7] Case C-221/89 *Factortame*, para. 20.

determined establishment in the broadcasting context to be 'the place in which a broadcaster has the centre of its activities, in particular the place where decisions concerning programme policy are taken and the programmes to be broadcast are finally put together'.[8] None the less, despite the definition highlighting the importance of the location of the editorial team for determining establishment in the broadcasting sector, this element of the test would only become relevant if there were more than one location within the Union which could be considered to be a broadcaster's place of establishment.[9] Reception as a criterion remained excluded.

This approach was maintained, with the exception of the *De Agostini* case,[10] in subsequent cases which came before the ECJ on this point prior to the amendment of the TWFD.[11] The EFTA Court has taken a similar line.[12] The issue of editorial control has resurfaced as the TWFD undergoes its second review, this time not in the context of determining the location of the broadcaster but in determining the type of service (see further below).

Although this basic principle of establishment may have been clear since *Commission* v. *UK*, the ECJ's later jurisprudence identifies a number of refinements. In *VT4*[13] the issue of double control arose. The Belgian authorities sought to regulate the retransmission by cable or satellite broadcasts originating from (and regulated by) the UK. The company was established in a '*Factortame*' sense in the UK; not only was the company incorporated under English law but senior management was based in the UK and some programme decisions were made there. Equally, however, VT4 had a physical presence in Belgium and some programme decisions were made there. Given that the definition of broadcasting in the original draft directive had been amended by the deletion of any reference to 'retransmission' to ensure that member states' regulatory authorities should not exert secondary control in such circumstances, it is not surprising that the ECJ ruled against the Belgian authorities, despite the fact that the programmes were aimed at Flanders.

---

[8] Case C-222/94 *Commission* v. *UK*, para. 58.

[9] See Advocate-General Lenz's views in Case C-14/96 *Criminal Proceedings against Paul Denuit* [1997] ECR I-2785.

[10] Joined Cases C-34-36/95 *Konsumerntombudsmannen* v. *De Agostini (Svenska) Forlag AB and Konsumerntombudsmannen* v. *TV-shop i Sverige AB* [1997] ECR I-3843.

[11] Case C-11/95 *Commission* v. *Belgium* [1996] ECR I-4115, Case C-14/96 *Denuit*, Case C-56/96 *VT4 Limited* v. *Vlaamse Gemeenschap* [1997] ECR I-3143.

[12] Joined Cases E-8 and 9/94 *Forbrukerombudet* v. *Mattel Scandinavia A/S and Lego Norge A/S*, Report of the EFTA Court, 1 January 1994–30 June 1995, p. 115.

[13] Case C-56/96 *VT4 Limited* v. *Vlaamse Gemeenschap*.

Such an approach, although it prohibits two sets of regulation, does not address the question of which regulatory authority should have the right and the responsibility to regulate. The problem is illustrated perhaps more clearly in the earlier case of *Denuit*,[14] which concerned a company which was established in the UK but which broadcast to Belgium. Editorial decisions were made in the USA, as the company established in the UK was the subsidiary company of an American company. Despite the fact that the UK had the least to do with the actual programming broadcast, the ECJ, in the interests of protecting the internal market and the one-stop shop principle, held that the Belgian authorities could not regulate the service. The Belgian authorities argued that, given the British rules, which at that time, distinguished between domestic and non-domestic satellite services, the UK authorities were not regulating the service. Arguably, then, there was no duplication of regulation; indeed, unless the Belgian authorities regulated, there was an absence of regulation. The ECJ rejected this argument. Member states cannot use another member state's failure to comply with Union law to justify their own failure to comply with Union law.

VT4 raised another issue; that of the 'abuse' of Union law to avoid national regulation. This issue had arisen in the context of broadcasting before in the cases of *TV10*[15] and *Veronica*.[16] In its early jurisprudence in *van Binsbergen*,[17] the ECJ had accepted that Union law should not be used to avoid national regulation. This principle is sometimes referred as anti-avoidance or the circumvention principle. It was extended to the broadcasting sector in *TV10* and *Veronica*, both cases which concerned broadcasters establishing themselves in Luxembourg, a state which permitted the broadcasting of advertising, but broadcasting at the Dutch audience, thereby circumventing the Dutch restrictions on advertising. In the first of the two cases, *Veronica*, the ECJ accepted that the establishment in Luxembourg was motivated by a desire to avoid the Dutch rules. It then held that Dutch legislation could in this situation be applied to the

---

[14] Case C-14/96 *Denuit.*
[15] Case C-23/93 *TV10 SA* v. *Commissariaat voor de Media* [1994] ECR I-4795.
[16] Case C-148/91 *Vereniging Veronica Omroep Organisatie* v. *Commissariaat voor de Media* [1993] ECR I-487.
[17] Case 33/74 *Van Binsbergen* v. *Bestuur van de Bedrijfsvereniging voor de Metaalnijverheid* [1974] ECR 1299, para. 13: 'a member state cannot be denied the right to take measures to prevent the exercise, by a person providing services whose activity is entirely or principally directed towards its territory, of the freedom guaranteed by Article [49] for the purpose of avoiding the professional rules of conduct which would be applicable to him if he were established within that state . . .'.

broadcaster. What the ECJ did here was not state that the anti-avoidance principle was an exception to the free-movement right, but instead that the company could not rely on those rights as it was, in reality, established in the Netherlands. This is a clearly different approach to establishment from that taken under the TWFD, though, as we have noted, the two tests of establishment (that in TWFD and that with regard to Article 43 EC) are not exactly the same.[18]

The implications of the *Veronica* judgment were examined more closely in *TV10*, with an emphasis on the circumstances in which the anti-avoidance principle would be applied. Since the early case of *van Binsbergen*, it seemed that the central concern addressed by the ECJ was that evasion of national rules was taking place; the nature of the national rules evaded in a given case did not seem significant. In *Veronica*, a slightly different approach can be identified. The ECJ had emphasised that the Dutch rules in question were aimed at protecting a public interest, although the ECJ also mentioned that the broadcaster was 'improperly evad[ing]' the Dutch regulation.[19] This arguably shifts the focus of the inquiry from the person (and possibly that person's motivation) to the national rules[20] and, in particular, limits the permissible interests protected by national rules to those viewed under Union law as being in the public interest.[21] By contrast, in *TV10* both the Advocate-General and the ECJ adopted a formulation in which a requirement for the anti-avoidance principle to apply was that the national rules being evaded were not incompatible with Union law.[22] This formulation of the anti-avoidance or circumvention principle is arguably wider than that used in *Veronica*, as it is not necessarily limited to circumstances in which 'overriding interests' in the sense of Union law (that is, goals Union law recognises as being in the public interest; see chapter 4) are in issue. Although the precise scope of permissible national rules is not clear,[23] the focus is once

---

[18] See, e.g., ECJ's assumption in Case C-14/96 *Denuit*, para. 23.

[19] As we have seen in ch. 5, the ECJ has accepted that measures designed to protect media pluralism are in the public interest, though it has found very few of them in practice to be acceptable under Union law, viewing most of them as disproportionate.

[20] L. Hell Hansen, 'The Development of the Circumvention Principle in the Area of Broadcasting', *Legal Issues of European Integration* 25 (1998/2), 111, p. 122, for criticism in the lack of clarity in the ECJ's reasoning here.

[21] For a discussion of the scope of derogations in Article 46 EC and interests of overriding public interest, see, e.g., L. Woods, *Free Movement of Goods and Services in the European Community* (Aldershot: Ashgate, 2004), ch. 12, esp. pp. 249–54.

[22] Case C-23/93 *TV10*: Advocate-General Lenz, Opinion paras. 12–15; judgment, paras. 20–1.

[23] There may, for example, be problems with the acceptability of rules perceived as disproportionate to their aims; see further ch. 4.

again on the body seeking to rely on arguments about the right to freedom of movement. These cases suggest that a company which establishes in one member state and broadcasts to another to evade the receiving state's system of regulation aimed at protecting media diversity and freedom of expression would find itself subject to the receiving state's rules. The ECJ's theory underlying this point is not so clear.

In some ways, it seems that the focus of the ECJ's approach is on wrong-doing, not on the substance of the rules evaded, as we can see in *TV10*, which narrowed the scope of the anti-avoidance principle in another important aspect. In *TV10*, the ECJ appeared to set down a two-stage test: the broadcaster's output should be directed wholly or principally towards the member state seeking to claim jurisdiction; and the broadcaster must have established itself in another member state in order to enable it to avoid the rules in issue.[24] Although an approach focussing on the beneficiary of the free-movement right seems to broaden the scope of action left to member states, the formulation here seems to limit the application of the principle to cases of deliberate, and therefore blatant, evasion. This formulation is much narrower than the early formulation in *van Binsbergen*. Although it might be argued that the question of whether the broadcaster was directing its broadcasts wholly or principally at another member state is an objective question of fact, neither the ECJ nor the Advocate-General gave any indication as to what factors should be taken into account. A difficulty arises as, in adopting a two-stage test, the ECJ is reintroducing the question of motive, implicit in its comments in *van Binsbergen*,[25] into the anti-avoidance equation. The question, then, is how would one prove motive? As noted in the cases brought under the TWFD, many of the factors that one might rely on to show intent to evade, or indeed the fact that a broadcast is aimed at another member state, are based on assumptions about where the nationals of particular member states would 'normally' be working. They are therefore based on assumptions contrary to fundamental principles of Union law, which prohibit discrimination based on nationality and assumptions such as the Dutch not normally working in Luxembourg.

Given that the question of establishment turned out to be crucial for the application of TWFD, and especially given the difficulties encoun-tered in cases such as *Denuit* and *VT4*, the potential application of the anti-avoidance principle within the context of TWFD was important, par-ticularly from the perspective of the receiving member state's regulatory

---

[24] Case C-23/93 *TV10*, para. 26.   [25] Case 33/74 *van Binsbergen*, para. 13.

authorities. In *VT4*, the regulatory authorities argued that the sole reason that the company established itself in the UK was for the purpose of avoiding the monopoly granted to VTM on the broadcasting of advertising. It therefore constituted a blatant case of forum shopping, or regulatory arbitrage; that is, choosing one's place of establishment with a view to affecting the law applicable to one's activities. The referring court did not raise this question in its reference to the ECJ, which therefore did not address the issue.[26] The Advocate-General, however, did, suggesting that the *TV10* principle should continue to apply even after the entry into force of the TWFD, although he suggested a very restrictive interpretation of that principle.[27]

The matter of jurisdiction within the terms of the TWFD also arose in *de Agostini*, which, on the face of it, concerned similar patterns of facts to the Belgian cases. A broadcaster established in the UK was broadcasting to Sweden in contravention of a number of the Swedish rules on advertising, both advertising aimed at children and misleading advertising. The Advocate-General in this case adopted an analysis which followed the ECJ's approach in *Commission* v. *UK* and the Belgian cases. Although he did recognise the potential application of the anti-avoidance principle, he emphasised that it should not be read too widely.[28] The ECJ, however, took a different approach. Instead of looking at formal criteria relating to where the broadcaster was established, which assumes that the TWFD is the relevant piece of legislation, it considered the subject-matter of the TWFD and whether the TWFD was the only Union act to take into account. That is, did the TWFD harmonise the field exhaustively, even if only at a minimum level? By referring to the recitals, it became apparent the TWFD was not the only possible piece of relevant legislation. The TWFD envisaged that, in the field of advertising, other Union measures existed which would also govern advertising, though the terms of the recitals are not limited to specific directives. This fact opened the way for the ECJ to mitigate the impact of its rulings regarding jurisdictional allocation of power, by removing the subject-matter of the dispute from the scope of the TWFD at an earlier point in the analysis. The issue for the ECJ was not one of whether the matter concerned broadcasting rather than another form of communication service, but whether the TWFD

---

[26] Note that the EFTA Court in a similar case under the TWFD did not adopt the anti-avoidance principle: Cases E-8 and 9/94 *Mattel and Lego*.

[27] In this he took the same approach as he had done in Case C-11/95 *Commission* v. *Belgium*.

[28] Cases C 34-6/95 *de Agostini*, Opinion of the Advocate-General, para. 45. For criticism of this approach, see Hansen, 'Circumvention Principle', pp. 132–3.

was the end-point of the legal analysis within the broadcasting sphere. In *de Agostini*, there turned out to be a difference between the rules relating to children, which the ECJ determined were covered entirely by the TWFD in its provisions relating to the protection of minors in the context of advertising, and the misleading advertising provisions. As well as being dealt with by the TWFD, the prohibition of misleading advertising was harmonised within the context of advertising generally. Surprisingly, the ECJ also held that the recitals which referred to other Union measures also implied that there might still be room for member state action within the scope of areas which the TWFD co-ordinated but did not harmonise.[29] The ECJ stated that member state national rules on matters co-ordinated by the TWFD would be permissible provided that they did not constitute a secondary means of control over broadcasts, which would undermine the TWFD. This statement is problematical. In its analysis, the ECJ seems to treat the problem relating to advertising as separate from that concerning broadcasting, which overlooks the fact that, as advertising is content, it is hard to distinguish between broadcasting and advertising in this way. It is questionable whether, in practice, *de Agostini* saves many national laws as, given the link between advertising and the broadcasting service, it is hard to imagine a situation where national advertising rules would not act as a secondary means of control.

Prior to the revision of the TWFD the issue of jurisdiction was clear, though giving rise to concern. The possibility of using the anti-avoidance principle to relocate establishment to the receiving member state within the terms of the TWFD was slim. Questions of editorial decision-making notwithstanding, formal institutional criteria were of greater weight than those relating to the substance of the broadcast content itself. Some member states and some commentators were worried that the approach adopted by the ECJ, although it did not follow exactly that of the Commission, was orientated towards the commercial considerations of broadcasting. That is, it did not seem to take into account the cultural aspects of broadcasting, allowing no place for member state sensitivity in these areas and overlooking the interests of citizens. The earlier approach in *Veronica* and *TV10* allowed some scope for member states to clamp down on those broadcasters which were deliberately 'playing

---

[29] A similar approach has been taken with respect to the e-Commerce Directive (Directive 2000/31/EC), discussed in J. Hörnle, 'Country of Origin Regulation in Cross-border Media: One Step Beyond the Freedom to Provide Services?', *International and Comparative Law Quarterly* 54(1) (2005), pp. 89–126.

the system' so as to evade inconvenient national rules, the scope of this approach was limited and also unclear. Once the TWFD was enacted, the scope of the anti-avoidance doctrine was narrowed down still further. The problem for the ECJ in this context is that an over-broad interpretation of the anti-avoidance principle can be used to undercut entirely the free-dom of establishment and the freedom to provide services.[30] Although *de Agostini* might, as discussed, provide some legal space for national rules, this would apply to limited types of content, mainly advertising-based content, and give rise to other practical problems. *De Agostini* illustrates one of the ironies underlying the TWFD, in that it is in the areas in which the member states have recognised the greatest need for action, such as the protection of minors, that the internal market rules operate the most clearly to bring the level of protection down to the lowest level within the Union (see chapters 4 and 10). Despite the fact that the TWFD allows member states to take action to impose higher standards on broad-casters within their jurisdiction, these standards cannot be imposed on broadcasters established elsewhere. As ever, the ECJ's toleration of reverse discrimination functions so as to trigger a downward spiral in standards to the lowest level.

The 1997 Amending Directive

Although the 1997 Amending Directive retains the principle of the 'one-stop shop', namely that there should only be one regulator throughout the Union in respect of a given broadcaster, it recognises that the variety of factual situations was not adequately dealt with by the interpretation given to the previous version of Article 2. The revised Article 2, relying heavily on the approach taken by the ECJ in its case law, details various factual permutations and the impact thereof on the determination of jurisdiction. The ultimate fall-back position, however, is that of the Commission, the use of the *Factortame* definition of establishment.[31]

Although the Amending Directive, in reaffirming the 'one-stop shop' principle, recognises internal-market concerns, it also takes note of the

---

[30] In the context of freedom of establishment, see the development of the case law in Case C-212/97 *Centros* v. *Erhvervs-og Selskabsstyrelsen* [1999] ECR I-1459 etc; is part of the development of case law to do with the difference between access to the territory/market versus professional rules for behaviour in the market?

[31] This remains in the draft second amending directive: Commission, *Proposal for a Directive amending Directive 89/552/EEC*, COM (2005) 646 final, 2005/0260 (COD), SEC (2005) 1625 and 1626, p. 15, Article 2(5).

anti-avoidance principle by making express reference to it in Recital 14. This suggests that, despite the difficulties noted earlier in the ECJ's rulings in this area, the anti-avoidance principle remains available to the regulatory authorities in recipient member states to allow them to take action against broadcasters which are playing the system. Recitals are not, however, legally binding provisions, and there is no expression of the principle in the operative parts of the directive. Given that recitals are aids to interpretation, one might suggest that the jurisdiction clause be read in the light of Recital 14. If the anti-avoidance principle is seen as affecting the determination of establishment, as it did in *TV10*, the lack of a legally binding anti-avoidance principle in the TWFD complicates an already confused state of affairs. The problem is exacerbated by the fact that some of the criteria that can be used to identify the abuse of free-movement rights, such as location of workforce, are also used to determine jurisdiction within the TWFD. There thus seems to be the possibility of blurring the test for establishment with that for the application of the anti-avoidance principle.

The draft second amending directive (DSAD) introduces provisions which allow member states to counter 'abuse or fraudulent conduct', subject to compliance with certain procedural requirements although the wording changed through the legislative process.[32] Crucially, DSAD does not define what it meant by 'abuse or fraudulent conduct', specifying that the requirement to act is to be proven on a case-by-case basis. Recital 23 to DSAD indicates that the provision is intended to codify the ECJ's jurisprudence in this regard. Given the somewhat unclear line of reasoning the ECJ has adopted, it is interesting that the recital refers to only some of the ECJ's decisions in this area: *van Binsbergen, TV10* and *Centros*. This suggests that the limitations imposed by the *Veronica* line of reasoning will not find their way into the TWFD; it does not help to clarify the precise circumstances in which the provision may be used. The vagueness of this drafting is a serious weakness in the provision, opening the way for inconsistencies in the way it is used, which provides no benefit either to promoting the internal market or respecting the cultural competence of the member states.

The jurisdiction clause as it currently stands is structured so as to identify a range of possible factual circumstances, starting with the simplest, and moving on through a range of more complicated company structures.

---

[32] See draft second amending directive COM(2005)646 final, Article 2(7)–(10). See also appendix.

Jurisdiction is determined by applying the criteria set out in paragraphs 3–5, starting with (3)(a). The relevant provisions provide:

(3) For the purposes of this Directive, a broadcaster shall be deemed to be established in a member state in the following cases:

a the broadcaster has its head office in that member state and the editorial decisions about programme schedules are taken in that member state;

b if a broadcaster has its head office in one member state but editorial decisions on programme schedules are taken in another member state, it shall be deemed to be established in the member state where a significant part of the workforce involved in the pursuit of the television broadcasting activity operates; if a significant part of the workforce involved in the pursuit of the television broadcasting activity operates in each of those member states, the broadcaster shall be deemed to be established in the member state where it has its head office; if a significant part of the workforce involved in the pursuit of the television broadcasting activity operates in neither of those member states, the broadcaster shall be deemed to be established where it first began broadcasting in accordance with the system of law of that member state, provided that it maintains a stable and effective link with the economy of that member state;

c if a broadcaster has its head office in a member state but decisions on programme schedules are taken in a third country, or vice versa, it shall be deemed to be established in the member state concerned, provided that a significant part of the workforce involved in the pursuit of the television broadcasting activity operates in that member state.

(4) Broadcasters to whom the provisions of paragraph 3 are not applicable shall be deemed to be under the jurisdiction of a member state in the following cases:

a they use a frequency granted by that member state;

b although they do not use a frequency granted by a member state nor a satellite capacity they do use a satellite capacity appertaining to that member state;

c although they use neither a frequency granted by a member state they do use a satellite up link situated in that member state.

(5) If the question as to which member state has jurisdiction cannot be determined in accordance with paragraphs 3 and 4, the competent member state shall be that in which the broadcaster is established within the meaning of Art. [43] et seq. of the Treaty establishing the European Community.

The article is arranged in a hierarchical manner. This works accordingly: if you do not fall into the first situation, then you move on to consider the other possibilities. Subparagraph 4 operates only if 3 does not apply, and 5 comes into play only if neither 3 nor 4 does.

Although the TWFD in its amended form recognises some of the problems in the area of jurisdiction, it is not trouble-free. Looking at the amended text, it can be seen that paragraph 3 is more sophisticated than its predecessor. Although the starting-point in 3a takes a fairly straightforward approach, paragraph 3b recognises that there may be more complicated corporate structures than the one mentioned in paragraph 3a. This is evidenced by the separation of the criteria of 'head office' and 'editorial decisions on programme schedules'. Whilst this distinction is aimed at making the case for jurisdiction more clear cut, it actually obscures the issue. By failing to define clearly what constitutes 'editorial decisions on programme schedules' or 'the head office', the criteria of establishment are confusing and potentially incompatible. Further, the definition adopted will have a profound impact on where establishment lies in a given case. The meaning of the term 'editorial decisions about programme schedules' is itself very problematic. The assumption made in Article 2 is that the editorial decisions and programme-scheduling are done in the same place. This is not necessarily the case. Editorial decisions tend to be policy-oriented decisions made by the Director of Programming, or a person who is senior in the management hierarchy. Decision-making about local programme-scheduling, however, is often a commissioning decision and may be made by a Commissioning Editor based in the receiving member state, that is, someone further down the corporate hierarchy.[33]

Even assuming this difficulty can be addressed, we still need to identify the level of autonomy ascribed to the notion of editorial decision-making. This may vary widely between different broadcasters, particularly depending on where and how an individual broadcaster sources its content. The same content and scheduling may be broadcast to different member states, changed only in relation to dubbing or subtitling, meaning the local offices, in practice, have little autonomy. By contrast, it may be possible for branch offices or subsidiaries to have a greater degree of control over scheduling, or even over some elements of programme content. In this case, it is debatable whether the internal-market rationale should apply to those channels which customise programmes for their own particular markets, in effect creating a different product. In this instance, the

---

[33] C. Murroni and N. Irvine (eds.), *Quality in Broadcasting* (London: IPPR, 1997).

impact of programme-classification or scheduling requirements on the internal market will need to be reconsidered.

The operation of the jurisdiction clause becomes even more problematic when we consider the impact of interactive television and the various additional services that may be provided in addition to 'standard' or 'traditional' television. Editorial services for electronic programme guides (EPGs) may be provided by a different entity from that providing the content. In addition, some interactive services, as well as splitting the location of the service between provider and recipient, may not have much editorial content at all. Further, as we shall see below, there are problems with the concept of editorial decision-making when the broadcaster is merely retransmitting pre-packaged bundles of channels. We can thus see, as suggested in chapter 1, that changes in the broadcasting environment affect the operation of regulatory systems, as categorisations appropriate to an environment at one stage of its evolution do not fit well with it at a later stage of its evolution.

Once the location of the head office and the location of the editorial decisions are separated, the question of establishment is determined by a third factor outlined in Article 3b 'a significant part of the workforce involved in the pursuit of television broadcasting activity'. Again, this phrase has not been defined, or distinguished from any of the other terms used in the provisions. It is not clear whether dubbing and subtitling to render programming appropriate to national markets is sufficient to constitute some form of editorial input, or whether it should merely be seen as falling within the 'pursuit of television broadcasting activity', or whether it can be seen as both broadcasting activity and editorial activity. Clearly, the determination of the meaning of terms and phrases like 'head office', 'editorial decisions on programme schedules' and 'a significant part of the workforce involved in the pursuit of the television broadcasting activity' is important if we are to understand fully how a broadcasting company's structures interrelate and so ascertain which member state has jurisdiction. In paragraph 3b any failure to identify the member state which has jurisdiction leads, by default, to consideration of the head office as the place of establishment. Given that 'head office' may not do anything but act as a legal or financial base, and that it may not even see or control content for which it is technically responsible, it would seem to be more sensible to have, as the default position, the country in which editorial decisions are being made. Problems arise, of course, were this to be a third country state, as has been the case where American companies are providing content for their European subsidiaries.

Paragraph 3c highlights the difficulty of trying to identify jurisdiction when a third country, which is responsible for editorial decisions about programme schedules, is located outside the Union. Given the nature of the media industry, with the sector being dominated by a few transnational conglomerates, this may be increasingly likely to be the case. In such a case, jurisdiction is established in the member state in which the head office is located, provided that a significant part of the workforce which is involved in the pursuit of television broadcasting activity is also located there. As in *Paul Denuit*, this may not always be the case. In recognition of this point, paragraph 4 locates jurisdiction with the member state in which the satellite link or licence is located. Applying this to *Paul Denuit*, the country containing the satellite uplink, Luxembourg, could have been the country which held jurisdiction, even though editorial decisions about programming schedules were made in the USA and the content received in Belgium. Even if a programme/channel is not intended for reception in the Union, it, according to the terms of Article 2(4), can fall within the jurisdiction of a member state if the broadcaster is using capacity connected with a member state or an uplink in a member state. This could bring a number of channels not intended for the European market but using the Astra satellite within the Luxembourg jurisdiction, although there are some safeguards against this.[34]

A further change introduced by the 1997 revision of the TWFD was one that might not seem to have an immediate impact on the definition clause: that is, the definition of broadcaster, introduced in Article 1. It is, however, significant because it outlines the scope of the TWFD. Member states will have jurisdiction over broadcasters as understood in the terms of the TWFD, which might, or might not, coincide with the concepts used in the individual member states' regulatory regimes. According to Article 1(b) of the current TWFD:

> 'broadcaster' means the natural or legal person who has editorial responsibility for the composition of schedules of television programmes within the meaning of (a) and who transmits them or has them transmitted by third parties.

It can be seen that there are parallels between the concepts used here and those used to determine jurisdiction. There are similar problems with a lack of clarity as to the meaning of the terms used. The term 'broadcaster' seeks to determine some boundaries: the reference to television

---

[34] See draft second amending directive COM(2005)646 final, Article 2(6).

programmes refers to the definition of television broadcasting itself, and seeks to exclude data services. The key concept in the definition is 'editorial responsibility'. It operates to distinguish between content-based decisions and transmission decisions, thus re-emphasising the boundary between content and delivery mechanisms, again a difficult boundary to draw (see chapter 6). This still leaves unclear the question of what is 'editorial responsibility'. It is doubtful if the idea of editorial responsibility is adequate or entirely appropriate in a multi-channel environment, when companies may well be reliant on prepackaged American offerings with windows left for regional advertising or some programming. It seems editorial responsibility has to cover a wide range of circumstances reflecting the new economic reality of a vertically integrated market. The breadth of these circumstances is unhelpful for policymakers who wish to identify certain points in the broadcasting process that in their view need to be regulated. As Gibbons notes, it is not necessarily the top end of the supply chain which is central, despite the fact that it has the closest link to the traditional idea of editorial responsibility.[35]

The impact of technological change on regulatory categorisations is further complicated in the Union, since there are a number of regimes which regulate electronic communications. When the TWFD was enacted, the nature of broadcasting and thus the type of activity regulated by the TWFD seemed fairly clear if not self-evident. Broadcasting was defined in the TWFD by reference to the transmission of television programmes, with some data services being specifically excluded. As we shall see when discussing advertising (see chapter 9), this definition of broadcasting is problematic. We argue here that the definition may be inadequate. The nature of broadcasting is not so clear in these days of narrowcasting, webcasting and interactive television. The problem was becoming evident by the 1997 revision of the TWFD, when, although the actual definition of broadcasting remained the same, the distinction between near video on demand (NVOD) and video on demand (VOD) was introduced to delimit the scope of the TWFD. Without actually discussing the nature of broadcasting, it seems the European institutions have determined that the boundary between broadcasting and other 'information society' services lies here (see chapter 3). The term 'information-society service' is defined as 'any service normally provided for remuneration, at a distance, by

---

[35] T. Gibbons, 'Jurisdiction Over (Television) Broadcasters: Criteria for Defining "Broadcaster" and "Content Service Provider"', in *The Future of the 'Television without Frontiers Directive'*, Schriftenreihe des Instituts fur Europäisches Medienrecht (EMR) 29, (2004) p. 57.

electronic means and at the individual request of a recipient of services'.[36] Information-society services can be delivered via all digital communication platforms such as the Internet, 3G mobile phones and also by digital television. Although television broadcasting itself within the meaning of the TWFD is not an information-society service, because its programmes are not provided at individual request, a distinction between near video on demand (NVOD) services which broadcast to many viewers at once and video on demand (VOD) services which are broadcast to individuals has been made: NVOD is caught by TWFD; VOD is not. The difference appears to lie in the individuality of the service rather than its interactivity. NVOD is still delivered to mass audiences; although that audience may have some freedom to select a start time that suits each viewer's individual convenience, their choice is exercised within the framework of a predetermined set of options as to content and timing. VOD is not subject to these constraints. The significance of the distinction is that, currently, information-society services are subject in general terms to much lighter touch regulation than is broadcasting.[37] The viewing experience within an information-society context is therefore less carefully controlled.

In this, the TWFD is consistent with earlier views, particularly those expressed by the Commission, about the mass nature of broadcasting. Some of the problems of the boundary between broadcasting and information-society services were considered by the ECJ in *Mediakabel*,[38] which concerned pay-per-view (PPV) television. The service offered was available as follows: a subscriber had the option of ordering a film from a catalogue offered by Mediakabel; any order would be made separately, using the subscriber's remote control or telephone using a personal identification code and paying by automatic debit. After payment, the subscriber would receive an individual key which would allow him to view one or more of the sixty films on offer each month, at the times indicated on the television screen or in the programme guide. Mediakabel argued that this service was accessible only on individual request and that it should therefore be classified not as a television broadcasting service but as an information-society service supplied on individual demand within the meaning of the third sentence of Article 1(a) of Directive 89/552. The

---

[36] Art. 1 of Directive 98/34/EC as amended by Directive 98/48/EC, OJ [1998] L 217, p. 18.

[37] Definition of geographical jurisdiction might vary also: note the exception clauses in the e-commerce directives which allow for different public interest objectives to be taken into account than are listed in TWFD. For a discussion of the jurisdiction clause and exclusions in the e-commerce directive, see J. Hörnle, 'Country of Origin Regulation', *passim*.

[38] Case C-89/04 *Mediakabel BV* v. *Commissariaat voor de Media*, judgment 2 June 2005.

ECJ held that the manner in which images are transmitted is not a determining element in the assessment as to whether a service is broadcasting
or an information-society service. In this, the ECJ was following its tradition of technology neutral assessments under TWFD. The ECJ argued
that

> a pay-per-view television service, even one which is accessible to a limited
> number of subscribers, but which comprises only programmes selected by
> the broadcaster and is broadcast at times set by the broadcaster, cannot be
> regarded as being provided on individual demand.[39]

Whether this distinction remains viable with the introduction of personal
video recorders (PVRs), Internet access via television programmes and
television delivery via mobile telephone is debatable. Further, the 'push'
versus 'pull' distinction which is sometimes used to justify this boundary
is problematic. It is based on viewer choice, that is, viewers have chosen to
select and watch information-society services such as VOD, in that they
have chosen to pull the information. There is, it is argued, less need for
regulation of these services. The implicit contrast is that in the traditional
broadcasting environment viewers did not have the range of choice and
therefore content provided to these viewers needed to be more heavily
regulated. Whether this argument justifies treating VOD, which from the
viewers' perspective is not readily distinguished form NVOD, differently
from NVOD is highly questionable, as the same content may be shown
by both VOD and NVOD. As we noted in chapter 5, it is also debatable whether such an approach respects the much-vaunted principle of
technological neutrality.

The proposed solution of the European Parliament, and one that had
been raised earlier during the consultation on convergence but rejected,
was that there should be one content directive (covering all electronic
content, including television). Quite apart from the question of whether
it is possible to make a clear boundary between content and transmission,
this proposal would raise some difficult questions about the appropriate
level of regulation. Typically, point-to-point communications (and those
in which the viewer is active in selection of material rather than passive)
have been subject to lighter levels of regulation than the traditional point
to multipoint broadcast media. Additionally, the Internet breaks down
national boundaries to a greater degree. In the light of this development and the earlier introduction of satellite direct to home (DTH)

---

[39] Case C-89/04 *Mediakabel*, para. 32.

broadcasting, we can no longer talk about closed national information systems. The new technologies therefore bring into question some fundamental assumptions about the broadcast media, its function and the way its content is distributed.

These issues were discussed during the review process of the TWFD in 2005, with the Commission putting forward a proposal which sought to introduce a broader directive covering all audiovisual content, but with certain types (that is point-to-multipoint transmissions by whatever technology) being subject to a greater level of regulation. To this end, DSAD contains a definition of 'audiovisual media service' as well as television broadcasting although it too was amended during the legislative process.[40] Given the scope of audiovisual media service is potentially broad, the recitals state that DSAD does not cover non-economic activity, as well as personal correspondence by email.[41] Given the breadth of the ECJ's approach to the scope of services,[42] it is questionable how many services will actually be excluded by this definition.

A basic level of obligations is imposed on all media service providers;[43] broadcasters remain subject to extra obligations. The recitals note that 'the importance of audiovisual media services for societies, democracy and culture justifies the application of specific rules' to audiovisual media services. Interestingly, there is no attempt to justify why traditional broadcast media are subject to more stringent rules, although the explanatory memorandum highlights the importance of not restricting the market in developing services, thus suggesting a commercial emphasis to the underlying rationale of DSAD. The distinction between the two is the linear or non-linear nature of the service. Broadcasting is defined as a linear audiovisual service. Although a linear service is not defined, DSAD contains a definition of 'non-linear service', being 'an audiovisual media service where the user decides upon the moment in time when a specific

---

[40] For a description of all the elements in the 'audiovisual media service' definition, see Commission, *Non-paper on Definitions in the Proposal for an Audiovisual Media Services Directive*, February 2006, available on http://europa.eu.int/comm/avpolicy/regul/regul/_en.htm#4. See also appendix.

[41] Draft second amending directive COM(2005)646 final, Recitals 13–16.

[42] See, e.g., Joined Cases C-51/96 & 191/97 *Christelle Deliège* v. *Ligue Francophone de Judo et Disciplines Associées ASBL et al.* [2001] ECR I-2549, discussed in L. Woods, *Free Movement of Goods and Services*, pp. 172–4.

[43] These concern the protection of minors, a prohibition on the incitement to hatred, a requirement that the media service provider be identified, a requirement that commercial communications should be identified as well as some qualitative restrictions on commercial communications.

programme is transmitted on the basis of a choice of content selected by the media service provider'. Thus, DSAD draws the line for the higher obligations between NVOD and VOD. As the recitals to DSAD note, the notion of editorial responsibility is 'essential for defining the role of the media service provider' and consequently for the services covered. This indicates, as we have suggested above, that editorial responsibility is about scheduling decisions and content-packaging rather than decisions about the content in individual programmes. In this context, the meaning ascribed to editorial responsibility is counter-intuitive. Although the proposed changes mean we are less likely to have to decide which Union measure to apply (TWFD or e-Commerce Directive), nevertheless the distinction between broadcasting and information-society services remains, given the graduated approach proposed in DSAD. The question of jurisdiction will be reformulated, however, as to whether the basic regime for all audiovisual media services applies, or whether the more stringent broadcasting regime is applicable.

Conclusion

The operation of the jurisdiction clause has allowed forum shopping on the part of some broadcasters. Forum shopping threatens individual member states' approach to broadcast regulation, despite the recognised division of competence between the Union and the member states. Although to a certain extent this process had occurred under the treaty provisions, particularly Article 49 EC as relating to services, the impact of the TWFD, and particularly the ECJ's approach to jurisdiction, seems to have exacerbated this tendency. The issue of jurisdiction remains contested as member states seek to protect their cultural concerns against the impact of commercial considerations in a framework which seems to allow the dislocation of regulation and favour internal market goals.

Although the doctrine existed to allow 'exceptions' to the treaty freedoms in the form of the circumvention or anti-avoidance principle, this has been interpreted increasingly narrowly, and the ECJ has not, in practice, used it in the context of the TWFD. Despite some concern by a number of member states, this is the approach that continues to be adopted, even in a Union that, post-Nice, has not only some level of cultural competence but provisions in the Charter of Rights that recognise the importance of press (and media) diversity and pluralism. Instead, the ECJ's approach in *de Agostini* has highlighted problems with the scope of the TWFD and the fact that the original directive (and, indeed, the Amending Directive) have not fully dealt with the difference between cross-border provision of broadcasting as a communication service and the provision of different types of content.

In this context, we have seen that the idea of a broadcaster, which under-pins this distinction, has become ever more contested in an increasingly multinational environment, in which content is created, packaged and transmitted by different combinations of operators. The question, here, is whom should the TWFD be regulating and by what legislation? Tech-nological and industry developments have thus rendered the scope of broadcasting, and consequently a regulatory system based on the concept of broadcasting, unclear. There have been consequent difficulties for those operating (whether that be the industry players, the regulators or even policymakers) in that environment, which affect the viewing experience.

The changing environment also brings into focus the different types of service which may be accessed by viewers in the broadcasting environment generally. Again, boundaries of competence come into play, as different regimes impose different standards and provide different levels of protec-tion for the viewer, which the viewer may not necessarily be aware of. In particular, broadcasting regimes may focus on the needs of citizens, whilst the regulatory framework in respect of other information-society services may focus more on consumers, particularly those who are active and able to choose their own diet of content. Although DSAD seeks to clarify the proper scope of the TWFD, our concern is that it has merely reformulated the question rather than addressing the problem of the boundary between regimes.

9

Advertising placement and frequency: balancing the needs of viewers and commercial interests

Introduction

Advertising, and its proper control, are and have been contentious areas. The cross-border character of television reach, a consequence of the development of satellite technology, caused further regulatory concerns regarding jurisdiction and the control of advertising. This was particularly problematic in the light of different national approaches to the regulation of advertising.[1] The Television without Frontiers Directive (TWDF)[2] contains specific provisions to deal with advertising, so as to create Union minimum standards, but it is questionable to what extent these rules protect all viewers, whether citizen or consumer.[3]

As we argued in chapter 1, within both the commercial and public service domains, viewers have different capacities to select, engage with or opt out of content, including advertising. With the changing broadcasting environment, discussed in chapter 3, broadcasters and advertisers are adopting new advertising techniques the better to target audiences. Some of these techniques make it more difficult to separate what we shall refer to as editorial and commercial content. Editorial content refers to the informational or entertainment narrative structure, order or plot of programmes. Commercial content includes all forms of advertising, ranging from conventional adverts, interactive adverts, sponsorship and

---

[1] Case 52/79 *Debauve* [1980] E.C.R. 833, para. 12 *et seq.*

[2] Council Directive 89/552/EEC of 3 October 1989 on the co-ordination of certain provisions laid down by law, regulation or administrative action in member states concerning the pursuit of television broadcasting activities OJ [1989] L 298/23, as amended by Directive 97/36/ EC OJ [1997] L 202/30.

[3] One group so far not considered, but that should also be included within the purview of judging advertising, is that of those who create individual content items – programme producers, actors, presenters, musicians and playwrights. This group has an interest in preserving the integrity of programming, which could be affected by advertising breaks that are too frequent, or commercial breaks occurring at an inappropriate place. As yet this group is only served by rules concerning frequency or placement and not aesthetics.

product placement. The assumptions underlying the TWFD suggest that, in general, consumers are served by attempts to limit market distortions and unfair competition,[4] while citizens are served by seeing advertising superintended in ways which (should) preserve editorial freedom and independence.[5] Even at a conceptual level, the approach adopted in TWFD seems inadequate; the problems have been compounded by the interpretation of the relevant provisions.

After briefly elaborating the relationship between viewers, advertisers and broadcasters, this chapter discusses the rules on advertising placement, frequency and quantity. It provides a description of the relevant provisions before analysing their weaknesses, and identifies the impact of new techniques, whether arising from technology or commercial practice, on the regulatory framework and consequently the viewing experience. The Commission's view is that technological convergence requires an integrated approach to information-society and audiovisual policies.[6] The danger is that such an interpretation will reflect a lowest common denominator approach to regulation, so as to encourage new services (in general funded by advertising) to develop without regard to the quality of those services and the interests they might serve. The needs of passive viewers particularly seem unlikely to receive adequate attention.

Relationship between broadcasters, advertisers and viewers

Advertising and the media have coexisted for hundreds of years and have become mutually dependent. Policymakers recognise this, but also that advertising should be subject to controls. There is a need to balance a range of different views and interests; and opinions about the value of advertising differ markedly. Consideration of the viewers' position regarding advertising can be approached from a variety of perspectives. Pluralist views about advertising recognise the benefit of advertising as a means of providing consumer choice. Conversely, neo-Marxist views are critical of the corrupting effect of advertising, because they believe it encourages excessive and wasteful consumption, promotes a consumerist society and reinforces certain lifestyles over others. Post-modern cultural critics generally point to the problems inherent in the commodification of culture, the trivialisation of contemporary life and the pervasive surreptitious and

---

[4] TWFD, Recitals 17.   [5] TWFD Recital 8.

[6] Commission, *Communication i2010 – An Information Society for Growth and Employment* [SEC (2004)1028] COM (2004) 541 final. See also ch. 5.

subliminal character of advertising, especially in the context of broad-casting services. In short, advertising can be seen either as a positive or negative service, and of some or no value to viewers.

Using the distinctions made in chapter 1 between the commercial and public service domains of the viewing experience, advertising can be understood in the following ways. From consumers' points of view, advertising is positive (see chapter 2). It can act as an aid to increased understanding when wishing to make consumption choices; it can stim-ulate or improve market fairness; it can increase knowledge of product ranges; and it can both stimulate and meet personal demands. From the citizens' points of view, advertising may be dismissed as a necessary but harmless (or not, if neo-Marxists and post-modern cultural critics are to be believed) if inconvenient nuisance. Overall, these two views are, for us, a reflection and a specific manifestation of the tension between trade and non-trade values already identified in chapter 4.

There is also a more worrying side to these two views. From the point of view of consumers, advertising could equally be judged to be a reflection of market distortions (created through, for example, corporate dominance, size or monopolistic position), thereby limiting consumer choices, or subverting what neoclassical and liberal economists refer to as consumer sovereignty. While the former regard it as an ideal and the latter generally regard it as a reality of free markets, both would agree that advertising can, through its own dominance and power of persuasion, distort choice and market relations.[7] Similarly, advertising can be judged from the point of view of citizens to be something which delimits and trivialises the public sphere, especially when we regard political advertising or promotion[8] as a form of advertising.[9] Advertising can also be a serious threat, or an actual impediment, to editorial freedom and independence, because of a broadcaster's reliance on adverting revenue (a case of 'don't insult the sponsor or threaten our major advertising accounts'). In either of these cases the regulators have before them extremes to concern themselves

---

[7] Attributed to Henry Ford. Although such modern advertisers would ironically tempt you with the 'old black' or the 'new black', but then such is their artfulness.

[8] The German Government paid €50,000 in order to have its development aid policy pro-moted positively. Although the plot of the programme seems to have been influenced by the German Government's payments, there was no mention of it in the text of the credits of the series. Epd-Medien, 82 of 1 October 2005, cited in BEUC, *Revision of the 'Television without Frontiers' Directive: BEUC position paper*, BEUC/X/023/2006, p. 5.

[9] This is not the place to talk of the relationship between advertising and propaganda, but the latter is obviously a threatening delimitation of the public sphere derived as it is from advertising techniques.

with; extremes which threaten both the consumer and citizen equally, and which in their purest form reflect how advertising may, unless regulated, degenerate into systematic attempts at large-scale or mass persuasion, which controls and manipulates information and imagery to such an extent that viewers are misled. For the broadcaster, choices exist: exercise self-restraint; or face imposed rules. The former has a mixed history and the latter are necessarily inconsistent, because different advertising rules apply in different member states, to different media and to different types of products.

Overview of placement rules

Within the TWFD the advertising rules can be divided into five categories: first, those requiring the identification of advertising as such (Article 10); secondly, those relating to content standards (including the prohibition of certain types of advertising, Articles 12–16; see chapter 10); thirdly, the linked rules regarding placement, that is the question of where advertising may be broadcast; fourthly, frequency, which relates to how often (Articles 10 and 11); and fifthly, quantity (Article 18 and 18a). A separate article, Article 17, deals with sponsorship, and there are specific rules regarding teleshopping channels.

The placement rules attempt to provide a balance between the various interests represented in the broadcasting sector, though it is not particularly clear as to the emphasis on the different interests protected. Recital 26 states:

> Whereas in order to ensure that the interests of consumers as television viewers are fully and properly protected, it is essential for television advertising to be subject to a certain number of minimum rules and standards . . . .[10]

This recital implies that the main concern of the advertising rules is consumer-oriented. By contrast, other recitals highlight the importance of content diversity and quality in the broadcasting environment, issues which are linked, though not exclusively, to the citizen-based model of viewing.[11] None the less, most of the interests identified seem to be principally those of the broadcaster and of consumer viewers. The fact that the role of advertisers and the weighting to be given to their interests is not specifically addressed in the recitals may have been a factor in the difficult

---

[10] See also Recital 27 TWFD.   [11] Recitals 4, 44 and 45, Directive 97/36/EC.

case law on Article 11 discussed below. It is notable that the *Explanatory Memorandum to the Convention on Transfrontier Television* (CTT), the treaty negotiated within the Council of Europe at broadly the same time as TWFD was enacted, states that the CTT, and its equivalent frequency rules, aims to establish a reasonable balance between the financial interests of the broadcaster and advertiser, on the one hand, and the interests of viewers, authors and creators of programmes, on the other.[12] The assumption underpinning the CTT seems to be that the interests of the broadcasters are commercial, and in some respects are in an adversarial relationship with the needs of the viewer. The TWFD is not so clear on its position about this relationship.

Although advertising is permitted in principle, despite previous prohibitions in some member states, it is limited, in particular as to quantity, frequency and placement. Individual member states may impose more restrictions on broadcasters established within that state's jurisdiction,[13] although some concerns have been expressed as to the amount of discretion member states should be permitted in this regard.[14] Although this may go some way to alleviating the concerns of the more interventionist member states,[15] such member states cannot impose standards higher than those set down in the TWFD on broadcasters established in another member state.[16]

One of the problems encountered in the regulation of advertising is how to identify the difference between commercial broadcasting (which consists of advertising, sponsorship and other forms of commercial communications) and editorial content (which, broadly speaking, consists of the programmes). Although there are difficulties with this distinction, discussed below, the TWFD attempts to distinguish between the two types

---

[12] Council of Europe, *Explanatory Memorandum to the Convention on Transfrontier Television*, para. 245 and Case C-245/01 *RTL* v. *Niedersächsische Landesmedienanstalt für privaten Rundfunk*, [2003] nyr, judgment 23 October 2003, paras. 62–3 and 65.

[13] Article 3(1) TWFD. There are technical arguments about the relationship between this general provision permitting member states to impose higher standards and Article 20, which applies in terms of domestic broadcasts, and which allows member states the possibility of laying down 'other' rules. At a practical level, it may be that this issue is of limited significance, as Article 20 is expressed to apply without prejudice to Article 3.

[14] Commission, *Issues Paper: Commercial Communications* (2005), p. 5.

[15] Note comments of Advocate-General Jacobs in Joined Cases C-320, 328, 329 and 337–9/94 *RTI* v. *Ministero delle Poste e Telecomunicazioni* [1996] ECR I-6471, who argued at para. 30 of his opinion that '[s]ince . . . the Directive is a minimum harmonisation measure, I consider any ambiguity in the Directive should be construed in favour of a broad discretion for Member States when implementing its provisions'.

[16] Joined Cases C-320, 328, 329 and 337–9/94 *RTI* , para. 45.

of material via what are sometimes called the principles of separation and of due recognition.[17] They are supported by the requirement that there should be no confusion between the editorial and commercial material.[18] Both these principles find legal form in the requirement in Article 10 that advertising should occur between programmes and should be identifiable as such. Article 10 further specifies that certain advertising techniques, which would blur the boundaries between editorial content and advertising, should be prohibited. So, subliminal techniques,[19] as well as surreptitious advertising,[20] are not permissible.[21] The issue of product placement in this context has been extensively discussed during the current review of the TWFD (see further below and appendix).

Advertising *during* programmes is the exception rather than the rule and is therefore subject to conditions.[22] In a traditional linear television environment, separation is normally regarded as a temporal matter rather than as a spatial consideration; certainly the text of Article 11 can be read as reaffirming such a view. This interpretation (including the more detailed rules described in the next paragraph) has come under threat with the advent of non-linear services, as we shall see below. Article 11 illustrates another concern: that advertising can impair the broadcasting service itself, by disrupting the flow of the programming. Article 11(1) therefore refers to the need to protect the 'integrity of the programme'. In so doing, it seeks to protect not just viewers but also authors (or other right-holders) of the programme itself.[23] Thus any exception to the principle that advertising occurs between programmes and not during them should be interpreted in the light of the underlying principles in Article 11(1); that is, since commercial breaks during a programme are themselves exceptions, they must not undermine the integrity of any programme.[24]

The remaining subparagraphs in Article 11 provide exceptions to the general principle that programmes should not be interrupted by commercial breaks. They can be seen as defining a number of general rules regarding the frequency of advertising. These are: the 20-minute rule;

---

[17] Article 10(1) TWFD; see also Recital 37 of Directive 97/36/EC and Article 18a(1), in relation to teleshopping windows.

[18] See Commission, *Interpretative Communication*, para. 19, referring to the *Explanatory Report to the European Convention on Transfrontier Television*.

[19] Article 10(3) TWFD.

[20] Defined in Article 1(d) TWFD. On product placement see also Article 17(1)c, concerning sponsored programmes.

[21] Article 10(4), TWFD.   [22] Article 11 TWFD.

[23] Case C-245/01 *RTL*, paras. 62–3.   [24] Case C-245/01 *RTL*, Opinion, para. 36.

the autonomous parts rule; and special rules that apply to specific types of programme. The TWFD, however, contains no rules about the interruption of one programme by another, for example a film by the news, which might be equally detrimental to a programme's narrative integrity. It is therefore uncertain what the legislator's views are on this particular matter and whether this lack of rules implies an implicit value judgment, indifference, confusion or lack of competence in this area. The TWFD also contains no rules about the frequency of particular advertisements; it seems possible, subject to practical considerations on the part of the broadcaster and advertiser, to broadcast repeatedly the same advertisement within the permitted advertising breaks.

The 20-minute rule can be seen as constituting the general frequency rule and, as the nomenclature might suggest, the basic principle is that each successive internal advertising break after the first such break must be at least 20 minutes after its predecessor. There is no minimum period before the first advertising break is permitted. This rule does not apply in certain programmes. This category concerns all types of programmes which are made up of autonomous parts (such as the broadcast of a football match), and in respect of such programmes advertising breaks may only be taken between the parts, and not during the parts themselves.

Three particular types of programme have been identified as needing greater protection from inappropriate or excessive advertising: first, those with a certain type of audience, for example children's programmes; secondly, certain types of cultural or informational programmes, for example religious programming and news; thirdly, 'audiovisual works such as feature films and films made for television (excluding series, serials, light entertainment programmes and documentaries)'.[25] All three are regarded as in need of protection from an overly commercialised environment, although the reason for the special treatment of the third category of programmes is not clear. One argument is that its narrative nature requires fewer interruptions, otherwise its dramatic integrity is lost. Another argument for a protectionist stance is that the popularity of films with audiences suggests that this style of programme is more likely to be abused by broadcasters inserting a lot of advertising. The extra limitations affect frequency of advertising breaks (films); specify the minimum length of programme that can be interrupted (documentaries, news, children's programmes); and include an absolute prohibition on advertising during a religious service. With the exception of the latter,

[25] Article 11(3) TWFD.

the 20-minute rule will also apply to frequency of advertising, save where the programme is in autonomous parts. Although this collection of provisions is not entirely coherent, these provisions reflect concerns about the impact of broadcasting and protection of certain citizens' interests in relation to particular types of programming.

Specific rules apply to sponsorship and teleshopping. The relevant provisions contain both content and placement rules, although content will not be discussed here (see chapter 10). In addition to introducing the principle that sponsorship must be identified as such,[26] the provisions relating to sponsorship emphasise the importance of editorial independence of programme makers.[27] As noted, the news may not be sponsored.[28] Although the producers of certain products are excluded from sponsoring programmes, the news is the only excluded category of programming. It therefore seems religious programmes may be sponsored, which does not seem to fit in with the 'special treatment' awarded to such programmes in relation to the permissibility of advertising breaks. From the foregoing, it is reasonable to argue that any coherence about the principles being protected by prohibiting advertising breaks is undermined.

Article 18 deals with permitted quantity of advertising in respect of channels other than teleshopping channels. Article 18(1) provides that the maximum amount of advertising spots, teleshopping spots and other forms of advertising (excluding teleshopping windows regulated by Article 18a) is 20 per cent of transmission time; advertising spots cannot take up more than 15 per cent of daily transmission time. To prevent all advertising slots being concentrated in the peak evening viewing hours, with obvious adverse consequences for viewers through the risk posed to the integrity of works, Article 18(2) specifies that no more than 20 per cent of a given clock hour may be devoted to advertising spots and teleshopping spots. In making the relevant calculations, Article 18(3) specifies that self-promotion and public service announcements are not included. These rules are applied to channels devoted to teleshopping, except for the restrictions on the amount of teleshopping content itself.

Problems arising from the operation of the advertising rules

Article 10 sets the principles by which advertising may be lawfully broadcast; it does not define advertising itself. A definition is found in the general definition section, Article 1 TWFD. Advertising is there defined as

---

[26] Article 17(1)(b) TWFD.   [27] Article 17(1)(a) TWFD.   [28] Article 17(4) TWFD.

any form of announcement broadcast whether in return for payment or for similar consideration or broadcast for self-promotional purposes by a public or private undertaking in connection with a trade, business, craft or profession in order to promote the supply of goods or services, including immobile property, rights and obligations, in return for payment.[29]

The definition section identifies other forms of commercial content, such as sponsorship and teleshopping, which are distinct concepts from that of advertising, although sponsorship, at least, could fall within the definition of advertising. All these forms of commercial content should be viewed in contrast to editorial content. The draft second amending directive (DSAD)[30] follows the broad approach of distinguishing commercial communications in general from editorial content, by introducing an overarching concept of 'audiovisual commercial communication' in contrast to 'audiovisual media service'.[31]

As noted, Article 10 is based on the principles of separation of editorial and commercial content and identification of commercial content. If these principles are not complied with, however, it can sometimes be difficult to identify advertising. One area in which it is not clear whether we are dealing with advertising or not is the use of products during programmes, and the boundary between acceptable product placement and surreptitious advertising. A particular difficulty is the identification of surreptitious advertising, a problem which may have adverse consequences for the values (such as editorial independence, as well as protection of viewers directly) which the advertising rules aim to protect. Although Article 10(4) prohibits surreptitious advertising, there is a weakness in this prohibition. It has been noted that the terms of Article 10 are phrased in quite technical language and the provision does not therefore cover all forms of commercial influence.[32] Within the terms of Article 1(d), which defines surreptitious advertising in TWFD, it is the commercial intent behind the placement of the product on the part of the broadcaster that seems important and this may be difficult to

---

[29] Article 1(c). Note the definition in the CTT is broader than this.
[30] Commission, *Proposal for a Directive amending Directive 89/552/EEC*, COM (2005) 646 final, 2005/0260 (COD), SEC (2005) 1625 and 1626.
[31] Articles 1(a) and 1(f), draft second amending directive, COM (2005) 646 final.
[32] G. Schuman, *Regulation of Advertising in the New Television without Frontiers Directive: Background Paper for the Plenary* EPRA/2001/08, 26–8 September 2001, p. 6, suggested an alternative principle: 'Advertisements and advertisers shall not influence programming content in any way.'

prove.[33] In its *Interpretative Communication*, the Commission suggested that an appropriate test would be one of 'undue prominence', whether this is in terms of recurring presence, or the manner in which the product or service is presented.[34] This approach leaves difficult questions of assessment to the national regulatory authorities, meaning that assessments could vary between member states.

The difficulties of preventing surreptitious advertising or regulating product placement,[35] especially where the editorial content originates from outside the Union or, in general, outside the broadcaster's control, have been noted.[36] Whether the solution is to abandon regulation of this phenomenon or to distinguish between acceptable forms of product placement and unacceptable surreptitious advertising poses the following dilemma. Should concerns regarding competition between broadcasters and programme makers for revenue be prioritised over those which aim to protect viewers (particularly vulnerable groups such as children) and the integrity of content? We might have quite different views on the answer depending on the type of product and programme involved. The news, for example, receives special treatment in respect of frequency of advertising breaks and the sponsorship rules because of its significance for informing the public. On this basis, the acceptance of surreptitious advertising or even product placement in such programming is undesirable.[37]

These issues have been discussed in the context of the second review of the TWFD. In general, it seems accepted that product placement is here to stay, at least by advertisers and commercial broadcasters. Their concern is that, with the development of technologies which allow viewers to sidestep watching advertising (via the use of devices such as personal video recorders (PVRs)), integrating the advertising in programmes is

---

[33] A drafting solution to this problem would be to remove the reference to 'by the broadcaster' in the definition of 'surreptitious advertising' in Article 1(d).

[34] Commission, *Interpretative Communication*, para. 33.

[35] Product placement can be considered to be the prominence of commercial products, trade marks and business logos within an editorial programme such as the broadcast of sport events, game shows or films; note also the difficulties arising from comments about ancillary products or services within editorial content.

[36] Council of Europe, *Standing Committee of Transfrontier Television Final Version of the Discussion Document prepared by the Delegate of Austria on Questions concerning Advertising, Sponsorship and Teleshopping* (T-TT (2004)013), 15 September 2004.

[37] See in respect of the proposed Article 3(h) of the draft second amending directive, BEUC, *Position Paper*, BEUC/X/023/2006, pp. 4–6.

the only way to maintain an income stream.[38] Whether one accepts this argument, that PVRs change viewers' relationship to advertising or not,[39] policymakers within the Union seem to have accepted this technology-based argument and have sought to address industry concerns. The new proposal, to enhance competitiveness of the Union broadcasting industry, allows product placement subject to certain conditions.[40] Surreptitious advertising remains prohibited.[41]

The crucial distinction between surreptitious advertising and product placement is that surreptitious advertising 'might mislead the public as to its nature'. How this distinction is to be made in practice is unclear. A number of respondents to the Commission's *Issue Paper on Commercial Communications* did comment that permitting product placement should not mean that the rules protecting particular types of programming should be undermined. It seems DSAD applies the general rules for advertising to product placement. It is, indeed, debatable whether a solution such as informing viewers at the beginning of a programme that product placement will occur during the programme is in all instances, or for all viewers, sufficient protection (see chapter 1). It also does not address the impact that product placement may have on the actual content of the programme. In the American context, screenwriters have complained that the need to attract and retain finance through product placement has put them under pressure to develop plots or characters in certain ways that they would not otherwise have chosen to do.[42]

The separation principle raises other issues. There are two underlying problems: the first relates to the definitions of advertising and other terms; the second concerns the framework within which the regulatory system has been designed to operate, that is the traditional, linear broadcasting environment. The difficulty with the separation principle is that it relies on understanding what a programme is in terms of a specific unit of content, as opposed to its commercial content. Although advertising is defined,

---

[38] Parliament, Press Release 'How to Modernise European Television Rules', 20060529-IPR08506, 2 June 2006, p. 1. Contrast analysis by BEUC, *Position Paper*, pp. 4–5.

[39] We argue that the use of the PVR is, in this context, no different in principle from fast forwarding through the advertisements using a video recorder or DVD player, and is in the same family of action as using the mute facility or leaving the room.

[40] Draft directive COM (2005) 646 final, Article 3(h).

[41] Draft directive COM (2005) 646 final, Article 3(g)(a).

[42] Writers Guild of America, west, *Press Release*, 'Entertainment Guilds Call for Industry Code of Conduct or FCC Regulation for Product Integration in Programming and Film – Guilds Issue White Paper Report on the Runaway Use of Stealth Advertising in Television and Film', 14 November 2005, available at www.wga.org/subpage_newsevents.aspx?id = 1422

the concept of a programme is not. It seems 'programme' is taken as self-evident. With the introduction of new advertising techniques, boundaries between editorial and commercial content may become blurred.[43]

It seems that the conception of 'programme' used in the advertising provisions envisages editorial content to refer to a specific item with a coherent structure.[44] Such an approach implies that the editorial content will have a beginning and an end (and, presumably, a middle). We then can identify the point between the end of one programme and the beginning of the next, during which advertising is permissible; or where we can identify the duration of the programme in order to identify the number of permissible internal advertising breaks. The difficulty is that we have no criteria by which to identify the beginning and end of a programme. Of course, it is possible to suggest such criteria, whether by form (opening and closing credits) or by substance (when the action draws to a close, the end of a game, for example).[45] Problems arise with the development of some relatively recent approaches to scheduling and channel formats. A rolling news channel need not demonstrate either the formal criteria of opening and closing credits as the news feed is continuous, nor is there any necessary narrative coherence to enable the end of the action to be identified. News programmes tend to be made up of lots of short news items. This means that there would be a greater reliance on criteria relating to the form of the programme and it is such formal criteria that would seem more open to manipulation. Other forms of television channels also illustrate this difficulty, for example, music channels based on the broadcast of successive pop videos.

The difference could be significant: lots of short programmes might allow for greater advertising frequency than the 20-minute rule might allow, or even as the autonomous parts rule would permit. Whereas internal advertising is subject to rules on quantity of advertising and frequency within programmes, advertising between programmes is subject only to the requirement that 'isolated advertising and teleshopping spots shall remain the exception.'[46] On this basis, the overall quantity rules

---

[43] The concept of a teleopromotion, recognised in Joined Cases C-320, 328, 329 and 337–9/94 *RTI* , does not yet seem to have made it into the English language: advertorial and infomercial are both found in the *Oxford English Dictionary*.

[44] L. Woods and A. Scheuer, 'Advertising Frequency and the Television without Frontiers Directive', *EL Rev* 29 (2004), 366–84, p. 374.

[45] See Woods and Scheuer, 'Advertising Frequency', pp. 374–5 for a more detailed discussion of these points.

[46] Article 10(3) TWFD.

in Article 18 become more significant in protecting viewers from excessive advertising. As we shall see, quantity rules become significantly more problematic in a digital, interactive environment. The determination of the beginning and end of a programme will have significance for identifying the nature of the programme and, consequently, the rules that apply to it.

Another concern arises in respect of the relationship between the two main frequency rules: the 20-minute rule; and the autonomous parts rule, which apply in the alternative. Applying one or other rule might affect permitted advertising frequency, as some programmes broadcast in autonomous parts (such as a boxing match with its temporal structure of highly specified rounds and rests) might permit very frequent advertising breaks.[47] At the other end of the scale, a broadcast motor race might not permit any such 'natural' or temporally specific breaks. A pragmatic compromise has been reached which permits broadcasters to allow some advertising breaks in more flexibly structured events.[48] Problems remain, however, in regard to what constitutes an interval; does it include an interruption in play, perhaps because of an injury to one of the players, a wicket taken or a pit stop, etc.?[49] The Commission's *Interpretative Communication* leaves this question open, although it does specify that Article 11(2) 'does not cover single accidental breaks'.[50] Does this mean that rain stopping play at Wimbledon (not, in most years, an isolated occurrence) could constitute a break?

For some broadcasting or scheduling techniques, it is not necessarily clear whether the programme is a series of programmes or one programme, possibly in autonomous parts. This can be seen in the case of children's programming, in which omnibus programmes are made up of a mixture of content. This can range from a situation where there is effectively a series of programmes linked by extended continuity announcements, through to a programme which has more editorial content surrounding other individual programme elements, which might be seen as constituting programmes in their own right.[51] The precise

---

[47] See *Explanatory Memorandum* to the CTT for types of programmes which are viewed as being in autonomous parts for the purposes of the CTT.

[48] Commission, *Interpretative Communication*, paras. 23–4.

[49] Council of Europe, T-TT (2004) 013, p. 15, notes the need for flexible interpretation of the equivalent provision in the CTT where artificial breaks might be justified; creating artificial breaks is, however, not permissible. See also document T-TT (2002) 19 regarding interruptions in play.

[50] Commission, *Interpretative Communication*, para. 23.

[51] See Woods and Scheuer, 'Advertising Frequency', pp. 376–7.

boundary between a series of programmes and programmes in parts is not entirely clear. Given the extra protection awarded to children's programming regarding the amount of advertising, the distinction might be important.

The issue of genres generally raises problems, as it does in other contexts such as the application of the quota rules (chapter 11 and, possibly, the determination of the scope of public service broadcasting (PSB), chapter 13). We have seen that some types of programming, for example news, have been awarded special protection. The scope of these protected genres has not been defined. The issue of the definition of genre types arose in *RTL*, concerning the scope of the provisions relating to 'audiovisual work'. This term is defined in Article 11(3) by a non-exhaustive list, with certain categories of programming being specifically excluded from its scope. In *RTL*, the broadcaster sought to argue that a number of films, which normally fall clearly within the scope of Article 11(3), fell outside its scope as they constituted a series, one of the categories of programming excluded from Article 11(3). The European Court of Justice (ECJ) rejected this argument, endorsing the view of the Advocate-General that, for a series to exist, the individual programmes making up the series must either share a continuing dramatic narrative or share characters. In coming to this conclusion, the ECJ emphasised that Article 11(3) should be interpreted in the light of its purpose; accepting the broadcaster's argument 'would make it possible for the increased protection to be circumvented and would therefore risk rendering it illusory'.[52] In making this statement, the ECJ emphasised the role Article 11 plays in balancing the competing interests in the broadcasting environment, and the need to protect the interests of the viewers and programme rights holders. The emphasis in *RTL* on the underlying purpose of Article 11 contrasts with the approach taken in the earlier *ProSieben* case.[53]

ProSieben concerned the calculation of the length, or in the terms of the TWFD, the 'scheduled duration'[54] of a programme for the purposes of calculating the number of breaks permitted by both Article 11(3) and Article 11(5). The argument centred on the question of whether the net or the gross principle should be used, that is, whether the advertising breaks

---

[52] Case C-245/01 *RTL Television GmbH* v. *Niedersächsische Landesmedienanstalt für privaten Rundfunk*, judgment 23 October 2003, para. 103.

[53] Case C-6/98 *Arbeitsgemeinschaft Rundfunkanstalten* (ARD) v. *Pro Sieben Media AG* [1999] ECR I-7599. For commentary, see R. Mastrioanni, 'Commentary on Case C-6/98 *Arbeitsgemeinschaft Rundfunkanstalten* (ARD) v. *PRO Sieben Media AG' CMLRev* 37 (2000), 1445.

[54] The CTT uses the term 'duration', which is arguably different in meaning.

themselves should be included in the calculation to find the programme's length.[55] Viewers' interests, assuming that they lie in limiting the amount of commercial breaks, would lie in just counting the length of the editorial material itself; those of the advertisers and broadcasters would lie in taking the combined figure. Despite the fact that it is illogical to suggest that one determines the legality of an advertisement by reference to the fact that it has already been broadcast, the ECJ took the approach that calculates duration by reference to the advertising plus the editorial content. Such an approach undermined the protection in Article 11(3) and 11(5). It would also seem to be inconsistent with the approach in the later *RTL* case, with its express reference to the interests of viewers and rights holders.

It is questionable which case reflects the better approach, following the review process of the TWFD. In the review, the rules relating to the insertion of advertising breaks have come under threat, particularly from commercial broadcasters and advertisers. Consumer groups (i.e. the groups representing the interests of consumers which responded to the second TWFD review) have not been so keen on any relaxation of these rules. None the less, DSAD proposes a significant 'simplification' or liberalisation of the rules, in that the 20-minute rule and autonomous parts rule have been deleted. Broadcasters can thus choose when to insert advertising breaks, the suggestion being that broadcasters will automatically do so at natural breaks in the action. Whilst some broadcasters may do so, there is a clear possibility that some broadcasters might abuse the relaxation of the rules and insert many advertising breaks, possibly many mini-spots. The rules relating to special types of programmes have been consolidated into a rule which permits one advertising break for every 35 minutes, arguably removing some of the difficulties arising from the different approaches, both as regards different types of programme and between advertising and sponsorship. Whether it has done so at an unacceptable cost by watering down the protection awarded to some programmes, notably religious programmes, is debatable. More significantly, however, news programmes and children's programmes receive greater protection than under the current system. In this regard, at least, DSAD seems sympathetic to viewers' interests and has raised the ire of some broadcasters.[56]

The calculation of frequency of advertising breaks, as well as their overall quantity, becomes more problematic when we consider split-screen

---

[55] For practical difficulties in determining scheduled duration, see Woods and Scheuer, 'Advertising Frequency', pp. 379–81.

[56] ITV, Channel 4 and Five, *The Proposed Audiovisual Media Services Directive: ITV, Channel Four and Five Perspective* (2006), p. 2. Contrast views of BEUC, *Position Paper*, p. 10.

broadcasting. It would seem that split-screen advertising, which occurs only during commercial breaks, should not cause a problem. The position with regard to commercial material (even self-promotional material) being broadcast at the same time as editorial material is more difficult; it is this aspect that is dealt with as 'split-screen advertising' within the *Interpretative Communication*. On one view, such advertising should not be permitted, as it does not respect the principle of separation. Some have taken the view that the principle of separation need not be limited to just temporal separation, but can be satisfied also by spatial separation, provided that the advertising feed is identifiable as such.[57] Spatial separation is when the advertising feed is confined to one part of the screen, the editorial content being broadcast in another, clearly defined, window.

Although this is a pragmatic solution, it does not correspond to the wording of the TWFD and reflects an approach to regulation that arguably sees the application of the rules as optional. It seems that where the rules do not fit industry practice the rules are changed, rather than industry practice limiting itself to what is permitted by law. None the less, this is the approach that the *Interpretative Communication* suggests in relation to Article 10 and, in principle, to Article 11.[58] The following caveats are added: the consent of rights holders must be sought and in any event the split-screen advertising must not prejudice the integrity of the programme. Presumably such an approach could limit, for example, the amount of the screen which it would be permissible to devote to advertising, and also affect the question of whether commercial audio feeds would be permitted. This still leaves problems in the calculation of overall frequency and quantity of advertising.

The issue of split-screen broadcasting is one of a group of issues arising from the development of digital technology which was simply not addressed by the TWFD, either in its original form or when it was amended in 1997. As the Commission noted in its *Interpretative Communication*, when referring to the earlier *Communication on Principles and Guidelines for the Community's Audiovisual Policy in the Digital Age*,[59] 'the point is not to restrict the development of new advertising techniques but to ensure that basic principles . . . continue to apply'.[60] Interactive television

---

[57] See Council of Europe, *Opinion on Split-Screen Advertising*, No. 9 (2002), which identifies criteria against which the acceptability of split-screen advertising may be assessed.

[58] Commission, *Interpretative Communication*, para. 46.

[59] Commission, *Communication on Principles and Guidelines for the Community's Audiovisual Policy in the Digital Age*, COM (1999) 657 final.

[60] Commission, *Interpretative Communication*, para. 37.

can introduce further new techniques not expressly dealt with by the TWFD. 'Interactive services' is a term that covers a broad range of services that can be provided over communications infrastructure (see chapter 3): seen broadly, it could also cover services provided over the Internet. The Union, shortly after it amended the TWFD, enacted the Information Society Directive.[61] As we saw in chapter 8, services which fall within that directive should not be dealt with under the TWFD, though the borderline between the two may not always be clear.[62] Certainly, a number of different varieties of interactive television services may be identified.[63] After its 2000 consultation exercise, the Independent Television Commission (ITC), the former television regulator in the UK, commented that the distinguishing characteristic of interactive television services was

> the ability of viewers to interact with TV programmes by one of two methods: by changing the content which appears on the screen – for example to access background information, to change camera angles, to view more than one picture at a time, or to view associated text at the same time as a main picture; or by providing information to the broadcaster through a return path, usually a telephone line – for example to order a product, to exercise 'votes' on options provided by a programme or to participate in an on-screen quiz show.[64]

The Commission has suggested that interactive advertising is an information-society service and therefore falls outside the scope of the TWFD. The Commission has also suggested that 'as long as the viewer has not voluntarily chosen to enter the interactive environment, the context is one of a linear broadcast of television programmes governed by the Television without Frontiers Directive'.[65] This division does not

---

[61] Directive 98/34/EC laying down a procedure for the provision of information in the field of technical standards and regulations OJ [1998] L 204/37, as amended by Directive 98/48 OJ [1998] L 217/18.

[62] Case C-89/04 *Mediakabel*, judgment 2 June 2005.

[63] The ITC identified three categories: enhanced programme services, which can be divided into two groups – editorial enhancements and advertising enhancements; and advertising enhancements to advertising. 'Guidance to Broadcasters on the Regulation of Interactive Television Services', February 2001.

[64] ITC, *Guidance to Broadcasters on Interactive Television Services*, February 2001, para. 4. It should be noted that using the Internet as a means of access to television broadcasting, even if it is provided on an 'unedited basis' (such as the 24-hour access to the 'Big Brother' house), does not necessarily constitute interactive television. Equally, using a television to access the Internet would not seem to constitute broadcasting; certainly the broadcasters would have little control over Internet content unless provided in a 'walled-garden' environment.

[65] Commission, *Interpretative Communication*, para. 58.

necessarily reflect the approach adopted by the regulators in each of the member states in this regard.

In this context, it is notable that one of the issues discussed in the *Commercial Communications Issues Paper* was a new definition of 'audiovisual commercial communication' which would have sub-categories such as traditional advertising, product placement and interactive advertising. It was proposed that a basic tier of rules would apply across all audiovisual commercial communications, with more stringent rules applying to specific categories of advertising transmitted in a more traditional environment.[66] This approach seems to have been adopted in DSAD, though how one draws the boundaries between the categories and where they lie is as yet uncertain (see chapters 8 and 10).[67]

Interactive television changes the relationship between viewer and broadcaster. The passive role of the viewer in traditional broadcasting changes to one in which viewers make more choices about what they get to see (see chapter 1). This fact has been used to suggest that interactive television should not be regulated as heavily as traditional television (in so far as it is viewed as television at all) (see chapter 8). Viewers' choices in such a context might, however, not be informed choices, as they might not know whether they are going from editorial material to commercial material. As far as the key concepts of separation and identification are concerned, unregulated use of interactive television could be seen as problematic in this regard. The introduction of commercial material during the programme, in addition to the 'scheduled' interruptions, becomes possible. It becomes more difficult, if not impossible, to assess whether the '20-minute rule' or the 'autonomous parts rule' has been satisfied when it is the viewer who is choosing when to click on the icon or button, and there is therefore no fixed point at which advertising starts. Of course, given the proposed deletion of these rules, this might cease to be a problem, at least from a regulator's perspective, although it may well remain a difficulty for the viewer.

The problem that a viewer might not be making an informed choice about accessing commercial material also contravenes the principle of identification. It has been suggested that the solution to this problem is to require an intermediate screen between the programme content and the commercial interactive content.[68] Requiring an intermediate screen

---

[66] Commission, *Commercial Communications Issues Paper*, p. 2.
[67] Draft second amending directive COM (2005) 646 final, Article 1(g)–(k).
[68] ITC, *Guidance to Broadcasters on Interactive Television* (2001), p. 7.

means that when viewers choose to proceed, they are doing so in the knowledge that they are interrupting the editorial material for commercial material, at least dealing with the issue of identification and knowledge. None the less, viewers would still not know the type of material for which they have interrupted their viewing until they have already exercised that choice. The ITC therefore suggested that this first 'page' of interactive content should contain at least some editorial material. Presumably the programme itself could indicate when interactive editorial material designed to enhance programme content is available.

It may be that broadcasters can find some way to distinguish between 'pulling' editorial material and 'pulling' commercial material; for example, by using different coloured buttons. The interactive icon or button itself is on the screen at the same time and therefore not separate from the programme; one could argue that this constitutes a form of 'surreptitious advertising', depending on the information included on that button.[69] Although the viewer is exercising some choice, it must not be forgotten that it is the broadcaster which has chosen to introduce the interactive feature and therefore controls the choice of content or services available. In the ITC's 2000 consultation, some concern was expressed about these points, as well as the impact on linear-programme integrity if commercial content is unlimited. Because of the potential impact on programme integrity, the frequency at which interactive advertising material may be accessed should be subject to the frequency rules; and the rules in Article 11(5). The DSAD expresses the idea that the separation principle should not prevent new forms of advertising; the identification principle is not so limited.

The rules on quantity may seem to be one of the least problematic provisions of those relating to advertising, and yet it is not as simple as it appears. There are a number of specific drafting problems, for example, concerning the identification of clock hour, and even what constitutes a 'day'.[70] Some commentators have noted that, given the hourly maximum on advertising, the daily limits are unnecessary, and this view has also come through in the opinions of some respondents to the Commission's *Issues Papers*.[71] There are other problems which highlight once again the difficulties in delineating clearly between different types of content. These problems concern not just the boundary between commercial and editorial

---

[69] The ITC has suggested that the button cannot be sponsored: see ITC *Guidance on Interactive Television*, p. 6.

[70] Commission, *Interpretative Communication*, para. 9 *et seq.*

[71] This question was also raised in the *Commercial Communications Issues Paper*.

content but also distinctions between different types of commercial communications. The TWFD distinguished between a number of different types of commercial communication: advertising; teleshopping; advertising spots; advertising windows; sponsorship; surreptitious advertising; product placement; and self-promotion. Different rules apply to these different forms of communication. The interrelationship between the rules can give rise to difficulties, as different regimes apply to the different types of commercial communication.

In particular, further problems arise concerning the relationship between Article 18 and the provisions dealing with sponsorship. It has been suggested that, despite the reference in Article 18(1) to 'other forms of advertising', sponsorship should not be included in any calculations for the purposes of Article 18. To include it in the calculation would limit the amount of traditional spot advertising permitted. It would seem that this argument has some textual support. Sponsorship, which is defined differently from advertising,[72] is subject to its own regime under Article 17. Certainly, it would not be included in Article 18(2) calculations. None the less, although the regulatory regime is based on a distinction between sponsorship and advertising, the boundary between the two is not clear, and it is possible that the broad definition of advertising could include some forms of sponsorship. Certainly, the practice could blur the boundaries, as an example from the UK illustrates. Heinz sponsored a programme on healthy eating. The programme maker was found to have taken steps to erect a 'Chinese wall', which meant that the editorial process was not influenced by Heinz and so no finding of a violation was made. The ITC did note that this case lay close to the boundary of what would be acceptable and stated that '. . . generic references to the sponsor's products came very close to having an overall promotional effect for Heinz . . . .'[73]

The regulations also depend on the distinction between teleshopping and other forms of advertising. Teleshopping is defined in Article 1(f) as 'direct offers broadcast to the public with a view to the supply of goods or services, including immovable property, rights and obligations, in return for payment'. Whether this definition is sufficient, especially in the light

---

[72] 'Sponsorship', defined at Article 1(e), 'means any contribution made by a public or private undertaking not engaged in television broadcasting activities or in the production of audio-visual works, to the financing of television programmes with a view to promoting its name, its trade mark, its image, its activities or its products'.

[73] ITC, *Programme Complaints and Findings Report* 22. See also comments of BEUC, *Position Paper*, p. 4.

of interactive television and the development of e-commerce in general, is another question. In its submission on the review of the TWFD, the Association for Commercial Television argued that the definition of teleshopping needed to be amended to make it clear that this activity did not fall within the definition of advertising in Article 1(c), a point with which the EBU concurred during the same exercise.

A further distinction concerns the boundary between advertising, the purposes of the advertising calculation and the categories excluded by virtue of Article 18(2), that is, self-promotional activities. The problems relating to self-promotional activities are twofold: first, this category's precise scope needs to be identified; secondly, there is a definitional question of whether self-promotion is seen as constituting a form of advertising or not. Broadcasters' own promotional activities fall within the scope of the TWFD.[74] The definition of advertising in the TWFD specifically includes 'broadcast for self-promotional purposes',[75] although the recitals recognise that this was at the time of the first review of a new area and that provisions concerning self-promotion may be subject to particular review in the future.[76] Further, we can see the only express reference to self-promotional activities lies in Article 18(3), which specifies that it is for the purpose of that article alone, i.e. the calculation of amount of advertising. Advertising does not include 'announcements made by the broadcaster in connection with its own programmes and ancillary products directly derived from those programmes', a statement which reflects the terms of Recital 34.[77] This would suggest that the placement rules on advertising do not affect such self-promotional broadcasts, although Recital 39 throws some doubt on the matter. It states:

> whereas it is necessary to make clear that self-promotional activities are a particular form of advertising in which the broadcaster promotes its own products, services, programmes or channels; whereas, in particular, trailers consisting of extracts from programmes should be treated as programmes . . .

There is conceptual confusion here. Further, as with the case for the interruption of editorial content by editorial content (for example, when a

---

[74] The provisions on self-promotion were introduced by the 1997 amendments, at quite a late stage in the drafting process, at the request of the British Government.

[75] Article 1(c) TWFD.   [76] Recital 39 TWFD.

[77] Article 18(3) also refers to public service announcements and charity appeals broadcast free of charge. This latter reference is somewhat surprising as an integral part of the definition of advertising is that the 'announcement' is broadcast 'in return for payment or for similar consideration'.

film is interrupted by an advertisement for another film), it would seem that the TWFD distinguishes between, and makes value judgments about, the impact of self-promotional activities by contrast to advertising. It is questionable whether such an approach reflects any concerns about protecting viewer interests in programme integrity, as the purpose seems to be simply to further the interests of the broadcaster which wants to increase viewing figures. In one sense, viewers here are being treated both as those who can be persuaded to consume further programmes, but also as potential commodities to be sold to advertisers.

This problem will only be exacerbated by new broadcasting techniques and even some approaches to programme scheduling. Confusion lies in the field of interactive television, split-screen television and subscription television. It is not clear how this situation can be addressed when, for example, a broadcaster uses a split screen during a programme to advertise how to subscribe to that channel. Equally unclear is the question of whether the analysis should be different if the broadcast contains information about another channel, when that channel is broadcast by the same broadcaster, or when the information relates to the product of another company, or its website (which may carry advertising).

A final problem relates to the introduction of new technologies, notably split-screen broadcasting. The assessment of quantity is problematic when we have two video feeds, one of which is broadcasting commercial content and the other programme content. One might argue, taking a pragmatic view of the TWFD, that the regulatory framework should be concerned with the majority of the screen, perhaps ignoring advertising that does not take centre stage or is not intrusive. This is a reasonably generous interpretation, allowing broadcasters a greater amount of freedom to broadcast commercial communications than might otherwise be the case. Quite apart from departing from a natural interpretation of the text, it leaves the unresolved problem of how to analyse split-screen broadcasts which are much more evenly divided between commercial and editorial material. It also ignores the issue of whether a screen split between audiovisual and video only, on the one hand; and between two audiovisual feeds, on the other, should be treated in the same way. Trying to solve the problem by looking at the proportion of the screen used for commercial advertising, and applying the total amounts permitted on a *pro rata* basis, adds further complications and may, for this reason alone, be thought undesirable.

Unsurprisingly, the quantity rules have also been under consideration as part of the TWFD review process. DSAD proposes the abolition of the daily limit on advertising (but retaining the hourly limits), as well as the quantitative restrictions in Article 18a. The other issues relating to Article 18 do not seem to have been addressed. In this, some industry pressure has been resisted to give some protection to viewers' interests in editorial content and, arguably, those of rights holders. The lack of certainty remaining regarding many techniques opens the possibility for advertisers and broadcasters to push the limits of what is acceptable.

Conclusion

The rules on placement and quantity of advertising aim to balance the competing interests of different groups: consumers, citizens, broadcasters, advertisers and programme producers. There are a number of weaknesses in these provisions, partly arising out of difficulties in the drafting of the TWFD itself, resulting from different perceptions as to the appropriate balance to be drawn; and partly as a consequence of the changes in the broadcasting environment. These changes can be seen to be technologically determined but, in fact, are also as a result of the increasing commercialisation of the broadcasting sector. Although the Commission's *Interpretative Communication* provides some clarification, fundamental disagreement as to the appropriate level of protection seems to remain. Even the ECJ has not been consistent as to the approach it should take: whether it should emphasise the discretion of a member state; whether limitations on the four freedoms should be restrictively interpreted; or whether the overall purpose of the TWFD (and its particular provisions) should be taken into account in determining the scope of the various broadcasters' activities.

Unsurprisingly, this area has been one that has been identified as being in need of particular review. Whatever the views as to the level of protection required, it seems clear that simplification or clarification of these rules is in order. This suggestion serves more generally, raising concerns about the level of detail appropriate to legislation at the Union level, a fact of which the Union itself seems to be aware (see chapters 4 and 10). The review process should consider the key concepts to be used in the regulation of advertising. In particular, a decision should be made as to whether spatial as well as temporal separation is appropriate, and whether identification of advertising as such, without formal separation devices, suffices.

In coming to the original balance between different interests, policy-makers seem to have reflected on a variety of different assumptions about the viewing experience and the degree of protection viewers require. From the viewpoint of citizens, a lack of control of advertising may pose a problem if it threatens or impedes editorial freedom and independence, and undermines the quality and integrity of programming. For consumers, advertising may be helpful and informative if the consumer is considered in the context of the product market generally, or it may simply be a nuisance and off-putting, or, worse, distort choice and market relations, generally spoiling the viewing experience.

Given the development of technology which allows viewers effectively to screen out unwanted content, one might think that some of the more complicated rules are unhelpful and unnecessary. None the less, it should be remembered that some content is more sensitive than others to commercial interruption, and some viewers are more in need of protection than others. The claims of viewers should not be overlooked, despite the potential of technology to empower them. Furthermore, we need to be wary of the extent to which it is claimed that technology is producing new solutions for viewers so as to minimise the need for regulation. Too often, these claims are overstated. Claims about technology are not necessarily a complete replacement for legislation. Equally, given that advertisers are also technically adept and that it is the nature of advertising agencies to find other ways to reach viewers, for example by product placement, such adroit new ways of advertising need to be monitored. Otherwise, advertising could become a threat to one of the fundamental concerns of the TWFD: programme integrity and, consequently, the quality of the viewing experience.

10

Negative content regulation

Introduction

Negative content regulation places restrictions and prohibitions on the broadcasting of certain types of material in order to protect viewers. A sensitive and contentious area even within a single member state, negative content regulation is even more problematic in the Union and external factors have exacerbated this. Increased numbers of channels has led to a fight for audience share, and some broadcasters have pushed at moral and cultural boundaries to attract viewers. At the same time, negative content regulation is increasingly being seen as unnecessary since viewers, in a multi-channel environment, have the technology to filter out unwanted programming. Traditional regulatory measures, on this reasoning, can be replaced not only by soft-law approaches but by technology. As we shall argue, these developments may not be entirely desirable[1] as they make assumptions about viewers' ability, and do not take into account personal and environmental factors affecting both consumer and citizen viewers (chapter 1).

Although crucial to the viewing experience, content regulation within the Union is problematic because it falls across boundaries in competence. Member states may determine their own regulatory system in the light of standards obtaining within their respective territories, although their

---

[1] See, e.g., the discussion by R. Brownsword, 'Code, Control, and Choice: Why East is East and West is West', *Legal Studies* 25(1) (2005), 1–21; see p. 19, where he discusses the advantages and disadvantages to two broad approaches to regulation which discourage and encourage individual viewer responsibility. Techno-regulation serves to delimit human activity, so compliance is enforced through technological limits rather than personal choice. The danger here is that users will no longer feel any moral responsibility when making choices, relying instead on the system to decide what is or is not acceptable. In contrast, regulation can, via a variety of means and codes, deliver moral, cultural and social messages which engage users, encouraging them to use self-control and take responsibility for judgments about what is, or is not, acceptable. These different approaches to individual responsibility appear to be particularly pertinent in the area of negative content regulation, where users, particularly parents, are being encouraged to use technology such as the V-chip to control their children's viewing.

complete freedom to regulate content is constrained by the EC Treaty (see chapter 4). The approach taken to jurisdiction (chapter 8) generally in the Television without Frontiers Directive (TWFD)[2] means that viewers may be able to receive broadcasting which is regulated by a different member state from that in which they are established, and whose rules and regulations about programme content may be unfamiliar. Viewers may therefore be able to access programming which does not necessarily reflect the standards to which they are accustomed and expect, and on which they may base their choices about viewing. To the extent that the Union tries to take action it is to minimise differences across regulatory regimes, as it is constrained by the lack of express cultural and moral competence. With both Union level and the member states limited in the type and extent of action they may take, it is difficult to find mechanisms for effective protection of viewers from harmful content. The solution currently adopted seems to be a move towards informal and co-ordinating measures.

The first part of this chapter briefly reviews the negative content provisions provided in the TWFD and in other provisions (the *Green Paper on Human Dignity*[3] and Council Recommendation[4]). The second part of the chapter considers particular problems that arise from these provisions. We then go on to consider alternative approaches based on co-regulation, information provision and the use of technology instead of traditional regulation. Finally, we question whether such measures to restrict broadcast content are an adequate, neutral and appropriate way to protect the interests of viewers.

General issues arising from negative content regulation

The provisions that constitute the system of negative content regulation in the Union raise a range of issues for regulators. All engender questions about the level of freedom of expression and the need to ensure

---

[2] Council Directive 89/552/EEC of 3 October on the co-ordination of certain provisions laid down by law, regulation or administrative action in member states concerning the pursuit of television broadcasting activities OJ [1989] L298/23, as amended by Directive 97/36/EC OJ [1997] L 202/30.

[3] Commission, *Green Paper on the Protection of Minors and Human Dignity in Audiovisual and Information Services*, COM(1996)483, final.

[4] Council, *Recommendation on the Development of the Competitiveness of the European Audiovisual and Information Services Industry by promoting National Frameworks aimed at achieving a Comparable and Effective Level of Protection of Minors and Human Dignity*, 98/560/EC 24 September 1998, OJ [1998] L 270.

that a diversity of views is represented. There is general agreement among Union regulators that even shocking and extreme speech may need protection, but that this must be balanced against the harm the speech may do (see Recital 8, TWFD and Article 10 ECHR). The right of minors to be shielded from material that may impair their development, the ban on incitement to hatred and the right of reply are all linked to the protection of human dignity, which itself is recognised as a general principle of Union law.[5] For those member states that recognise human dignity as a constitutional principle,[6] it becomes 'a universal European postulate', which 'sets qualitative standards in the field of the media'.[7] The desire to respect human dignity within broadcasting content may, however, sometimes clash with the particular interests of broadcasters often expressed in terms of freedom of expression. Here the category of 'broadcaster' includes owners, programme makers as well as advertisers, and we shall assume that each will have their own and different interests and motives for broadcasting particular types of content. Programme makers and advertisers may reject attempts to control their content, claiming that their artistic integrity and creativity are undermined. Broadcasters, owners and advertisers may, however, be using different types of speech, which attract different levels of protection. Typically, commercial speech, a term which is of uncertain meaning,[8] has attracted a lower level of protection than other types of speech, such as political speech.[9] This lower level of protection is linked to the idea that the free expression of a range of political views, among certain other types of speech (such as artistic, literary, philosophical and so on), contributes to the development of a public sphere or public spheres, where it is believed that

---

[5] See C-377/98 *Netherlands* v. *Parliament and Council* (Biotechnological Inventions) [2001] ECR I-7079, but contrast Case C-36/02 *Omega Spielhallen – und Automatenaufstellungs- GmbH* v. *Oberbürgermeisterin der Bundesstadt Bonn*, judgment 14 October 2004.

[6] E.g., in Germany, and other member states, human dignity is a constitutional right. Article 1 of Basic Law for the Federal Republic of Germany (Grundgesetz, GG) states that: 1) Human dignity shall be inviolable. To respect and protect it shall be the duty of all state authority.

[7] ARD and ZDF, *Statement of the Position of ARD and ZDF on the Topic Paper for the Liverpool Conference on Audiovisual Policy: protection of young people and human dignity*, Right of Reply, 6 September 2005, p. 1.

[8] For a review of the problems in this area, see C. Monro, 'The Value of Commercial Speech', *Cambridge Law Journal* (2003) 62(1), 134–58, *passim*.

[9] See *Casado Coca* v. *Spain* (94) 18 ECHR concerning advertising, allowing national authorities a wide margin of appreciation in the regulation of commercial speech. See more recently on the boundary between political speech and advertising: *VgT Verein gegen Tierfabriken* v. *Switzerland* (24699/94), judgment 28 June 2001, (2002) 34 EHRR 4.

rational critical debate can occur (see chapter 2). The values attributed to freedom of expression can mean that concerns about harmful speech, even that infringing human dignity, can be outweighed. The issue is made more difficult because different cultural and moral values within member states mean that pan-Union agreement about what constitutes 'harmful' content, and what the boundaries of permissible speech are, is difficult to achieve. Thus question of race and religious beliefs, which can be a particularly sensitive issue in societies which are becoming increasingly multicultural, are usually subject to keen, and even acrimonious, debate when issues of control and protection are raised.[10]

Despite the concerns outlined in chapter 1 about whether regulation adequately protects viewers with different skills and requirements, it has generally been recognised that children as a group are more vulnerable and therefore deserve greater levels of protection.[11] Attempts to protect minors generally focus on certain types of content agreed to be the most likely to harm them: violence; pornography; inducement to use alcohol, tobacco or drugs; encouragement to gamble; and, more recently, the problems that have arisen via the Internet, namely the possibility of anonymous contact between children and adults. The protection of minors from such a broad range of harmful content is becoming increasingly difficult due to technological change and convergence, as we shall see below. Whether the regulatory systems that are in place, and which are based on a traditional broadcasting environment, are adequate is questionable.

Current Union provisions for the control and restriction of content

Despite the difficulties in finding a balance between the competing interests which are acceptable across the Union, the TWFD contains a number

[10] In September 2005 the Danish newspaper *Jyllands-Posten* published twelve cartoon depictions of the Prophet Mohammed. Its editors said that the publication was part of an experiment to overcome what they perceived as self-censorship by illustrators to produce pictures of the Prophet Mohammed. The cartoons were highly offensive to Muslims, not only did they provide graphic depictions of the Prophet, which is forbidden, they also appeared to associate the Prophet (and by implication all Muslims) with terrorism. The offence that was given, seen by many as disrespect for Islam, led to mass protests, violence and loss of life. Human rights law obliges governments to protect religious freedom and religious minorities, but the cartoon controversy also raised questions about the limits imposed by human rights law, particularly the right to freedom of expression, on governments' ability to suppress speech.

[11] B. Gunter, J. Harrison and M. Wykes, *Violence on Television: Distribution, Form, Context and Themes* (Mahwah, NJ: Lawrence Erlbaum Associates, 2003), pp. 153–7.

of provisions which seek to provide a base level of negative content regulation. Two groups of provisions in the TWFD identify types of content which may be restricted in the public interest: Articles 12–16; and Articles 22 and 22a. A further provision, Article 2a, provides the procedural mechanism whereby member states may seek to prevent harmful content from being received within their jurisdiction.

Articles 12–16 are concerned with advertising and teleshopping, and place restrictions on broadcasters to ensure that they will not

> prejudice respect for human dignity, include any discrimination on grounds of race, sex or nationality, be offensive to religious or political beliefs, encourage behaviour prejudicial to health or to safety or encourage behaviour prejudicial to the protection of the environment.[12]

Articles 13 and 14 refer to the types of products that cannot be advertised or sold via teleshopping, namely, cigarettes, other tobacco products, medicine products and medical treatment available only on prescription in the member state under whose jurisdiction the broadcaster falls. Prohibitions relating to advertising and teleshopping for alcoholic drinks are found in Article 15, which states that such advertising 'may not be aimed specifically at minors or, in particular, depict minors consuming these beverages'.[13] Article 16 is concerned with upholding prohibitions to ensure that 'television advertising shall not cause moral or physical detriment to minors' and specifies the criteria with which advertisers must comply. These criteria prevent advertisers from 'directly exhorting minors to buy a product or service by exploiting their inexperience or credulity', and advertisers are prevented from 'directly encouraging minors to persuade their parents or others to purchase the goods or services being advertised'. The rest of the article seeks to protect minors from material

---

[12] Article 12 TWFD.

[13] Eurocare, *Response to the Issue Paper for the Audiovisual Conference in Liverpool: Commercial Communications of Alcoholic Beverages*, p. 4, refers to Article 15, which was first established as a way to help member states regulate their rules for alcoholic drinks commercials. Eurocare note that marketing practices have changed, but the rules appear to have stayed the same. In particular, the development of sponsorship in sport is a problem. Article 15 TWFD is the only provision under Union law governing the advertisement of alcohol but, although it prohibits the specific targeting of minors, the ubiquity of sports sponsorship ensures that alcohol advertising is very prevalent. Similarly, product placement of alcohol is not protected by Article 15. Eurocare advocate that 'in the absence of a uniform definition of "children", "children's programmes" and of "products aimed at children" in the Directive' product placement should not be used before 10 p.m. and that this new rule should be added to Article 15. This argument seems to have been unsuccessful.

that shows them 'in dangerous situations', although this is qualified by the word 'unreasonably'.

Articles 22 and 22a are particularly focused on the protection of minors and of public order. Article 2a TWFD provides that member states must ensure freedom of reception and may not restrict the transmission within their jurisdiction of television programmes broadcast from other member states. Article 22 is the only exception to this principle. The original version of Article 22 was amended by the 1997 directive to make it clear that there were two separate categories of material in it. These categories should be read as two different categories, rather than, as some broadcasters had suggested, as forming one group of offending material. Such an interpretation would have provided a lower level of protection, as it would then have been sufficient to satisfy the requirements of the TWFD if offending material were inaccessible to minors. Effectively, this interpretation would have removed the category of prohibited material now found in Article 22(1). The European Parliament had suggested broader ranging restrictions, but these were not adopted by the Council.[14] The resulting text fell between the two positions. Article 22 TWFD now provides:

1. Member states shall take appropriate measures to ensure that television broadcasts by broadcasters under their jurisdiction do not include any programmes which might seriously impair the physical, mental or moral development of minors, in particular programmes that involve pornography or gratuitous violence.
2. The measures provided for in paragraph 1 shall also extend to other programmes which are likely to impair the physical, mental or moral development of minors, except where it is ensured, by selecting the time of the broadcast or by any technical measure, that minors in the area of transmission will not normally hear or see such broadcasts.
3. Furthermore, when such programmes are broadcast in unencoded form Member States shall ensure that they are preceded by an acoustic warning or are identified by the presence of a visual symbol throughout their duration.

---

[14] European Parliament, *Decision on the Common Position Adopted by the Council with a View to the Adoption of a European Parliament and Council Directive Amending Council Directive 89/552/EC on the Co-ordination of Certain Provisions Laid Down by Law, Regulation or Administrative Action in Member States Concerning the Pursuit of Television Broadcasting Activities* (C4–0380/96–95/0074(COD)), A4–346/96.

An additional provision, Article 22a, was inserted, which requires member states to 'ensure that broadcasts do not contain any incitement to hatred on grounds of race, sex, religion or nationality'.

Essentially, there are three categories of material which justify member-state action: that contained in Article 22a, which broadly deals with incitement to hatred of various types; and two categories concerning material which might be perceived to affect minors. Of these two, the first category concerns material that might seriously impair minors' well-being, while the second category considers material that is only 'likely to impair' their development. Member states may take different measures in relation to these types of material which suggests that material in Article 22(1) may be prohibited, whereas it is sufficient if material of the type described in Article 22(2) is identified. There is no similar distinction between different types of hate speech.

The problems with negative regulation in the TWFD

The one-stop shop approach which underlies the TWFD (see chapter 8) means that for member states, their freedom to introduce and enforce negative regulation is limited. In addition to these problems of competence, or perhaps resulting from them, these limitations to some extent affect member states' ability to protect their cultural identity and general moral standards, but also fail to provide common standards throughout the Union. There are a number of problems with the drafting of these provisions in the TWFD which we shall discuss in three broad groups: the first relates to definitions of the terms used in the provisions; the second group looks at the relationship between the provisions themselves as well as overarching principles of Union law; and the third group involves some practical implications of the approach, in particular that found in Article 2a.

A number of terms in both the advertising provisions and Article 22 are vague. For example, the reference to minors in dangerous situations is not clear; the qualification of this requirement introduces vagueness to the provision about what might actually be deemed to be unreasonable. The advertising provisions are broader than Article 22, in that they specifically refer to the concept of human dignity. It may be surprising in itself that Article 22 does not contain any such reference, but the concept of human dignity is problematic in terms of its scope, in that it is both broad and vague. The concerns to protect human dignity imply broader considerations,[15] namely that some types of content may undermine our respect for our fellow human beings. Content that treats subjects in the broadcast media as being no more than their gender, colour of skin, religion, sexuality or ethnic group is regarded as damaging. In particular, it is argued that such treatment reflects contempt for the value and worth of others. Once again, the variety of cultural and moral approaches across the Union to such issues means that different views exist about what is or is not acceptable for broadcasting. It is also questionable the degree to which the prohibited content identified in Article 12,[16] which relates to discrimination on grounds of race, sex or nationality rather than hatred, and which refers to material which is offensive to religious or political beliefs, covers the same ground as the prohibition in Article 22a. It may be that there is a difference and that the terms of Article 12 are broader than Article 22, as a result of the lower level of protection awarded to the freedom of commercial speech.

It is worth noting that Article 22 is aimed only at the protection of minors; arguably, similar material which affects adults would not be covered. This is important, as Article 22 envisages two responses to problematic material: it might be either prohibited entirely; or, where it is of a lesser threat and appropriate devices are used, still broadcast. By distinguishing between the type of material in Article 22(1) and 22(2), member states are able to make judgments about not only if particular types of content should be shown but when and with what type of warning or level of protection.

These provisions are vague and rather general in scope, and Recital 40 recognises that 'it is necessary to clarify the rules for the protection

[15] See, e.g., Commission, *Green Paper on the Protection of Minors and Human Dignity;* Council of Europe, *Compilation of responses to the questionnaire on 'Big Brother' type programmes;* Council of Europe, *European Convention on Transfrontier Television, Standing Committee on Transfrontier Television,* T-TT(2002) 9; Council of Europe, *European Convention on Transfrontier Television, Standing Committee on Transfrontier Television,* Opinion No 1/2002 of the Conseil Supérieur de l'Audiovisuel of the French Community of Belgium; Council of Europe, *Opinions and Recommendations adopted by the Standing Committee on Transfrontier Television, Statement no.1 on human dignity and the fundamental rights of others* (2002), p. 19.

[16] Eurocare, *Response to the Issues Paper,* p. 6, supports the idea that rules on human dignity (Article 12) should be applied to all audiovisual commercial communications, both linear and non-linear. Currently, sponsorship slogans are not covered by these rules and Eurocare suggests that specific implementing arrangements should be adapted to the characteristics of each category of audiovisual content services and specified within the TWFD. This element seems to have been accepted: see proposed amendments to Article 3 TWFD.

of the physical, mental and moral development of minors'. The types of problematic content particularly identified in Article 22 are 'pornography' and 'gratuitous violence', although it is left up to member states to determine the specific definition of these terms and what content may be seen to 'seriously impair' minors. A lack of clarity in relation to precise definitions of these terms, or the lack of specific examples provided by the TWFD, means that they are open to different types of interpretation.[17] As we have noted, Articles 22(1) and 22(2) are tied in to youth protection. Given that some material may be banned whether or not minors may access it, for example if it is encrypted, it is questionable whether Article 22(1) is really about youth protection, or whether it is concerned to allow member states to uphold more general moral values. None the less, quite apart from issues about the level of impact a programme might have, it seems that any offending content will need to be tied back to an impact on youth. This can be seen in the EFTA Surveillance Authority Decision on *Canal + Gul* and others.[18] In these cases, the authority noted that the Norwegian legislation made a 'sufficient link between the prohibition of pornography in the General Civil Penal Code and the powers of the Mass Media Authority to restrict retransmissions under the Broadcasting Act', but that the assessment of the link was a matter for national law.

In a way, this approach respects the diversity of the member states. From the examples of action taken by member states under Article 2a to date,[19]

---

[17] The problem of definition and enforcement of an agreed common definition in this regard was discussed by Mediawatch-uk in its response to *The Revision of the 'Television Without Frontiers Directive*, p. 4. Mediawatch-uk suggest that in the absence of any real control in this area, the best way to protect minors 'is to bring forward effective sanctions against those who market and transmit, by whatever means, "pornography and gratuitous violence"'. D. Keller and S. G. Verhulst, 'Parental Control in a Converged Communications Environment: Self-regulation, Technical Devices and Meta-Information', *Final Report for the DVB Regulatory Group* (Oxford: Programme in Comparative Media Law and Policy, University of Oxford, 2000), p. 7, briefly discuss the problems in achieving a workable definition of the terms 'illegal, harmful or offensive content' and the consequent difficulties in achieving a balance between protecting children against material which is deemed to be 'unsuitable' whilst ensuring freedom of expression. See also S. G. Verhulst, 'Protection of Minors in the Media', in Rossnagel (ed.), *Television and New Media in Europe: Legislation, Liberalisation, Self-Regulation*, Schriftenreihe des Instituts für Europäisches Medienrecht, 22 (Munich and Berlin: Jehle Rehur, 2001), 35–52, p. 37.

[18] EFTA Surveillance Authority *Decision Canal + Gul and others*, PR(03)25.

[19] Commission *Opinion XXX TV* C(95) 2678 final; Commission *Opinion Rendez-Vous Television* C(96) 3933 final; *R. v. Secretary of State for National Heritage, ex p Continental Television* [1993] 2 CMLR 333 (Div.Ct.) and [1993] 3 CMLR 387 (CA), the resulting reference to the ECJ, Case C-327/93, *Red Hot Television* was removed from the register and

it seems the Commission is unwilling to interfere with a member state's assessment on whether material triggering the application of Article 2a exists.[20] In the *TV1000 Sverige* Case,[21] the EFTA Court had to decide whether member states had the freedom to determine their own standards or whether Article 22 'introduced a common standard for what "might seriously impair the physical, mental or moral development of minors"', or whether the provision 'left it up to each individual Union and EFTA country' to determine the degree of pornography which would have this effect.[22] The Commission's *Green Paper on Human Dignity* had, as we shall see later, noted the wide variety of approaches throughout the various member states and the difficulty of creating a common understanding. Against this, allowing member states to determine their own standards would impair the functioning of the common market. The EFTA Court, given that the TWFD gives no guidance on the type of programming to be caught by Article 22, suggested that it was for each member state to determine what was acceptable in respect of its own jurisdiction subject to the oversight mechanism now contained in Article 2a TWFD.[23]

In this approach, there are parallels to that taken in respect of the four freedoms in general, in which member states, in practice, retain a significant degree of freedom to determine public morality under Articles 30 and 46 EC, subject always to the idea that any measures taken are necessary and proportionate (see chapter 4). In this context we could argue that there is a difference between the four freedoms and the provisions of the TWFD, as Article 2a specifies the type of measures to be taken by the member state. It is therefore more difficult to argue that a member state's response is disproportionate, although examples may be found.

---

the broadcaster went bankrupt. See also EFTA Surveillance Authority Decision *Canal* + *Gul and others*, PR(03)25; *KommAustria X-Gate Multimedia Broadcasting 2000.*

[20] Erotica Rendez-Vous challenged the Commission's decision in Case T-69/99 *Eurotica Rendez-vous Television Danish Satellite TV A/S* v. *Commission*, [2000] ECR II-4039, but was unsuccessful on procedural grounds.

[21] See E-8/97 *TV 1000 Sverige AB* v. *Norwegian Government* [1998] 3 CMLR 318.

[22] The case concerned the original form of Article 22; the same principles arise in relation to the revised version of TWFD.

[23] Contrast the approach of the ECJ in Joined Cases C-34–6/95 *Konsumerntombudsmannen* v. *De Agostini (Svenska) Forlag AB and Konsumerntombudsmannen* v. *TV-Shop i Sverige AB* [1997] ECR I-3843, in which a Swedish rule prohibiting advertising aimed at children was held not to fall within rules permitted by the directive. For discussion, see R. Craufurd Smith, 'Sex and Violence in the Internal Market: The Impact of European Community Law on Television Programme Standards', *Contemporary Issues in Law*, (1998), 135–53, p. 148. One might argue that there is a distinction between the two cases as *De Agostini* concerned advertising rather than editorial content.

For example, state action is over-broad when it affects all the channels within a broadcaster's portfolio rather than just the offending channel.[24]

There are a number of questions about the relationship between the different provisions. Article 2a relates only to the type of material precluded by Article 22. It does not relate to Articles 12–16, which contain a wider range of content standards. On the face of it, member states would seem to be unable to prohibit broadcasts in which advertising violated the content standards set out in Articles 12–16, arguably lessening the level of protection for the viewer. Presumably, however, if the advertising also violated the standards in Article 22, member states could act: Article 22(1) at least does not seem to be restricted to television programmes. Of course, the problem with this interpretation is that the definition of television broadcast*ing* in Article 1a refers to television programmes. As we have seen in chapter 8, this arguably excludes advertising. Such an interpretation is not only problematic in terms of the issues discussed in chapter 8, but might undermine protection of content standards.

A more general question is whether it is possible to rely on the four freedoms and their derogating provisions in addition to, or instead of, Article 2a. This could be significant in two ways: first, the treaty derogating provisions are broader than the terms of Article 22; secondly, there may be a greater role for the proportionality assessment. This general question links back to the issues raised by *de Agostini* about the scope of the TWFD and, in particular, the question of which fields are co-ordinated by it (see chapter 8). On the one hand, Recital 44 states that the TWFD constitutes 'the essential harmonisation necessary and sufficient to ensure the free movement of television broadcasts in the Community'. The word 'sufficient' suggests that all public policy interests have been adequately regulated by the TWFD. On the other hand, as Advocate-General Jacobs suggested in *de Agostini*, there is a distinction between 'the fields co-ordinated by the directive and the specific matters regulated by it'.[25] This suggests that the fields co-ordinated by the TWFD are not necessarily exhaustively regulated by it. The suggestion gains support from the fact that Recital 17 specifically refers to the possibility of other legislation having an impact on areas that also fall within the scope of TWFD. Further, the Commission, in its original *TWF Green Paper*, suggested that there was a distinction between 'laws to protect public

[24] Craufurd Smith, 'Sex and Violence in the Internal Market', pp. 146–7.
[25] Joined Cases C-34–36/95 *de Agostini*, Opinion of the Advocate General, para. 81.

morals in the sexual sphere', and 'special laws to safeguard minors' in the context of sex and violence.[26] The Commission suggested that it would be better to wait to identify whether differences in member states' rules relating to morality in general created barriers to the free movement of television services, before attempting to introduce Union standards in this regard. It is arguable therefore that public morals in the sexual sphere lie outside the scope of the TWFD. The European Court of Justice (ECJ) in *Commission* v. *Belgium* indicated that, although the TWFD undoubtedly contained rules dealing with public policy, public morality or public security, they were not exhaustive.[27] On this basis, there may still be scope for member states to act to protect public morals and other public interests more generally outside the scope of the TWFD, although any such action must be non-discriminatory and proportionate. It also should comply with the requirements of Article 10 ECHR.[28]

On a more pragmatic note, it can be seen that the enforcement mechanism established by Article 2a is complex, long-winded and operates after the event. The Article 2a mechanism may be hard to operate in practice, as it gives unscrupulous broadcasters time to exploit the jurisdiction clause (see chapter 8) and move from member state to member state, thus making it difficult to identify the regulatory authority with initial jurisdiction to take action.[29] Co-operation between member states' regulatory authorities could prove crucial in minimising the impact of this loophole.

The distinction between different types of content recognises that digital technology has changed, and will continue to change, the way in which people watch television and the extent to which they can control what they see. It is no longer practical for regulators to view programmes in advance of broadcasting, an issue recognised in Recital 41. However, this means that measures must be in place to allow broadcasters, regulatory bodies and viewers to judge the nature and suitability of the content. A variety of measures may be possible, ranging from information about content

---

[26] Commission *Green Paper on the Establishment of the Common Market for Broadcasting*, COM(1984)300 final, p. 286.

[27] Case C-11/95 *Commission* v. *Belgium* [1996] ECR I-4115, para. 92.   [28] Article 6 TEU.

[29] The issue of using the right of free movement to try to avoid national regulation was confronted in the broadcasting sphere in the case of Case C-23/93 *TV10 SA* v. *Commissariaat voor de Media* [1994] ECR I-4795. This ruling seems to have been narrowed down however by the ECJ in, e.g., Case C-11/95 *Commission* v. *Belgium*. See further ch. 8 and Commission, *Proposal for a Directive amending Directive 89/552/EEC*, COM(2005)646 final.

available on electronic programme guides (EPGs), warnings, watershed arrangements (where certain types of programme content are subject to restrictions based on different times of the day when they may or may not be broadcast), age-based classifications, content descriptions and advisories.

Impact of technology on regulation

The TWFD was updated in 1997 to take account of technological and market developments. In 1999 the European Parliament and the Council recognised that it would be necessary to bring together industries and other parties in order to examine ways in which audiovisual content could be evaluated and assessed, particularly in relation to the development of the Internet. In particular, the concern was to share best practice across the Union in relation to protection of minors and vulnerable parties from content provided across different platforms[30] A refocussing of the institutions' approach occurred in relation to the notion of responsibility, with the Union institutions promoting greater user or audience awareness (particularly that of parents controlling their children's viewing, but also for children[31]) via measures to increase media literacy.[32]

---

[30] See the *Community Action Plan* adopted 21 January 1999 to promote the safer use of the Internet by combating illegal and harmful content on global networks (also referred to as the Safer Internet Action Plan). See also Decision No. 276/1999/EC, OJ [1999] L 33/1, which was extended in 2003 for two more years by the European Parliament and the Council, Decision No. 1151/2003/EC amending Decision No. 276/1999/EC, OJ [2003] L 462/1. The Union aims to promote the safer use of the Internet by combating illegal and harmful content on global networks. This provision also includes measures to encourage the exchange of information and co-ordination with relevant actors at national level and has special provisions for the accession countries.

[31] See also www.mediasmart.org.uk This is a non-profit-making media literacy programme for primary schoolchildren.

[32] Commission, *Second Evaluation Report from the Commission to the Council and the European Parliament on the application of the Council Recommendation of 24 September 1998 concerning the protection of minors and human dignity*, COM(2003)776; Commission, *Proposal for a Recommendation of the European Parliament and of the Council on the protection of minors and human dignity and the right of reply in relation to the competitiveness of the European audiovisual and information services industry*, COM(2004)341, final. See also ARD and ZDF, *Statement of the Position of ARD and ZDF*, p. 3. In this response, ARD and ZDF recognise that the stress on parental responsibility is particularly problematic in the context of non-linear services, particularly the Internet, where children may have more knowledge about the service and ways of avoiding filtering devices than do their parents. The broadcasters propose that member states should be encouraged 'to seek suitable measures, especially media competence and media training programmes, which will enable children and young people to use the services responsibly'.

A Communication from the Commission in 1997[33] had paved the way for the 1998 Council Recommendation,[34] which was the first legal instrument[35] at Union level aimed at using national frameworks to achieve the protection of minors and human dignity. These frameworks together were intended to provide a comparable and effective level of regulation and would cover all forms of delivery from broadcasting to the Internet. The Recommendation suggested that in the new multi-media environment, where an almost unlimited amount of content can be accessed from around the world, there was a need for a self-regulatory approach to supplement the legal framework, as well as a need for international co-operation.[36] Two evaluation reports provided by the Commission,[37] which have verified the progress made by member states with reference to self-regulatory measures, codes of conduct and technical educational measures in this area, have shown that there are significant differences across the Union, particularly in relation to the effective regulation of new digital services. This lack of uniformity raises questions about the extent to which the sharing of information by member states can result in common Union standards and practices.[38] Problems encountered when attempts are made to harmonise content standards are particularly an issue in relation to the standardisation of rating systems designed to help viewers assess the content of programmes (see further below).[39]

Given that different types of content delivery mechanism create different types of relationship with the viewer, it could be argued that different

---

[33] Commission, *Communication from the Commission on the follow-up to the Green Paper on the protection of minors and human dignity in the audiovisual and information services, together with a proposal for a Council Recommendation concerning the protection of minors and human dignity in the audiovisual and information services*, COM(97)570 final.

[34] Council, *Recommendation on the development of the competitiveness of the European audiovisual and information services industry*.

[35] A recommendation is listed in Article 249 EC as one of the acts of the Union but it is not legally binding.

[36] Council, *Recommendation on the development of the competitiveness of the European audiovisual and information services industry*, p. 2.

[37] Commission, *Evaluation Report from the Commission to the Council and the European Parliament on the application of the Council Recommendation of 24 September 1998 concerning the protection of minors and human dignity*, COM(2001)106, final; Commission, *Second Evaluation Report*.

[38] See Commission, *Proposal for a Recommendation on the protection of minors and human dignity*. This Proposal follows on from the *Second Evaluation Report from the Commission to the Council and the European Parliament on the application of the Council Recommendation of 24 September 1998*.

[39] See Commission, *Second Evaluation Report concerning the protection of minors and human dignity*, pp. 15–17.

levels of content regulation should be applied across a variety of platforms. The problem with this argument is that it is becoming more difficult to distinguish between 'television broadcasting' services and information services (see chapter 8).[40] Such distinctions are increasingly problematic within the context of digital television, due to its ability to facilitate individual requests for services through the interactive elements now provided, particularly via interactive digital television (iDTV) services. The consensus of policymakers and those representing industry interests is that lower levels of regulation could be required for encrypted services, or those requiring an identification number to access programmes via pay TV, than for mainstream unencrypted free-to-air services. The use of encryption or pin numbers means that, in theory, material that may be harmful to minors, but which is not illegal, can easily be broadcast on a restricted basis, thus upholding freedom of expression and complying with Article 22(2) TWFD.[41] The Commission argued that it would be unnecessary to reinvent a new regulatory framework for broadcast content that is transmitted via a variety of platforms. The European Parliament argued any regulatory measures which are taken in the future need to be flexible enough to take account of media convergence, but 'should be set down in Content Framework Package of graduated levels of regulation',[42] as well as meet the broader goals relating to the Union's aim to be the most dynamic and competitive economy by 2010.[43]

As we have seen in chapter 3, technological developments have meant that a distinction can be drawn by policymakers between linear and non-linear services. Viewers are expected to take more responsibility in respect of their own viewing choices in the case of non-linear services. The approach adopted in the draft second amending directive (DSAD)

---

[40] Case C-89/04 *Mediakabel BV* v. *Commissariaat voor de Media*, judgment 2 June 2005.
[41] Encryption is not always sufficient as there may be errors in the encryption system, as can be seen in the case of a viewer who complained that he received The Fantasy Channel, normally an encrypted service, when he had not asked for it: ITC, 'Television X-The fantasy channel: NTL, EPSOM', *Programme Complaints and Findings*, January 2002. Problems also arise in regard to scheduling errors: see, e.g., ITC, 'Channel U', *Programme and Complaints Bulletin 13* and more recently, Ofcom, 'Streak Party', *Ofcom Programme Complaints Bulletin*, Issue 45, 23 July 2005. Similar difficulties arise with regard to advertising: ITC, 'Television X-Text', *Advertising Complaints Bulletin*, 15.
[42] European Parliament, *Report on Television Without Frontiers* (2003/2033(INI)), A5-0251/2003 final (The Perry Report, PE 312.581/DEF), section 10, p. 8.
[43] See also Commission Communication, *i2010 – A European Information Society for growth and employment*, COM(2005)229 final, p. 5.

envisages two different tiers of rules for the two types of services.[44] The first tier, found in Articles 3c–3h, contains the basic rules for all audiovisual media services and relates to negative content requirements, such as the protection of minors. These rules apply to all audiovisual content services, including advertising, both linear and non-linear, and are minimum standards. As a consequence, some of the specific provisions for television broadcasters, such as Articles 12 and 22(a), have been abolished. Articles 3c–3h require all content providers to be restrained in equal ways when issues of incitement to hatred, and harm to minors arise.

Articles 3d and 3e DSAD currently contain the provisions relating to linear and non-linear services as follows:

Article 3(d) states that:

> Member states shall take appropriate measures to ensure that audiovisual media services under their jurisdiction are not made available in such a way that might seriously impair the physical, mental or moral development of minors.

Article 3e states that:

> Member states shall ensure by appropriate means that audiovisual media services and audiovisual commercial communications provided by providers under their jurisdiction do not contain any incitement to hatred based on sex, racial or ethnic origin, religion or belief, disability, age or sexual orientation.

There are two aspects to the proposed changes with regard to viewer protection: the scope of the provisions; and the regulatory mechanisms by which they are to be implemented. At a general level an approach that allows gradated regulatory density conforms to the principle of proportionality. The second tier of rules would place further requirements on linear audiovisual services and arise from rules derived from the current TWFD. The principle of subsidiarity is also respected, if member states are allowed to impose stricter national regulation on content standards.[45]

---

[44] Explanatory Memorandum, Commission, *Proposal for a Directive of the European Parliament and of the Council amending Council Directive 89/552/EEC on the Co-ordination of Certain Provision laid down by Law, Regulation or Administrative Action in Member States concerning the Pursuit of Television Broadcasting Activities*, COM(2005)646 final, 2005/0260 (COD), SEC(2005)1625 and 1626, pp. 10–11.

[45] In their *Statement of the Position of ARD and ZDF*, German public service broadcasters ARD and ZDF argue that, if non-linear services are included in the content directive, then

More specifically, proposed Article 3d is different from Article 22 in that it focusses on the making available of services (irrespective of impact), whereas Article 22 attaches to the impact of the content itself. Article 3d is wider than Article 22, if it is possible to make non-harmful content available in a harmful way. Seeing gambling might not be harmful, but making interactive gambling programmes available might be.

Looking at Article 3e, there are two issues to consider. Firstly, it contains no reference to human dignity. This weakens the protection for viewers regarding the advertising content, although not for programme content. Secondly, as amended by DSAD, the enforcement provision in Article 2a allows member states to take action only in relation to the matters mentioned in Article 3e, that is hate speech in its various forms. The current version of Article 2a permits member states to take action against incoming broadcasts on the basis of content harmful to minors (Article 22(1) and 22(2)), thus weakening the protection mechanism in this regard. Whether the proposed changes, at least in this latter aspect, will be acceptable to the other institutions is questionable.

Moving to the second aspect of viewer protection, the suggestion is that regulation could be effected by different forms of regulatory intervention involving state regulation, co-regulation and self-regulation, as well as co-operation between different member states. The Commission envisages such regulation to be in keeping with its 'legislative strategy which aims at combining regulation [with] more flexible instruments which allow member states, industry and citizens to cooperate at the Union level on the basis of the experience on the ground' (see chapter 4).[46] The Commission is seeking to facilitate this 'bottom-up' action through collaboration between self-regulatory and co-regulatory bodies. Some have, however, argued that co-regulation or self-regulation would be inappropriate, although any regulation needs to continue to be carefully balanced

member states should be allowed to provide stricter national regulations for those services, 'in particular if the social significance of those services becomes increasingly closer to that of the linear services', p. 4.

[46] Commission, Press Release, *Enhancing the effectiveness of the protection of minors and of human dignity in audiovisual and information services: the European Commission proposes a new Recommendation*, IP/04/598, 6 May 2004, p. 1. The European Commission adopted a proposal for a Recommendation of the European Parliament and of the Council on the protection of minors and human dignity and the right of reply in the European audiovisual and information services industry. The Recommendation is a follow-up of the Commission's *Second Evaluation Report concerning the protection of minors and human dignity*.

against freedom-of-expression rights.[47] Furthermore, as recent cases illustrate, legal and statutory intervention is still required to protect viewers from hate speech, perhaps more so as increasingly channels from outside the Union are available within its territory and are problematic in terms of their content.[48] Further, as argued earlier, it is questionable to what extent identification of common Union standards is possible when specific decisions about the nature of content which must be banned, or which can be shown subject to restrictions, are dependent on the various cultural and social values that exist in different member states.[49] In a devolved regulatory system, it is unlikely that any agreement on common Union standards for programme content will occur. In particular, the potential for effective co-regulatory and self-regulatory control of content that is harmful to minors is weakened. As we have seen, although prevention of harm to individuals and respect for human dignity can be found in a number of the existing TWFD provisions, the use of self-regulation and co-regulation to address such complex issues appears problematical, given that these types of regulation themselves evade clear definition and may be interpreted in different ways.[50]

The exploration of these different regulatory mechanisms has highlighted difficulties about how lighter forms of regulation, perceived as necessary for technological and economic development of the Union, can

[47] Commission, *Issues Paper for the Liverpool Audiovisual Conference: Protection of minors and human dignity, right of reply*, July 2005, 3.

[48] See, e.g., the Al-Manar case. Al-Manar was launched in Lebanon as a terrestrial station and has belonged to Hezbollah culturally and politically since it began broadcasting. The French satellite Hot Bird 4, owned by the Eutelsat organisation, allows it to transmit over a wide footprint. In December 2004 the French Conseil d'Etat ordered the French-based Eutelsat Company to shut down Al-Manar broadcasts, following accusations that its programmes were anti-Semitic and could incite hatred. Al-Manar complied voluntarily to stop broadcasting on the following day in order to avoid other Arab programmes of the same multiplex being shut down. See also Danish Radio RPJ TV, the Kurdish satellite channel registered in Denmark, Med TV, which had its licence withdrawn by UK authorities and Medya TV, to whom French authorities refused to grant a licence.

[49] Certain member states have complained about the entry of unsuitable material into their territories. E.g., Sweden prohibits advertising aimed at children, and in the UK there have been several cases in which the national regulator has sought to make a proscription order which seeks to ban the input of pornographic broadcasting. See, e.g., Red Hot Television, TV Erotica, Rendez-vous Television, Satisfaction Club TV, Eurotica Rendez-Vous and Eros TV have been proscribed in the United Kingdom. Section 177 of the Broadcasting Act 1990 enabled the Secretary of State to declare a foreign satellite service as unacceptable. See Case T-69/99 *Eurotica Rendez-vous*.

[50] C. Palzer, 'Co-regulation of the Media in Europe: European Provisions for the Establishment of Co-regulation Frameworks', *IRIS Plus* 2002, p. 6.

be reconciled with honouring pan-Union values and standards. Member states and the Union institutions increasingly use codes of conduct (often drawn up by industrial stakeholders), alongside existing regulatory rules. In the law-making process, they take advice and receive input from industry, user groups and other interested parties, though it is unlikely that all have an equal voice. The issue of how, in practice, these different approaches can be reconciled with non-negotiable standards and rights is far from settled. If member states increasingly withdraw from using statutory regulation in favour of bottom-up action through collaboration between national self-regulatory and co-regulatory bodies, the problem of developing accessible systematised codes of conduct and practice remains unaddressed. The result is that there is no system in place that can effectively help users to make informed decisions about the nature of the content they might wish to watch, use or purchase. Without an international code of some sort (see the next section) what is acceptable in one part of the Union and not in another will inevitably produce confusion as well as risk causing offence.[51] This is particularly problematic as the lighter touch regulation proposed is predicated on informed viewers and viewer choice.

Technology as a regulatory mechanism

In its *Second Evaluation Report on Human Dignity*, the Commission suggested collaboration between member states' regulatory and co-regulatory bodies,[52] which will lead to an 'exchange of best practices concerning such issues as a system of common, descriptive symbols which would help viewers assess the content of programmes'.[53] We question below the extent to which the use of information-based guidance is feasible or desirable.

A variety of measures may be possible, ranging from content descriptions available on EPGs or in other textual formats, warnings, watershed arrangements and age-based classifications. Age-based categories for rating programmes are used throughout Europe. Problematically, they vary significantly in different member states and there appears to be continued resistance to the possibility of pan-Union standards to be adopted in this area in relation to broadcasting. Member states still apply the 1998

---

[51] T. McGonagle, 'Co-regulation of the Media in Europe: The Potential for Practice of an Intangible Idea', *Iris Plus*, 2002, p. 3.
[52] Commission, *Second Evaluation Report*, p. 18.   [53] *Ibid.*, p. 18.

Council Recommendation[54] in different ways.[55] Reluctance to adopt a pan-Union system of age-based ratings for broadcasting may, however, not necessarily be as problematic as it might first appear.

The use of age-related ratings systems as the only means to identify the suitability of a programme for children elicits concern. Age-based categories make specific assumptions about the psychology of the television audience, which may be either inaccurate or incorrect.[56] Such categories are based on the assumption that children have distinct types of reactions to content depending on their age. The adoption of this view has been questioned as not reflecting an adequate understanding of child development.[57] Academic studies have criticised age-based ratings in that they tend to treat all children under 13 as a homogeneous group, ignoring the fact that they may be psychologically diverse.[58] The age boundaries, in some respects, seem arbitrary: any decision to rate a programme suitable or not suitable for a particular age group is generally based upon very subjective and judgmental criteria. Indeed, different families may have different concerns about the content of a television programme which are specific to their own values, or their judgment of the specific needs of their own child. Age-based ratings may therefore influence viewers in different ways.[59] In theory, this may render a universal standard for all children of the same age irrelevant and ineffective. Furthermore, there is some evidence that age-based ratings may invite audience reactions which are the opposite of those intended.[60] Labelling of programmes with age-based restrictions, which assert that the content is not suitable for a child of a particular age, can cause a 'boomerang effect', whereby children are actually more attracted to material simply because it is restricted (sometimes called 'the forbidden-fruit effect').[61]

---

[54] Commission, *Second Evaluation Report*, p. 17.
[55] Outside the field of broadcasting, the Pan European Games Information (PEGI) age-rating system has provided a single system for interactive games throughout the Union.
[56] B. Gunter, 'Avoiding Unsavoury Television', *The Psychologist*, 13(4) (2000), 194–9, p. 195.
[57] D. Kunkel, 'Why Content, Not Age of Viewers, Should Control What Children Watch on TV', *The Chronicle of Higher Education*, XLIII (21),(1997), B4-5, p. 1.
[58] B. J. Wilson, D. Linz and B. Randall, 'Applying Social Science Research to Film Ratings: A Shift from Offensiveness to Harmful Effects', *Journal of Broadcasting and Electronic Media*, 34 (1990), pp. 443–68, cited in Gunter, 'Avoiding Unsavoury Television', p. 195.
[59] M. Krcmar and J. Cantor, 'The Role of Television Advisories and Ratings in Parent–Child Discussions of Television Viewing Choices', *Journal of Broadcasting and Electronic Media*, 41(summer), 1977, 393–411, p. 395.
[60] Gunter, 'Avoiding Unsavoury Television', p. 197.
[61] B. J. Bushman and A. D. Stack, 'Forbidden Fruit Versus Tainted Fruit: Effects of Warning Labels on Attraction to Television Violence', *Journal of Experimental Psychology: Applied*,

Given that age-based categories vary across Europe, and indeed across the world,[62] coupled with growing evidence that they may not be a particularly effective way of labelling content, a push towards the adoption of such standards in the Union may not be helpful. In any event, we have seen the review of the TWFD refocus regulatory control towards a lighter touch approach with greater responsibility for viewers justified by greater choice and by the existence of filters. This means that the pressures placed on a parent to filter or monitor children's viewing are increasing, particularly in the area where material is not banned, but may be deemed harmful. The assumption behind this lighter touch approach is that parents must exercise the authority vested in them to protect their children, particularly when non-linear forms of broadcasting allow viewers to bypass other regulatory controls such as watershed scheduling arrangements. This is an assumption replete with its own assumptions about modern parenthood.

Although the use of encryption systems and pin numbers obviously offers parents some control over children's viewing, they have to rely upon content descriptions, increasingly provided via EPGs. Despite the fact that EPGs are becoming more important for viewers seeking to make an informed choice from a growing range of options, there are weaknesses. Not only are there problems about the neutrality of the information provided[63] but difficulties also arise in relation to the way the technology operates. None the less, information or descriptions of content when coupled with an age-based rating give some guidance as to the suitability of the programme. The incorporation of informational advisories into the age-based ratings scheme has resulted in a combination of two different types of labels: an age-based evaluative system; and an information system. In contrast to the subjective, judgmental evaluative age-based ratings system, information labelling systems (despite their potential lack of neutrality) do not seek to make judgments regarding those for whom the content is appropriate. This means that parents are left to make decisions about what type of content is suitable for their child, based on the information given. There are issues here about the relative ability of parents to assess the information provided, returning us to the distinction between

---

2(3), 1995, 207–26, p. 208; Kunkel, 'Why Content, Not Age of Viewers, Should Control What Children Watch on TV', p. 31.

[62] Gunter, Harrison and Wykes, *Violence on Television*, p. 251.

[63] See also ch. 6 for a discussion about the relationship between the content of EPGs, the location of a channel on an EPG and broadcasters' concerns about resulting viewers' choices.

active and passive viewers (see chapter 1). Consequently, the comprehensibility and usefulness of the information becomes more important as a guide to viewing decisions.

An analogy has been drawn between the content labelling of programmes and nutritional labelling which provides information about the content of the food without making judgments about whether a person should eat it or not.[64] Equally, such labelling may not be neutral as it can highlight the 'healthy' aspects of a food, for example, low fat, while downplaying the less healthy aspects, for example, high in sugar.[65] The food metaphor continues. The 'tainted-fruit' explanation is based on the assumption that more information about a programme may repel viewers from watching if they confront explanatory material that makes them feel uncomfortable, or it is not of interest.[66] This latter point ties into concerns about whether increased niche programming and the development of technology such as personal video recorders (PVRs) and EPGs facilitate the viewer in obtaining a wide diet of programming, or instead operate to reinforce existing preferences (see chapters 3, 11 and 13).

The Working Group on the Protection of Minors and Human Dignity reported in 2005 that a mixed range of views exists about the value of a common European rating system. Some members of the Working Group took the view that 'a single mandatory or voluntary content classification for audiovisual content in the Union is unnecessary and inappropriate'.[67] Those in favour of common standards argue that their development is related to the need to provide more efficient consumer information. Alongside this debate, there are also those who are concerned about the need to recognise and respect the range of cultural differences across the Union, and fear that a single-content classification system would necessarily be insensitive to local mores. In theory, better information should be helpful to parents and allow them to make better judgments about the

---

[64] H. L. Chen, 'Young Adolescents' Responses to Evaluative and Informational Labelling Systems for TV', *Paper Presented at the International Communications Association Conference*, San Francisco, California, May 1999, p. 5.

[65] Sometimes there may be a problem of information overload, where 'the explosion of availability may actually cause problems for consumers who have to select appropriate and relevant information'; see G. Howells and T. Wilhelmsson, *EC Consumer Law* (Aldershot: Ashgate, 1997), p. 12. In relation to broadcasting, there may be an issue about the nature and style of packaging, rather than a problem arising from the sheer number of broadcast channels.

[66] Gunter, 'Avoiding Unsavoury Television', p. 198.

[67] Final Report of the Working Group 1: *Protection of minors and human dignity, right of reply*, p. 2.

suitability of programming for their children (assuming, that is, that they have the capacity, the time and the interest to do so). Problematically, the basis for much television content classification remains grounded in an unclear understanding of audience psychology and the effect that censorship of material has on young viewers' desire to watch unsuitable programming. An attempt to harmonise common descriptive symbols, pictograms or content descriptions rather than age-based ratings seems, on the basis of current research, to be more sensible.

The need for common-evaluation criteria and standards and comparable measures to evaluate content has been recognised as essential to any proposed type of pan-Union technical filtering system. Such a system, such as the V-chip, could in principle use both age-based ratings and information systems. The V-chip allows viewers to block programmes based on their rated levels of specified content (e.g. violence, sex, bad language). It is designed specifically to enable adults to block programmes they think are unsuitable for their children (or others). Despite the European Parliament's suggestion, this technology has not been adopted in the Union due to different technical standards in member states. None the less, the feasibility of such technology has been explored at length by the Commission in response to requirements laid out in Recital 42 TWFD.[68] In addition to the difficulties involved in standardising Union technology, there are larger problems inherent in the use of the V-chip as a protection measure and its interrelationship with information systems (such as EPGs), through which individuals make decisions about the suitability of content.[69] There remains the problem about whose standards and judgments are to be incorporated into the technical filtering system and also into the descriptions or age-based ratings.[70] The question of

---

[68] In 1999 the European Commission, under obligation, carried out its enquiry into the desirability, practicability and effectiveness of the V-chip and programme content rating systems as a way of improving parental control over television: see Commission, *Study on Parental Control of Television Broadcasting Communication*, COM(1999)371.

[69] Concerns were also raised by the Commission regarding technological blocking devices, perceiving them as 'upstream censoring' which may violate freedom of expression.

[70] For a discussion of some of the problems of relying on private actors to enforce government policy, see, e.g., J. Boyle, 'Foucault in Cyberspace: Surveillance, Sovereignty and Hardwired Censors', *University of Cincinnati LR* 66 (1997), 177–205. Discussing the use of the V-chip in the United States, he comments at p. 202, 'The V-chip seems to be merely a neutral facilitator of parental choice. The various acts of coercion involved (the government making the television company insert the thing into the machine, the public–private board choosing which ratings criteria will be available for parents to use) simply disappear into the background. Finally, the distributed privatized nature of the system promises that it might actually work; though admittedly, state administration of the television system poses fewer headaches than state administration of the Internet.'

who would undertake to provide and develop neutral content descriptions that would be applicable across the Union remains unanswered. In any event, we should remember that reliance on information technology and the viewer not only changes the relationship between the viewer and the regulatory system but may result in some viewers failing to make active choices, instead relying on the default positions programmed in by the technology. Regulation has been devolved to the viewer, but in this instance, in effect, returns to an industry player. An industry player, however, might not have primary regard to the public interest (which is at least what regulators claim to do) or to the needs of citizen viewers.

It is clear that concern about the protection of minors and the incitement of hatred retains a broad consensus across the Union. None of the new provisions addresses the problems which will continue to arise in terms of the different approaches member states may take in developing systems for labelling content and the difficulties which viewers face when attempting to make informed choices about which content is suitable for themselves and for their children.

Conclusion

Technological development has affected the ability of member states to control the nature of content which is received within their own borders, and consequently affected their approach to regulation. The TWFD contains certain provisions constituting negative content regulation. We have seen, however, a number of problems arising with the drafting and application of these provisions, perhaps influenced by the limited Union competence in this area. The sensitivity of the area seems to have resulted in a drift towards more informal mechanisms. While a potential exists to establish standardised symbols or content descriptions across the Union, the provision of a common Union age-based ratings seems unlikely, again given the diversity of member states' approaches. Given the critical nature of research on the value of age-based ratings, abandoning any attempts to harmonise them perhaps need not be of concern. Other ways of informing viewers about the nature of content broadcast (for example, EPGs) have the potential to be more helpful. There is a need, however, to address the neutrality of the content on the EPG, who provides it and for what purpose. Using technologies as part of the regulatory schema, in the anticipation of greater viewer self-reliance, may avoid a host of problems, but attention needs to be paid to the needs of vulnerable or passive viewers. Equally, while the involvement of industry participants in regulatory structures (via co- or self-regulation) may make those structures more flexible, care should be taken that they do not only reflect the interests of industry at the expense of viewers.[71]

[71] E.g., Bertelsmann, *Comments on the Commission Consultation, Protection of Minors and Human Dignity; Right of Reply*, p. 10, commented that harmonisation of standards would endanger successful self-regulation regimes and advised that the Commission continue not to intervene in effective self-regulation schemes; Bitkom, *Comments on the Rules Applicable to Audiovisual Content Services: Issue Paper 5*, p. 3, also commented that a general harmonisation of standards in relation to protection of minors or right of reply would undermine successful self-regulation; mediawatch-UK, *Revision of the 'Television Without Frontiers' Directive, Protection of Minors and Human Dignity; Right of Reply*, p. 2, expressed concern about the effectiveness of the current system in relation to protection of minors, and questioned whether member states should be left to define 'incitement to hatred' subjectively, arguing that the best means to ensure incitement to hatred on the grounds of race, sex, religion or nationality is prohibited is to enshrine safeguards in the Universal Declaration of Human Rights. For further responses to the TWFD Consultation, see http://europa.eu.int/comm/avpolicy/revision-tvwf2005/2005-contribution.htm.

11

Positive content regulation: quotas

Introduction

As we argue in chapter 1, the viewing preferences of citizens require a diverse range of programming. The consequences of an increasingly competitive, international media market mean, however, that broadcasters tend to adopt successful formulas based upon tried-and-tested programming formats which are repeated. This approach leads to the safe, the similar and the familiar endlessly occupying programme schedules. Positive content regulation could operate to counter this tendency. The problem as far as the Union is concerned, as we saw in chapters 4 and 5, is that it has limited competence in this regard. If content quotas aimed at protecting citizens' interests are justified by reference to cultural policy, plurality or diversity, the Union does not have direct legislative competence. The Television without Frontiers Directive (TWFD),[1] which includes content quotas, is based on internal market considerations. These considerations result in the quotas being shaped by industrial and commercial concerns, the most typical being the need for a return on investment and the utilisation of national skills pools. The consequence is that quotas are not assessed by reference to the quality of broadcast content, but by reference to formal criteria. Even if things were otherwise, the use of quotas would remain problematic. Some see them as contrary to freedom of expression, while for others they are contrary to international trading rules. The different viewpoints of the member states in this regard are well known, and the lack of agreement led to the quota obligations being phrased in opaque and non-binding terms.[2]

---

[1] Council Directive 89/552/EEC of 3 October 1989 on the co-ordination of certain provisions laid down by law, regulation or administrative action in member states concerning the pursuit of television broadcasting activities OJ [1989] L 298/23, as amended by Directive 97/36/ EC OJ [1997] L 202/30.

[2] B. de Witte, 'The European Content Requirement – Five Years After', *Yearbook of Media and Entertainment Law* (1995) 101–27, p. 104.

This chapter assesses the nature and functioning of the quota system. In doing so, it will consider the scope of the works covered by the two types of quota: the 'European quota'; and the 'independent works quota', and the nature of the obligations contained in Articles 4–6 TWFD. We then assess, in light of the underlying problem of Union competence, the question of whether they address cultural or commercial concerns, and whether they achieve a balanced and effective result. In this assessment, we shall consider the influence of the quotas on the viewing experience and thus the degree to which different viewers' needs are addressed.

Overview of quota provisions

Whereas the negative content regulations are aimed at prevention of harm, positive content can be viewed in general terms as seeking to stimulate 'good' quality content. The assessment of the content's quality links regulation with the social, cultural and educational objectives of broadcasting (see chapter 2), an approach which resonates with the viewing requirements of the citizen viewer. As we suggest in chapter 1, passive citizen viewers are traditionally and typically dependent on a narrow range of providers supplying a diverse range of content.

Within the TWFD, Articles 4–6 fulfil this positive function. They introduce two types of quota: one focusing on 'European works' (Article 4(1)); the other on 'independent European works' (Article 5). The member states are under an obligation, 'as far as practicable and by appropriate means', to ensure that the majority of transmission time is reserved for European works, and that 10 per cent is reserved for independent European works. Alternatively, this quota may be satisfied by reference to the broadcasters' programming budget. In this sense, the independent works quota is not just a quota which relates to transmission time but also relates to the production of works to satisfy the independent works quota. The 'European quota', by contrast, is concerned purely with transmission. Transmission can be linked to the commodification of cultural products, as it provides the means of their distribution for consumption. The production (of independent works) is more closely linked to the creation of the work and stimulating the creative industries. Although the programme production industries are commercial entities falling within industrial policy, it is also possible to see them as contributing to expressions of culture through broadcasting. They also improve the diversity of content on offer. Following this argument, the independent quota has clear cultural objectives.

'European works' and 'European independent works' are both defined in Article 6. Two elements of these definitions are common to both categories: first, the notion of a 'work'; and secondly, that the work be 'European'. The TWFD does not consider the nature of a 'work', except to the extent that certain genres are excluded from the calculation of transmission time: news, sports events, games,[3] advertising, teletext services and teleshopping.[4] Article 6(1) identifies three possible categories of European work:

a works originating from a member state;
b works originating from a European state that is party to the Council of Europe Convention on Transfrontier Television;
c works which originate from other European states.

To a greater or lesser extent, all these categories require production control to be in the hands of a body established within the Union: these conditions in the case of (a) and (b) above being found in Article 6(2);[5] and in the case of (c) in Article 6(3). Article 6(3) further requires that the production be made within the context of a bilateral agreement relating to audiovisual policy between the Union and the relevant European country.[6] Article 6(4) extends the scope of 'European' to productions within the framework of co-production agreements with third countries: again production control must vest in a body established within the Union and the majority of the funds must come from the Union.

So far the definition of control has focused on the producers. Article 5 recognises that programming, which does not fall within Article 6(1) but which is made mainly with authors and workers residing in one or more member states, will proportionately be considered to be a European work

---

[3] Interestingly, the TWFD does not define the notion of games. The EBU has arrived at a definition which distinguishes between game shows and quiz shows. Gameshows, according to this definition, are programmes whose format is a competition developed for television involving tests of knowledge, intelligence or skill. Quiz shows are similar to game shows, but place less emphasis on prizes and more emphasis on testing the competitors' intellectual ability.

[4] These last two categories were inserted by Directive 97/36, the Amending Directive.

[5] Interestingly Article 6(1)(a), which was altered by the Amending Directive, does not cross-refer to Article 6(2), but Article 6(2) specifies that Article 6(1)(a) is subject to the conditions set out in Article 6(2). Presumably this is an error that crept in during the amendment process and Article 6(1)(a) should be understood as being subject to the requirements in 6(2).

[6] This provision is amended in the draft second amending directive (DSAD): Commission, *Proposal for a Directive amending Directive 89/552/EEC*, COM(2005)646 final, 2005/0260 (COD), SEC (2005) 1625 and 1626.

to the extent that the European producers have contributed to the production costs. Why financing would make a production 'European', when those involved in its production would not justify such an assessment, is far from clear. Equally, the idea that a work may be found to be 'European' according to a certain percentage is difficult to explain.

Independent works are defined as European works which are created by 'producers who are independent of broadcasters'. It is again not clear from the terms of the TWFD whether this requirement relates purely to the legal structure of the company, or whether it relates to the company's freedom of editorial control. This matter is discussed further below.

Definition of European works

Despite a lack of evidence to show the effectiveness of cultural policy in the formulation of a European identity,[7] Union policymaking continues to focus on the importance of television as a means to foster some type, albeit vague, of pan-European culture (or sense of belonging to the Union), whilst also celebrating the Union's cultural diversity through a variety of programmes for audiovisual and civic participation (see chapter 5).[8] Law can sometimes clarify concepts which, outside the legal context, are contested. Unfortunately, this does not seem to be the case in relation to culture. Certainly, the TWFD does not seek to define European culture; neither does the EC Treaty. The state-aid provisions also refer to culture (see chapter 13); in practice, this has tended towards a view of culture as linked to heritage, though the point has not been expressly discussed and certainly not by the European Court of Justice (ECJ).[9]

The influence of the media is not, however, limited to cultural concerns in the usual sense of broadcasting highbrow programming. Messages which reinforce the values associated with a common European identity, culture or citizenship may be found in a range of genres. Arguably, it is this

---

[7] C. Belot and A. Smith, 'Europe and Identity: A Challenge for the Social Sciences', in U. Hedetoft (ed.), *Political Symbols, Symbolic Politics: European Identities in Transformation* (Hampshire: Ashgate Publishing Limited, 1998), p. 99.

[8] See similarly Commission, *'Non-Paper' on Short Reporting* (2006), available http://europa/ eu.int/comm/avpolicy/regul_en.htm#4, noting the importance of the free circulation of programmes about other member states.

[9] L. Woods, 'The Application of Competition Rules to State Aids for Culture', in *Culture and Marché, ERA Forum 1-2005*; and 'Culture in the European Union', in van Empel (ed.), *From Paris to Nice: Fifty Years of Integration in Europe* (The Hague: Kluwer Law International, 2003), pp. 109–29.

aspect (broadcasting a broad range of programming that reflects different dimensions of European culture) that the quota provisions are, in practice, protecting, even if this was not at the forefront of legislators' minds when they agreed the provisions. Indeed, Articles 4 and 5 emphasise that media regulation should have regard to 'broadcasters' informational, educational, cultural and entertainment responsibilities to its [*sic*] viewing public'. This point re-emphasises the assumptions that European policymakers have made about the values ascribed to the broadcast media (see chapters 2 and 5). It could be argued that 'informational' here should not be seen narrowly, but as relating more generally to political information, as well as cultural and educational matters. Furthermore, Recital 44 to the Amending Directive recognises the need to protect television's public interest role, without clarifying what, in the context of the TWFD, that term means.

Against this background, one might have thought that the idea of promoting European culture through the broadcast media would require programming that reflects those public interest concerns identified in chapter 2. As a corollary, positive programming requirements should also, it seems, pay heed to ensuring that programming which fulfilled these needs was broadcast. It is here, however, that weaknesses in the quota rules emerge. We believe that to satisfy or protect citizens' interests in broadcasting, the quota rules require certain general quality standards. As we have noted, there are no such quality standards included in the quota rules. In so far as quality is dealt with, it is dealt with in a negative sense, through the prohibitions on certain unacceptable types of programming (see chapter 10). This does little or nothing to prevent the quotas being met by programmes that are of poor quality and which do not therefore meet informational, educational and cultural aims or goals (no matter how vague), even when the genres of programming acceptable to satisfy those obligations are broadly understood.

The other approach to ensuring that public interest programming is broadcast is to require certain genres, which are perceived as particularly appropriate to filling public interest needs, to be broadcast (see also discussion of scope of public service broadcasting (PSB) in chapter 13). In this context, such content would typically be news, current affairs programmes and documentaries, as well as programming which might reflect a highbrow view of culture rather than popular culture. Surprisingly, then, when we look at the quota requirements, the programmes excluded from the calculation of the transmission time taken up with European works are news and current affairs programmes. Whether this means that current affairs and news are excluded from the concept of 'European culture' or not, it certainly seems that the quota provisions do not seek to encourage the broadcasting of these types of programmes. Before we are too heavily critical of the TWFD in this context, it should also be noted that programming of a type that might be typically seen to be pandering purely to consumer interests, such as game shows, is likewise excluded from the quota calculation.

The reliance on a genre-based test can be analysed in two ways. On the one hand, the TWFD, by not dealing with quality of content, is merely respecting the division of competence within the Union (see chapter 4). Recital 13 to the original Directive specifically states that the TWFD, in setting down the minimum rules needed to guarantee freedom of television services, does not affect member states' competence with regard to the content of programmes. It is, however, difficult to maintain the argument that the TWFD does not contain content rules. Quite apart from the quota rules themselves, the negative regulations found in relation to harmful content (see chapter 10) are rules relating to content of programming.

On the other hand, the exclusion of certain categories of content from the quota calculation has arisen out of a desire to focus the quotas on fictional or artistic rather than journalistic elements of the media industry. Specifically, this means seeking to stimulate the film and television production companies, which are in competition with companies worldwide, particularly with the American production houses.[10] By contrast, although the expansion of 24-hour niche news channels has increased competition between news providers seeking to capitalise on the opportunities offered by digital technology in a global news market, there is less competition between national news providers as such on the traditional linear channels. Any competition that exists between such news providers is only a reflection of the competition between channels and their attempts to retain and attract viewers.

The distinction made in the TWFD between factual programming and entertainment-based programming therefore raises the question of whether this element of the quota requirements is really driven by a desire to protect European culture or citizens' interests, or is motivated by industrial concerns.[11] In the light of the media's widely regarded role as the 'fourth estate', the exclusion of news is a somewhat surprising omission,

---

[10] See Recitals 19 and 20 of the original TWFD, which link the quotas, including the independent works quota, to the development of the European audiovisual industry.

[11] The recitals to each of the directives have noted the industrial aspect of the mass media and the production houses particularly; the proposed amending directive with its reference to

especially given the concerns expressed about the lack of interest in, and knowledge of, the Union held by the average European citizen.[12] Of course, we should note that the significance and value of news is just one aspect of what is deemed necessary to serve the public interest and provide cultural programming. In this context, the excluded categories take another content group out of the calculation, that of sport. As we noted in chapter 1, sport, as the TWFD itself recognises (see chapter 12), is significant in terms of generating senses of identity and belonging, no matter how partial the groups which are represented by those sports are. However, what remains outstanding in this particular context is the question of whether the extension of the TWFD to a broader range of audiovisual media services, as suggested in the Draft Second Amending Directive (DSAD),[13] should extend the possibility of the quotas rules to, for example, on-line games. The reason behind the question is that, without doubt, the on-line games industry is an important part of popular culture and especially youth culture.[14] It has a similar structure in terms of the development of content (and arguably similar distribution problems) to the film industry.[15] If a broader range of services is to be subject to quota requirements, further work needs to be done on whether the categories on which the quotas are based remain appropriate.

Defining cultural programming *per se* is itself difficult, but these difficulties are compounded by the fact that such programming is also required to be 'European'. Within the EC Treaty, and particularly Article 151 EC, there is a tension between two approaches to the meaning of European. One approach sees it as deriving from a pan-European cultural identity. The second adopts the idea of 'unity in diversity', which recognises all the different cultures and languages which together make up the Union.[16] This latter idea can be found in the TWFD, with its references to maintaining the cultural diversity of the member states. In one respect, the tension here is not unique to the Union. Although it is tempting to talk

the i2010 Information Society is no exception: Proposal for a Directive amending Directive 89/552/EEC, COM(2005)646 final, Recital 7.

[12] See the Commission, *Communication on an information and communication strategy for the European Union*, COM(2002)350 final, and the efforts made by the Directorate-General Press and Communication to improve the so-called democratic deficit. DSAD itself noted the importance of pluralism in the news, COM (2005) 646 final, Recital 26.

[13] DSAD, COM(2005)646 final, Recital 35.

[14] For their own view of the significance of games, see European Games Developer Federation, *Statement of the Reform of the Directive 'TV without Frontiers'*, p. 1, available at www.europarl.eu/

[15] *Ibid.*, p. 2.   [16] See also Article I–3 of the proposed Constitution.

of the member states as if each had a homogeneous culture, such a view would be simplistic. In many member states, the citizenry can often have multiple facets to their cultural identities, variously derived from a region, an ethnic group and or religious group.

The ECJ has, indeed, taken the diversity of a population into account on occasion. In one of the *Dutch media cases*[17] (discussed chapter 5), the ECJ noted the 'social, cultural, religious and philosophical' diversity of the Netherlands, although on the facts the Dutch rules were held to be disproportionate to their aim, which was the protection of the plurality of the media. None the less, diversity seems particularly difficult for the Union to express, and the matter is therefore never adequately addressed. This failure to consider the different interests in this area has consequences for any coherent understanding of what is meant by the word 'European'. In particular, it is unclear whether the European interest is the same as an individual member state's interests, or whether a discussion of a member state's interests exhausts all the possible interests within that member state. In short, a requirement based on an ill-defined idea of 'European' is inadequate to ensure that a culturally diverse range of programmes is broadcast, whether this be in respect of programmes broadcast by other member states or minority voices within a particular member state.

This difficulty can be seen in the way European works are described; the TWFD merely refers to 'works originating from member states'. This phrase conflates the idea of 'European' with the member states, both individually and in conjunction. It is, on the terms of the TWFD, impossible to require pan-European productions. The requirement is satisfied by productions originating from any of the member states. In one sense, the terms of the TWFD are understandable. Discrimination on grounds of nationality is inconsistent with the fundamental principles of the Union; this is expressed in the general principles found in the EC Treaty, and which have formed an important element of the ECJ's jurisprudence on the free movement of people. The principle of non-discrimination also forms an important element in the concept of European citizenship. In the *Garcia Avello* case,[18] Advocate-General Jacobs linked non-discrimination to cultural diversity. This approach would seem to be fundamentally inconsistent with regulations which sought to distinguish between the nationals of the different member states. Although the proposition may seem

---

[17] Case C-288/89 *Stichting Collectieve Antennevoorziening Gouda* v. *Commissariaat voor de Media* [1991] ECR I-4007, para. 13.

[18] Case C-148/02 *Garcia Avello* [2003] judgment 2 October 2003, Opinion, para. 72.

non-contentious at a general level, it has led to problems which arise in three linked ways.[19]

First, as can be seen from the above discussion, a system which does not allow us to distinguish between a conflation of all, or more than one of, the member states and individual member states means that European productions in this sense include domestic productions. Thus, although national rules would not be permitted to discriminate directly on grounds of nationality, in practice broadcasters can, and do, broadcast material produced in the same member state as that in which they are established. The *Impact Study*,[20] commissioned by the Commission in accordance with Article 25(a) TWFD, reinforces this concern. It found that while the number of European works being broadcast grew from 1993 to 2002, the number of non-domestic European works has risen more slowly.[21] Language requirements imposed in national regulatory systems may also reinforce this tendency.[22] Language requirements can be phrased in a neutral manner, so that they do not directly discriminate against imported content. In this context, it is notable that the original TWFD contained in

---

[19] One problem which we have seen is the 'abuse' of Union law; if Union law does not distinguish between nationality, it is very difficult to run an argument that says a national of member state A is abusing Union law rights to avoid home regulation if that national sets up business in another member state but targets production at the state of origin. The key element in this argument relates to assumptions about where a national of state A lives and to whom he or she should be broadcasting. See further ch. 8, and contrast Case C-148/91 *Vereniging Veronica Omroep Organisatie* v. *Commissariaat voor de Media* [1993] ECR I-487 and Case C-23/93 *TV10 SA* v. *Commissariaat voor de Media* [1994] ECR I-4795, noted by P. Wattel, *CMLRev* 32 (1995), 1257, with Case C-56/96 *VT4 Ltd* v. *Vlaamse Gemeenschap* [1997] ECR I-3143, and discussion in L. Woods and J. Scholes, 'Broadcasting: The Creation of a European Culture or the Limits of the Internal Market?', *Yearbook of European Law 17* (1997), 47–82, *passim*. More generally, see Case C-212/97 *Centros Ltd* v. *Erhvervs-og Selskabsstyrelsen* [1999] ECR I-1459; and A. Kjellgren, 'On the Border of Abuse: The Jurisprudence of the European Court of Justice on Circumvention, Fraud and Abuses of Community law', in M. Andenas and W.-H. Roth, (eds.), *Services and Free Movement in EU Law* (Oxford: Oxford University Press, 2002), *passim*.

[20] David Graham and Associates Limited, *Study on the Impact of Measures concerning the Promotion and the Distribution and Production of TV Programmes (Community and National) provided for under Article 25(a) of the 'Television without Frontiers Directive'*, (2005) available http://ec.europa.eu/comm/avpolicy/docs/library/studies/finalised/4-5/27-03-finalreport.pdf.

[21] Recital 21 to the original TWFD envisaged that member states might want to impose stricter standards, and specifically in relation to the definition of European works. This option does not seem to have dealt with this particular problem and, indeed, may contribute to it through the imposition of 'culturally' driven requirements. The *Impact Study* notes that 25 per cent of the qualifying transmission time in Greece is required to be devoted to works produced in Greece, p. 96.

[22] David Graham and Associates, *Impact Study*, p. 12 and pp. 94–6.

the recitals, especially Recital 25, a specific acknowledgment that member states retain the competence to maintain an 'active policy in favour of a specific language'.[23] Language policy is also linked to the term 'independent producers' in the Amending Directive.[24] None the less, it might be harder for a non-national broadcaster or production company to satisfy such a requirement, especially where that broadcaster is not established in the same language area. This constitutes indirect discrimination contrary to Article 49 EC.[25] It could be argued that programming that is not broadcast in the national/regional language of the recipient viewing population is not going to be watched by many people and is therefore unlikely to remain commercially viable, meaning that, in practical terms, such questions are unlikely to arise often. None the less, language rules have the effect of reinforcing a preference for national programming. Although the extent to which such rules are permissible has been the subject of some debate,[26] once again, we see a tension between the stated need of creating a single broadcasting market and the desire to protect the cultural diversity of the member states.

Secondly, if the development of European culture requires pan-Union productions, the possibility of national productions counting towards a broadcaster's European quota might undermine the development of European productions. Of course, better understanding between the various member states might be achieved by the swapping of programming between them, but this view overestimates the power of television and, as we have seen, is not required by the terms of the TWFD. National markets may instead be reinforced; certainly, they may remain segmented from one another within the Union.[27] The *Impact Study* shows that audiences throughout the Union tend to have a preference for American products over European works originating from other member states. DSAD maintains the quota rules. Indeed, given that non-linear services have the potential, at least partially, to replace traditional services, DSAD requires member states to 'ensure that media service providers under their jurisdiction promote, where practicable and by appropriate means, production of and access to European works'.[28] The quotas requirements are potentially

[23] The TWFD implicitly recognises the problems of language, albeit in the context of viewing the internal market as fragmented: see Recitals 20 and 22 of the original TWFD.

[24] Amending Directive, Recital 31.   [25] See further ch. 4.

[26] See, e.g., de Witte, 'The European Content Requirement', p. 107.

[27] The conclusions of the David Graham and Associates' *Impact Study* support this contention, pp. 13–14.

[28] Draft second amending directive, COM (2005) 646 final, Article 3(f)(1); see also Recital 35.

extended to non-linear services by this provision. Although this point is not addressed in the substance of DSAD, Recital 36 to the proposal specifically draws attention to the desirability of member states making provision for broadcasters to include an adequate share of co-produced European works, or of European works of non-domestic origin. As it is only contained in the recitals, this is not a binding obligation. It has also met with some resistance from those who argue such an obligation imposes unnecessary costs on new media service providers. The cost argument is not new and has been used by broadcasters operating in the traditional environment, as we shall see below.

Thirdly, the conflation of European with individual member states has given rise to more problems, as has been noted by a number of commentators.[29] As some of the recitals to the TWFD note, some member states have weaker domestic broadcasting markets than do others. This is particularly the case for the smaller and/or linguistically isolated member states. According to our analysis of the quota regime, given that no distinction is permissible on grounds of nationality, broadcasters may choose to buy content from broadcasters or production houses in the other member states (especially those in the same language group) in preference to productions from the same member state. Factors influencing this choice could relate to quality or, more likely, cost. Although the reference to language policy requirements may be acceptable in some circumstances, and may operate to protect linguistically isolated states (providing a domestic market is viable), this will not operate to protect small states with a much larger neighbour in the same language group.[30] We are then faced with a difficult question: is it better for these states to be dominated by programming from another member state (or possibly by co-productions) rather than by non-European productions, specifically American programming? The argument in favour of programming from other member states implicitly suggests that there is a core common ground between the member states and, crucially, a difference between European values and American values, thus justifying ring-fencing the Union market. Whilst some analysts have claimed to identify core common European values,

---

[29] Lupinacci, 'The Pursuit of Television Broadcasting Activities in the European Community: Cultural Preservation or Economic Protectionism?', *Vanderbilt Journal of Transnational Law* (1991), 113–54, p. 127.

[30] Any lack of protection for minority languages raises concerns about any effect this may have on expressions of cultural identity within the Union. See, e.g., D. Crystal, *Language Death* (Cambridge: Cambridge University Press, 2000), p. 36. In the case of the Welsh language, the local media in particular have played a large part in preserving the language and preventing its decline: Crystal, *Language Death*, p. 88.

they have omitted to establish how these differ from American values.[31] Additionally, their analysis does not adequately deal with the fact that minority values, including those from smaller member states, may still not be adequately protected if unity in diversity as a principle is to be maintained.

As noted above, some member states contain distinct regional groups or significant minorities. The definition of European works does not itself exclude the works of such groups from the scope of the quota provision necessarily. Indeed, certain cross-border groupings may be protected in some respects by the broad definition of European; this may encourage the broadcasting of some minority programming.[32] None the less, the exclusion of certain types of programming from the quotas calculation may mean that broadcasters might not have the incentive to select those types of programming for broadcast. The problem is that some of these, notably, but not exclusively, news and sports events, are often vehicles for regional and sub-regional productions. Their exclusion means that there are few genres left which can provide European content at the sub-national level. This has an impact not only on the content itself but on the viability of production houses in the provinces. The production of 'European works' could thus be skewed towards production and monitoring of national works, from whichever member state, thereby reinforcing a view of 'European' which is made up of majority groups' cultures. One is left with the impression that the dominant concern in the quota provisions is to protect the underlying producers, as part of European industry. Any cultural benefit to an aggregated notion of citizen is a by-product of a desire to protect European industry and consideration of the position of minorities within the Union has not received great attention. This may not, of course, be malice aforethought, but rather the consequence of the difficulties in marrying up abstract concepts with specific criteria for their identification.

Criteria for assessing 'European'

We have seen that there are some difficulties with the idea of European works at a level of principle. Some of these problems are linked to how

---

[31] See, e.g., H. Wallace, 'The European that Came In from the Cold', *International Affairs* 67(4) (1991), pp. 648–64, referred to by C. Shore and S. Wright (eds.), *Anthropology of Policy* (London: Routledge, 1997), pp. 165–92.

[32] For the position of minorities more generally, contrast W. Kymlicka, *Multicultural Citizenship* (Oxford: Oxford University Press, 1995) and J. Waldron, 'Minority Culture and the Cosmopolitan Alternative', *University of Michigan Journal of Law Reform* 25 (1992), 751.

'European' is seen: that is, tied into the concept of a member state. There is a further level of difficulty which relates to how we establish which productions are made in which member state (a different form of the establishment problem found in jurisdiction; see chapter 8). The approach adopted in the TWFD is a structural approach, that is, it looks at the location of the companies or other bodies which are producers (in a broad sense) of content rather than the substance of the content itself. This is a pragmatic solution to what would otherwise be an approach based on the subjective assessment of content. None the less, this structural approach protects European culture (however defined) only if one accepts that the place of residence or establishment has a necessary link with the content of the programming produced; in other words, that such content will automatically reflect the culture of the originating member state. As we shall show, there are problems with this approach, and they are greater in some contexts than others. We suggest that the creative elements of programming rather than structural (and financial) questions about production companies should be central to any assessment of a link between production and cultural worth. This element is not equally present in all situations.

The assumption about the link between place of business and culture is not sound. Too much depends on questions of establishment and residence; these criteria do not necessarily say anything about the nationality of the bodies (natural or legal) involved. It is more likely, to the extent that a causal link can be identified, that it is nationality, cultural or religious identity, rather than current place of establishment, that influences any resulting programming.

An added complication appears when we consider the term 'producer'. Whereas the author[33] and actors are individuals, the term 'producer' has two possible meanings, which could affect the determination of whether a particular work should be considered European or not. It could mean the producer of the relevant project itself, or the production company responsible for the project.[34] The loyalties or identities of bodies corporate may

---

[33] Presumably, the author is not necessarily the copyright holder in a given script or outline, but the person who actually wrote it.

[34] It is unclear here whether the Union means production company by the term 'producer' or is referring to the specific individual who has the role of producer in respect of a programme. The recitals do not help: Recital 27 of the Amending Directive distinguishes between a programme maker and producer, potentially indicating that it is the personal sense of producer that is meant; whereas Recital 31 seems to refer to production companies by its use of the word producer, as does Recital 23 to the TWFD. The Commission, *Suggested Guidelines for the Monitoring of the Implementation of Articles 4 and 5 of the Television*

cause difficulties in this context. The first problem is a matter of general principle. We are not convinced that, by contrast to the position for an individual, companies have a cultural identity, as opposed to corporate culture, which finds its way into the creative element of any programming. Secondly, even if we accept that there might be some form of corporate cultural identity, tying a company down to a particular nationality or set of national interests is not easy. While it may be possible to identify some companies that are chauvinistic, or culturally determined, most contemporary corporate structures prove to be remarkably agnostic and independent of nationality, and more concerned with economic performance. Corporate bodies have shareholders and, although the company itself may be established within the Union, the shareholders, or some of them, may not be European. In the increasingly globalised environment of transnational corporations in which ownership of media companies is concentrated into increasingly few hands, it seems likely that companies established under the laws of one of the member states may be owned by a body established outside the Union.

The TWFD does nothing to stop this.[35] The approach adopted in the quotas provisions raises the questions of the level of impact that the nationality of the shareholder has on the cultural content of the programmes produced by the production company. As we shall see below, the Commission has noted in successive reports on the application of Articles 4 and 5, that being a subsidiary of a non-Union company has had significant impact on the ability of the subsidiary to comply with the quotas requirements; there is a link between non-Union ownership and editorial policy. Although the impact of editorial policy relates to the broadcasting of content, rather than its production, it is arguable that similar problems (favouring content from the same state as the shareholders) could occur in the production arena. Further, it would seem likely that, in the long term, any profits made by the production company will find themselves repatriated to the shareholders. Such an outcome hardly supports the long-term development of the European audiovisual production industry, one of the goals, if not the main goal, of the TWFD.

without Frontiers Directive, 11 June 1999, point 5.4 states, however, that 'A producer is considered to be established in a European State if the company is a going concern which has a permanent staff involved in both production and commercial operations at the European level.' This would seem to be aimed at excluding paper companies. It clearly also suggests that the Commission is viewing 'producer' as meaning a production company.

[35] The TWFD does not cover media mergers; there is some debate about the Union's competence in this regard (see ch. 4), though currently the issue of media pluralism is being debated as part of the review of the TWFD.

Furthermore, this approach does not take account of the pressures of a commercial and global market-place on business decision-making, which affects decisions on content. It assumes that writers and producers will produce a programme that reflects their cultural background. This is not necessarily the case. Even assuming a 'pure' European programme remains possible in an environment in which programme makers have never been exposed to 'non-European' influences, companies making choices about the nature of content might not want to commission such programming. Companies will tend to place commercial factors ahead of cultural prerequisites. This aspect can be seen in the quota provisions, with their references to the need to build world-class European production houses. The Amending Directive itself recognised this. Recital 27 states:

> broadcasting organisations, programme makers, producers, authors and other experts should be encouraged to develop more detailed concepts and strategies aimed at developing European audiovisual fiction films that are addressed to an international audience.

It could be argued that the need to appeal to a worldwide (or non-European) market would have an impact on the types of content choice made. Consequently, Union broadcasting policy through the TWFD appears to have encouraged the process of homogenisation and the dilution of national (or European) culture, in the interests of making a programme as broadly acceptable as possible.[36]

Commercial pressures are not limited to production companies, but may also affect broadcasters. The Commission has noted the tendency to use archive and stock material from the parent company or other subsidiaries, rather than European material, by a number of subsidiaries of American companies based throughout the Union. This may, given the increasingly international nature of the media industry, be a problem without a solution. Certainly, it is an issue that has been raised during the review process, but whether the economic decisions of parent companies are a good enough reason for 'exempting' some channels from the quota provisions is questionable. If the principle were to be applied more generally, many obligations on the broadcasters would be completely undermined. Such an argument could be put forward in the context of negative regulation in respect of matters relating to the time particular

---

[36] More information on the tactics used to improve the rate of export of programmes are discussed by J. Harrison and L. Woods, 'Television Quotas: Protecting European Culture?', *Entertainment Law Review* (2001), 5–14, p. 12.

programmes were scheduled, a decision similarly beyond the control of broadcasters. It has also been used in the context of surreptitious advertising or product placement in relation to the advertising placement rules (chapter 9). This weakness illustrates the problem of the subject-matter of regulation: should the regulation be aimed at those who transmit pre-order channels; or should it be those that package the channel in the first place? This reflects the problems in relation the definition of broadcaster in the TWFD, where it is not clear whether the regime is applicable to those who create and bundle the content to be broadcast, or those who are the point of contact with viewers and provide the framework through which viewers can access content. The appropriate scope of broadcaster is the subject of some discussion (see chapter 8), as is the question of at which point of the distribution chain regulatory obligations bite. We believe that an approach which focuses on the viewing experience would place responsibility for content on the company through whose framework the viewer accesses content.[37]

The commercialisation of the television environment has created a second set of problems that affect the diversity of broadcast content. It has led broadcasters and production companies to choose perceived safe options in terms of programme styles. In particular, the buying and selling of programme formats which have proved popular has become common.[38] Although such a work must satisfy the test for a 'European work' (or even a 'European independent work') in terms of those employed on the project, it is debatable whether the resulting programme would necessarily portray European values, as the values of the programme will have been incorporated in the original format. There are two points. First, this returns us to the observation we made earlier about the importance of the creative element in identifying cultural values in a production. Secondly, it is arguable that a lot of popular formats contain little that is culturally stimulating. The repetition of similar formats undermines a viewing experience traditionally built upon a broad range of content and genres, a problem that is

---

[37] E.g., the Discovery channels are provided by an American company. This content can be accessed across a number of platforms in the UK. If we look at digital terrestrial television, Freeview provides the framework through which viewers can access that content. The actual transmission is carried out by a further company, Crown Castle, which has no responsibility for content.

[38] The term 'formats' is used to refer to the tendency for certain types of programmes to share common unifying features, usually relating to the way the show is organised, such as use of guests or main characters, or even studio set-up. Generally, programmes which have common unifying features fall into the genres of sitcoms and gameshows, although they are not so limited.

reinforced by technology which enables bulk recording of the same type of programme material.[39]

As noted above, Article 5 opens up the possibility that works may be considered partly European, the proportion of 'Europeanness' to be determined by reference to the amount of funding that originates from within the Union. The requirement of European control is absent. Quite apart from the question of whether it is possible to determine something to be partly 'European' in cultural terms, we doubt that it is entirely appropriate to determine that proportion by reference to funding rather than content. In this context, it should be noted that the TWFD gives no clue as to how to assess 'mainly' for the purposes of Article 5. Would 51 per cent satisfy this requirement, or does it mean virtually all involved should be European? Moreover, it does not distinguish between types of employee and some (such as the author or director and even the actors) may have more impact on the European feel of the end product than others, such as sound technicians, special effects people and wardrobe staff. It is possible, however, for this last group of more technical jobs to outweigh the former numerically. This distinction reaffirms our concerns about the degree of emphasis that is placed on structural issues rather than on creative aspects of content production.

Equally difficult to determine (because it is not quantifiable) is any accurate assessment about the level of creativity required to make a programme. Some are genuinely creative; others formulaic; and still others mere copy-cat programmes. In the advertising chapter (chapter 9), we saw the difficulties for the application of Article 11 arising from omnibus magazine programmes for children made up from different programming elements. The same example illustrates the problems with the idea of making a programme within the terms of the TWFD. Some elements of these programmes are original, but others are often bought in; for example, cartoons from the Disney Corporation. The elements of the omnibus programme can be complete programmes in themselves which are inserted into the magazine framework. Whilst it is arguable that a programme comprising part original and part sourced material is 'made' for the purposes of Article 5, such a conclusion does not seem to be justified if all the elements were complete programmes bought from elsewhere. This point has additional significance in assessing the quota rules against cultural measures: whose cultural values are represented in the case of an assemblage of (American) cartoons or music videos?

---

[39] For a more detailed discussion of this point, see Harrison and Woods, 'Quotas', p. 12.

Independent productions

It is assumed that the idea of what is 'European' that applies to 'European works' applies also to 'European independent works'. There is no further clarification of this term in the operative part of the TWFD. Whether the term 'independence' relates purely to the legal structure of the company, or whether it relates to the company's freedom of editorial control, is not clear from the terms of the TWFD. It may be that editorial independence could be ensured even within the subsidiary of a broadcaster. Equally, formal structural independence does not guarantee editorial independence, as we shall see below. If the two concerns, formal structural independence and actual independence of opinion, are not interdependent, surely the focus on any criteria must be aimed at ensuring the latter rather than the former. Of course, industrial policy might militate towards the protection of small- and medium-sized enterprises, which could cover those producers that are structurally independent from broadcasters. Quotas then could operate to provide those companies with a market for their works.

The Commission's Suggested Guidelines[40] emphasise that the definition of 'independent' should be understood in the light of Recital 31 of the Amending Directive, which identifies ownership as one issue to be taken into account but refers also to other considerations, such as the amount of production supplied to the same broadcaster and the ownership of any secondary rights. All of these might affect a production company's freedom of action, as a company might think twice before offending its major source of income. There are, however, problems with referring to Recital 31. The guidance in itself is vague. It lists criteria that can be taken into account, but it does not specify whether these are by way of example or a cumulative minimum. The phrase 'such as' excludes the possibility of an exhaustive definition. It has, none the less, been suggested that Recital 31 should be clarified to make it clear that the criteria identified are a necessary minimum and that other additional criteria may be used. Further, the list is linked in with the principle that lesser used languages should be protected. It could be argued that this linkage operates to limit the scope of 'independent producers', though seeing the language policy requirements as an additional, optional, factor which could be taken into account would, in our view, be better.

---

[40] Commission, *Suggested Guidelines for Monitoring the Implementation of Articles 4 and 5*, 11 June 1999, available at http://ec.europa.eu/comm/avpolicy/info_centre/library/legal/index_en.htm p. 4.

The lack of definition does give member states considerable latitude in this area, quite apart from the possibility of imposing higher standards via Article 3. Potentially, a wide variety of interpretations of this phrase could arise, with possible adverse consequences for the creation of an internal market. Although member states cannot stop broadcasts coming in that comply with a potentially wider conception of independent producer used by another member state, a narrow version will have an impact on the choice of production sources selected by broadcasters established within that member state's jurisdiction. This may affect the internal market in audiovisual content production, if not the supply of broadcasting itself. Further, it is a problem that is likely adversely to affect production companies in member states with small broadcasting markets, as such companies are less likely to be independent because of conditions on their home market.[41] DSAD does not seek to solve the difficulties in this area, as it does not introduce a clarification of the term.

Application and enforceability

One argument that has been put forward to justify the inclusion of the quotas in the TWFD, despite the dubious status of quotas in international law, is that they are not legally binding obligations. Some commentators[42] have suggested that this obligation is political rather than legal, as Commissioner Bangemann also stated when the TWFD was agreed. Certainly, the minutes of the Council meetings would support this viewpoint. It should be noted, however, that the opinions of the political organisations are not conclusive in determining the extent and nature of Union law obligations; the final arbiter of the extent and meaning of Union law is the ECJ.[43] Thus, the comments of the political institutions are not determinative as to whether the quota provisions are legally binding or not.[44] It must not be forgotten that the quotas are provisions of a Directive and the EC Treaty describes Directives as being legally binding, even if member states have some discretion as to how the obligations contained in Directives are achieved.[45]

In theory, the Commission could take action against recalcitrant member states under Article 226 EC. This is supported by the TWFD: not only

---

[41] The Nordic Public Service Broadcasters, *Comments on the Review of the 'Television without Frontiers' Directive* (2006), available http://www.europarl.europa.eu/, p. 3.
[42] De Witte, 'European Content Requirement', p. 114.   [43] Article 220 EC.
[44] Case C-292/89 *R.* v. *Immigration Appeal Tribunal*, ex parte *Antoinissen* [1991] ECR 745.
[45] See Article 249 EC.

are the member states under an obligation to report on the implementation of the quotas, which indicates that these obligations are to be taken seriously, but Article 4(3) obliges the Commission to ensure the proper application of Articles 4 and 5. The reporting obligations additionally mean that the Commission should be able to identify when breaches occur. Indeed, some of the cases which have already come before the ECJ on the TWFD have implicitly recognised the obligation on the member states to take steps to ensure that broadcasters try to comply with the quota requirements.[46] All these factors imply that Articles 2–4 contain legally binding obligations, even if those obligations are somewhat unclear in their terms.

Additionally, although it may not be possible to require that member states ensure the quota rules are adhered to strictly, the requirements could be seen as a standstill provision, that is that member states' performances in this regard cannot get worse. Each year's achievement is then the minimum that can be attained the following year. The ECJ has taken this approach in other areas where aspirational wording has been used.[47] Although the Commission has not specifically focused on this point, it has noted in its reports when individual broadcasters' performances have deteriorated.[48] Even if this approach is not adopted here, the wording of Article 4(2) does still provide a minimum, calculated by reference to the relevant member state's performance in 1988 (save for certain transitional provisions).[49] Problematically, whereas Article 4 is drafted by reference to the member state's average performance, the subsequent obligations really fall on individual broadcasters. This leads to the question of whether a member state's performance can remain stable, when internally some broadcasters are improving whilst others are not, or possibly even getting worse. The Commission notes this possibility, suggesting that it is looking to the performance of individual broadcasters, albeit through the intervention of the national regulator.[50] The European Parliament has, however, criticised an approach which relies on the performance of broadcasters taken across all their channels, instead advocating

---

[46] See Case C-14/96 *Criminal Proceedings against Paul Denuit* [1997] ECR I-2785.

[47] Case 203/80 *Cassati* [1981] ECR 2595.

[48] See, e.g., comments on NRK AS and NRK2 in Norway referred to in Commission, *Fourth Report on the Application of Article 4 and 5 of Directive 89/552/EEC, as amended by 97/36/EC.*

[49] This reference remains the same; there is no mention of the new member states. Presumably their position is dealt with in the relevant accession treaties.

[50] Commission, *Third Report on the Application of Article 4 and 5 of Directive 89/552/EEC, as amended by 97/36/EC.*

an assessment which looks at compliance with the quota obligations on a channel-by-channel basis, which is more difficult to satisfy. According to the European Parliament, such an approach is particularly important in member states in which the concentration of broadcasters is high.[51] Neither of these two approaches reflects the nature of the wording of the TWFD which is addressed to the member states.

Further, it is unclear which factors will be taken into account when determining whether it is practicable to carry out the obligation. A broadcaster will see its revenues and profit margins as hugely significant; regulators may not agree, although there is always the danger of regulatory capture, especially where those regulators are uncertain of their power to act. The Union does not usually accept economic difficulties as good justification for failure to comply with Union law, but here the recitals to the TWFD specifically make reference to the fact that such considerations may be taken into account.[52] Clearly, then, economic considerations also have a role to play in the operation of the quotas. None the less, although in the Commission's report on the implementation of the quota provisions a number of broadcasters refer to the cost of European productions (VT4 and RTL-TVi, for example), the Commission and national regulators have, in some cases, still sought to challenge the relevant broadcasters' non-compliance with the requirements.

This issue of cost may be of particular significance if we take into account the position of new service providers. Currently the TWFD does not cover information-society services, audiovisual content via 3G mobile telephones and on-demand services. Such service providers do not, therefore, have the cost of supplying potentially expensive European productions, arguably putting them at an advantage when compared with traditional broadcasters. This distinction may seem a trifle harsh in some contexts, for example when we consider the narrow boundary between video on demand (VOD) and near video on demand (NVOD). The European Parliament has noted the danger of creating a two-speed audiovisual sector in this regard. Even if 'digitalisation and interactivity represent opportunities for both the industry and the consumers, more choice does not necessarily mean either better quality or greater quantity of European works'.[53] The recitals to DSAD suggest that, in so far

---

[51] European Parliament, *Report on the Application of Article 4 and 5 of Directive 89/552/EEC, as amended by 97/36/EC, for the period 2001–2002*, A6-0202/2005 (*Weber Report*), para. 6, p. 5.

[52] Recital 30 to the Amending Directive.   [53] Parliament, *Weber Report*, para. 31, p. 8.

as non-linear services substitute for traditional broadcasters, they should 'continuously and efficiently promote the distribution and production of European works'.[54] This suggestion has caused outcry on the part of the new media service providers.

Conclusion

The use of quotas has given rise to the following problem. Given that their purpose is concerned with aims such as promoting a European culture, concerns with European works and so on, they are ambiguous and confusing. This raises the issue of whether quotas can ever be expressed clearly enough to protect these aims and whether they are, in fact, the appropriate vehicle for achieving such aims. The Commission, in its reports on the application of Articles 4–6, suggests that there has been an increase, in general terms, of European works and independent works, and that therefore the quota requirements have been successful. To some degree, this statement is supported by the *Impact Study*. This argument rather misses the point. The mechanism of a quota, whether in respect of production or transmission, is not in issue here. Rather, the problem is the criteria for the identification of a 'European work', and for independent works and the values that they seek to promote or protect. The problem for European works is that we do not have a sense of 'European'; the factors that are used are financial or structural, rather than cultural, thus implying that the objectives are industrial. Of course, viewers may none the less benefit, but the lack of safeguards suggests that citizens, at least, are less securely and directly protected. The concerns are compounded when we look at independent productions. They are simply inadequately defined, thus potentially undermining the effectiveness of the quotas in ensuring diversity of content.

Although, in principle, we support the continued inclusion of the quotas, further thought needs to be given as to what is meant by 'European', 'European work', 'European independent work' and 'European culture', especially given the importance and value of the broadcast media to the Union. Given the difficulty in defining these terms and in defining genres, content and quality in the broadcasting sphere, it is understandable that structural criteria appear attractive (or at least an answer). None the less, it hardly looks convincing in public interest terms, if we are seeking to ensure a diverse range of programming of interest to citizen viewers is

---

[54] Draft second amending directive, COM (2005) 646 final, Recital 35.

broadcast. As other interested parties have suggested,[55] it may be that on their own quotas are insufficient, and that alternative measures, such as the MEDIA programmes (see chapter 5), should continue to support the production of programming that is at least distinctive and original, even if we cannot guarantee its 'European-ness'. We might then see a greater range of diverse content being available, a state of affairs which would surely enrich the viewing experience.

[55] Nordic Broadcasters, *Comments on Review*, p. 2, Ofcom, *Ofcom Position Paper – European Works*, 24 April 2006, available www.europarl.europa.eu/, para. 5, p. 2.

12

Privatisation of sport and listed events

Introduction

We have seen in chapter 2 that broadcasting is perceived as fulfilling certain social and cultural functions. To enable it to do so, certain types of content must be available to all viewers. Desirable content here includes news and current affairs programmes, wider factual and learning programming, and certain other events which are also perceived to facilitate social and cultural identity formation, particularly sport. Typically, sport has been available free to air on mass-audience channels. Passive viewers could access, and take for granted, certain mainstream sporting events. Yet sport is a valuable commodity, something that consumer viewers were, and are, willing to pay for. Premium content such as sporting rights was, and still is, central to the ability of broadcasters (and providers of new media services) to enter the market and remain there. This strategy has been facilitated by technological change, particularly through subscriber management systems and encryption technologies which enable the exclusion of those not willing or able to pay. Certain types of content have become commodified and privatised rather than generally available. The phrase 'content is king' is true for pay TV, whose model of the viewer is a consumer who is willing and able to pay. Serving the citizen viewers' interests is not the concern of the private sports broadcasters.

This chapter explores how different value systems interrelate in European broadcasting policy and the consequences this has for the access rights of different viewers, as well as different broadcasters, to sporting events. We look at the role of European competition law (Articles 81, 82 and 86)[1] and consider the addition of the listed events provision to the Television without Frontiers Directive (TWFD);[2] how it works in practice;

---

[1] Article 81 prohibits private sector anti-competitive agreements; Article 82 prevents the abuse of a dominant position and Articles 81 and 82 are applied to the sector by Article 86(1).

[2] Council Directive 89/552/EEC of 3 October on the co-ordination of certain provisions laid down by law, regulation or administrative action in member states concerning the pursuit

and certain weaknesses in the system. This chapter identifies the balance that exists between economic and non-trade priorities to assess what sort of viewing experience is likely to be respected and whether an appropriate level of protection is accorded to different viewers (see chapter 1).

Conflicting policy considerations

There are tensions between the need to protect or support the public interest within broadcasting (chapter 2) and the desire to develop a successful broadcasting market[3] (chapter 3). The approach towards sport equally has a double-sided aspect. On the one side, sport is seen to have special characteristics and, in this context, Union policymakers have periodically acknowledged the potential cultural importance of sport as part of the process of Union integration and of the formation of a European collective identity.[4] Attempts to harness the integrative potential of sport are made more difficult by the limited competence that the Union has regarding sport (see chapter 4).

On the other side, these non-commercial concerns coexist with the view that professional sport is a large-scale business operation. Sports firms should not be treated any differently from industrial undertakings and therefore the economic aspect of sport is subject to Union law.[5] None the less, the Commission seems to go to great lengths to emphasise the distinctive nature of sport, and the ways in which certain rules are necessary to enable sports events to take place, such as the rules of the relevant sport itself. The extent to which sport should be specifically taken into account in Union law has attracted a good deal of debate. The Constitutional Treaty's Article III-182 for the first time provides the Union with a legal base to provide a supporting role to member states in the social, educational and cultural aspects of sport. It is not, however, certain whether this treaty will ever come into force.

Despite the recognition of the importance of sport and the possible social and cultural benefits of broadcasting it to a European public, the commercial benefits of televised sport have proved to be a vital business

---

of television broadcasting activities OJ [1989] L298/23, as amended by Directive 97/36/EC OJ [1997] L 202/30.

[3] Including for these purposes new media services, such as 3G content on mobile phones.

[4] Council, *Reports of the Ad Hoc Committee on a People's Europe to the European Council*, (Second Addoninno Report) (1985) Supplement 7/85 Bull EC, p. 26, para. 5.9.1.

[5] See Case 36/74 *Walrave and Koch* [1974] ECR 140. The ECJ's ruling in the *Walrave* case established that Union law applies to sport, in so far as the practice constitutes an economic activity within the Union.

strategy for pay TV broadcasters and certain sporting organisations. Sport is well understood as being the following: it is a way to access a significant market share of viewers; to generate a subscriber base for pay TV companies; to break into a competitive market; and, in some instances, to generate high returns on pay-per-view (PPV) events. Particular sports events, such as Premier League football in the UK, have been used to drive up viewer subscriptions, a strategy which was referred to by Rupert Murdoch as using televised sport as a battering ram to increase sales and the global reach of his television interests.

Televised sport is equally significant for those reliant on public funds. As well as ensuring an audience (significant for those broadcasters justifying receipt of a licence fee or other state support), given the significance of sport to citizens, arguably public service broadcasting (PSB) should carry sport. Public service broadcasters or free-to-air television operators who try to acquire sports rights, however, are often priced out of the market by PPV or pay TV operators.[6] Although the types of sports used as a driver of pay TV take-up may vary between the member states, across the Union the end result is the same: without regulatory intervention, these sports become too expensive to be acquired by free-to-air television.[7]

A mutually beneficial relationship has emerged between television and sport at a general level. Competition between broadcasters seeking to acquire the rights to broadcast sporting events means that, in practice, there is very little that can be described as mutual. With regard to the viewer, the relationship which is established between the purchaser and seller of sport rights will act as a determinant of the viewing experience, if an event can be watched, when it can be watched and by whom (an issue that in part is addressed in the listed-events provision). Although the relationship between media and sport is not new and has accompanied the growth of mass commercialised spectator sport from the end of the nineteenth century,[8] it has grown and developed in the light of the range of new technologies provided first, by satellite technology; and second,

---

[6] The Commission has said that public service broadcasters can acquire sports rights but must not distort the market in respect of state aid. Commission, *Public Service Broadcasting and State Aid – Frequently Asked Questions*, Memo/05/73 (2005), p. 3.

[7] See, e.g., BSkyB in the UK, Kirch in Germany, Berlusconi in Italy and Vivendi in France, who have made direct rights deals with sporting organisations.

[8] M. Roche and J. Harrison, 'Cultural Europeanisation through regulation?: The Case of Media-sport in the EU', *Working Paper Presented at the IAMCR Conference, Media Sport Working Group* (Barcelona, 2002), p. 21.

since the late 1990s, by digitalisation. There has been a move away from the sharing of sporting events, through the infrastructures and collective values of national public service broadcasters, to an exploitation of multi-million-pound sectoral market opportunities. The ability of satellite technology to provide 'live' sporting events from around the world to hundreds of millions of people has further raised the value of sporting events, especially those that include premier or elite sports clubs.

Given the value ascribed to sport by the Union, how has it responded to these developments? Two approaches are evident: negative and positive. A negative approach can be identified where sport is covered by the exceptions to general EC Treaty provisions; in particular, the free movement of people,[9] and in the sport/broadcasting context through the application of, or exception from, competition rules. In this, we can see parallels to the development of a negative cultural policy, discussed in chapters 4 and 5. A positive approach has developed through the 1997 Amending Directive, which introduced the listed events system, and the 2000 Nice Treaty Declaration on Sport. Both these policy instruments share the same, or similar, ideas: namely that sport is 'special' and the broadcasting of some sporting events to the whole population is desirable. The extent to which competition law and the four freedoms could, or should, take sport's allegedly special status and nature into account is less clear. Within the context of broadcasting, it is the competition rules which have had the most impact. We shall now consider how the Commission and the courts have responded to the dual, but related, concerns of sport and broadcasting.

Competition law and the exclusive rights to sporting events

The above developments in the sports-rights market led the Commission to consider the scope of European competition rules in the context of

---

[9] See, e.g., Case C-415/93 *URBSA v. Bosman* [1995] ECR I-4921, which removed the power of professional football clubs to control the careers of players associated with them. Even if players were at the end of their contracts, the players' current club could charge transfer fees from other clubs. In 1995 the ECJ, petitioned by the player Marc Bosman, ruled that this power was illegal and an infringement on the free movement of workers in the Union's single market, under Article 39 EC. Henceforth, all players in professional football and other similar sports would have the legally enforceable right against their employing club to a free transfer to another club on the expiry of the period of their contract with the employing club.

Article 81, which prohibits anti-competitive agreements (see chapter 4).[10] In particular, it began to investigate the collective sale of rights such as the sale of a season's games by a national football association or league, on the ground that this procedure might not be in the public interest. Issues of access both for the broadcaster and the viewer arose, as the collective sale of rights to a few broadcasters meant that the number of games available was being restricted to people who subscribed to particular broadcasting platforms. These sorts of issues also raised questions about market foreclosure and abuse of a dominant position under Article 82, as often it is only the established pay TV operator that is in a position to bid for sporting content (see chapter 6).

Certain consistent themes can be identified from the cases in this area. An early case concerned Screensport.[11] In 1988 Screensport (a satellite broadcast sports company) filed complaints with the Commission. One of the complaints concerned a joint-venture between the EBU and News International in respect of their joint-venture company, Satellite Sport Services Limited (SSSL). In 1988 the EBU and News International had signed two exclusive rights agreements (a services agreement and a facilities agreement) with SSSL. The EBU had also signed the Eurosport Consortium Agreement in order to share sporting broadcasts among seventeen of its members. Screensport complained about the dominant position of SSSL in the Union sports broadcasting market. The Commission approached the complaints about the EBU and SSSL by splitting the cases into two. The first addressed the granting of exclusive rights to SSSL and the second related to the EBU's exclusive sports rights agreement within the Eurovision system. In the first case the Commission ruled in favour of Screensport, arguing that the EBU's exclusive rights agreement with SSSL was an infringement of Article 81(1) as the joint venture excluded third-party access. This issue of ensuring access would become a significant theme in the Commission's decisions in the media and communications sectors, as we shall see below (and see chapters 6 and 7).

The Commission considered the second case in 1993, and was supportive of the EBU's exclusive rights deal between the Union's public service broadcasters.[12] Here, the Commission recognised the importance

---

[10] Some mergers such as the *NewsCorp/Telepiu* merger also raised similar issues about access to premium content such as sporting rights.: *Newscorp/Telepiu*, Commission Decision, COMP/M.2876, 2 April 2003. See ch. 7.

[11] Commission Decision, Case IV/32.524 *Screensport/EBU* OJ [1991] L 63.

[12] Commission Decision, Case IV/32.150 *EBU/Eurovision* OJ [1993] L 179 of 22.07.1993 (overturned by the CFI).

of public service broadcasters' ability to provide free-to-air access to sporting events and the public service broadcasters' role in serving the public
interest. The public service broadcasters were exempted from Union competition rules under Article 81, and allowed to hold exclusive rights to
broadcast sports based on the EBU's Eurovision system. Despite the
Commission's recognition of a public interest dimension to the EBU's
acquisition of sports rights, the decision was later overturned. The Court
of First Instance (CFI) ruled against the Commission's decision to allow
the EBU exemption,[13] particularly as a number of private groups had
been denied membership of the EBU. The Commission subsequently re-
adopted an exception in respect of the EBU's joint buying arrangements
following a change in the EBU's rules, but again this was overturned by
the CFI on the basis that the rules did not ensure third-party access to
sporting rights that would not otherwise be broadcast.[14]

Screensport introduces themes which can still be seen in Commission decisions today, notably that a greater number of potential services
is desirable to stimulate competition (this approach can also be seen
in media mergers; see chapter 7) and that sport should be viewed as
having specific characteristics. This point was re-emphasised in a proposed joint-venture deal between the European Sports Network (ESPN);
Générale d'Images (GdI) and Canal+ to acquire the television interests
of WH Smith (WHSTV).[15] In its decision, the Commission recognised
the transnational nature of sports broadcasting because of its ability to
cross national, cultural and linguistic boundaries, and hence the matter
was judged to be a 'European issue'.[16] The recognition of the European
issue operated to bring the case within the Commission's competence
(see chapter 4).

A number of comments have been made about the Commission's
approach to the joint selling of rights: that it illustrates the beginning
of an expansion of competence into cultural fields; that it shows some

---

[13] Joined cases T-528/93, T-542/93, T-543/93 and T-546/93 *Metropole télévision SA and Reti
Televisive Italiane SpA and Gestevisión Telecinco SA and Antena 3 de Televisión* v. *Commission*
[1996] ECR II-649.

[14] EBU *Eurovision*, Commission case IV/32.150 OJ [2000] L 151/18, Joined cases T-185,
216, 299-300/00, *Métropole Télévision SA (M6), Antena 3 de Televisión, SA, Gestevisión
Telecinco, SA and SIC - Sociedade Independente de Comunicação, SA* v. *Commission* [2002]
ECR II-3805.

[15] Commission Decision, Case IV/M.110 *ABC/Générale des Eaux/Canal+/WH Smith* OJ
[1991] C 244.

[16] A. Harcourt, *The European Union and the Regulation of Media Markets* (Manchester:
Manchester University Press, 2005), p. 48.

regard for the specific nature of sport and also for the position of public service broadcasting (PSB); and that, in trying to allow a broad range of broadcasters access to content, it is also concerned with ensuring access on the part of the viewers to a wide range of broadcast content. In short, in recognising the specific nature of sport, it is focusing on not just consumers' interest but, arguably, also that of citizens. As we have seen in chapter 7, the legitimacy of the Commission taking into account Article 81 assessments has been challenged; it has been argued that the Commission should take a purely economic approach. Whatever the rights and wrongs of that debate, the fact is that Article 81(3) was not designed to deal with cultural and broadcasting policy, factors which may affect the Commission's efficacy in this regard. Certainly, joint selling continues to be an issue, as the *UEFA*,[17] *Bundesliga*[18] and *English Football Association Premier League* (FAPL)[19] cases, all of which concern the joint selling of the rights to broadcast football matches, illustrate.

Certain points of settled jurisprudence can be identified. In the case of sports rights, a rather narrow product market can be defined (on the significance of product market see chapter 7).[20] Holders of rights to specific sporting events have a market power that competing broadcasters cannot easily match, as the sporting events are rarely substitutable from the perspective of viewers. In principle, then, such agreements are likely to fall within the scope of Article 81, having an impact horizontally (the prevention of clubs competing in the sale of rights),[21] and restricting the content available to competing broadcasters. Such agreements therefore also have vertical effects, that is, an effect on different points in the supply chain.

Many agreements can be justified under Article 81(3) (see chapters 4 and 7). It is argued that joint selling creates efficiencies through the provision of a single point of sale for a branded league product. This allows viewers to watch the progress of the league as a whole, rather than just

---

[17] Commission Decision, COMP/C.2-37.398, *UEFA* OJ [2003] L 291/25.

[18] Commission Decision, COMP/C.2-37.214, *Bundesliga*, 19 January 2005.

[19] Commission Decision, COMP/38.173 *English Football Premier League* (FAPL), C(2006)868 final, 22 March 2006, Annex containing FAPL commitments.

[20] See Commission Decision IV/36.888, *Football World Cup* OJ [2000] L5/55, in which the Commission noted that one sport is not substitutable for another, that another tournament was not substitutable for the World Cup and even the women's World Cup was not substitutable for the men's. More recently, see Commission Decision COMP/M.4066, *CVC/SLEC*, concerning Formula One and Moto GP.

[21] The feasibility of clubs selling their respective rights is, apparently, a factor the Commission also takes into account: T. Toft, *Sport and Competition Law* Comp/C.2/TT/hvds D(2005), p. 5.

individual games. To benefit from this argument, new media rights must not be unduly constrained by an agreement and any period of exclusivity must be limited. Thus in *UEFA*, the new selling arrangements included a division of the rights into fourteen different packages with the same media (for example, there were three live television packages) and across different media (radio, universal mobile telecommunications system (UMTS),[22] Internet, as well as television).[23] The football clubs were also allowed to sell certain rights in parallel with UEFA, on a non-exclusive basis. The aim was to ensure that rights were not unused. Contracts were limited to three years' duration.

It seems from this that the Commission has sought to balance conflicting interests, but a more sophisticated analysis is required. Although the needs of viewers are taken into account, in that the branding of the games as a league allows a viewer to go to one broadcaster to follow all relevant games, there are some weaknesses in this position. Fans of sports clubs or teams also want access to their own particular club, which introduces the dimension of specificity to their requirements. Depending on the position of the club in a league, or its popularity, viewers may find that their club or particular sporting interest is simply not shown on television. Thus, although branded as a league, the games that specific groups of fans, or other viewers, might want to watch may not be covered. In order to counter the effect of this, the Commission has insisted on the segmentation of the rights, so that more games (with greater representation of clubs) are shown on television. Nevertheless, the question remains: is the argument that following a league in its entirety, which the Commission accepts justifies joint selling, consistent with commitments that require the matches to be split among different broadcasters? In this scenario, viewers will probably have to subscribe to a number of different suppliers. This issue has bedevilled the question of viewer access to sport since *Screensport*, because the obligation to distribute rights to sporting events among broadcasters seems to be 'platform blind' within the broadcasting sphere. We have seen that a 'technology-neutral' approach to platforms within competition law is not always beneficial to viewers (chapter 7). Further, although consumers have the choice of which sporting package

---

[22] UMTS increases broadband capacity, data speeds and new broadband service capabilities from second-generation mobile networks to 3G-mobile technology.

[23] Similarly, in the *Bundesliga* case media rights were divided so as to give more than one broadcaster the opportunity to obtain the rights. See Commission, *Press Release, Competition: German Football League commitments to liberalise joint selling of Bundesliga media rights made legally binding by Commission decision*, IP/05/62, 19 January 2005.

to buy, there is no direct focus on the fact that viewers might have some form of citizen-based right to access certain forms of sporting events or information (chapter 1).

Furthermore, it seems that breaking the rights up into packages reveals a weakness in the process-based nature of competition law intervention, as can be seen in the case of the joint selling of matches to British and Irish television companies on an exclusive basis by the FAPL. The sale of broadcasting rights in this way meant that, in practice, only one quarter of all the Premier League matches were broadcast live (138 in total) and only one company, BSkyB, could afford to purchase the rights. In June 2001 the Commission opened an investigation into the joint selling arrangements and the FAPL applied for negative clearance under Article 81(1) or, if this failed, an exemption under Article 81(3).[24] In response the Commission emphasised that any possible 'efficiencies and benefits that joint selling could provide in the media markets were negated by the commercial policy pursued by the FAPL'.[25] The Commission's main concern was that the joint and exclusive sales of packages of media rights created, among other things, barriers to entry, limitations on the development of products and markets and further media concentration.[26] The FAPL's formal reply denied that the arrangements restricted competition, but it still issued an invitation to tender for media rights for the 2004–7 seasons.[27] In an attempt to address the monopoly which BSkyB held over the FAPL matches, a newly structured package of rights was developed. This initially consisted of three main tranches of live games known as gold,[28] silver[29] and bronze[30] packages. The three packages were designed to create more competition between broadcasters, lessening the possibility of BSkyB controlling all the live rights and increasing the chances that a terrestrial broadcaster, such as the BBC or ITV, might be able to re-introduce live Premier League football free-to-air for the first time since 1992. The invitation to tender also included a traditional highlights

---

[24] European Commission, *Notice published pursuant to Article 19(3) of Council Regulation No 17 concerning case COMP/C2/38.173 and 38.453 – joint selling of the media rights of the FA Premier League on an exclusive basis* (2004/C 115/02), section 3.

[25] Commission, *Article 19(3), Notice* section 7.

[26] *Ibid.*, section 7.   [27] *Ibid.*, sections 8, 10 and 11.

[28] The gold package consisted of 38 matches on Sunday afternoon at 4 p.m.

[29] The silver package consisted of 38 matches on Monday evenings, midweek and Sunday at 2 p.m.

[30] The bronze package consisted of a further 62 matches on Saturday afternoon at 1 p.m. and 5.15 p.m. The Premier League later broke up the bronze package of 62 games into two separate packages of 31 games each.

package; a new package of rights that enabled a broadcaster or club channel to screen 'near live' matches, which would be available from midnight on the match day.

Ultimately, the attempt to encourage more than one broadcaster to screen live Premier League football games failed.[31] In August 2003 all four live packages were bought by BSkyB, as it was the only UK broadcaster that could afford them.[32] DG Competition has continued to make clear its objection to the monopoly of FAPL football matches held by BSkyB, and negotiations between the current Competition Commissioner and the Chief Executive of the FAPL have led to an agreement between the Commission and the FAPL to end BSkyB's monopoly of live Premier League matches in the tender for rights for matches from 2007. The 138 matches were broken down into 6 packages of 23 games, which can be distributed via television, broadband and mobile telephone. Crucially, no single broadcaster was permitted to bid for all of them. The further breaking up of the packages into balanced units seemed to encourage greater competition from other broadcasters, such as NTL, Setanta and perhaps the free-to-air broadcasters. Despite these changes, the new rules could, in theory, still have allowed BSkyB to win a majority of the packages (in theory up to five),[33] meaning that they could retain their dominance of pay-TV football in the UK.[34] In fact, Setanta paid £392 million for a three-year deal to the rights to 2 of the packages, 46 matches per season.[35] BSkyB took the bigger share, paying £1.31 billion for the remaining 4 packages, comprising 92 games per season.

---

[31] The BBC purchased the rights to show Premier League highlights from 2004.

[32] In April 2004 sealed bids for the fourth tranche of rights were received from the free-to-air broadcasters, the BBC, ITV, Channel 5 and from Setanta Sports. They all fell well below a minimum reserve price of £1.5 million per game established by BSkyB and Sky Sports held on to the exclusive rights for the whole of the Premiership for another three years.

[33] BSkyB's head of sport has indicated that, in order to get the same sort of exclusivity gained from owning the rights to the majority of matches, BSkyB would pay the same amount of money in 2007 for fewer games. D. Timms, 'Sky: We'd Pay the Same again for TV Football', www.mediaguardian.co.uk, 7 December 2005.

[34] A more equitable agreement has been reached in Germany, whereby the German football league and the Commission have agreed to legally binding commitments in the sale of packages of media rights. These rights are to be split into 9 different packages: 5 for television, 2 for the Internet and 2 for mobile phone streaming. The Commission hopes that this arrangement will act as a template for sports rights sales in the Union. See Commission, *Competition: German Football League commitments to liberalise joint selling of Bundesliga media rights made legally binding by Commission decision*, IP/05/62, 19 January 2005.

[35] O. Gibson, 'Setanta Starts Fund Raising and Seeks New Investor', *Guardian*, 24 May 2006, available www.media.guardian.co.uk/print/O,,329487802-105236,00.html/.

The difficulties that DG Competition has faced in challenging the dominance of BSkyB over the rights to Premier League football have been illustrative of the problems that arise when there is no credible competitor in the broadcasting sector. For several years meaningful choice and access for viewers to televised FAPL games has been undermined and the interests of citizen viewers overlooked. Although Setanta has won the rights to 46 games, it has access to the least attractive times in the schedule. It plans to offer some of the games via Freeview to homes not served by Sky Sports, as well as via broadband Internet services, in both cases as a subscription service. Although BSkyB remains a dominant player in televised Premier League football, its monopoly position has now been challenged. None the less, the availability of sport on FTA television remains limited. This point perhaps underlines the importance of outcome-orientated regulation, seen in TWFD Article 3a, discussed below.

The Commission's decisions in the media sector have shown a preference for commitments allowing third-party access, which then allows the main exclusive contract to be permissible under Article 81(3). This approach has been criticised with respect to the position of new media services. For example, the *UEFA* and *Bundesliga* decisions do not appear to provide for Internet access rights to third parties, although UMTS operators do seem to be protected. This may be because football leagues do not have the necessary transmission licences to exploit UMTS rights themselves, and therefore need to co-operate with UMTS operators.[36] Further, the requirement that the parties with the rights to sporting events should sub-license part of those rights has given rise to adverse comment. Although more than one broadcaster might now have access to the rights, in effect the approach adopted by the Commission transforms the main contract holder into a wholesaler, with whom competing broadcasters must deal. This is not a replacement for competition in the market for the rights themselves, but a form of secondary or fringe competition. Competitors are at the mercy of an operator, possibly in a dominant position, and it has been argued that the way a number of the commitments in this regard have been phrased means that the system allows the main contract holder to charge high prices to its competitors. Not only might this mean that cheaper prices for viewers do not materialise but, if the margins are too tight, it will not be cost effective for other broadcasters to buy the extra rights, resulting in no extra choice for viewers, whether seen

---

[36] D. Geradin, 'Access to Content by New Media Platforms: A Review of the Competition Law Problems', *Entertainment Law Review*, 30(1) (2005), 68–94, p. 90.

as citizens or consumers. It remains to be seen whether such behaviour would be prevented by Article 82.

A final set of problems relates to the appropriateness of the treatment of sport as special. Weatherill suggests that forms of social solidarity which envisage grass-roots involvement are not necessarily well served by exclusive broadcasting agreements.[37] Here, social solidarity could be equally well served by allowing a more competitive market for the rights to sporting events, resulting in lower prices and perhaps a greater range of games on offer, even on free-to-air television. The proceeds of such competitive sales could then be redistributed in accordance with a principle of encouraging participation in sport from which forms of social solidarity are derived. Of course, this argument is unlikely to find favour with the leagues selling the rights, or the pay TV broadcasters, which have used exclusive sporting rights to such advantage in developing their subscriber bases. Ironically, arguments used to support the special nature of sport, which might be thought initially to support the citizens' interest, actually operate against them in practice, as they merely justify the disapplication of competition and trading rules to big business.

It should be noted that the Commission's claim to respect sport as a cultural phenomenon is probably overstated. Commissioner Monti, in respect of one of the Commission's decisions on UEFA's rules, stated that the decision 'reflects the Commission's respect for the specific characteristics of sport and its cultural and social function'.[38] The decision itself is, however, based on a routine application of competition law, based on a market analysis. Although the specific nature of the market for broadcasting rights is addressed, the decision does not focus on the cultural and social function of sport.[39] One can also see similar sleights of hand in other broadcasting rights cases. In the *UEFA* decision, the Commission is concerned with efficiencies not the rights of citizen viewers, although the two may overlap. This may be a result of the competence constraints on the Commission noted in chapters 4 and 5, which the European courts seem quite keen to police,[40] as ideas such as the cultural and social function of sport do not fit easily in the categories of benefit identified in Article 81(3).

---

[37] S. Weatherill, 'Sport as Culture in EC Law', in R. Craufurd Smith (ed.), *Culture and European Union Law* (Oxford: Oxford University Press, 2004), p. 129.

[38] Commission, *Press Release, Commission clears UEFA's new Broadcasting Regulations*, IP/01/583, 20 April 2001, cited in Weatherill, 'Sport as Culture', p. 131.

[39] Weatherill, 'Sport as Culture', pp. 131–2.

[40] Harcourt, *The European Union and the Regulation of Media Markets*, p. 48.

The Union's vision of cultural citizenship, fostered through free and diverse access to very popular sporting events, has been undermined through measures that facilitate the exclusive purchase of broadcasting rights and the inability of the Commission to facilitate viable competition from free-to-air broadcasters. Today the relationship between sport, broadcasting and citizens' viewing is now to be found in the policy of the listed events system that ensures sporting occasions of national importance are available on free-to-air television.[41]

The listed events system

The privatisation of certain sporting events contradicts the central public service value of universality (see chapter 2) and reflects trends in the commodification of information and the commercialisation of the broadcasting environment.[42] Different types of universality exist, but all are related to the ability of viewers to have access to and to be able to receive a diverse range of content which is free to air. Providing universal service is therefore a way of ensuring that viewers have access to a common stock of knowledge and a shared viewing experience (chapter 1). In the context of broadcast sport, two broad positions can be identified. The first is whether we should be 'concerned if the public have to pay to watch major sporting events on television . . . the public will, after all, have to buy tickets to gain entry to a real match or competition'.[43] The second is that citizen viewers should have access to certain televised sporting events, although this, of course, begs the question of which televised sporting events should be universally available via free-to-air broadcasting.

In 1997 the TWFD was amended by the inclusion of Article 3a to recognise the value and importance of general public access to major events, the broadcasting of which should be guaranteed. Some of these protected events were identified in the preamble of the TWFD, referring generally to events in which national teams or participants take part in key international events, but also leaving it open to member states to decide which events should be protected.

---

[41] Roche and Harrison, 'Cultural Europeanisation Through Regulation?', p. 27.

[42] G. Born and T. Prosser, 'Culture and Consumerism: Citizenship, Public Service Broadcasting and the BBC's Fair Trading Obligations', *Modern Law Review*, 64(5) (2003), 657–87, p. 671.

[43] R. Craufurd Smith and B. Böttcher, 'Football and Fundamental Rights: Regulating Access to Major Sporting Events on Television', *European Public Law*, 8(1) (2002), 107–33, p. 111.

Article 3a may be broadly broken down into two elements. The first is set out in paragraph (1):

> Each member state may take measures in accordance with Community law to ensure that broadcasters under its jurisdiction do not broadcast on an exclusive basis events which are regarded by that member state as being of major importance for society in such a way as to deprive a substantial proportion of the public in that member state of the possibility of following such events via live coverage or deferred coverage on free television.

Thus, it can be seen that the TWFD gives the member states the freedom to take action in this area, if they so choose, by drawing up a list of events considered to be of major importance for them. Member states are free to choose whether to take action and, if they so choose, which events to protect, and some member states still choose not to have any listed events.[44] Listed events may not only be sporting events but could be cultural events, such as the San Remo Italian Music Festival. Article 3a(2) requires member states to notify the Commission of those events that they have chosen to list and the measures taken to implement the list. The Commission is under a responsibility to verify that the member states' measures are compatible with Union law. It has, however, been left to member states to determine whether the listed events should be available via whole or partial live coverage, or whole or partial deferred coverage. It also gives member states the freedom to determine what is a 'substantial proportion of the public', allowing the member states to take different views on what percentage of the population should have access to particular events.

There is no definition of events of major importance, but the preamble gives some guidance, stating that they should:

> meet certain criteria, that is to say be outstanding events which are of interest to the general public in the European Union or in a given member state or in an important component part of a given member state.[45]

It seems clear that a member state may act to protect events that are of international, national and, significantly, subnational importance. This recital introduces two further elements: (1) that the event is outstanding, though what this means is unclear; and (2) that the event is of interest to the general public. This seems to require a factual assessment of what

---

[44] For an up-to-date list of listed events in Union member states, see www.obs.coe.int/ oea_publ/iris/iris_extra/sports_rights_tv.pdf.en.

[45] Amending Directive, Recital 21.

people are interested in, although, arguably, it may also include events that it is felt that people should be interested in. Some may argue that, given its popularity, Premier League football should be protected under these guidelines. Those uninterested in football, or those football fans only interested in their own non Premier League team, would presumably disagree.

Although the TWFD is clearly drafted in broader terms, the examples given in the preamble are all major sporting events, a preference that is reflected in many of the member states' choice of important events. These sporting events, however, vary greatly between different member states, as Article 3a is not intended to be a harmonising measure. Even when there is agreement on the inclusion of an international sporting tournament on the member states' lists, their approaches differ as to how much of that tournament they list. For example, the UK placed the whole of the 2002 and 2006 World Cup games on its list. In contrast, Germany listed only those games involving the national team, the semi-finals and the final, and Italy listed only those matches involving the national team and the final.

The TWFD does not seek to establish a single European list of major events, although in its consultation on revisions to the TWFD, the Commission reconsidered the advisability of introducing rules for the broadcasting of events of major importance to society. In practice, although not all member states have taken the opportunity to list events, there does seem to be a core group of such events, based around certain sporting events, notably the Olympic Games, the Football World Cup and the Football European Cup, although Wimbledon and the Tour de France also seem reasonably popular. These last two events are interesting as examples of national events which have developed to gain international significance.

The Commission also questioned whether the concept of 'a substantial proportion of the public' should be harmonised. The question of whether the current possibility for member states to introduce a list of events should be made binding was also considered.[46] In its *Issues Paper*, the Commission noted that there was a preference not to harmonise the concept of 'a substantial proportion of the public',[47] as this differed in accordance with the audiovisual landscape in each member state. Attempts to

---

[46] Commission *Issues paper for the Liverpool Audiovisual Conference: Right to information and right to short reporting*, July 2005.

[47] *Ibid.*, p. 2.

harmonise these provisions would be problematic. The Commission has not, in its draft second amending directive (DSAD),[48] attempted to do so. A patchwork of different rules will continue to exist for the foreseeable future.

The second element of Article 3a, set out in paragraph (3), is mandatory. In effect, this constitutes a requirement on all member states to respect other member states' choices about their individual selections of listed events deemed to be of major importance to each of them. Given the structure of the TWFD and the differing national systems of regulation across the Union, it would be easy for a broadcaster to avoid the listed-event rules in one member state by establishing itself in another member state and broadcasting back to the member state of origin. The recipient member state would not have jurisdiction to stop the broadcaster (chapter 8) and, arguably, the host member state would not have the power to do so even if it, too, had listed the event, because the broadcaster would not be precluding the broadcast of the relevant event in the host member state.[49] It is clear that the drafters of the TWFD had this concern in mind.[50] Thus Article 3a(3) requires member states to

> ensure, by appropriate means, within the framework of their legislation that broadcasters under their jurisdiction do not exercise the exclusive rights purchased by those broadcasters following the date of publication of this Directive in such a way that a substantial proportion of the public in another member state is deprived of the possibility of following events which are designated by that other member state in accordance with the preceding paragraphs . . .

In some respects this is a variant of mutual recognition found throughout Union law, and in the TWFD itself, in the jurisdiction clause.

Weaknesses in the listed events system

There is no limitation on the member states' discretion both as to the number of events that are listed and as regards the level of protection allowed (i.e. whether live coverage or highlights must be available). The

---

[48] Commission, *Proposal for a Directive amending Directive 89/552/EEC*, COM(2005)646 final, 2005/0260 (COD), SEC (2005) 1625.

[49] Furthermore, Article 49 prohibits restrictions on the export of services just as much as imports – see Case C-384/93 *Alpine Investments BV* v. *Minister van Financiën* [1995] ECR I-1141.

[50] See Recital 19 TWFD.

'optional' nature of the protection awarded reflects a lack of agreement as to the desirability of such intervention and, perhaps, a lack of certainty as to Union competence in this regard. Arguably, subsidiarity is being respected. This, together with a reliance on co-operation between member states, however, leads to potential weaknesses in the system. For example, unlike the position with other general content concerns (Article 2a), there is no mechanism within the TWFD to remedy the position where the relevant member state takes no action to protect the listed events in one member state from being broadcast exclusively to that member state by a broadcaster under its jurisdiction. Given that member states should not take unilateral action to stop such broadcasts, in such an instance a member state would be reliant on the Commission taking action, or would need to take action itself under Article 227 EC, both of which would take time and almost certainly apply only after the event had been broadcast.

Further, although member states may choose to list similar events, there is no guarantee that the free-to-air broadcasts will be of the same type in each such member state. This raises the issue of the scope of the 'right' to see major events. Is it the case that a major event must be shown live, or are we concerned with just the transmission of information about it, in which case delayed coverage or highlights might suffice? As noted in the context of football matches, sport has other particular characteristics which make the relationship between it and television particularly compelling for both the viewer and the broadcaster. It is ephemeral in that it is predominantly watched and enjoyed live. Part of the significance of a major event is the fact that the event is viewed by a lot of people at the same time. It has an immediacy and a contemporaneity which brings people together and promotes collective identities. If part of the purpose of listed events is to enhance and build European cultural citizenship and a European sense of identity, the system appears to fail, for no other reason than free-to-air audiences are now often deprived of watching some major sporting events in the same way and at the same time as each other and pay TV consumer viewers.

The negotiations and the litigation relating to the rights to broadcast the 2002 Football World Cup highlighted further weaknesses in the listed events system. Kirch had paid £249 million for the rights[51] and it planned to exploit this investment by breaking them into packages to be sold on an exclusive basis to the highest bidder at an auction. A range of European

---

[51] *Ibid.*, p. 125.

pay TV operators were expected to bid for the rights. Problematically for Kirch, and for pay TV broadcasters in the UK, the list of events drawn up by the then regulator, the Independent Television Commission (ITC), included all 64 of the World Cup games which were required under UK regulations to be broadcast free to air. A pay TV operator wishing to purchase the rights had to risk the possibility that the regulator might not agree to the games being broadcast on an exclusive PPV basis. The ITC, following the judgment of Lord Hoffman in the *TV Danmark 1*[52] case (discussed below), argued that the free-to-air broadcasters, ITV and the BBC, should be allowed to bid first. While free-to-air broadcasters knew if their price was too low the rights owner might sell them to a pay TV operator, the latter were also aware that the ITC could prevent the broadcasting of the games on an exclusive basis. When the BBC and ITV put together a joint bid of £55 million for the rights to the World Cup games in 2002 and 2006, Kirch, which had asked for £170 million, challenged the scope of the UK's list.[53] Kirch argued that the UK regulations infringed the right to freedom of expression, the right to property and the right to pursue an economic activity. The ECJ had previously ruled that these rights are not absolute and may be restricted in the pursuit of other public interest goals.[54] Finally, a £160 million pound deal was agreed with Kirch, the BBC and ITV for the rights to all 64 games in the 2002 and 2006 World Cup tournaments.[55]

Craufurd Smith and Böttcher consider that, in fact, these actions 'may indicate no more than the failure of media companies such as Kirch and TV Danmark 1 to understand the social and cultural importance of the rights at their disposal'.[56] In the case of these two companies, their actions may be seen as determined measures solely aimed at maximising their own revenues and finding ways to evade national and Union legislation

[52] *R.* v. *Independent Television Commission, ex parte TV Danmark 1 Ltd* [2001] UKHL 42.
[53] Case T-33/01 *Infront WM AG* v. *Commission* [2005], nyr, judgment 15 December 2005.
[54] Case 5/88 *Wachauf* v. *Germany* [1989] ECR 2609, para. 18, cited in Craufurd Smith and Böttcher, 'Football and Fundamental Rights', p. 129.
[55] The television rights to show the World Cup in the UK were owned jointly by ITV and the BBC. ITV and the BBC had, together, agreed to pay £160 million for the rights to show the 2002 World Cup and the 2006 World Cup in Germany, although they had only paid £3.35 million between them for coverage of the 1998 World Cup in France. The ITV/BBC deal with Kirch was agreed in October 2001 after a year of negotiations. Kirch originally asked for £170 million for the British rights to cover only the 2002 World Cup. In the end an overall price of £160 million was agreed for the rights to show both the 2002 and 2006 World Cups. ITV and BBC paid more than they had wanted to for the rights and much less than Kirch hoped to sell them for. See www.le.ac.uk/so/css/resources/factsheets/fs12.html
[56] Craufurd Smith and Böttcher, 'Football and Fundamental Rights', p. 132.

aimed at protecting the public interest.[57] The activities of Kirch and TV Danmark 1 raised unresolved issues relating to the absence of a mechanism by which a fair price for rights can be established at an early stage in the sale of rights to events which have been listed and the degree of freedom member states have in drawing up their lists under Article 3(a).

The issue of what is a fair price that can be expected of a free-to-air broadcaster in respect of a listed event is difficult to assess. If prices are set too low, the rights holder may just refuse to sell the rights, meaning that there is no televised coverage of the relevant event at all. This spoiling tactic may be countered through the use of competition policy at a European level. Article 82 precludes the abuse of a dominant position and, as regards intellectual property rights, the ECJ has held that the refusal to license the rights in television listings magazines constituted an abuse (see chapter 7).[58] It required the rights holder to license the rights at a reasonable price. Ultimately, however, the question is what constitutes a reasonable and fair price, and whether, given the perceived need for intervention in the market, the market price is the appropriate one. In addition, the question of whether the price should be set at a different level for public service broadcasters, to take into account their particular social and cultural remit, has not been satisfactorily addressed. Essentially this question asks whether Article 3a is about ensuring that the events are broadcast free-to-air, or whether it is about ensuring that public service broadcasters have a chance to buy the rights. The latter approach is a poisoned chalice for public service broadcasters. It is so for two reasons. First, it only provides for the possibility of bidding, which invariably means being outbid since they are constrained by limited public funding. Secondly, if they are successful, they are likely to have been so at the expense of having adequate funding remaining for other types of programming equally central to their PSB remit.

This issue occurs again in the context of Article 3a(3). The distinction between a process-based view of Article 3a(3) and a result-based view of that provision was discussed in the *TV Danmark 1* case. The reasoning in the case was heavily influenced by the way the UK has chosen to implement its obligations under Article 3a(3). The UK had already introduced a system to protect listed events within the UK, which effectively meant that the ITC had to consent if any broadcaster wanted to broadcast any

---

[57] *Ibid.*, p. 132.

[58] Joined Cases C 241 and 242/91P *Radio Telefis Eireann (RTE)* v. *Commission* (Magill) [1995] ECR I-743.

listed event exclusively. In making its decision, the ITC had to have regard to a code on the issue which it had published. In particular, the code stated that:

> any invitation to express interest in the acquisition of rights must have been communicated to broadcasters in both the free to air and pay TV categories; the price sought must be fair and reasonable and non-discriminatory, taking into account previous fees, time of day of coverage; potential revenue associated with the event; and competition in the market place.

The requirements of Article 3a(3) were grafted on to this system. Where a broadcaster established in the UK wished to broadcast an event listed by another member state for reception in that member state, again ITC consent would be required, and again by reference to the ITC code. In the *TV Danmark 1 Case*, which concerned a broadcaster which sought to broadcast the Danish World Cup matches exclusively to Denmark, the ITC also had regard to the legal position in Denmark, which would have required TV Danmark 1 to offer to share the rights with the public service broadcasters established there. This TV Danmark 1 was unwilling to do. The ITC therefore refused its consent, resulting in a judicial review action of its decision.

TV Danmark 1 argued that, in the light of the code, the ITC should have been looking at the way the rights were acquired in the first place, taking into account subsequent matters, such as the way in which the proposed rights would be exercised. TV Danmark 1 was unsuccessful in the English High Court, but the Court of Appeal[59] overturned the High Court judge's finding. The Court of Appeal took a perverse approach to the interpretation of Article 3a. Although it adopted a standard European approach to interpretation by referring to the Recitals of the TWFD, it did not emphasise the Recitals which seemed most particularly to refer to Article 3a. The Court of Appeal therefore held that the object of Article 3a was not unqualified: competition in sports rights was also an object of the TWFD. The ITC on this reasoning should have restricted itself to verifying that the free-to-air broadcaster had had its fair chance, rather than ensuring any particular end result. Further, according to the Court of Appeal, where there was a fair auction, the viewing populace had not been deprived of the possibility of viewing; the auction provided the possibility, it just did not provide the fact of such viewing.

---

[59] *R. v. Independent Television Commission*, ex parte *TV Danmark 1* [2001] 1 WLR 741 CA, [2001] ECC 11, 103.

The House of Lords reversed the Court of Appeal's judgment.[60]
Although the House of Lords recognised that there is a tension between
various policies in the TWFD, it concluded that these had already been
taken into account in the limitations imposed on member states in terms
of the events that could be listed and the requirement to notify the
Commission of such listings. According to the House of Lords, the implementing provisions in the Broadcasting Act 1996 and the ITC code did not
give effect to the UK's responsibilities under Article 3a(3), it merely put
the ITC in the position of doing so. Further, 'possibility' in this context
means the possibility of switching the television on to a free-to-air channel and watching the event. It does not mean the theoretical possibility
that a public service broadcaster had the chance to acquire the rights. The
Court of Appeal's view that all that was required was a fair auction undermines the effectiveness of the listed-events provisions. Were the Court of
Appeal's interpretation correct, the Government might as well have left
the listed sporting events to market forces. Reducing the ITC's review to
checking that there is a fair and reasonable price would make the whole
regulatory structure pointless.

Although the case is a judgment of the English Courts and therefore
not binding on other member states or on the European institutions, it is
significant as it highlights two different perspectives taken by legal institutions in their interpretation of broadcasting policy. The view adopted
by the Court of Appeal, essentially process-based, focussed on competition and the market participants. The House of Lords, by looking at the
end result, assumed the purpose of the regulation was to protect citizens'
interests. The latter is a view that, as we have argued throughout, is all too
easily overlooked, and Union broadcasting policy is more often likely to
be influenced by the supposed benefits of formal choice.

The actions of Kirch and TV Danmark illustrate a particular approach
to freedom of expression, one which assumes it is acceptable to own
information and which does not take into account a citizen's right to
information.[61] The ability of commercial broadcasters to privatise certain
broadcast events invites the question as to whether a fair balance between
commercial and other non-trade values is being struck. One possible solution is to ensure that free-to-air broadcasters have a right to transmit short

---

[60] R. v. Independent Television Commission, ex parte TV Danmark 1 [2001] UKHL 42.
[61] Such a view contradicts Article 6 of the Treaty of European Union (Maastricht), which
stipulated that the Union would respect fundamental rights guaranteed by the European
Convention for the Protection of Human Rights and Fundamental Freedoms, which in
Article 10(1) protected the right to freedom of expression.

extracts from televised sporting events, although this solution ignores the importance attached to viewing the event, as opposed to learning about the outcome subsequently. In its *Issues Paper* the Commission noted that the current TWFD does not address the issue of short reports,[62] and that views about its desirability were mixed. Some considered that a statutorily harmonised right to access newsworthy events (where newsworthy events appear to be synonymous with events which, when broadcast, are seen to serve public interest) should be established at the European level. Other member states were less eager to see a statutory measure established. Private broadcasters and rights holders, who would lose some of their claim to exclusivity, opposed the idea that viewers had an automatic right to such content, and argued that the issue of access to newsworthy events should remain a matter for voluntary codes.

Clearly, what is deemed to be in the public interest varies, but the Commission, in the interests of transnational freedom of information, suggested that non-discriminatory access to broadcast extracts for use in information programmes should be given by one member state to another. Article 3b of DSAD provides that member states are to ensure that

> Broadcasters established in other Member States are not deprived of access on a fair, reasonable and non-discriminatory basis to events of high interest to the public which are transmitted by a broadcaster under their jurisdiction.

Decisions still need to be made about the conditions upon which such free transfer of information would occur, but Recitals 26 and 27 in DSAD appear expressly to link the broadcasting of sporting events on an exclusive basis with the right to use short extracts for the purposes of general news programming. Two issues arise: first, should events that could attract a mass audience be broadcast free-to-air in the public interest, either in their entirety, or as a short report classed as a newsworthy event? Secondly, if some events are to be broadcast on an exclusive basis, what price should a broadcaster be charged for transmitting short reports? This last aspect, as the experience of Article 3a shows, is likely to give rise to problems.

Conclusion

The broadcasting of sport demonstrates a range of tensions between commercial and citizens' interests which occur within Union broadcasting

---

[62] Commission, *Issues Paper: Right to Information*, p. 1.

policy generally. The Union assumes that both the broadcasting and sporting sectors are important industries with economic value, but are also the mechanism through which an involved citizenry can be developed, and through which a sense of European identity and culture may be fostered. As the relationship between the media industry and the sport industry has become increasingly enmeshed, so they are now increasingly dependent on each other: the sport industry for the money it receives from broadcasters; and the broadcasting industry for the money it derives from showing sport on a commercial basis. This relationship of mutually reinforcing economic benefits between television and sport institutions, constantly facilitated by technological development, is already having noticeable practical implications for the viewing experience. On the one hand, new technology could foster greater interest via the potential to televise a variety of sporting events to a diverse range of people. On the other hand, the way in which new technology is being exploited by the broadcasting sector and certain sporting institutions serves to restrict viewers' access to content. The issue of how important is this exclusion of viewers from access to the broadcasting of certain sporting events is dependent upon the extent to which sport is seen to be central to the needs of citizen viewers, or the desires and satisfaction of consumer viewers. In the case of citizen viewers, the perceived concern is that access to sport is important, either as a matter of the right to receive information or because of sport's special role in society and importance to the individual viewers themselves. In the case of viewers as consumers of sport, both broadcasting and sport lose their special status, save to the extent that they are, particularly in combination, a very desirable commodity.

The Union has recognised that there are major difficulties in coping with the complexity of broadcasting sport. Its ability to act is limited by the vehicles it can use to do so: with no express competence, much of the scope for Union action is developed within the context of competition law. This raises difficult questions as to whether the Commission should, or has the competence to, take sport's special nature into account and the effectiveness of such action in a heavily commercialised environment. Perhaps as a response to the competition decisions in this area, there has been specific legislative activity in this area by the Union's institutions. The listed-events system in the TWFD is clearly an attempt to protect the special status of certain key events, particularly sporting events, for the Union citizen. However, the viability of the listed-events system as a mechanism to protect access to televised sporting events and to ensure diversity of broadcast sport content is under constant pressure. Given that member states have the freedom to choose which events they protect, there are bound to be differences, both in the scope of and the level of protection awarded to, in the terms of the TWFD, 'events of importance to society' across the Union. The *TV Danmark 1* case clearly illustrates that a member state will be heavily reliant on the regulatory structure of another member state, and its willingness and ability to enforce that system, to ensure that listed events remain available free-to-air. In the light of this, as we have argued, it remains uncertain and questionable the extent to which conflict over access rights to televised sport is adequately addressed by the Union.

13

State aid: constraints on public service broadcasting

Introduction

The provision of public service broadcasting (PSB) in the Union is defined and supported through the various national broadcasting systems. The problem within the Union is a familiar one: such provision is often in conflict with general Union trade objectives, here the rules on state aid. The increased numbers of channels (chapter 3) have challenged the rationale for intervention in the broadcasting market, and the value and justification for PSB has been the subject of continued debate, both at national and European level. The proper scope of PSB is being reconsidered in relation to what should be funded, given the increased range of services that could be offered in a digital environment. Of paramount concern here is that if PSB caters for the viewing interests of citizens, particularly those who are passive (see chapter 1), what level and nature of service should a citizen viewer be entitled to expect from a public service broadcaster?

With the vulnerable position of PSB as a backdrop, this chapter first outlines some of the different approaches to PSB within the Union. It then considers the difficulties in attaining PSB objectives in the light of conflicting policy goals, and takes into account the interplay between Union and national competence. We then consider the impact of other Union policies, notably competition and state aid, on PSB in the absence of specific Union legislation, and question whether PSB, with its role of protecting the citizen viewer, continues to remain viable.

Approach to PSB in the Union

The identification of a role for PSB in Europe has been based upon the agreement by the member states and particular institutions of the Union that PSB has 'social, cultural and democratic functions';[1] and is vital for

---

[1] Council, *Resolution of the Council and Representatives of the Governments of the Member States concerning PSB* OJ [1999] C 30/1, para. B.

ensuring democracy, pluralism,[2] social cohesion and linguistic diversity,[3] points that are recognised in the Protocol on PSB and reaffirmed in the Council Resolution on the subject.[4] The European Parliament has linked the value of PSB to social and political cohesion via its ability to act as 'an aid to informed citizenship'.[5] A connection is made between the type and range of programming that is produced and a range of ambitious, and rather abstract, goals such as the development of informed citizenship, instilling a sense of civic responsibility, fostering social cohesion and a sense of belonging to a community.[6] Although PSB is seen to have an important remit by institutions within the Union, the organisation, definition and fulfilment of this remit remain a matter for member states and not the Union.[7]

Given this freedom accorded to member states, the systems of PSB vary across the Union, with different types of PSB organisations supplying a public service. The Commission has required that each member state establish its own definition and scope of PSB,[8] but different levels of progress have been achieved in the various member states.[9] In addition, the European Parliament has called on public service broadcasters to aim

[2] Media pluralism is recognised *inter alia* by the Union as being a crucial element of the democratic process, both in member states and in the Union as whole. Protection of media pluralism entails a variety of different instruments applied at different levels (see ch. 7) and PSB is seen to make an important contribution. The protection of pluralism has been a consistent concern of the European Parliament and the Council of Europe. The Commission, while not taking any formal initiative in the area, has recognised the importance of PSB, while leaving member states to use PSB to promote and protect media pluralism. See the Amsterdam Protocol and Commission, *Communication on the Application of State Aid Rules to Public Service Broadcasting* (2001/C 320/04), OJ [2004] C 320/5.

[3] Council, *Resolution concerning PSB*; European Parliament, *Motion for a Resolution on the future of public service television in a multi-channel digital age*, Committee on Culture, Youth, Education and the Media 11/7/96 A4-0243/96; European Parliament, *Resolution on the role of public service television in a multi-media society* 19/9/96 A4-0243/96. See also Council of Europe, *Recommendation of the Committee of Ministers to Member States on the Guarantee of the Independence of Public Service Broadcasting*, R (96)10.

[4] Council, *Resolution concerning PSB*, p. 1.

[5] European Parliament, *Resolution on the role of public service television in a multi-media society*, para. B.

[6] J. Harrison and L. M. Woods, 'European Citizenship: Can European Audiovisual Policy make a Difference?', *Journal of Common Market Studies*, 38(3) (2000), 471–94, p. 472.

[7] Member states' decisions about the organisation and financing of PSB must meet particular criteria of good governance that the member states themselves set out.

[8] Commission, *Communication on the Application of State Aid Rules to PSB*, section 11.

[9] N. Tigchelaar, 'State Aid to Public Broadcasting – Revisited: An overview of the Commission's practice', *European State Aid Law Quarterly* 2 (2003), 169–81, p. 169.

to develop 'quality standards and guidelines for programme content',[10] which appears to be an attempt by the Parliament to identify a specific mechanism through which broadcasters can achieve PSB.

Traditionally, the ability of PSB to address the high expectations placed upon it has been linked to a requirement that public service broadcasters must provide a diverse range of quality broadcasting, free-to-air.[11] Thus one area of concern for the Union has been the issue of access to PSB, an issue which has technological, infrastructure and content considerations (see chapter 2). Article 31 of the Universal Service Directive[12] sets out the basis on which member states may impose must-carry obligations on the transmission of specific public interest content on different platform operators (see chapter 6). Despite difficulties in guaranteeing equality of access, in practice PSB is still seen as the vehicle that is most likely to ensure 'broad public access, without discrimination and on the basis of equal opportunities'.[13] The privatisation of certain types of information, however, means that, in practice, consumerism rather than citizens' interests is being prioritised by commercial broadcasters and policymakers (see chapter 12).

Public service broadcasters are encouraged by the European Parliament to make new technology available to public institutions and in public places.[14] The lack of clarity relating to the scope and definition of PSB in Union policy documents, however, has led to questions being asked by commercial competitors about the extent to which a state aided broadcaster can, or should, use state aid to fund expansion into the digital sector. Some public service broadcasters have taken advantage of the expansion in spectrum provided by the development of satellite and digital transmission technologies to launch a variety of entertainment and information channels and to enter into partnerships with the commercial sector.[15] Given that public service broadcasters are expected to take a

---

[10] European Parliament, *Motion for a Resolution on the Future of Public Service Television in a Multi-channel Digital Age*, n. 35.

[11] European Commission, High Level Group on Audio-visual Policy, *The Role of Public Authorities in the Media*, ch. 3, October 1998 OJ [1999] C 3020/5.

[12] Directive 2002/22/EC on Universal Service and Users' Rights Relating to Electronic Communications Networks and Services OJ [2002] L 108/51.

[13] Council, *Resolution Concerning PSB*, n. 4.

[14] Parliament, *Resolution on the Role of Public Service Television in a Multi-Media Society*, para. E.

[15] In 2001 the BBC gained permission from the Commission to start nine new digital services on radio and television: see NN 63/01 OJ [2002] C 23, 1. In contrast, the Commission has requested that Germany and The Netherlands clarify the role and financing of their public service broadcasters, particularly in relation to the scope of their online activities.

lead in 'the development of new services'[16] and the Council[17] has stated that 'the public service remit must continue to benefit from technological progress', any prevention of such activity by the Commission may seem to be contradictory, even though public service broadcasters' actions may be seen by some commercial competitors to distort competition.

Lack of consistency and clarity seem to pervade much Union policy relating to PSB. Despite the support for PSB from the European Parliament and Council, and attempts made to define it by the Commission, none of their documents addresses, at least not explicitly, the question of *who* carries out PSB functions.[18] The PSB remit can be specifically linked with a particular broadcasting organisation (or organisations). This linkage has traditionally been the case with state broadcasters given responsibility for PSB within a particular member state. Alternatively, PSB could be seen as being a series of separate functions, which can be carried out by any broadcaster (or combinations of broadcasters) no matter what the broadcaster's legal structure, provided that the end goals of PSB are satisfied by the type of broadcasting in issue.[19]

The lack of clarity about what programmes or content actually constitute PSB is also linked to the question of whether the scope of PSB is to be defined by reference to types of content. For example, current affairs programmes, and access to interactive content about health, public affairs or education, may be seen to be 'PSB' content, while reality TV shows (despite audience participation through voting), for example, are not. Alternatively, should PSB be defined by criteria, such as quality, innovation and accessibility, rather than by genre? Although the European Parliament has focused on quality and innovation as constituting PSB requirements, there has been no determination at the Union level as to how these PSB requirements, or indeed PSB itself, should be defined. If definition by genre becomes the determining factor, a clear list of what falls within and outside the PSB remit, and why, would be needed. Quite apart from the difficulties in establishing the scope of particular genres,

---

[16] Parliament, *Resolution on the Role of Public Service Television in a Multi-Media Society*, para. 7.

[17] Council, *Resolution Concerning PSB*, para. 3.

[18] J. Harrison and L. M. Woods, 'Defining European Public Service Broadcasting', *European Journal of Communications*, 16(4) (2001), 477–504, p. 484.

[19] Section 264(11) a–f of *The Communications Act 2003 (c. 21)* (London: HMSO, 2003) lists the relevant television services, 'which (taking them all together over the period as a whole) fulfil the purposes of public service television broadcasting in the United Kingdom' (*ibid.*, Section 264(3)a). The specific public service remits for licensed providers are set out in Section 265.

noted also in relation to the quotas rules (chapter 11) and the advertising frequency rules (chapter 9), this determination would require particular value judgments to be made about what is PSB programming or content, and what is not; why this is the case, and why such judgments make the case.

Conflicting policy concerns

In addition to these definitional issues, there is another, perhaps more significant, difficulty. It is based in the relationship between the Union and the member states, and also in the relationship between various policy goals in the Union. Briefly, the problem relates to the fact that member states' support for PSB can be seen as distorting competition and could therefore be viewed as contrary to the rules in the EC Treaty, notably those relating to state aid. Member states' systems must, to survive, either not constitute a distortion of competition or fall within the exceptions contained within the treaty, a fact which clearly limits member states' freedom of action in areas of policy, for example, cultural policy, and one which also affects the determination of state provision of services in areas which some member states may feel are properly their preserve.

None the less, the introduction of a new provision in the Treaty of Amsterdam (ToA) provided evidence of recognition of the importance of issues which go beyond economic and commercial issues by expressing concerns about the impact of a free-market approach on social and cultural aspects of European society. Article 16 EC provides that

> the Community and member states, each within their respective powers and within the scope of this Treaty, shall take care that such services [of general economic interest] operate on the basis of principles and conditions which enable them to fulfil their missions.

Services of general economic interest (SGEI) are market services that discharge general interest tasks and are subject to specific public service obligations by the member states.[20] The provision indicates mixed goals,

---

[20] In parallel, the term 'universal service' designates a set of general interest requirements which should be met by undertakings operating in certain sectors such as telecommunications and the postal service to ensure that everyone has access to essential services of a specified quality at an affordable price. In the absence of clear case law on this point 'the Commission has no power to take a position on the organisation and scale of the public task . . . provided that the aid in question does not benefit the activities pursued in competitive sectors or exceed what is necessary to enable the undertaking concerned

however. While Article 16 EC emphasises the importance of public services generally, and the ability of member states to provide such services in the manner of their choosing, it also states that public services must be subject to the competition provisions. This is an example of conflicting competences and the precise scope of this provision and the way it operates in practice is unclear. On the one hand, it emphasises the need to ensure that public services are carried out, and by member states, but on the other hand, it re-emphasises the existing division of power between the Union and the member states.

The PSB Protocol conveys a similar mixed message. Although the importance of PSB (seen broadly) is emphasised, as is the role of the member states in determining the proper scope and funding of PSB, the freedom of the member states in this regard is limited by reference to the competition provisions. The fact that the PSB Protocol is of interpretative status can be viewed similarly. Member states were concerned enough to agree to the PSB Protocol, but were not so concerned, or not inclined to agree, to more specific provision in the treaty. The Commission highlighted the limits on the role of member states in its explanatory note on the PSB Protocol, stating that funding for public service broadcasters 'must not alter the terms for business to an extent incompatible with the public interest . . .'. Thus, the understanding of public interest through the Competition Directorate-General's views (and those of the European courts) on SGEI remains vital to the determination of the permitted scope of PSB. This determination may, however, entail a different view of the public interest, based on the value of the benefits of a competitive market, rather than that used by the member states when justifying PSB. Again, there are mixed messages here. In its *Communication on PSB*, the Commission has provided itself with the task of verifying 'whether or not member states respect the Treaty provision', thus limiting 'the role of the Commission . . . to checking for manifest error'[21] on a case-by-case basis.[22] In this way the Commission does not 'question the nature or the quality of a certain product', other than to ensure that, in the wording of the Protocol, the 'democratic, social and cultural needs of each society'[23]

---

to perform the particular task assigned to it'. See Case T-106/95 *FFSA* [1997] ECR II-229, para. 192; also see Commission, *Communication on Services of General Interest in Europe* OJ [1996] C 281/3.

[21] Commission, *Communication on the Application of State Aid Rules to PSB*, section 36. See also European Commission, NN 88/98 *BBC News 24*.

[22] See Commission, *XXVIIIth Report on Competition Policy* (1998), para. 273.

[23] *Ibid.*, section 36.

are met. This might suggest a hands-off approach, and indeed this may be the case[24] with regard to the initial view of scope, but the Commission retains the right to review the proportionality of the measure adopted, a factor which may be crucial in the determination of the acceptability of the measure,[25] thus having a limiting effect on member states' freedom of action. We doubt whether the Commission, especially DG Competition, is the best placed institution to assess the needs of an individual member state's society.

In any event, both Article 16 EC and the Protocol indicate that not only are there tensions in and between Union policies and their interpretation by different Union institutions but also that there are different views held between member states and the Union as to the proper scope of competence in the area of PSB. The impact of other cross-cutting provisions, such as Article 151(4) EC (discussed in chapter 4), is unclear. Although according to this provision culture should be taken into account in the determination of other policies, such as competition and state aid, a fact which the Commission seems to have recognised,[26] this has yet to occur. Despite high expectations from some commentators,[27] the concern remains that the scope of member states' freedom in preserving their cultural interests in the face of commercial imperatives will be judged in the economic context of competition policy.

Overview of legal state aid framework

Article 87(1) prohibits aids that are likely to distort competition and thus affect inter-state trade. It does so because it regards such aid as incompatible with the EC Treaty. The article provides that:

---

[24] Though contrast the approach of the Commission to the French international news channel N 54/2005 OJ [2005] C 256/25. There it was argued that as the channel was aimed at countries other than France it could not fall within the notion of France's cultural and democratic needs. In assessing the acceptability of the aid under Article 86(2), the Commission said that the assessment was not to be done on the basis of the protocol or its Communication, p. 9, para. 40.

[25] Note also the impact of the *Altmark* 'criteria' here, see below: Case C-280/00 *AltmarkTrans GmbH* v. *Nahverkehrsgesellschaft Altmark GmbH* [2003] nyr, judgment 24 July 2003.

[26] Commission, *First Report on the Consideration of Cultural Aspects in European Community Action*, COM(1996)160.

[27] See authors cited by L. Mayer-Robitaille, *Application of EC Competition Policy regarding Agreements and State Aid in the Audiovisual Field* (Strasbourg: Audiovisual Observatory, 2005) IRIS Plus, p. 6.

Save as otherwise provided in this treaty, any aid granted by a member state or through state resources in any form whatsoever which distorts or threatens to distort competition by favouring certain undertakings or the production of certain goods shall, insofar as it affects trade between member states, be incompatible with the common market.

Articles 87(2) and 87(3) provide for exceptions to this prohibition. Article 87(2) provides for exceptions which are automatically compatible with the common market. Those in Article 87(3) are cases which may be compatible with the common market, including Article 87(3)(d), which potentially permits 'aid to promote culture and heritage conservation', subject always to the common interest as determined by the Commission.[28]

In addition, Article 86(2) provides that, although competition rules apply to undertakings entrusted with the operation of SGEI, the rules do so 'insofar as the application of such rules do not obstruct the performance in law or in fact, of the particular tasks assigned to them'. Ultimately any assessment under Article 86(2) must also ensure that the development of trade is not affected 'to such an extent as would be contrary to the interests of the Community'. In general terms, should state aid be found, Article 86(2) EC may still protect the grant of the aid. This provision would seem to be an attempt by the drafters of the treaty to recognise that there are societal goals which may not be adequately served purely by the operation of the market or the creation of the common market.

To fall within the state-aid rules a number of criteria must be satisfied. There is a five-stage test of interlinked elements which trigger Article 87. The elements are: (a) the measure must be specific rather than general; (b) the existence of 'aid'; (c) granted by a member state from state resources or a public body;[29] (d) which distorts/threatens to distort competition; and (e) affects trade between member states.

---

[28] Different rules apply to 'new' and as opposed to 'existing' aid, as we shall see in the case of NOS the management organisation of the Dutch public service broadcasters: Commission, Press Release, State Aid: Commission orders Dutch public service broadcaster NOS to pay back €76.3 million excess ad hoc funding, IP/06/822, 22 June 2006, p. 2.

[29] In the Italian case, the benefits received by RAI were awarded by a public body, Cassa Depositi e Prestiti: see Commission, Press Release, Commission opens formal procedure regarding certain aid measures for public broadcaster RAI (Italy) and raises no objections to other measures, IP/99/532, 20 July 1999. Article 87 also covers aid which is financed out of the public purse but administered by private bodies. In the BBC News 24 case the licence fee is a form of taxation and the funds obtained thereby were viewed as constituting state funds, even though the money is collected by a private company on behalf of the BBC.

Looking at the first element which must be satisfied to show state aid, a distinction is made between aid and general rules relating to economic policy. General rules relating to economic policy which affect the industry sector as a whole usually fall outside Union supervision, remaining the responsibility of member states. Therefore the ability to deduct tax from the costs of investment from income and corporation tax liability would not constitute aid. Conversely, rules which benefit a given sector (for example, the broadcasting sector) would be aid.

The second element requires that the member state's intervention must favour 'undertakings'.[30] Although to constitute state aid there must be a benefit, the actual purpose of the aid is irrelevant. Rather, it is the effect of the government intervention that is important for determining the existence of aid and whether it is compatible with the common market.[31] The general position then under Union law is that financial support provided to a public service broadcaster by a member state has the potential to be seen as state aid under the provisions in Article 87 EC.

Given the complexities surrounding PSB, it is perhaps not surprising that the Commission's approach should reveal some hesitation and inconsistencies. As member states opened up their markets to broadcasting, commercial companies began to complain about the distortion in the broadcasting market caused by state or public subsidy given to public service broadcasters. Initially, the Commission appeared unsure as to what approach to take in its assessment of the complaints made by broadcasters in Spain (complaint made by Gestevision Telecinco against RTVE), France (complaint made by TF1 against France 2 and 3) and Portugal (complaint made by SIC against RTP).

A preliminary point is whether PSB operators should be considered as economic actors, given that many do not aim to make a profit and operate free-to-air. The institutions (notably the Commission's Competition DG), however, have typically taken a very broad view of what constitutes an economic undertaking and, according to existing case law, broadcasters, whether under PSB obligations or not, have economic interests. Although there is no exchange of goods and services for payment between broadcaster and viewer, this does not mean that public service broadcasters have no impact in the market-place. In particular, public service broadcasters compete for viewers, which will have an impact on advertising

---

[30] 'Undertakings' have been defined very widely by the Union and apply to all bodies or persons which are carrying out an economic activity.

[31] Case 173/73 *Commission* v. *Italy* [1974] ECR 709, para. 27.

and sponsorship revenue for commercial broadcasters and some public service broadcasters even compete for advertising revenue.[32] When the Commission finally took a decision in the complaint in the Portuguese case in 1996,[33] it found that the funds paid by the Portuguese state to the public service broadcaster, RTP, did not constitute state aid under Article 87(1) EC, as they were paid to offset the costs of public service obligations and were a compensation for the money spent by the broadcaster. This reasoning appears to take the view that the provision of funding was not seen to favour the undertaking in this case. This decision was later annulled by the Court of First Instance (CFI),[34] which took the view that such grants did constitute aid, but that their purpose should be taken into account when assessing the aid's compatibility with the common market, or when considering the application of Article 86(2).

In the case of *BBC News 24*, the Commission's assessment of state aid seems to have been based on two criteria: first, that the BBC was in receipt of a positive benefit; and secondly, that the state aid compensated charges normally included in the costs of an undertaking.[35] Given that a lessening of costs has been found to constitute aid, it could seem strange that the Commission found that must-carry rules do not involve state aid, presumably because the link between the benefit and the state action is indirect; the benefit is actually provided by the private undertaking obliged to carry the specified content.[36] Presumably preferential access to radio spectrum would constitute state aid.[37]

Of significance in this context is the way the Commission's approach to the assessment of aid has changed. In the Portuguese case, it took a compensation approach; whereas cases such as the *BBC News 24* case show a move to the hypothetical investor test. According to this test, the actions of the state are judged by reference to the action a private investor would be assumed to have made in similar circumstances. This view, also articulated in the Commission's *Communication on State Aid* in 2001,[38] follows the

---

[32] Commission, Case IV/M.566 *CLT/Disney/SuperRTL*, Decision 17 May 1997.
[33] Commission Decision, NN 141/95 Financing of the public Portuguese television OJ [1997] C 67.
[34] Case T-46/97 *Sociedada Independent de Comunicação SA* v. *Commission* [2000] ECR I-2125.
[35] Case C-256/97 *Déménagements-Manutention Transport SA* [1999] ECR I-03913.
[36] Commission Decision C2/2003 (ex NN 22/02) *Denmark/TV2* C(2004) 1814, final para. 68; Summary Assessment C2/2004 (ex NN 170/03) *Ad hoc measures to Dutch public broadcasters and NOS and NOB*, OJ [2004] C 61/8. On must carry rules, see ch. 6.
[37] *Denmark/TV2* C(2004) 1814, paras. 28–31.
[38] Commission, *Communication on the Application of State Aid Rules to PSB*, section 33.

approach of the CFI in *FFSA*[39] and the annulment of the Commission's earlier ruling in the Portuguese case. Following these cases, the position appeared to be that state financing of public services constituted state aid under Article 87(1), but might be justified under Article 86(2). Such funding would, therefore, have to be subject to Commission scrutiny. Furthermore, increasing pressure would be placed upon member states to clarify and justify their methods for funding public service broadcasters. This position, however, now has to be understood in the light of the *Ferring*[40] and *Altmark* decisions, discussed below.

The third element which must be shown to satisfy the test for the existence of state aid is that the aid is granted by member states or through state resources. This is fairly easily seen in the context of PSB. State aid has been found in several cases: the subsidies[41] received by France 2 and France 3;[42] the loan guarantees by the state which were lower than commercial rates of interest, or deferred loans and reduction of taxation or tax exemptions, received by RAI,[43] and the licence-fee funding received by Kinderkanal/Phoenix[44] and BBC News 24. These cases all involved state resources, whether directly or indirectly. In some contexts, there can be an overlap between this element and the second element of the test, the existence of aid.

The fourth element of the test for state aid requires a distortion of competition and the fifth element that the aid affects inter-state trade, even if the benefits in issue are small.[45] In practice, these two elements are often linked, competition being considered in the context of competition between operators in different member states' markets. In the recent DVB decisions, however, the Commission focussed on the impact

---

[39] Case T-106/95 *FFSA and Others v Commission* [1997] ECR II-229.

[40] Case C 53/00 *Ferring v. Agence Centrale des Organismes de Sécurité Sociale (ACOSS)* [2001] ECR I-9067.

[41] In the broadcasting sector, aid can come from a variety of sources. It can comprise both direct and indirect state funding, which could take the form of a licence fee, or may arise through other *ad hoc* measures such as tax exemptions, debt-rescheduling, capital increases, subsidies, asset re-evaluations, state loans or state guarantees.

[42] Commission, *Press Release, Commission enjoins the French government to submit information on the existing nature of the financing scheme of the public broadcasters France 2 and France 3*, IP/99/81, 3 February 1999; Commission, Press Release, *Commission opens formal procedure regarding State aid to public broadcasters France 2 and France 3*, IP/99/531, 20 July 1999.

[43] From Cassa Depositi e Prestiti; see above.

[44] European Commission, NN 70/98 *Kinderkanal and Phoenix* OJ [1999] C 238/03.

[45] See Case T-214/95 *Vlaams Gewest v. Commission* [1997] ECR II-717.

on competition between different distribution platforms rather than on competition between service providers from different member states.[46] This seems to be a variant of the technology-neutral approach found in other areas. Otherwise, the Commission's approach has been that there is a distortion of competition if the effect of the aid is to protect a domestic industry against imports. Consequently, a direct impact on any trade between member states is not necessary, it is enough if the measures give the recipient of state aid an advantage over other Union competitors involved in intra-Community trade.[47] This reasoning was adopted in the decision regarding aid granted to the French television production company *Société française de production* (SFP).[48] Although the French government argued that funding given to SFP would not affect inter-state trade, because only 10 per cent of video production was intended for the international market, the Commission rejected its case. The Commission's reasoning was SFP was placed in an advantageous position in the context of the Union, as other operators from member states would be unable to enter or compete as effectively as SFP in the French market because of its subsidy. The size of SFP's export market was not seen to be of primary importance; rather, the distortion to the Union's internal market was in issue.[49] When the Commission evaluates the impact of state aid on trade between member states, it does not engage in a measurement of a causal connection between the benefit gained by the recipient of state aid and any loss suffered by a competitor. In the *BBC News 24* case, the Commission noted that it is sufficient if the recipient is put in a position whereby it can 'offer a service on conditions which cannot be matched by any other commercial operator'.[50]

---

[46] Commission, *Press Release: State aid – Commission rules subsidy for digital terrestrial TV (DVB-T) in Berlin–Brandenburg illegal; explains how digital TV can be supported*, IP/05/1394, 9 November 2005, p. 1. The Commission identified support mechanisms that would be viewed favourably: funding for rollout in areas where population is not dense; compensation for costs of simulcasting; subsidies to consumers for the purchase of STB; compensation to broadcasters for early cessation of analogue broadcasting licences, p. 2. The Commission seems to have dealt with the two issues together in the French International News Channel Case: Commission Decision – N 54/2005, *International News Channel)* C(2005)1479 final, p 6, para. 28.

[47] Case 730/79 *Phillip Morris v. Commission* [1980] ECR 303.

[48] Commission Decision, *Société française de production* (97/238/EC) OJ [1995] L 95/19.

[49] Commission, *SFP*, part VIII. SFP has subsequently received aid, but justified under Article 87(3)(c): Commission Decision 98/466/EC OJ [1998] L205/68; Commission Decision N 797/2001 *France/SPF* C(2002)2593 final OJ [2003] C71/3.

[50] NN 88/98 *BBC News 24*, para. 30.

Problems in identifying aid

Decisions as to whether or not aid confers any advantage to a recipient have been controversial. At one point, it seemed that the European courts and the Commission had adopted the market-investor principle. As others have noted, the use of the hypothetical investor test in the context of the provision of public services generally is self-defeating, given the nature and purpose of public services.[51] By definition, they involve choices that are not determined by profit-seeking behaviour, but rather by social concerns. Given the scope of PSB obligations, the answer to the question posed by the hypothetical investor test would usually be negative, and so the money the broadcasters receive would be considered as aid, which, if the other elements of Article 87(1) were satisfied, would then have to be justified under Article 87(2) or (3), or under Article 86(2). Thus, in the German *Kinderkanal and Phoenix* and the British *BBC News 24* cases (although the British government tried to argue that the licence fee was reimbursement for expenditure for carrying out PSB obligations), the broadcasters were deemed to have received state aid.[52]

Further clarification on state aid was needed. A few weeks after the Commission's *PSB Communication* was adopted, the European Court of Justice (ECJ) gave a ruling in *Ferring* on whether the new tax introduced by the French authorities on direct sales of medicines to pharmacies constituted state aid. The ECJ considered that,

> provided the tax on direct sales imposed on pharmaceutical laboratories corresponds to the additional costs actually incurred by wholesale distributors in discharging their public service obligations. . . . The tax may be regarded as compensation for the services they provide and hence no state aid within the meaning of Article 87 of the Treaty.[53]

This seems to be a move away from the market-investor test and a move back towards the compensation approach the Commission took in the Portuguese case.[54] Some have criticised the approach in *Ferring*, arguing that the judgment suggests that only two categories relating to state aid

---

[51] A. Bartosch, 'The Financing of Public Broadcasting and EC State Aid Law: An Interim Balance', *European Competition Law Review*, (1999), 197–204, p. 200; M. Ross, 'State Aids and National Courts: Definitions and Other Problems – A Case of Premature Emancipation?', *Common Market Law Review*, 37 (2000), 401–23, p. 411.

[52] NN 70/98 *Kinderkanal and Phoenix*; NN 88/98, *BBC News 24*, para. 24.

[53] Case C-53/00 *Ferring v. Agence Centrale*, [2001] ECR I-9067, para. 27.

[54] Commission Decision, NN 141/95 *Financing of the public Portuguese television*, OJ [1997] C 67.

are possible: either incompatible aid; or non-aid. If such an analysis is accepted, Article 86 loses any purpose in relation to state aid, as 'fair compensation is no aid and over-compensation is always incompatible'.[55]

The *Altmark* case gave the ECJ the chance to clarify the problem of advantage to the recipient and the question of whether or not compensation for SGEI is state aid.[56] The ECJ established the principle 'that a compensation that does not exceed what is necessary to cover the minimum possible costs incurred in the discharge of public service obligations is not state aid'.[57] The ECJ indicated that the compensation given to an efficient operator is not aid, whereas compensation given to an inefficient operator may still be compatible aid. This appears to be a step towards the protection of non-trade considerations, as the change means, at a level of principle, that support for PSB that satisfies the *Altmark* test will not be aid and will, therefore, not have to be assessed for its compatibility with the common market.

The difficulty is that, under the *Altmark* ruling, the basis on which the existence of aid is determined is by reference to four specific criteria. First, there must be clear public service obligations; secondly, pre-established parameters for determining the compensation; thirdly, there is no over-compensation; and fourthly, that there is either selection of the operator through tender procedure, or a determination of compensation with reference to costs of a typical, well-run undertaking. Problematically, the criteria to determine whether aid exists or not under *Altmark*, in practice, seem similar to tests used to justify aid under Article 86(2), particularly as regards the proportionality of funding (see below). Certainly, in its post-*Altmark* decisions, the Commission has rarely concluded that the *Altmark* conditions have been fulfilled.[58] *Altmark* does not add greatly to the conceptual clarity in this area.

In *BBC Licence Fee*,[59] which pre-dated *Altmark*, the Commission considered whether the expansion of the activities of the BBC through the provision of nine new digital services, which fell outside the scope of the

---

[55] S. Santamato and N. Pesaresi, 'Compensation for Services of General Economic Interest: Some Thoughts on the *Altmark* Ruling', *Competition Policy Newsletter*, No. 1, Spring (2001), 17–21, p. 17.

[56] *Ibid.*, p. 17.   [57] *Ibid.*, p. 21.

[58] See, e.g., N 37/2003 *BBC Digital Curriculum* OJ [2003] C 271/47, para. 23 – note that the scheme was accepted under Article 86(2) EC; see also NN 170/03 *NOS/NOB*, but contrast NN 31/2006 *Funding for RTP*, 5 July 2006, paras. 73–6: see Commission Press Release, *State aid: Commission endorses restructuring plan for Portuguese public broadcaster RTP*, IP 06–932.

[59] Case NN 63/01 *BBC Licence Fee* OJ [2003] C 23, para. 30.

traditional PSB task of providing free-to-air channels to a mass audience, could be accepted as a public service. In this case, the Commission ruled that the BBC was fulfilling a public service task and that no aid was found. It did, however, spell out the need for a 'clear and precise identification of the activities covered by the public service remit, and the conditions under which these have to be performed [as being] important for non-public service operators, so that they can plan their activities'.[60] These criteria are used by the Commission in order to assess the proportionality of the funding.[61] However, three cases (RTP, RAI, and France 2 and France 3) were re-examined in 2003 in the light of the *Altmark* case, and the principles set out in the Commission's *PSB Communication* of 2001. All three cases followed the same pattern, whereby the Commission found that the conditions provided by Article 87(1) were, in fact, met and consequently the funding given to these broadcasters was deemed to be state aid. When considering more specifically the condition that the state measure must confer an advantage, the Commission applied the *Altmark* test. All three cases failed to meet the second criterion listed in the *Altmark* judgment, namely that 'the parameters on the basis of which the compensation is calculated have been established beforehand in an objective and transparent manner'.[62] It would seem that it is particularly difficult for public service broadcasters to pass the *Altmark* test and therefore to escape the qualification of state aid, as many have been established and funded for a considerable period of time and certainly before the need for clear identification became apparent.[63] Such an approach re-emphasises the Commission's ability to review PSB funding, arguably undermining the impact of the change from hypothetical investor to compensation approach found in *Ferring* and *Altmark*. If this is the correct interpretation of *Altmark*, it is certainly not clear from the text of the ECJ's judgment.

The approach of the Commission in response to the ECJ's rulings appears to emphasise the need for member states to be very precise about the nature of their broadcasters' PSB remit and parameters through which, and by which, public service broadcasters are eligible for compensation in

---

[60] Case NN 631/01 *BBC Licence Fee*, para. 36.

[61] M. Varney, 'European Controls on Member State Promotion and Regulation of Public Service Broadcasting and Broadcasting Standards', *European Public Law*, 10(3) 2004, 503–30, p. 525.

[62] Case C-280/00 *Altmark*, para. 95.

[63] In a 2005 memo, the Commission noted that in all cases involving PSB post-*Altmark*, the Commission had found that the *Altmark* criteria had not been satisfied: Memo/05/73, p. 1.

the digital age.[64] The problem is that more specific obligations are inherently less flexible, a difficulty which is compounded when the types of service which might be offered are changing rapidly. Recently broadcasters in Ireland, the Netherlands and Germany, in the light of their on-line activities,[65] have been asked to implement a clear definition of their public service remit; show clear separation of accounts, distinguishing between public service and other activities; show adequate mechanisms to prevent overcompensation of public service activities; and to ensure that an independent (national) authority checks compliance with these rules. Although the Commission is not necessarily questioning the ability of public service broadcasters to offer on-line services as part of their remit, it is concerned to ensure that the scope and remit of public service broadcasters in this area is determined by the member states concerned and not by the broadcasters themselves.

Exceptions to the state-aid provisions

Given the economic focus of the state-aid provisions and the specific value and role of broadcasting (see chapter 2), the cultural exception in Article 87(3)(d) might initially seem to be relevant. However, the use of this cultural exception does not seem to have been raised when the question of state aid for public service broadcasters is discussed, despite the obvious links between the film and television sectors and culture. In the *BBC News 24* case, the UK did not suggest that the cultural exception be used. The Commission noted this fact, but then commented that the exception would not be relevant in any event, as BBC News 24 dealt with information rather than cultural needs.[66] It is questionable as to the extent it is possible to make such a clear distinction between news, information and culture.[67] Moreover, it is hard to draw any clear lines in the Commission's approach in the various decisions dealing with Article 87(3)(d), save that any interpretation of the provision is likely to be narrow. Although

---

[64] M. Varney, 'European Controls on Member State Promotion and Regulation of Public Service Broadcasting and Broadcasting Standards', p. 523. Note approach on funding concerning SMS-services, *NOS/NOB*.

[65] Commission, *Press Release, State aid: Commission requests Germany, Ireland and The Netherlands to clarify role and financing of public service broadcasters*, IP/05/250, 3 March 2005, p. 1.

[66] NN 88/98 *BBC News 24*, para. 36.

[67] Similarly, in N 70/98 *Kinderkanal*, the Commission stated that 'the educational and democratic needs of a member state have to be regarded as distinct from the promotion of culture', p. 3.

aid for the promotion of cultural products in the Irish language was authorised under Article 87(3)(d), aid for local television stations in the French-speaking community in Belgium was unsuccessful. The Commission focused on the fact that the stations had to produce 'full-time news, animation, cultural development and education programmes'. According to the Commission, these 'may not be considered as being directed entirely or specifically at the promotion of culture within the meaning of Article 87(3)(d)', without explaining the lack of connection any further.[68] Given that aid to national film industries can fall within 87(3)(d), it is not clear why television programming does not. Further, the boundary between the production industries for film, television production and the dissemination of broadcasting has not been investigated. As a general comment, the Commission does not seem to have expressly considered the impact of Article 151(4) EC in its decisions in this context either. Rather, the Commission has tended to view PSB as a matter for resolution under Article 86(2), without necessarily considering culture in much detail if at all.[69]

Article 86(2) is an exception which is addressed only to the type of undertaking specified in Article 86(2). There are two elements to this provision: the service in question must be an SGEI; and the undertaking in question must be entrusted with that responsibility by a member state. Broadcasters entrusted with PSB obligations fall within the category of undertakings to which Article 86(2) is addressed: the public-interest nature of broadcasting is generally accepted, fulfilling the first element; and most PSB providers operate under national legislation, fulfilling the second. Interestingly, it seems that the public-service nature of their mission need not relate to the member state which is conferring the obligation. In the Commission decision concerning the International News Channel, which was supported by the French Government but effectively incapable of reception in France, that undertaking was still held to fall within Article 86(2).[70]

None the less, there are problems that arise when considering the scale of member state support. The scope of protection awarded by Article 86(2)

---

[68] Commission Decision, N 548/2001, *Belgium (French-speaking community)*, OJ [2002] C 150/7.

[69] Commission, *Communication on the Application of State Aid Rules to PSB*, p. 8; although film production is regularly exempted under this provision, television is rarely considered in this context. See L. Woods, 'The Application of Competition Rules to State Aids for Culture', in *Culture et Marché ERA-Forum* 1/2005, p. 43.

[70] N 54/2005, *International News Channel*, p. 10, para. 43.

is itself limited by the requirement that any measure does not interfere with the Union interests. The Commission's *Communication on Services of General Interest in Europe* covers, among other sectors, the broadcasting field. In this document, the Commission attempted to identify how it would 'ensure smooth interplay between, on the one hand, the requirements of the single European market and free competition in terms of free movement, economic performance and dynamism and, on the other, the general interest objectives',[71] although, in practice, it was not particularly clear or helpful. The Commission clarified its policy in its *PSB Communication* of 2001,[72] where it stated that companies which provide SGEI shall only be subject to the rules of the treaty in so far as their application does not obstruct the performance of the assigned task, namely the company's ability to provide PSB. This is consistent with the terms of Article 86(2); indeed, it virtually repeats them. The communication states that state aid to public service broadcasters should be proportionate to the net costs of providing a clearly defined PSB task entrusted by the relevant member state to the undertaking.

There are two problems with this test. The first concerns the requirement that costs should be proportionate to funding (or vice versa). This seems very similar to some of the *Altmark* criteria for determining whether aid exists in the first place. Given the similarity between the two tests, there is a risk that funding found to be aid because it over-compensates cannot be proportionate for the purposes of Article 86(2), rendering the safeguard provided by Article 86(2) toothless. It is this argument we saw earlier used against the introduction of the compensation test. In our view, this problem is not a matter of principle affecting the compensation test itself, but the way the four *Altmark* criteria and the test for the application of Article 86(2) have developed that has caused this problem. A distinction between the two must be made, bearing in mind that the rule will always be wider than exceptions to that rule, but also taking into account our concerns regarding the impact of the *Altmark* criteria on the development of PSB (below).

Secondly, this test (as indeed does *Altmark*) requires a clear definition of the public service remit. This might cause problems where the scope or nature of the public service changes, particularly in response to changes in technology or societal expectations. In particular, this position has raised concerns when public service broadcasters have taken advantage of new

[71] Commission, *Communication on Services of General Interest in Europe*, para. 19.
[72] Commission, *Communication on the Application of State Aid Rules to PSB*, section 11.

digital opportunities. Public service broadcasters seeking to expand their remit in this way have argued that such activity should not be regarded as being commercial, but as an expansion of their PSB task.[73] We have some sympathy with this view, since to fulfil the PSB role broadcasters need to attract audiences which they are unlikely to be able to do if their services are outmoded or only delivered via outdated technologies, such as analogue transmission. However, the debate still continues about the extent to which loosely defined PSB activities constitute public service or 'mission creep',[74] which may confer advantage on the recipient of aid.

Impact on the scope and scale of PSB at the member state level

Although the definition of state aid remains problematic, *Altmark* is an improvement on the use of the hypothetical-investor test. The implication of the hypothetical-investor test seems to be that PSB functions are limited to uneconomic broadcasting functions, and thus PSB broadcasting is defined by reference to what commercial broadcasters will not, or cannot, do. BSkyB drew on this sort of argument when it challenged the BBC's 24-hour news channel, broadcast now on terrestrial, cable and satellite digital platforms. BSkyB's argument was that, as state aid is tied into loss-making activities, a broadcaster should not use public funds to provide a service that could be provided by the private sector, irrespective of the type of programming carried, because they believed that such a body receiving state aid would be at a competitive advantage. The problem arising from this argument is that some types of programming which would be of interest to citizens and which are universally available free-to-air, are potentially profitable, as the BBC News 24 example shows, and that accepting hypothetical-investor reasoning would open up the possibility that such programming might become the preserve of pay TV and sold as a commodity.

As we have noted, *Altmark* took a different approach. Although still tied in to the idea that broadcasters should only receive compensation for actual expense, there seems to be greater freedom to determine the scope

---

[73] S. Depypere and N. Tigchelaar, 'The Commission's State Aid Policy on Activities of Public Service Broadcasters in Neighbouring Markets', *Competition Policy Newsletter*, 2 Summer (2004), 19–22, p. 20.

[74] Depypere and Tigchelaar, *ibid.*, p. 19, refer to 'mission creep' as 'the process by which a mission's methods and goals change gradually over time'.

of PSB.[75] None the less, the second and third criteria in *Altmark* might raise problems for a vibrant PSB sector. The requirement to specify a PSB remit clearly and in advance may lead to PSB being constrained in a developing market. More significant is the question of over-compensation. It is not clear to us whether the assumption in *Altmark* is that public funding should be limited to the bare minimum to provide the service, that is, it is not a limitation on the type of service that is problematic, but the permitted quality. An approach to the third *Altmark* criterion should not take as its baseline the lowest possible cost, but instead the cost of the quality of programmes produced or sought to be produced by the broadcaster. Otherwise, there are likely to be adverse consequences on the ability of the public service broadcaster to invest in distinctive and innovative programming, which is expensive to produce, and which may further exacerbate the information divide that already exists between those who can afford multiple television subscriptions and those who cannot.

The state aid provisions do not explicitly address whether PSB functions can be split up and provided by different broadcasters, not all of whom receive state aid. Some types of programming, such as children's, news and sports coverage, can be provided commercially, but, in terms of programme type or quality, may be seen to have a PSB element. Arguably, PSB can be seen as a series of severable obligations, which, in principle, could be carried out by several broadcasting organisations, rather than a single PSB obligation that is carried out in its entirety by one broadcaster. Problematically, a division of PSB programming (without ensuring that there was universally accessible programming available) would undermine any potential that PSB has coherently and consistently to reflect cultural diversity, or to promote the conditions for social cohesion. Efforts to use PSB to encourage cultural tolerance or social cohesion via mass audience viewing of programmes will fail if the types of channels on offer become increasingly niche-oriented, and are the province of greater numbers of speciality channels. Under these circumstances, viewers trying to access a diverse range of quality programming may have to take out multiple subscriptions in order to achieve a varied programme diet. Such viewers would also have to be discerning and willing to search for content. The risk of this is that a fragmented PSB offering scattered among a number of channels is easy to miss. This would then require passive citizen viewers to become active, which they may not be capable of, whether for internal or external

---

[75] Commission, *Press Release, Commission requests Germany, Ireland and The Netherlands to clarify role and financing of public service broadcasters*, IP/05/250, 3 March 2005, p. 1.

reasons. The advantage with vertical diversity of content within one or two mass-audience channels is that, assuming a broadcaster can achieve viewer loyalty, viewers are more likely to receive a varied diet of programming than if they viewed only specialist or entertainment programming. As we suggested in chapter 1, regulators and policymakers need to be aware of the different viewers and viewing activities that require protection in the contemporary broadcasting environment. The state-aid rules do not assist in this process; indeed, it is possible to read *Altmark* as facilitating a move towards niche PSB channels, while undermining the possibility of funding high-quality channels.

Conclusion

While PSB is generally accepted at both European and national level to fulfil an important role,[76] particularly as regards protection of citizen viewers, there is little consensus as to the scope of PSB and the mechanisms by which it may be delivered. Problematically, PSB has different aspects which fall within several of the competences of the member states and the Union. Thus, while member states are concerned to ensure that PSB is provided, the Union institutions view PSB providers as economic operators, state support to which should not contravene the EC Treaty and in particular competition and common market rules. The definition of aid in the first instance is crucial for determining the boundary between acceptable and unacceptable member state support. A broad definition of aid seems to have been used in the 1980s and 1990s via the use of the market-investor test. This meant that member state support was likely to be considered aid and subject to review at the Union level in accordance with competition policy objectives. This approach curtailed, at a level of principle, member states' freedom to provide PSB as they saw

---

[76] There has been broad agreement at national and European level about the nature of these values which have been articulated in various compendia of PSB values prepared by both media professionals and academics. See, e.g., The Broadcasting Research Unit, *The Public Service Idea in British Broadcasting: Main Principles* (Luton: John Libbey, 1985), pp. 25–32; *The Report of European Broadcasting Union's (EBU) Perez Group, Conclusions of the TV Programme Committee's Group of Experts on the Future of Public Service Broadcasting* (EBU: mimeo 1983), p. 4; and, more recently, see G. Born and T. Prosser, 'Culture and Consumerism: Citizenship, Public Service Broadcasting and the BBC's Fair Trading Obligations', *Modern Law Review*, 64(5) (2003), 657–87; G. F. Lowe and T. Hujanen, *Broadcasting and Convergence: New Articulations of the Public Service Remit* (Göteborg: Nordicom, 2003), *passim*.

fit. As we have seen, the scope of exception is crucial and in this context Article 86(2) has been significant. The Commission has been sensitive to public-interest concerns, though this does not change the fact that it has, to a large degree, appropriated competence for PSB provision from the member states.

Even with the change in approach following the *Ferring* and *Altmark* cases, member state choices are still subject to review. All that seems to have changed is the question the review answers, and not the nature or basis of the review itself. Problematically for member states, this change to the review requires them to attempt to define PSB;[77] a task which has not been successfully undertaken by the Union itself. Defining PSB runs the risk of ossifying it and therefore preventing change, innovation and growth. This is because either a member state defines PSB too narrowly, forcing a PSB provider to go beyond its proper remit if it is to retain viewers in a changing broadcasting environment; or the member state defines PSB too broadly, so as to exceed its competence in the view of the Commission. If that were not enough, there is the persistent problem of avoiding a definition of PSB that is too vague, a problem which risks a failure to satisfy the *Altmark* criteria. The approach in *Altmark* raises concerns about the risk that, although PSB might be defined broadly, it could be inadequately funded. PSB may be allowed to expand across a range of digital channels, but a broad view of over-compensation could limit the funds available to provide quality programmes. In all of this, the Commission seems to have been a somewhat reluctant participant and increasingly pushed by private broadcasters to challenge PSB. It has not focused directly, if at all, on the consequences of this for the viewing experience and for citizen viewers specifically.

[77] D. McQuail, *McQuail's Mass Communication Theory* (London: Sage, 2000), p. 156.

PART III

14

Conclusions

We began from the position that broadcasting is important. Its importance is, from the perspective of different people, based in different factors. From one point of view, it is understood as being a result of its influence; alternatively, that importance arises from its economic value. Within the first point of view there are many positions and beliefs. Variously, broadcasting is said to be able to contribute to a nation's cultural sense of itself, to entertain, to educate, to inform and to provide social glue, but also to distort, to dumb down, to misrepresent and to contribute to social undoing. The second viewpoint is more straightforward. There are those who regard broadcasting purely as an industry, and there are also those who regard it as an evolving service at the heart of the new knowledge economy. Both would suggest that broadcasting be treated as an industrial sector, rather than as a public service. The two main viewpoints have consequences for the perception of the appropriate roles of the private sector and the public, respectively, and also for the role, scope and type of regulation. Typically, those who take the first viewpoint would endorse public intervention, whether in the form of an (independent) state broadcaster or close regulation in the public interest; the second viewpoint may be characterised as requiring little or no intervention, as the market is assumed to provide a range of services. Indeed, some would suggest regulation does damage, especially in hindering the development of technology and new services.

Within this book, we have argued that broadcasting is best understood as something that can contribute to social, political and cultural purposes. We have also suggested that this is something current Union regulation sometimes ignores, sometimes pays lip service to and sometimes struggles with. The nature of the contribution that broadcasting makes to these purposes is, for us, captured by the idea that, if viewers are regarded as citizens, then the nature of regulatory thinking is utterly different from that used when viewers are regarded as consumers in a market-place, whether this be at a national or European level. This distinction is pivotal (table 1, chapter 1). The consumer resides in the commercial domain, is market-based, economically determined, individualistic and regards content, in all forms, as capable of being purchased and owned. The citizen resides in the public domain and regards certain content as a social and civic asset which should be available to all, sees communication infrastructures as adding to the cultural fabric of collective identity and belonging, requires that certain civic functions are fulfilled by broadcasters and believes that the public purse, and not the personal purse, bears the cost of such a service.

A viewing experience which satisfies the needs of citizens implicitly contains not only certain types of content but also a range of content. The citizens' domain is also universally available, even if, in practice, viewers choose not to watch the wide range of programmes provided. Consideration of this domain brings into play issues of access as well as issues of range and quality of content. By contrast, in the consumers' domain, information may be owned and controlled for private rather than public interest; access here is not just about technology but, crucially, about ability and willingness to pay. It is in this domain that the distinction between active and passive viewers has a heightened significance. By contrast with assumptions underpinning the public domain, the content range of individual consumers will not necessarily be easily or readily available. Passive consumers are likely to be presented with a basic and limited level of service; those who wish to access premium content, for example, will have to engage with technology via conditional access systems (CAS) in pay TV and pay-per-view (PPV) systems.

In chapter 1, we noted the inherently majoritarian bias, or bias towards those who can pay, of a market-based model, which 'emphasizes the satisfaction of aggregated individual desires . . .'.[1] Yet aggregated individual choices are no guarantee of best collective results. Indeed, as argued in chapter 7, competition policy goals have difficulty accommodating issues such as freedom of speech, diversity and plurality. Thus, any approach which provides only an increased level of formal freedom, here expressed as freedom of choice, is providing only increased economic choices for those select groups who can afford to pay for the choices they wish to make. Effectively public information is becoming a private resource from which groups can be excluded. The 'cash limit' limits the scope of others to choose, either because they cannot match market prices or because they are unwilling to pay them. In either case, limits and restrictions to

[1] H. Shelanski, 'The Policy Limits of Markets: Antitrust Law as Mass Media Regulation', *Law and Economics Workshop*, University of California, Berkeley, Paper 7, 2003, p. 7.

choice are set by price and the viewing experience becomes restricted to conditional access controlled by cost.

We suggested that Union broadcasting policy is a by-product of three key factors which have caused a drift towards a regulatory framework that favours understanding viewers as consumers rather than as citizens. The three factors are: first, rapid technological changes; second, the increase in the commercialisation of the broadcasting sector; and third, the conflicting policies and disputed competencies within the Union. The first two are external to the Union, they originate from the general broadcasting environment; the latter is Union-specific. All three are structural; that is, they form the context within which Union broadcasting policy must be considered.

Rapid technological change has created new broadcasting players, generated new commercial alliances, brought down traditional market sector barriers, increased the value of broadcasting and has turned the sector from different and discrete parochial concerns into an international service market. Also, rapid technological change has meant that for each new technical development, issues surrounding viewing arise. These can be summarised as: access to content via infrastructure; and the nature and range of content available. Within the context of Union broadcasting policy, the interplay of technology (or arguments based on technology) and policy development is manifest and extensive. At its most basic, technological development can outpace regulatory structures, triggering new approaches to regulation. Technology has also been seen as variously facilitating, or replacing, the need for regulation. These views about the relationship between technology and regulation are leading to an increasingly technologically determined approach to regulation, that is, the existence of certain technologies is viewed as necessitating specific regulatory responses or withdrawals (chapter 3). In our view, this approach is overly simplistic and is an abdication of regulatory choice and responsibility.

An approach that relies on filtering systems, information and navigation systems overlooks the fact that such systems are not necessarily neutral in the way they operate and can encode private (commercial) interests into the architecture of the communications system. It is very rarely clear from the technology that these interests have been encoded, or whose interests have been represented. Although technology may empower some viewers and make new services available, not all viewers are able to access or use the technology to the same degree. As a sub-set of access to content are the twin poles of inclusion and exclusion, which are ideas that are more noticeably discussed under the rubric of social policy than broadcasting policy. This is regrettable because technological changes exacerbate the divide between the included and the excluded. It is here that broadcasting policy has lamentably failed to consider the implications of technological change from the perspective of citizen viewers. Relying on technology as means by which viewers organise and control their viewing experience again overlooks the fact that not all have the same capacity to negotiate and evaluate the content options available. As we have noted in the context of consumer policy, information is not, on its own, sufficient to allow people to make informed choices. Here, attempts to stimulate media literacy are derisory. There is, therefore, a risk that technology determines (e.g. the exclusion of programmes via filters) and perhaps contracts existing viewing choices (i.e. programming the personal video recorder (PVR) with all the same types of programme), rather than being a useful tool to expand choice in the tradition of public service broadcasting (PSB). As has been suggested in the context of the Internet, increased choice of sources and the possibility of personalised schedules can lead to a risk of fragmentation where reaffirmation of parochialism and narrow worldviews becomes more likely. Regulation at the European level has been based on ideas that have been driven by technological change. For example, we have seen the introduction of the principle of technologically neutral regulation. The boundaries of broadcasting have been drawn by the distinction between point-to-multipoint services, on the one hand, and point-to-point services on the other, sometimes equated to the distinction between push services and pull services. These principles are, as we have discussed, problematic for a number of reasons (chapter 8). Crucially, and unfortunately for the protection of viewers, these distinctions do not consider the viewing experience. Specifically, policy does not take into account whether viewers, from the look and feel of the services on offer, understand what type of content will be broadcast. The lack of knowledge about regulatory regimes (with their different levels of protection) and where they might begin and end means that viewers may not always or easily be able to make informed choices about the type of content or service they wish to access.

Our second factor concerns the increase in the commercialisation of the broadcasting sector, which can be seen in the growing influence of commercial entities in the sector. This influence can be seen in both the increasing economic size of the sector and its growing influence in policymaking decisions. The commercial sector, in conjunction with many policymakers, has generated arguments that can be summarised in the following ways. Broadcasting is at the heart of European economic prosperity, and here one of the following words would be used, revival, future, strength, prosperity and so on. In this way, the commercial broadcasting sector ties itself to the general aims of the Union, encapsulated in the Treaty of Rome, to improve standards through increased commerce (chapter 4). This finds its current expression in the Lisbon agenda and the i2010 initiative (chapter 5).

The Union has been perceived as, first, in need of economic revival, with the communications sector, including broadcasting, as having the potential to become one of its few global strengths. The sector therefore should be free as possible from constraints which stifle innovation and growth. Secondly, it is a dynamic Europe, but which is so only because of its grasp of the new economic opportunities opened up by the knowledge economy, in which the broadcasting sector is a vital part, and which therefore should be left alone to get on with what it has to do. In these arguments, the voice of the broadcasting industry has acquired for itself a persuasive and sometimes compelling set of justifications for deregulation. Here, we are asked to think of broadcasting's strengths, as they range from arguments about technological innovation, new services, greater choices and increased quality. Each, naturally enough, can be queried. That is not the point here, however. Crucially, the voice of the industry and its demands for lighter touch regulation, and other less formal regulatory mechanisms, have combined to put public intervention, especially PSB, on the back foot. We see this in the extensive lobbying during review procedures, the involvement of industry representatives on policy advisory committees, such as that advising Bangemann, and in the standard-setting committees. Industry has also the financial resources, which private individuals rarely do, to use particularly, but not exclusively, competition policy to challenge national regulatory regimes (e.g. state aid, case law on four freedoms, chapters 4 and 5). Competitors have also challenged decisions of the Commission exempting agreements on the basis of social concerns, rather than pure economic analysis.[2] Currently, Union broadcasting policy is based on consumer sovereignty and establishing a fair market for all. It rarely strays from this specific economistic and formal conception of freedom of choice. Commercial broadcasters and many policymakers continue to champion the cause of the viewer regarded as a

---

[2] See notably the series of challenges to the acquisition of sporting rights by the EBU, discussed in ch. 12. The establishment of TPS, carrying free-to air channels, discussed in ch. 7, was challenged by a private broadcaster in Case T-112/99 *M6* et al v. *Commission* [2001] ECR II-2459.

free consumer in a fair market on every occasion. The challenge is simple: PSB is subsidised, distorts the market and reduces consumer sovereignty. More aggressively, the commercial sector now says that it can fulfil a public service function just as well as the traditional suppliers of PSB, and that the arguments behind 'merit goods' do not stand up (chapter 2). Once again, voices within the European polity are forced to defend (albeit rhetorically) the idea of the citizen viewer and their 'naive' expectation that public funds should be used for broadcasting certain types of content.

Our thesis here is that this shift in European broadcasting towards commercial overstatement and public service understatement, commercial imperative over public purpose, and commercial language over the articulation of traditional public values, in essence combines commercial aggression and public-service defensiveness. The consequences for the viewing experience are potentially profound, and possibly disastrous for citizens. Commercial imperatives militate towards content that is formulaic, middle of the road, repetitive, safe and unchallenging, as broadcasters seek to ensure mass audiences necessary to attract premium advertising rates. This is especially so on those commercial channels which are available free-to-air or on basic subscription packages. For the active consumer, premium content, such as sport and films, is available, but only at a cost. The real cost of this privatisation of information is felt by those without means to access premium content, a development which undermines the principle of universality that has traditionally underpinned the public domain. The fragmentation of audiences between the commercial and the public domains (see table 1, chapter 1) reflects a shift from a communal viewing experience to a personalised and individualised one. Additionally, the need to permit the development of European 'giants' which can compete in the global market to some extent has driven merger decisions in the communications sector (chapter 7), as has the desire to have new services. The implications of such mergers for diversity of suppliers and content have not been adequately addressed by Union policymakers.

Our third factor related to the Union's competence. As we noted in chapter 4, the Union has limited competence, that is, it has only the powers to act conferred by the treaties. In many areas, the Union and its institutions share competence with the various member states. The question then arises about how such shared competence may best be managed in a system which accords priority to Community law but also, in relation to some policy areas such as culture, limits the type of action the

Union may take. This limitation may be seen by some as being positive, as it means that more sensitive, non-trade policy areas will receive greater protection from the member states. On this view, the limited competence respects subsidiarity and prevents 'competence creep' on the part of the Union. In our opinion, such a view is flawed. The fact that the Union has greater freedom of action in other areas is likely to mean that, in practice, the subsidiary areas of competence are influenced by the primary areas of Union competence, notably trade and competition. We suggested that Union competence in cultural matters is not autonomous from the Union's common-market policies and, consequently, has also not been coherent. The uncertainty surrounding the Union's competence in the area of culture can have adverse consequences for the protection of public service values in the broadcasting sector. Rather than allowing a clear division of competence, with a definite boundary between member states protecting their own cultures, and the Union protecting the internal market, the interplay between the two areas of competence has had some rather unfortunate consequences.

Limited competence has meant that the Union has not adopted specific legislation to allow public-interest concerns to be considered directly by the institutions, even though the difficulties such regulation would seek to address seem to be beyond the control of member states acting individually. This problem can be seen in the failed media mergers regulation (chapter 5). Now the issues are dealt with by the Commission under normal competition policy. Although the Commission does seek to take account of issues such as media pluralism, it is hampered by not having tools designed for this purpose to hand, and also runs the risk of being accused of illegitimate action (chapter 7 and, to a lesser extent, chapter 12).

In using what effectively are regulatory techniques in the competition context, we see here an example of the interplay between the two areas, a hybridisation which can also be seen in the Communications Package[3] (chapter 6). The Communications Package also illustrates another trend, that is, legislation picking up terminology and tests used in individual decisions by the European Courts and the Commission. We can also see, in the context of the introduction of the Television without Frontiers

---

[3] Directive 2002/21/EC Framework Directive; Directive 2002/20/EC Authorisation Directive; Directive 2002/19/EC Access Directive; Directive 2002/22/EC Universal Service Directive and Directive 2002/58/EC Data Protection and Electronic Communications Directive OJ [2002] L 108. There is also a decision on Radio Spectrum: Decision 676/2002/EC OJ [2002] L 108.

Directive (TWFD),[4] that the political institutions sometimes respond to circumstances created through judicial decisions. Whether this transplanting of legal concepts from one field to another is appropriate or desirable is questionable.

The operation of the four freedoms has had a deregulatory impact, arguably resulting in a market without a state, where market forces are unconstrained by regulation in the public interest. Even when the Union has sought to counteract the deregulatory tendencies of negative harmonisation through legislative activities, there are problems. As we have suggested, the harmonising competence of the Union lies in the creation of an internal market, here, in the services sector, the terms of which seem to suggest a move towards deregulation. This underpinning of policy by the internal market provisions has meant that the TWFD has been framed by free-trade considerations, and these seem in some instances to have a higher status within the TWFD than do cultural concerns (chapter 9), or influence the scope and nature of cultural provisions (chapter 11). The TWFD is also limited as a result of the Union's competence in terms of the extent of the content regulation perceived as legitimate. Although certain types of 'harmful' content are prohibited or restricted, it is the member states which have the power and responsibility to identify and enforce these matters. Forum shopping and inequalities in the system remain a possibility (chapter 8). Equally, the limitation can be seen in the interplay between the state-aid rules and the national PSB systems. We suggested that, by not focusing on the purpose of PSB and the actual viewing experience, there was a danger that PSB would become undernourished through the application of the state-aid rules (chapter 13), and that certain types of premium content (chapter 12) would fall outside its financial resources.

We have also argued that when the boundaries of Union competence come into range, the law-making institutions become more open to infighting in the institutions and to lobbying pressure, and seek to adopt less formal mechanisms for the agreement of Union standards. These actions allow industry voices to be heard, but do not necessarily take adequate account of the needs of viewers (chapters 9 and 10). An early example can be seen in the TWFD. In its original proposal, the Commission had included greater cultural provisions and the Parliament sought to make

---

[4] Council Directive 89/552/EEC of 3 October on the co-ordination of certain provisions laid down by law, regulation or administrative action in member states concerning the pursuit of television broadcasting activities OJ [1989] L298/23, as amended by Directive 97/36/EC OJ [1997] L 202/30.

these more extensive.[5] In order to get agreement in the Council, the proposals were watered down to constrain the TWFD more closely to trade matters (chapter 5). The push towards co-regulation and self-regulation can be seen in this light, as can soft law. Ironically, the extensive consultation procedures which the Union institutions adopt towards policy developments and legislative initiatives, whilst seeking to increase legitimacy and transparency of Union actions, may exacerbate this tendency to give a platform to commercial interests. In this context, the enthusiasm which Union institutions exhibit towards technology can be understood as providing them with new tools to solve difficult problems. A less neutral analysis would say that they are merely trying to avoid becoming involved in having to make contentious decisions in areas in which their competence is contested. The result of policy choices based on limited action, and an emphasis on consumer choice and the benefits of technology, have had the result that broadcasting policy within the Union is focussed on the active consumer.

The discussion so far has concentrated on the current position. As we have noted, Union law in this area is undergoing a process of revision. After a lengthy period of consultation, a draft second amending directive to the TWFD (DSAD)[6] was tabled by the Commission. The Commission has also started a review of the Communications Package. More generally, since 2000 competition law has been undergoing a modernisation process, with the decentralisation of enforcement of Article 81 having been introduced, and the replacement of the Merger Regulation with a new version. At the moment, the Commission is in a process of public consultation concerning the application of Article 82 to exclusionary abuses, that is, behaviour and business practices by dominant undertakings that are likely to prevent competitors from entering particular markets. With the vertically integrated nature of the broadcasting sector, together with its reliance on intellectual property rights, these practices have an impact on the possibility of viewers being able to access a diverse range of content. The question for us is whether these various developments and proposed changes improve the position as far as the impact of broadcasting policy on the viewing experience is concerned. Our main focus in addressing this question is the DSAD. Both the review of the Communications Package

---

[5] R. Collins, *Broadcasting and Audio-Visual Policy in the European Single Market* (London: John Libbey, 1994), p. 67. See also R. Negrine and S. Papathanassopoulos, *The Internationalisation of Television* (London: Pinter, 1990), p. 76.

[6] Commission, *Proposal for a Directive amending Directive 89/552/EEC*, COM(2005) 646 final, 2005/0260 (COD), SEC (2005) 1625 and 1626, Article 2(5).

and the consultation on Article 82 are at too early a stage to say anything meaningful about them here. The impact of the earlier review of Article 81 was not directly addressed to this area of policy, although, as we have identified in chapter 7, the move to an economics-based approach to the assessment of Article 81(3) consequent on the modernisation process is likely to affect the viewing experience adversely. In our view, by failing to address the three factors we have identified throughout (technological change, commercialisation and competence issues), and their impact on the viewing experience as delineated in chapter 1, the proposed changes to the regulatory environment continue to emphasise the active consumer, and even increase the policy drift in this direction.

Taking each of our factors in turn, we begin by examining how technological change and the arguments relating to its relationship with regulation have manifested itself in the DSAD. At a very general level, the DSAD is the child of convergence, as it introduces a common, albeit two-tier, content regulatory system, irrespective of the transmission technology used. The focus is the type of service; DSAD covers mass-media audiovisual services (audiovisual media services (AVMS) within the terms of DSAD). It could be argued that this proposed extension of DSAD addresses concerns we identified in chapter 8 about the proper meaning of broadcasting and, consequently, the scope of the broadcasting regime. This proposal clarifies the relationship of TWFD with other directives, but the introduction of a two-tier system merely relocates the problem. The boundary between the two regimes now falls within the TWFD. The end point of the broadcasting regime obligations remains the same, based on a distinction between push and pull. The argument underlying the distinction is based on consumer choice,[7] but without regard to how the services are perceived by viewers. In this context we have some sympathy with Ofcom's position,[8] that is, the TWFD should be limited to those services that 'look and feel' like broadcasting; the corollary of which is that all such services are subject to the higher level of protection typically found in a broadcasting regime.

The appropriate level and type of control over content and traditional and new services was discussed during the review. Underpinning much of the debate was the assumption that, in an age of channel abundance

---

[7] Given that 'push' and 'pull' services utilise different technologies, it may also be argued that the distinction is not technology neutral.

[8] Ofcom, *Ofcom Position Paper – Scope*, 24 April 2006, para. 10, p. 3, available http://www.ofcom.org.uk.

created and managed by technology, lower levels of regulation would not have a significant impact on the viewing experience. Certainly, the DSAD has the effect that, although more services are regulated, the regulation imposes a lower level of obligation with regard to negative content regulation and advertising content. DSAD contains a requirement in Article 3(c) that AVMS providers must give the viewer contact details for the AVMS provider, as well as details for the relevant regulator, if any. Although greater information is, in principle, beneficial, we question whether the underlying assumption behind this provision is that viewers should assume greater responsibility for challenging unacceptable content directly with the AVMS provider. Although the DSAD is silent on the subject of filtering devices, we reiterate here our concerns about using the rhetoric of consumer choice linked to technology as a replacement for regulation.

Advertising frequency rules in general have been simplified or relaxed. As Recital 42 to DSAD states: 'as the increase in the number of new services has led to a greater choice to viewers, detailed regulation with regard to the insertion of spot advertising with the aim of protecting viewers is no longer justified'. This position assumes that viewers will have a choice.[9] Of course, if all channels take advantage of the lighter regime, viewers will have a choice of intrusive advertising across a range of channels, or the choice that they have always had, that is the choice to switch off the television. In addition, we do not accept that technology (such as PVRs) gives viewers any greater control in this matter than that which they have had with earlier time-shifting technology, despite the claims of industry to this effect. Similarly, if product placement is to be allowed, then choice and the freedom to avoid advertisements are further diminished. PVRs can be used to fast forward through commercial breaks, but cannot screen out advertising wrapped up in editorial content.

The changes to the advertising rules bring us to our second factor, the increasing commercialisation of the sector and the impact of commercial interests on the regulatory framework. The proposed amendments in DSAD would clearly alter the current balance between industry interests and those of viewers (as well as programme makers and rights holders). The Commission in its *Fifth Report on the Application of the TWFD* noted

---

[9] European Parliament, *Press Release – How to Modernise European Television Rules*, 2 June 2006, quotes Walter Neuhauser of IP-Network/RTL as saying 'consumers no longer need to be protected from advertising since they can switch over or off', p. 1, available at www.europarl.europa.eu/news/expert/infopress_page/.

that regulatory authorities have tended not to monitor compliance with the advertising placement rules closely.[10] Pragmatic assessments of industry practice suggest that the rules should be altered to reflect reality, and it appears that, to some degree, this is the position that the Commission has adopted. As we argued in chapter 9, compliance with law essentially becomes optional. As the BEUC noted, amending the law accordingly gives commercial interests a further incentive for non-compliance with rules,[11] which may have a spill-over effect into other areas of regulation.

One particularly worrying development is the acceptance of product placement, although surreptitious advertising, in principle, remains prohibited. Allowing product placement has a number of linked consequences. Significantly, it blurs the boundary between editorial content and commercial content, although the separation principle is central to advertising regulation in many other areas. The blurring of this distinction pushes the viewing experience into an arena of consumption, again, further undermining the traditional public service domain. The impact of the proposed acceptance of product placement, as with the other changes to the advertising placement rules, means that we risk 'swimming in a sea of commercial communication'.[12] The emphasis is on viewers' choice, especially given that the DSAD envisages the use of distinctive signs and identification to warn viewers about product placement. As we have noted in chapters 1 and 10, an information-based approach is not always enough to protect viewers, especially the more vulnerable groups. Additionally, integrating commercial communications into programmes undermines, if not eradicates, viewers' ability to choose not to watch advertising. It may also adversely affect editorial independence and, consequently, the viewing experience generally. Although the rules prohibit product placement in news, documentaries and children's programmes, presumably to protect the public domain, we question whether this is enough. In all this, we see industry using or, more judgmentally, hijacking, technology-based arguments emphasising viewer choice to further industry interests in lighter touch regulation.

None the less, although industry interests have been taken into account to a significant degree, there are instances where the industry lobby, or sections of it, has been disappointed with DSAD, for example: the

[10] Commission, *Fifth Report on the Application of the Television without Frontiers Directive*, COM(2006)49, para. 3.5.3.
[11] Bureau Européen des Unions des Consommateurs (BEUC), *Revision of the 'Television without Frontiers' Directive: BEUC Position Paper*, BEUC/X/023/2006, 11 April 2006, p. 11.
[12] J. Murray, BEUC, quoted in Parliament, *How to Modernise*, p. 1.

extension of the base tier of regulation to all AVMS; the retention of quotas and listed events; as well as the introduction of short reporting; and the anti-avoidance clauses. Whether such disappointments constitute a consistent attempt to protect the viewing experience is unlikely; it is certainly insufficient given the other changes we have identified.

These issues bring us to our third factor; that of competence and its impact on the scope and types of regulation adopted. The anti-avoidance clauses introduced in Article 3(3) DSAD seek to return to the host member state some degree of control over the content transmitted for reception within its territory, specifically where the broadcaster abusively or fraudulently evades the host member state's regime. In this way, a member state's own cultural competence is re-emphasised over the free movement imperatives of the TWFD. Although this proposed change is hugely significant in terms of principle, as we suggested in chapter 8, the impact of these provisions is uncertain. They come into play in only limited circumstances, the scope of which is not clearly identified, and ultimately all such cases will be reviewed for their compliance with Community law by the Commission. It may be that this concession at the level of principle is based in the uncertain competence of the Union in the context of broadcasting's cultural, social and political purposes.

Uncertainty as to competence resurfaces in the context of content regulation. Although content regulation remains within the TWFD, the DSAD envisages that co-regulatory regimes are to be encouraged, no matter the significance of the principle that is to be protected. Indeed, Recital 25 suggests that co-regulation 'can play an important role in delivering a high level of consumer protection'. We question this assumption, as it may do no more than provide a conduit for industry voices, and note that the DSAD seems to give no thought to the question of whether such systems can ensure the protection of citizens, at any level whatsoever. We suggested in chapter 4 that there was a trend in the Union towards this sort of measure, but we believe that the introduction of co-regulation in this particular proposal may be linked to a certain defensiveness on the part of the Commission about the Union's competence, despite the extensive study of co-regulatory measures carried out at the request of the Commission (see chapter 5). In a similar vein, we can see that, despite obvious weaknesses in the existing systems for quotas and listed events, the Commission has chosen not to upset the existing balance of interests in these particularly sensitive areas. Unfortunately, these are areas that are particularly central to enhancing the citizens' viewing experiences.

Although the DSAD seeks to balance different interests in the developing broadcasting sector, it has not given adequate attention to the needs of all viewers. This, in conjunction with outstanding problems such as those encountered in relation to PSB, media mergers and an inadequate definition of universal content service in the context of access rules, means that the current regulatory focus is drifting towards supporting the viewing experience of the active consumer. To adopt a purely consumerist approach to viewing television is to evade questions about who is responsible for the availability, quality, diversity and, significantly, safety of broadcast content. To propose a caricature, the viewing environment of an active consumer is one in which the viewer is selfish, morally vacuous, with a perfect right to have a content range to match Nero's and who lives in a unitary and solipsistic world. While this caricature is extreme and risible, it is meant to show the potentially unsustainable and damaging nature of a purely consumerist approach, for two reasons. First, such viewers constitute a ridiculous caricature of human dispositions and should such viewers exist they demonstrate that they require our help, unless we show ourselves to be similarly disposed. Secondly, such viewers are a danger both to themselves, to us and to the continued existence of the public domain. We have argued throughout, and indeed European policymakers have accepted, that broadcasting has significance beyond a commercial value. To safeguard citizens' interests in the broadcasting context requires regulatory intervention, and obligations must be imposed on broadcasters, even if such imposition is unpopular with certain sectors and even with certain viewers. This is not to say that regulation should ignore the interest of consumers or industry; nor should it seek to return us to a broadcasting environment consisting of two channels in black and white. Rather, the regulatory regime cannot, should not and actually does not ignore the rights of consumers any more than they should ignore the rights of citizens, and it must do so in the light of technological developments. Both must coexist as a heuristic divide that balances real broadcasting issues. Our point is that such balance is currently missing and cannot be reinstated by reliance on technology alone. In sum, direct attention must be paid to the viewing experience to ensure that the matter is redressed.

APPENDIX

At the time of finishing the manuscript, the process of revising the TWFD had just begun. The manuscript therefore took into account the Commission's original proposed amending directive. The revision process is still not complete, though the Commission has produced an amended proposal.[1] The Council subsequently submitted informally to the European Parliament a document which reflected a political compromise, with a view to reaching an agreed text at the common position stage, as envisaged by paragraphs 16–18 of the *Joint Inter-institutional Declaration on Practical Arrangements for the Co-Decision Procedure* and on which the Council hopes to adopt a common position before the end of May 2007.[2] Although the Parliament's Committee on Culture and Education accepted the draft,[3] the procedure itself has drawn some criticism on the basis that this 'backdoor agreement' undermines the democratic function of the

[1] Commission, Amended Commission Proposal, COM(2007)170 final. The Commission also produced a working document which was a draft consolidated text: Draft consolidated amended AVMS directive 2007 (working paper) rev 3.
[2] Presidency of the Council, Amended Proposal for a Directive of the European Parliament and of the Council amending Council Directive 89/552/EEC on the coordination of certain provisions laid down by law, regulation or administrative action in member States concerning the pursuit of television broadcasting activities (Television without Frontiers) – final compromise text, Doc 9026/07, 27 April 2007; General Secretariat of the Council, Preparation of the Council Meeting 'Education, youth and Culture' on 24 and 25 May 2007: Amended Proposal for a Directive of the European Parliament and of the Council amending Council Directive 89/552/EEC on the coordination of certain provisions laid down by law, regulation or administrative action in member States concerning the pursuit of television broadcasting activities (Television without Frontiers) – political agreement, Doc 8640/07, 30 April 2007; General Secretariat of the Council Presidency of the Council, Preparation of the Council Meeting 'Education, Youth and Culture' on 24 and 25 May 2007: Amended Proposal for a Directive of the European Parliament and of the Council amending Council Directive 89/552/EEC on the coordination of certain provisions laid down by law, regulation or administrative action in member States concerning the pursuit of television broadcasting activities (Television without Frontiers) – final compromise text, Doc 8640/07 ADD1 COR 1, 2 May 2007.
[3] European Parliament, Press Release – Info, 'Reform of European television rules one step closer' – Culture, 08-05/07.

European Parliament.[4] Therefore although many commentators suggest that the proposal will not now change, it still has to secure the agreement of the Council and of the European Parliament in plenary.

Although the comments made in the body of the book remain valid, from this revised proposal a number of further points can be made:

1. The extension of the regulatory regime to 'audiovisual media services' seems, in principle, to be accepted though there is still much concern about the meaning of this term and thus the boundaries of the directive;
2. Likewise, the internal boundary between 'linear' and 'non-linear' services is accepted, but unclear in practice;
3. Changes have been made to the provisions dealing with co- and self-regulation;
4. The possibility of including 'anti-avoidance' provisions has been highly contentious;
5. Although the simplification of advertising rules has been agreed, the approach towards product placement has also proved divisive;
6. Special provision has been made regarding the advertising of junk food aimed at children.

Whilst we discussed the problems arising from the internal boundary in chapter 8, and the comments made then remain valid, some more needs to be said about the outer boundary of audiovisual media services. The essential concern has been to ensure that the scope of the directive is not too extensive, either in terms of strangling new services with limited impact or in regulating the views of private parties. The Commission was aware of this difficulty from the start, suggesting that audiovisual media services covered essentially moving images provided as a business which were not ancillary to another service. The devil is in the detail and both the Council and the European Parliament sought to tidy up the Commission's original drafting. The amended proposal now defines an 'audiovisual media service' as:

> a service as defined by Articles 49 and 50 of the Treaty which is under the editorial responsibility of a media service provider and the principal purpose of which is the provision of programmes in order to inform, entertain or educate to the general public by electronic communication networks within the meaning of Article 2(a) of Directive 2002/21/EC of the European

---

[4] See comments of Helga Trüpel reported at www.euractiv.com/en/infosociety/meps-agree-frequent-tv-ads/article-163647.

Parliament and of the Council. Such audiovisual media services are either
television broadcasts as defined in paragraph c) of this article or on-demand
services as defined in paragraph e) of the Article.

We do not have the space here to examine the meaning of this definition in detail. Certain points may none the less be noted. This version is
different from the amended proposal produced by the Commission and
indeed removes some of the difficulties with that definition. The definition does, however, remain problematic. The purpose that a service must
have in order to fall within the scope of the directive, that is the requirement to 'inform, entertain or educate', is broad to the point where it is
difficult to think of a content service which does not have one of those
objectives. Although this phrase may reflect the PSB remit, it does not
in practice operate so as to limit audiovisual media services to the mass
media. Further, editorial responsibility is a key concept, but problematic, as we have already identified. Although the directive now defines the
term, it does little to dispel the uncertainty about the level of decision
making caught as it refers to both the selection of programmes and their
organisation.

Further, the definition itself depends on the notion of a 'programme',
now defined as 'a set of moving images with or without sound constituting an individual item within a schedule or a catalogue established by a
media service provider and whose form and content is comparable to the
form and content of television broadcasting'. Examples of programmes
are then given. Again this might be an improvement on previous versions,
but essentially a programme is television-like content, which presupposes
we know what that is in the first place. The definition of television broadcasting in the directive does not help as it in turn is based on the definition
of audiovisual media service. There are also questions about the nature
and scope of a 'catalogue', in particular, does the catalogue have to be for
the purpose of providing an audiovisual media service, or will any listing
of content suffice? Resolution of the problems arising from such broad
definitions is likely to take time and continue after the directive comes
into force. Currently, the directive does not cover provision or distribution of audiovisual content generated by private users for the purposes of
sharing and exchange within communities of interest, but there remains
a lack of clarity here. The recitals refer to 'user-generated content' but
with no clarification as to what this term means, and it is far from a generally understood term of art. Social networking sites such as MySpace

and YouTube may also include material which is intended for wider distribution, such as video launches of music recordings and other videos and this raises questions as to whether the way in which such material is organised or presented actually constitutes a catalogue. It is also not clear how websites such as 18 Doughty Street (which has Talk TV, video blogs, an on-demand catalogue and daily schedule of 'programmes' made in a studio) will be treated within the scope of the directive.

A further difficulty arises from the lack of clear definition about what constitutes co- and self-regulation in the EU audiovisual context. In our concluding chapter we questioned the assumption in Recital 25 that co-regulation 'can play an important role in delivering a high level of consumer protection', particularly when implemented in accordance with the different legal traditions in member states. The variety of approaches to the interpretation of the meaning and constitution of co- and self-regulation which exist in member states means that different types of regulatory protection for viewers can be implemented for the same services across the EU. A new clause has been inserted into the agreed text which will enable these differences to continue to exist. The new wording states that:

> without prejudice to Member States' formal obligations regarding transposition, this Directive encourages the use of such instruments. This neither obliges Member States to set up co- and/or self-regulatory regimes nor disrupts or jeopardises current co- or self-regulatory initiatives which are already in place within Member States and which are working effectively.[5]

There is an additional provision which states that 'co-regulation should retain the possibility for State intervention in the event that its objectives are not met'.[6] These new provisions protect member states' own constitutional systems in the interests of freedom of expression and public interest objectives, allowing member states to continue to decide and define what constitutes co- and self-regulation. In particular, where there is an existing system which works, the new directive will not require it to be replaced with another system. Where self-regulation is allowed to flourish and is

---

[5] This wording was taken from Footnote 13 of the Council General Approach.

[6] This addition was a response to the European Parliament's amendments 36 and 37 and refers to amendments made to Recital 25 (see European Parliament *Report on the proposal for a directive of the European Parliament and of the Council amending Council Directive 89/552/EEC on the coordination of certain provisions laid down by law, regulation or administrative action in Member States concerning the pursuit of television broadcasting activities*, COM(2005)0646 – C6-0443/2005 – 2005/0260(COD), A6-03992006 final).

dominated by industry concerns, the level of viewer protection may be reduced. As we have already suggested, little or no thought has been given in the directive to the nature of the viewing experience and the need to protect all types of viewers' interests. The insertion of a clause recognising that co- or self-regulation may be insufficient, especially as regards the need to protect constitutional and human rights, suggests that some member states may have identified this problem.

The jurisdiction clause based on a formal notion of establishment has long been problematic. Articles 3(1a)–(1d) provide a procedure whereby a member state may take action against a broadcaster which is seeking to circumvent a member state's broadcasting regime. The version proposed here allows more scope to the member states to take action in such circumstances than the amended Commission proposal, which had adopted the suggestion of the European Parliament in this regard. The conditions for the provision to apply are that a broadcaster is providing a broadcast wholly or mostly directed towards the territory of a member state (other than the state in which the broadcaster is formally established). The recipient member state must contact the host member state, which is obliged to request the broadcaster to 'comply with the rules of general public interest in question'. This could constitute a formal limitation on the type of rules to be protected, though it is hard to imagine a rule which did not have some claim to protect the public interest. In any event, it would seem to be a matter of the member state's discretion as to which public interests to protect. If this does not lead to satisfactory results and the broadcaster has established itself for the purposes of circumvention (though not necessarily for the sole purpose of circumvention) a member state may take objectively necessary non-discriminatory and suitable measures against the broadcaster. Interestingly, this is all based on the recipient member state's assessment of the situation, though the compatibility of the measures remains to be assessed by the Commission. This then seems to be a reasonable compromise between the concerns of the member states in terms of the balance between cultural policy and viewer protection and the needs of the internal market.

The simplification of the rules on advertising has been discussed in chapter 9. Product placement was not, however, dealt with in any depth. Article 3f, which applies to all audiovisual media services, provides that product placement shall be prohibited, but that in certain circumstances it may be permitted. Member states are thus given the choice in relation to certain categories of content as to whether or not to permit product placement and a distinction is made between what might be termed incidental product placement and product placement which the product producer pays for. Paid-for product placement is not permitted in programmes for children (though whether this means programmes aimed at children or programmes which many children watch or are likely to watch is not clear). Certain products may not be 'placed' and in any event provisions specify producer independence and that viewers should be notified at the beginning of a programme and after commercial breaks.[7] The assumption here is that a warning divorced from content is adequate to protect vulnerable viewers, but given that a time lag will occur between the warning and the placement of a product, vulnerable viewers may still not be protected. Despite the introduction of the new placement rules 'undue prominence' and surreptitious commercial communication are still impermissible. Taking the same line as that taken in relation to advertising frequency,[8] industry interests here have won on a 'we do not comply with the law anyway so why regulate?' style argument, which may have long term repercussions in other areas. Shadow rapporteur, Helga Trüpel (Greens/EFA) criticised the deal, arguing that:

> [t]he introduction of a legal framework for product placement for the first time means there will be no escaping the creeping commercial incursion into private life. It goes completely against the principles of the UNESCO convention on cultural diversity that the European Union strongly supports and so do the Greens.[9]

Alternatively, it could be argued that, since the current version of TWFD prohibited only surreptitious advertising, the position has not changed that much. Further, in specifically addressing the issue, the matter of product placement is more clearly regulated than before. As suggested in chapters 9 and 14 the problem remains, at a level of principle, that the central rule of separation of commercial messages from editorial content has been undermined opening the possibility of further encroachment of commercial content in practice.

The final change is the introduction of a provision relating to junk food advertising aimed at children.[10] This obliges member states and the Commission to 'encourage media service providers to develop codes of conduct regarding inappropriate audiovisual commercial communication' in this area. Whilst on one level this is a step forward by including

---

[7] Recital 45 suggests that viewers be informed by a 'neutral logo'.
[8] Recognised in Recital 44.
[9] www.euractiv.com/en/infosociety/meps-agree-frequent-tv-ads/article-163647.
[10] Article 3(d)(2).

this policy area within the directive, it is not a legally binding code of conduct on the audiovisual media service providers. Whilst we might argue that there are competence problems here (see chapter 5), in addition to any political disagreement this approach seems to be a practical example of the move towards co- and self-regulation. Within the framework of the proposed directive, however, a problem arises, albeit one common to a minimum harmonisation system. There is no equivalence to the provision in relation to sporting rights which obliges member states to take steps to respect other member states' choices (chapter 12). Thus, if a member state encourages but fails to persuade audiovisual media service providers within its jurisdiction to adopt such a code, or the code adopted is minimalist in terms of its scope or obligations, the other member states – which may have adopted higher standards – may not prevent incoming broadcasts containing junk food advertising, leaving vulnerable viewers unprotected.

Our conclusions were that the directive as constituted was a compromise and that the revision process was subject to heavy lobbying. Against this background, the desire to find other non-legislative 'solutions' to public interest objectives (whether through the use of technology and media literacy arguments, or alternative regulatory mechanisms) can be readily understood. In our view, these types of 'solution' under-emphasise the needs of vulnerable groups. The final draft of the directive may seem to take viewers' needs and public interest concerns into account, by the extension of the directive's scope and by the inclusion of junk food provisions, but the underlying thrust has been deregulatory and certain key principles (such as the separation of editorial and commercial content) have been undermined. The full impact of these changes in practice will not be felt for some time; it is to be hoped that the Union decision makers got the balance right – that is, 'right' from the perspective of the viewer and not transnational media corporations.

BIBLIOGRAPHY

Ahlborn, C., Evans, D. and Pauilla, A., 'Competition Policy in the New Economy: Is Competition Law up to the Challenge', *European Competition Law Review* (2001), 156–67.

Analysys Ltd, 'Public Policy Treatment of Digital Terrestrial Television (DTT)', in *Communications Markets: Final Report for the Commission* (2005).

Ang, I. (ed.), *Living Room Wars* (London: Routledge, 1996).

Ariño, M., 'Competition Law and Pluralism in European Digital Broadcasting: Addressing the Gaps', *Communications and Strategies* 54(2) (2004), 97–128.

Barber, R., *Jihad vs McWorld* (New York: Ballantine Books, 1995).

Barendt, E., *Broadcasting Law* (Oxford: Clarendon Press, 1993).

Barnett, S., 'New Media, Old Problems: New Technology and the Political Process', *European Journal of Communication*, 12(2) (1997), 193–218.

Barnett, S. and Docherty, D., 'Purity or Pragmatism? Principles of Public Service Broadcasting', in J. Blumler and T. Nossiter (eds.), *Broadcasting Finance in Transition* (New York: Oxford University Press, 1991).

Bartosch, A., 'The Financing of Public Broadcasting and EC State Aid Law: An Interim Balance', *European Competition Law Review* (1999), 197–204.

Bavasso, A. F., 'Electronic Communications: A New Paradigm for European Regulation', *Common Market Law Review* 41 (2004), 87–118.

Belot, C. and Smith, A., 'Europe and Identity: A Challenge for the Social Sciences', in U. Hedetoft (ed.), *Political Symbols, Symbolic Politics: European Identities in Transformation* (Hampshire: Ashgate Publishing Limited, 1998).

Benkler, Y., 'From Consumers to Users: Shifting the Deeper Structures of Regulation', *Federal Communication Law Journal* 52 (1999), 561–79.

Bird and Bird, Market Definition in the Media Sector – Comparative Legal Analysis' *Study for the European Commission*, DG Competition (2002).

Blumler, J. (ed.), *Television and the Public Interest: Vulnerable Values in West European Broadcasting* (London: Sage in association with the Broadcasting Standards Council, 1992).

Bomberg, E. and Stubb, A., *The European Union: How Does it Work?* Oxford: Oxford University Press, 2003.

Born, G. and Prosser, T., 'Culture and Consumerism: Citizenship, Public Service Broadcasting and the BBC's Fair Trading Obligations', *The Modern Law Review*, 64(5) (2003), 657–87.

Bourgeois, J., and Bock, J., 'Guidelines on the Application of Article 81(3) of the EC Treaty or How to Restrict a Restriction', *Legal Issues of Economic Integration*, 32(2) (2005), 111–21.

Boyle, J., 'Foucault in Cyberspace: Surveillance, Sovereignty and Hardwired Censors', *University of Cincinnati Law Review* 66 (1997), 177–205.

The Broadcasting Research Unit, *The Public Service Idea in British Broadcasting: Main Principles* (Luton: John Libbey, 1985).

Brownsword, R., 'Code, Control, and Choice: Why East is East and West is West', *Legal Studies* 25(1) (2005), 1–21.

Bruck, P. *et al.*, *Report on Transnational Media Concentrations in Europe* (Strasbourg: Council of Europe, 2004).

Bureau Européen des Unions des Consommateurs (BEUC), *Revision of the 'Television without Frontiers' Directive: BEUC Position Paper*, BEUC/X/ 023/2006, 11 April 2006.

Bushman, B. J. and Stack, A. D., 'Forbidden Fruit Versus Tainted Fruit: Effects of Warning Labels on Attraction to Television Violence', *Journal of Experimental Psychology: Applied*, 2(3) (1995), 207–26.

Calhoun, C. (ed.), *Habermas and the Public Sphere* (Cambridge, Mass.: MIT Press, 1992).

Camesasca, P., *European Merger Control: Getting the Efficiencies Right* (Oxford: Hart Publishing, 2000).

Carter, E. J., 'Market Definition in the Broadcasting Sector', *World Competition* 24(1) (2001), 93–124.

Cave, M., and Crowther, P., 'Preemptive Competition Policy meets Regulatory Anti-trust', *European Competition Law Review* (2005), 481.

Chen, H. L., 'Young Adolescents' Responses to Evaluative and Informational Labelling Systems for TV', *Paper Presented at the International Communications Association Conference* (San Francisco, Calif., 1999).

Clegg, S., Hudson, A. and Steel, J., 'The Emperor's New Clothes: Globalisation and e-Learning in Higher Education', *British Journal of Sociology of Education* 24(1) (2003), 49–53.

Closa, C., 'The Concept of Citizenship in the Treaty on European Union', *Common Market Law Review* 29 (1992), 1137–70.

Cohen, S., *Folk Devils and Moral Panics* (Oxford: Blackwell, 1973).

Collins, R., *From Satellite to Single Market; New Communication Technology and European Public Service Television* (London; Routledge, 1998).

'Unity in Diversity? The European Single Market in Broadcasting and the Audiovisual, 1982–92', *Journal of Common Market Studies*, 32(1) (1994), 89–102.

Broadcasting and Audio-Visual Policy in the European Single Market (London: John Libbey, 1994).

Collins, R. and Purnell, J., *Commerce, Competition and Governance: The Future of the BBC* (London: Institute for Public Policy Research, 1995).

Commission, *Press Release, State Aid: Commission orders Dutch public service broadcaster NOS to pay back € 76.3 million excess ad hoc funding*, IP/06/822, 22 June 2006.

Discussion Paper on the Application of Article 82 EC, 2006.

Fifth Report on the Application of the Television without Frontiers Directive, COM(2006)49.

Communication on the Review of the EU Regulatory Framework for Electronic Communications Networks and Services, COM(2006)334 final, SEC(2006)816 and 817.

'Non-Paper' on Short Reporting, 2006, http://europa/eu.int/comm/avpolicy/regul_en.htm#4

Staff Working Document on the Review of the EU Regulatory Framework for Electronic Communications Networks and Services, SEC(2006)816, COM(2006)334 final.

Proposal for a Directive of the European Parliament and of the Council amending Council Directive 89/552/EEC, COM(2005)646 final, 2005/0260 (COD), SEC (2005)1625 and 1626.

Issues Paper for the Liverpool Audiovisual Conference: Commercial communications, July 2005.

Issues Paper for the Liverpool Audiovisual Conference: Protection of minors and human dignity, right of reply, July 2005.

Issues Paper for the Liverpool Audiovisual Conference: Right to information and right to short reporting, July 2005.

Communication on Accelerating the Transition from Analogue to Digital Broadcasting, COM(2005)204 final, SEC(2005)661.

Communication i2010 A European Information Society for growth and employment, COM(2005)229 final.

Explanatory Memorandum, Proposal for a Directive of the European Parliament and of the Council amending Council Directive 89/552/EEC on the Co-ordination of Certain Provision laid down by Law, Regulation or Administrative Action in Member States concerning the Pursuit of Television Broadcasting Activities, COM(2005)646 final, 2005/0260 (COD), SEC(2005)1625 and 1626.

Press Release, Competition, German Football League commitments to liberalise joint selling of Bundesliga media rights made legally binding by Commission decision, IP/05/62, 19 January 2005.

Public Service Broadcasting and State Aid: Frequently Asked Questions, Memo/05/73, 2005.

Press Release, State aid, Commission rules subsidy for digital terrestrial TV (DVB-T) in Berlin-Brandenburg illegal; explains how digital TV can be supported, IP/05/1394, 9 November 2005.

Press Release, State aid: Commission requests Germany, Ireland and The Netherlands to clarify role and financing of public service broadcasters, IP/05/250, 3 March 2005.

Press Release, Commission requests Germany, Ireland and The Netherlands to clarify role and financing of public service broadcasters, IP/05/250, 3 March 2005.

Press Release, Enhancing the effectiveness of the protection of minors and of human dignity in audiovisual and information services: the European Commission proposes a new Recommendation, IP/04/598, 6 May 2004.

Communication on the application of state aid rules to public service broadcasting, (2001/C 320/04), OJ [2004] C 320/5.

Guidelines on the Assessment of Horizontal Mergers and the Council Regulation on the Control of Concentrations between Undertakings, OJ [2004] C 31/3.

Paper for Focus Group: Regulation of Audiovisual Content, September 2004.

Guidelines on the Assessment of Horizontal Mergers and the Council Regulation on the Control of Concentrations between Undertakings, OJ [2004] C 31/3.

Interpretative Communication on Certain Aspects of the Provisions on televised Advertising in the 'Television without Frontiers' Directive, C(2004)1450, 23.03.2004, OJ [2004] C 102/2.

Communication i2010, an Information Society for Growth and Employment, SEC (2004)1028, COM(2004)541 final.

Guidelines on the application of Article 81(3), OJ [2004] C 101/97.

Proposal for a Recommendation of the European Parliament and of the Council on the protection of minors and human dignity and the right of reply in relation to the competitiveness of the European audiovisual and information services industry, COM(2004)341 final.

Communication on Interoperability of Digital Interactive Television Services, SEC(2004)1028, COM(2004)541 final.

Working Paper on Interactive Digital Television, SEC(2004)346.

Commission, Notice published pursuit to Article 19(3) of Council Regulation No. 17 concerning case COMP/C2/38.173 and 38.453 – joint seeing of the media rights of the FA Premier League on an exclusion basis (2004/C 115/02), OJ [2004] C 115/3.

Working Document An Approach to Financing the Transport of 'Must-carry' Channels, in relation to Article 31 of the Universal Service Directive, COCOM03-38, 2 September 2003.

Recommendation on Relevant Product and Service Markets within the Electronic Communications Sector susceptible to ex ante Regulation, COM(2003)497, OJ [2003] L 114/45.

Second Evaluation Report from the Commission to the Council and the European Parliament on the application of the Council Recommendation of 24 September 1998 concerning the protection of minors and human dignity, COM(2003) 776.

Green Paper on Services of General Interest, COM (2003) 270 final.

Working Document 'Must Carry' Obligations under the 2003 Regulatory Framework for Electronic Communications Networks and Services, 22 July 2002.

Working Document, the 2003 Regulatory Framework for Electronic Communications – Implications for Broadcasting, Doc. ONPCOM02-14, 14 June 2002.

Communication on an information and communication strategy for the European Union, COM(2002)350 final.

Communication on an Information and Communication Strategy for the European Union, COM(2002)350 final.

XXXIInd Report on Competition Policy, 2002.

European Governance: A White Paper, COM(2001)428 final.

Notice on Remedies acceptable under Council Regulation 4064/89/EEC and under the Commission Regulation of 447/98/EC, OJ [2001] C68/3.

Evaluation Report from the Commission to the Council and the European Parliament on the application of the Council Recommendation of 24 September 1998 concerning the protection of minors and human dignity, COM(2001)106 final.

Press Release, Commission clears UEFA's new Broadcasting Regulations, IP/01/583, 20 April 2001.

Public Consultation on the Convergence Green Paper: Communication to the European Parliament, the Council, the Economic and Social Committee and the Committee of the Regions, COM(1999)108.

Study on Parental Control of Television Broadcasting Communication, COM(1999)371.

Communication on Principles and Guidelines for the Community's Audiovisual Policy in the Digital Age, COM(1999)657 final.

High Level Group on Audio-visual Policy, The Role of Public Authorities in the Media, OJ [1999] C 3020/5.

Press Release, Commission opens formal procedure regarding State aid to public broadcasters France 2 and France 3, IP/99/531, 20 July 1999.

Press Release, Commission opens formal procedure regarding certain aid measures for public broadcaster RAI (Italy) and raises no objections to other measures, IP/99/532, 20 July 1999.

Press Release, Commission enjoins the French government to submit information on the existing nature of the financing scheme of the public broadcasters France 2 and France 3, IP/99/81, 3 February 1999.

Suggested Guidelines for the Monitoring of the Implementation of Articles 4 and 5 of the Television without Frontiers Directive, 11 June 1999.

XXVIIIth Report on Competition Policy, 1998.

Third Report on the Application of Article 4 and 5 of Directive 89/552/EEC, as amended by 97/36/EC, COM(1998)199.

Green Paper on the Convergence of the Telecommunications, Media and Information Technology Sectors, and the Implications for Regulation Towards an Information Society Approach, COM(1997)623.

Notice on Definition of the Relevant Market for the purposes of Community competition law, OJ [1997] C 372/5.

Communication from the Commission on the follow-up to the Green Paper on the protection of minors and human dignity in the audiovisual and information services, together with a proposal for a Council Recommendation concerning the protection of minors and human dignity in the audiovisual and information services, COM(1997)570 final.

Green Paper on the Protection of Minors and Human Dignity in Audiovisual and Information Services, COM(1996)483 final.

First Report on the Consideration of Cultural Aspects in European Community Action, COM(1996)160.

Communication on Services of General Interest in Europe, OJ [1996] C 281/3.

Report on the Application of Directive 89/552/EEC and a Proposal for a European Parliament and Council Directive amending Council Directive 89/552/EEC, COM(1995)86 final.

White Paper on Growth, Competitiveness and Employment: The challenges and ways forward into the 21st century, COM(1993)700 final.

XXVIth Annual Report on European Competition Policy, 1996.

Communication on Audiovisual Policy, COM(1990)78 final.

Television and the Audio-visual Sector: towards a European policy, European File 14/86, Luxembourg: Office for Official Publications of the European Communities, 1986.

Television without Frontiers: Green Paper on the Establishment of the Common Market for Broadcasting, COM(1984)300 final.

Communications Committee, *Implementation of Standards and Interoperability of Digital Interactive Television under the New Regulatory Framework*, Working Document COCOM, 02–31.

Coppell, J. and O'Neill, J., 'The European Court: Taking Rights Seriously?', *Common Market Law Review* 29 (1992), 669–27.

Cottle, S. (ed.), *Media Organization and Production* (London: Sage, 2003).

Council, *Press Release from the 2361st Council meeting on Culture held in Luxembourg*, 21 June 2001, 9755/01 (Presse 233).

Resolution of the Council and Representatives of the Governments of the Member States concerning PSB, OJ [1999] C 30/1.

Resolution of the Council and Representatives of the Governments of the Member States concerning PSB. OJ [1999] C 30/1.

Recommendation on the development of the competitiveness of the European audio-visual and information services industry by promoting national frameworks aimed at achieving a comparable and effective level of protection of minors and human dignity, 98/560/EC, OJ [1998] C 270.

Council, *Reports of the Ad Hoc Committee on a People's Europe to the European Council*, 1985 Supplement 7/85 Bull EC (*Second Addoninno Report*).

Council of Europe, *Standing Committee of Transfrontier Television Final Version of the Discussion Document prepared by the Delegate of Austria on Questions concerning Advertising, Sponsorship and Teleshopping* (T-TT (2004)013).

Compilation of responses to the questionnaire on 'Big Brother' type programmes, European Convention on Transfrontier Television, Standing Committee on Transfrontier Television (T-TT(2002) 9).

European Convention on Transfrontier Television, Standing Committee on Transfrontier Television, Opinion No.1/2002 of the Conseil Supérieur de l'Audiovisuel of the French Community of Belgium.

Opinions and Recommendations adopted by the Standing Committee on Transfrontier Television, Statement no. 1 on human dignity and the fundamental rights of others, 2002.

Recommendation of the Committee of Ministers to member states on self-regulation concerning cyber content, self-regulation and user protection against illegal or harmful content on new communications and information services, R(2001)8.

Recommendation of the Committee of Ministers to Member States on the Guarantee of the Independence of Public Service Broadcasting, R (96) 10.

The Media in a Democratic Society: Draft Resolutions and Draft Political Declaration, 1994.

Steering Committee on the Mass Media (CDMM), Committee of Experts on Media Policy, *Final activity report on the possibility of reaching agreement on a legal instrument relating to direct broadcasting by satellite DBS*, Document MM-PO (82) 24 (Strasbourg, 1982).

Craufurd Smith, R., 'Rethinking European Union Competence in the Field of Media Ownership: The Internal Market, Fundamental Rights and European Citizenship', *European Law Review* 29(5) (2004), 652–72.

'Article 151 EC and European Identity' in Craufurd Smith (ed.), *Culture and European Union Law* (Oxford: Oxford University Press, 2004).

'Sex and Violence in the Internal Market: The Impact of European Community Law on Television Programme Standards', *Contemporary Issues in Law* (1998), 135–53.

Craufurd Smith, R. and Böttcher, B., 'Football and Fundamental Rights: Regulating Access to Major Sporting Events on Television', *European Public Law* 8(1) (2002), 107–33.

Crisell, A., *Understanding Radio* (London: Methuen, 1986).

Crystal, D., *Language Death* (Cambridge: Cambridge University Press, 2000).

Curran, J., 'Mass Mass Media and Democracy: A Reappraisal', in J. Curran, and M. Gurevitch (eds.), *Mass Media and Society* (London: Edward Arnold, 2000), pp. 82–117.

'Television and the Public Sphere', in P. Holland, *The TV Handbook* (London, Routledge 1997).

Curran, J. and Gurevitch, M. (eds.), *Mass Media and Society* (London: Edward Arnold, 2000).

Curran, J. and Seaton, J., *Power without Responsibility* (London: Routledge, 2003).

Dabziger, K., *Socialization* (London: Harmondsworth, 1971).

Dahlgren, P., *Television and the Public Sphere: Citizenship, Democracy and the Media* (London: Sage, 1995).

Dashwood, A., 'The Relationship between the Member States and the European Union/European Community', *Common Market Law Review* 41(2) (2004), 355–81.

David Graham and Associates Limited, *Study on the Impact of Measures concerning the Promotion and the Distribution and Production of TV Programmes (Community and National) provided for under Article 25(a) of the 'Television without Frontiers Directive'*, 2005 available http://europa.eu.int/comm/avpolicy/stat/studi_en.htm#3

Depypere, S. and Tigchelaar, N., 'The Commission's State Aid Policy on Activities of Public Service Broadcasters in Neighbouring Markets', *Competition Policy Newsletter*, 2 Summer (2004), 19–22.

de Streel A., 'European Merger Policy in Electronic Communications Markets: Past Experience and Future Prospects', *The 30th Research Conference on Information, Communication and Internet Policy*, Virginia, 28–30 September 2002.

'The Protection of the European Citizen in a Competitive E-Society: The New E.U. Universal Service Directive', *Journal of Network Industries*, 4(2) (2003), 189.

'Market Definitions in the New European Regulatory Framework for Electronic Communications', *Info* 5(3) (2003), 27–47.

de Vries, S., 'Public Service, Diversity and Freedom of Expression and Competition Law', *Culture et Marché ERA-Forum* 1 (2005), 54–5.

De Witte, B., 'Trade in Culture: International Legal Regimes and EU Constitutional Values', in G. de Burca and J. Scott (eds.), *The EU and the WTO: Legal and Constitutional Issues* (Oxford: Hart, 2001).

'The European Content Requirement in the EC Television Directive – Five Years After', *Yearbook of Media and Entertainment Law* 101 (1995), 101–27.

Diss, R., 'The European TV Broadcasting Market', *Eurostat*, Theme 4, 24/2002, http://epp.eurosat.cec.eu.in/cache/ITY_OFFPUB/KS-NP-02-024/EN/KS-NP-02-024-EN.PDF.

d'Olivera, U. J., 'Union Citizenship: Pie in the Sky?', in A. Rosas and E. Anatola (eds.), *A Citizen's Europe* (London: Sage, 1995), pp. 58–84.

Doward, J., 'Sky Digital "Dumps" ITV', *The Observer*, 28 January 2001, 18.

Dutton, W. H., *Society on the Line: Information Politics in the Digital Age* (Oxford: Oxford University Press, 1999).

Eriksen, E. O. and Fossum, J. E., 'Democracy Through Strong Publics in the European Union?', *Journal of Common Market Studies*, 40(3) (2002), 401–24.

Eurocare, *Response to the Issue Paper for the Audiovisual Conference in Liverpool: Commercial Communications of Alcoholic Beverages* (2005).

European Broadcasting Union, *EBU contribution to the European Commission's call for input on the forthcoming review of the EU regulatory framework for electronic communications and services*, 30 January 2006.

EBU Comments on the Public Consultation on the EC Commission's Discussion Paper on the Application of Article 82 of the EU Treaty to Exclusionary Abuses, 2006.

EBU Comments on the EU Commission's Proposals for Directives Regarding the Review of the Regulatory Framework for Communication, 2000.

The Report of European Broadcasting Union's (EBU) Perez Group, Conclusions of the TV Programme Committee's Group of Experts on the Future of Public Service Broadcasting (EBU: mimeo, 1983).

European Parliament, *Press Release: How to Modernise European Television Rules*, 20060529, IPR08506, 2 June 2006.

Report on the Application of Articles 4 and 5 of Directive 89/552/EEC, as amended by Directive 97/36/EC for the period 2001–2002 (2004/2236(INI)), A6-0202/2005 (*Weber Report*).

Report on Television without Frontiers (2003/2033(INI)), A5-0251/2003 final, PE 312.581/DEF (*Perry Report*).

Report on the Commission Communication 'Towards a new Framework for Electronic Communications Infrastructure and Associated Services – The 1999 Communications Review' (COM (1999) 539 – C5-0141/2000 – 2000/2085 (COS)).

Motion for a Resolution on the Future of Public Service Television in a Multi-Channel Digital Age, Committee on Culture, Youth, Education and the Media, 11 July 1996, A4-0243/96, 1996.

Resolution on the Role of Public Service Television in a Multi-Media Society, 19 September 1996, A4–0243/96, 1996.

Decision on the Common Position Adopted by the Council with a View to the Adoption of a European Parliament and Council Directive Amending Council Directive 89/552/EC on the Co-ordination of Certain Provisions Laid Down by Law, Regulation or Administrative Action in Member States Concerning the Pursuit of Television Broadcasting Activities (C4-0380/96-95/0074(COD)), A4-346/96, 1996.

Resolution on the Role of the Media, OJ [1985] C 288/113.

Report on radio and television broadcasting in the European Community (Hahn Report), Document 1-1013/81, 1982.

Resolution on radio and television broadcasting the European Community, in European Communities of the European Communities, OJ [1982] C 87/109.

Working Documents, 346/77 (*Scelba Report*, 1977/78).

Faulks, K., *Citizenship in Modern Britain* (Edinburgh: Edinburgh University Press, 1998).

Feintuck, M., *The Public Interest in Regulation* (Oxford: Oxford University Press, 2004).

Media Regulation, Public Interest and the Law (Edinburgh: Edinburgh University Press, 1999).

Fikentscher, A., and Merkel, K., 'Technical Bottlenecks and Public Service Broadcasting', Regulating Access to Digital Television, Strasbourg: European Audiovisual Observatory, *IRIS Special*, 2004.

Franklin, B. (ed.), *British Television Policy: A Reader* (London: Routledge, 2001).

Galperin, H. and Bar, F., 'The Regulation of Interactive Television in the United States and the European Union', *Fed. Comm L.J.* 55 (2002), 61–84.

Garnham, N., 'Information Society Theory as Ideology', in F. Webster, *Information Society Reader* (London: Routledge, 2004), pp. 165–83.

Gauntlett, D., *Moving Experiences: Understanding Television's Influences and Effects* (London: John Libbey, 1995).

George, S. and Bache, I., *Politics in the European Union* (Oxford: Oxford University Press, 2001).

Geradin, D., 'Access to Content by New Media Platforms: A Review of the Competition Law Problems', *Entertainment Law Review* 30(1) (2005), 68–94.

Gibbons, T., 'Control Over Technical Bottlenecks: A Case for Media Ownership Law?', in *Regulating Access to Digital Television, IRIS Special* (Strasbourg: European Audiovisual Observatory, 2004).

'Jurisdiction over (Television) Broadcasters: Criteria for Defining "Broadcaster" and "Content Service Provider"', in A. Rossnagel *et al.* (eds.), *The Future of the 'Television without Frontiers Directive'*, Schriftenreihe des Instituts fur Europäisches Medienrecht (EMR) 29, (2004) pp. 53–61.

'Pluralism, Guidance and the New Media', in C. Marsden (ed.), *Regulating the Global Information Society* (London: Routledge, 2000), pp. 304–15.

'Concentrations of Ownership and Control in a Converging Media Industry', in C. Marsden and S. Verhulst (eds.), *Convergence in European Digital TV Regulation* (London: Blackstone Press, 1999), pp. 155–73.

Media Regulation (London: Sweet & Maxwell, 1998).

Gibson, O., 'Setanta Starts Fund Raising and Seeks New Investor', *Guardian*, 24 May 2006, www.media.guardian.co.uk/print/O,,329487802-105236,00.html/

'BBC and BSkyB Settle Satellite Dispute', *Guardian*, 13 June 2003, www.media.guardian.co.uk/print/0, 3294 77801-105236, 00. html/

Giddens, A., *The Nation State and Violence* (Cambridge: Polity Press, 1985).

Gomery, D., 'The FCC's Newspaper-broadcast Cross-ownership Rules: An Analysis', (Washington DC: Economic Policy Institute, 2002), www.epinet.org/books/cross-ownership.pdf

Gormley, L., *Prohibiting Restrictions on Trade within the EEC* (North Holland: Elsevier Science Publishers B.V., 1985).

Graham, A. 'Broadcasting Policy in the Multimedia Age', in A. Graham, C. Kobaldt, S. Hogg, B. Robinson, D. Currie, M. Siner, G. Mather, J. Le Grand, B. New and I. Corfield (eds.), *Public Purposes in Broadcasting* (Luton: University of Luton Press, 1999), pp. 17–45.

Gunter, B., 'Avoiding Unsavoury Television', *The Psychologist* 13(4) (2000), 194–9. 'Media Violence: Social Problem or Political Scapegoat?', *Inaugural Lecture*, Department of Journalism Studies: University of Sheffield, 1995.

Gunter, B., Harrison, J. and Wykes, M., *Violence on Television: Distribution, Form, Context and Themes* (Mahwah, NJ: Lawrence Erlbaum Associates, 2003).

Habermas, J., *Structural Transformation of the Public Sphere* (Cambridge: Polity Press, 1989).

Hall, S., 'Coding and Encoding in the Television Discourse', in S. Hall, D. Hobson, A. Lowe and P. Willis (eds.), *Culture, Media, Language* (London: Hutchinson, 1980), pp. 197–208.

Halloran, J., *The Effects of Television* (London: Panther, 1969).

Hans Bredow Institut Study on Co-regulatory Measures in the Media Sector, *Interim Report, Study for the European Commission, Directorate Information Society*, 19 May 2005, http://europa.eu.int/comm/avpolicy/stat/2005/coregul/coregul-interim-report.pdf

Harcourt, A., 'Regulation of European Media Markets; Approaches of the European Court of Justice and the Commission's Merger Task Force', *Utilities Law Review* 9(6) (1998), 276–91.

The European Union and the Regulation of Media Markets (Manchester: Manchester University Press, 2005).

Hargreaves, I., *Journalism: Truth or Dare* (Oxford: Oxford University Press, 2003).

Harrison, J. and Woods, L., 'Defining European Public Service Broadcasting', *European Journal of Communications*, 16(4) (2001), 477–504.

'Television Quotas: Protecting European Culture?', *Entertainment Law Review* (2001), 5–14.

'European Citizenship: Can European Audiovisual Policy Make a Difference?', *Journal of Common Market Studies* 38(3) (2000), 471–94.

Helberger, N., Scheuer, A. and Strothmann, P., 'Non-discriminatory Access to Digital Access Control Services', *IRIS Plus* (2001).

Helberger, N. and Springsteen, A., '*Summary of the Discussion' Regulating Access to Digital Television* (Strasbourg: European Audiovisual Observatory, 2004).

Held, V., *The Public Interest and Individual Interests* (New York: Basic Books, 1970).

Hell Hansen, L., 'The Development of the Circumvention Principle in the Area of Broadcasting', *Legal Issues of European Integration*, 25(2) (1998), 111–38.

Herman, E. and McChesney, R., *The Global Media* (London: Cassell, 1997).

Hervey, T., 'Mapping the Contours of European Union Health Law and Policy', *European Public Law* 8(1) (2002), 69–105.

Hoffmann-Riem, W., *Regulating Media: The Licensing and Supervision of Broadcasting in Six Countries* (London: The Guildford Press, 1996).

Hörnle, J., 'County of Origin Regulation in Cross-border Media: One Step Beyond the Freedom to Provide Services?', 54 *International and Comparative Law Quarterly* 89, (2005), 89–126.

Howells, G. and Wilhelmsson, T., *European Consumer Law* (Aldershot: Ashgate, 1997).

Hrbek, R., Oppermann, T. and Starbatty, J. (eds.), *Integration Europas und Ordnung der Weltwitschaft* (Baden-Baden: Nomos Verlagsgesellschaft, 2002).

Isin, E. and Wood, P., *Citizenship and Identity* (London: Sage, 1999).

ITC, *Guidance to Broadcasters on the Regulation of Interactive Television Services* (February 2001).

Programme Complaints and Findings Report 22, 8 September 2003, available at: www.ofcom.org.uk/static/archive/itc/uploads/PROGRAMME_COMPLAINTS_BULLETIN_NO_22.doc

Kaitatzi-Whitlock, S., 'The Privatising of Conditional Access Control', *Communications and Strategies* 25 (1997), 91–124.

Katsirea, I., 'Why the European Broadcasting Quota Should be Abolished', *European Law Review* 28(2) (2003), 190–209.

Keller, D. and Verhulst, S. G., 'Parental Control in a Converged Communications Environment: Self-Regulation, Technical Devices and Meta-Information', *Final Report for the DVB Regulatory Group* (Oxford: Programme in Comparative Media Law and Policy, University of Oxford, 2000).

Kelman, M., 'Legal Economists and Normative Social Theory', in *A Guide to Critical Legal Studies* (Cambridge, Mass.: Harvard University Press, 1987).

Kjellgren, A., 'On the Border of Abuse: The Jurisprudence of the European Court of Justice on Circumvention, Fraud and Abuses of Community Law', in M. Andenas and W. H. Roth (eds.), *Services and Free Movement in EU Law* (Oxford: Oxford University Press, 2002).

Kocsis, K., 'Ethnicity', in D. Turnock (ed.), *East Central Europe and the Former Soviet Union* (London: Arnold, 2001), pp. 88–103.

Krcmar, M. and Cantor, J., 'The Role of Television Advisories and Ratings in Parent–Child Discussions of Television Viewing Choices', *Journal of Broadcasting and Electronic Media*, 41 (1977), 393–411.

Krebber, D., *Europeanisation of Regulatory Television Policy: The Decision-Making Process of the Television Without Frontiers Directive from 1989 and 1997* (Baden-Baden: Nomos Verlagsgesellschaft, 2002).

Kunkel, D., 'Why Content, not Age of Viewers, Should Control what Children Watch on TV', *The Chronicle of Higher Education*, XLIII(21) (1997), B4–B5.

Kymlicka, W., *Multicultural Citizenship* (Oxford: Oxford Univesity Press, 1995).

Larouche, P., *Competition Law and Regulation in European Telecommunications* (Oxford: Hart Publishing, 2000).

Laswell, H., 'The Structure and Function of Communication in Society', in W. Schramm and D. Roberts (eds.), *The Process and Effects of Mass Communication* (Urbana: University of Illinois Press, 1948).

Le Grand, J. and New, B., 'Broadcasting and Public Purposes in the New Millennium', in A. Graham, C. Kobaldt, S. Hogg, B. Robinson, D. Currie, M. Siner, G. Mather, J. Le Grand, B. New and I. Corfield (eds.), *Public Purposes in Broadcasting* (Luton: University of Luton Press, 1999), pp. 113–36.

Lessig, L., 'The Zones of Cyberspace', *Stanford Law Review*, 48 (1996), 1403–11.
The Future of Ideas: The Fate of the Commons in a Connected World (London: Random House: 2001).

Levy, D., *Europe's Digital Revolution: Broadcasting, Regulation, the EU and the Nation State* (London: Routledge, 1999).

Lewis, G., 'Citizenship', in G. Hughes (ed.), *Imagining Welfare Futures* (London: Routledge/Open University Press, 1998), pp. 103–50.

Lippmann, W., *Public Opinion* (New York: Harcourt, 1922).

Lowe, G. F. and Hujanen, T., *Broadcasting and Convergence: New Articulations of the Public Service Remit* (Göteborg: Nordicom, 2003).

Lupinnaci, T., 'The Pursuit of Television Broadcasting Activities in the European Community: Cultural Preservation or Economic Protectionism?', *Vanderbilt Journal of Transnational Law*, 24 (1991), 113–54.

McCallen, L., 'EC Competition Law and Digital Television', *Competition Newsletter*, 1 February 1999, 4–16.

McCombs, M. E., 'The Agenda-Setting Approach', in D. D. Nimmo and K. R. Sanders (eds.), *Handbook of Political Communication* (California: Sage, 1981).

McCombs, M. E. and Shaw, D. L., 'The Agenda-Setting Function of Mass Media', *Public Opinion Quarterly*, 36 (1972), 176–87.
'The Evolution of Agenda-Setting Research: Twenty-Five Years in the Marketplace of Ideas', *Journal of Communication* 43:2 (1993), 58–67.

McGonagle, T., 'Changing Aspects of Broadcasting: New Territory and New Challenges', *IRIS Plus* 10 (2001).
'Co-Regulation of the Media in Europe: The Potential for Practice of an Intangible Idea', *Iris Plus* (2002).

McKinsey and Company, *Review of Public Service Broadcasting around the World* (London: McKinsey and Company, 2004).

McQuail, D., *McQuail's Mass Communication Theory* (London: Sage, 2005).
McQuail's Reader in Mass Communication Theory (London: Sage, 2002).

Media Performance: Mass Communication and the Public Interest (London, Sage, 1992).

Marenco, G., 'The Notion of Restriction on the Freedom of Establishment and the Provision of Services in the Case-Law of the Court', *Yearbook of European Law*, 11 (1991), 111–50.

Marsden, C., 'Introduction: Information and Communications Technologies, Globalisation and Regulation', in C. Marsden (ed.), *Regulating the Global Information Society* (London: Routledge, 2000), pp. 1–40.

'The European Digital Convergence Paradigm: From Structural Regulation to Behavioural Competition Law?', *Journal of Information Law and Technology*, 3 (1997), available on-line.

Marshall, T. H., 'Citizenship and Social Class', in T. H. Marshall, *Class, Citizenship and Social Development* (Greenwood: Westport, 1973).

Mastrioanni, R., 'Commentary on Case C-6/98 *Arbeitsgemeinschaft Rundfunkanstalten* (ARD) v. *PRO Sieben Media AG*', *Common Market Law Review* 37 (2000), 1445–64.

Masuda, Y., 'Image of the Future Information Society', in F. Webster (ed.), *Information Society Reader* (London: Routledge, 2004), pp. 15–20.

Mayer-Robitaille, L., 'Application of EC Competition Policy regarding Agreements and State Aid in the Audiovisual Field', *IRIS Plus* (Strasbourg: Audiovisual Observatory, 2005).

Miliband, R., *The State in Capitalist Society: The Analysis of the Western System of Power* (London: Quartet Books, 1973).

Mill, J. S., 'On Liberty', in S. Collini (ed.), *On Liberty and Other Writings* (Cambridge: Cambridge University Press, 1989), pp. 1–116.

Monro, C., 'The Value of Commercial Speech', *Cambridge Law Journal* (2003), 62(1), 134–58.

Monti, G., 'Article 82 and New Economy Markets', in O. Graham and F. Smith (eds.), *Competition, Regulation and the New Economy* (Oxford: Hart, 2004), 17–54.

'Article 81 EC and Public Policy', *Common Market Law Review* 39(5) (2002), 1057–99.

Morley, D., *The 'Nationwide' Audience* (London: British Film Institute, 1980).

Morley, D. and Brunsden, C., *Everyday Television: The 'Nationwide' Study* (London: British Film Institute, 1978).

Mulgan, G., 'Television's Holy Grail: Seven Types of Quality', in G. Mulgan (ed.), *The Question of Quality* (London: BFI, 1990), pp. 4–32.

Murdoch, G. and Golding, P., 'Corporate Ambitions and Communication Trends in the UK and Europe', *Journal of Media Economics*, 12(2) (1999), 117–32.

Murdock, G. and Golding, P., 'For a Political Economy of Communications', in R. Miliband and J. Saville (eds.), *The Socialist Register* (London: Merlin Press, 1973), pp. 205–34.

Murroni, C. and Irvine, N. (eds.), *Quality in Broadcasting* (London: IPPR, 1997).

Negrine, R. and Papathanassopoulos, S., *The Internationalisation of Television* (London: Pinter, 1990).

Nitsche, I., *Broadcasting in the European Union: The Role of Public Interest in Competition Analysis* (The Hague: T.M.C. Asser Press, 2001).

Nordic Public Service Broadcasters, *Comments on the Review of the 'Television without Frontiers' Directive*, 2006, www.europarl.europa.eu/

Norris, P., 'The Digital Divide', in F. Webster (ed.), *Information Society Reader* (London: Routledge, 2004), pp. 273–86.

A Virtuous Circle (Cambridge: Cambridge University Press, 2000).

Odudu, O., 'A New Economic Approach to Article 81(1)', *European Law Review*, 27 (2002), 100–5.

OECD, Competition Policy Roundtables: Media Mergers, 19 September 2003, DAFFE/COMP (2003), 16.

Ofcom, *Ofcom Position Paper, European Works*, www.europarl.europa.eu/, 24 April 2006.

Ofcom Special Report, *Consumer Engagement with Digital Communication Services*, www.ofcom/org.uk/research/cm/consumer_engagement/, 2006.

Oftel, *Ensuring Access on Fair Reasonable and Non-discriminatory Terms* (London: OFTEL, 1999).

Ogus, A., *Regulation: Legal Form and Economic Theory* (Oxford: Clarendon Press, 1994).

Outhwaite, W. (ed.), *The Habermas Reader* (Cambridge: Polity Press, 1996).

Palzer, C., 'Co-regulation of the Media in Europe: European Provisions for the Establishment of Co-regulation Frameworks', *IRIS Plus* (2002).

Papathanassopoulos, S., *European Television in the Digital Age* (Cambridge: Polity Press, 2000).

Peacock Committee, *Report on Financing the BBC*, Cmnd 9824, 1986.

Postman, N., *Amusing Ourselves to Death* (London: Methuen, 1985).

Potter, W. J., *On Media Violence* (London: Sage, 1999).

Ritter, C., 'Refusal to Deal and Essential Facilities: Does Intellectual Property Require Special Deference Compared to Tangible Property?', *World Competition*, 28(3) (2005), 281–98.

Roche, M., 'Mega-events, Time and Modernity: On Time-structures in Global Society', *Time and Society*, 12(1) (2003) 99–126.

Rethinking Citizenship (Cambridge: Polity Press, 1992).

Roche, M. and Harrison, J., 'Cultural Europeanisation Through Regulation?: The Case of Media-sport in the EU', *Working Paper presented at the IAMCR Conference*, Media Sport Working Group (Barcelona, 2002).

Ross, M., 'State Aids and National Courts: Definitions and Other Problems – A Case of Premature Emancipation?', *Common Market Law Review* 37 (2000), 401–23.

Roukens, T., 'What are We Carrying Across the EU These Days? Comments on the Interpretation and Practical Implementation of Article 31 of the Universal Service Directive', in *To Have or Not To Have Must-Carry Rules, IRIS Special* (Strasbourg: European Audiovisual Observatory, 2005).

Rouse, L., 'The BBC's Vision Thing', *Broadcast*, 28 July 2006, 15.

Sampson, T. and Lugo, J., 'The Discourse of Convergence: A Neo-liberal Trojan Horse', in G. Ferrell Low and T. Hujanen (eds.), *Broadcasting and Convergence* (Goteborg: Nordicom, 2003), pp. 83–92.

Santamato, S. and Pesaresi, N., 'Compensation for Services of General Economic Interest: Some Thoughts on the Altmark Ruling', *Competition Policy Newsletter*, 1, Spring 2001, 17–21.

Sarikakis, K., *Powers in Media Policy* (Oxford: Peter Lang, 2004).

Sauter, W., 'The Role of European Economic Law in the Information Society: Balancing Private Freedoms and Public Interests in the Context of Convergence between Telecommunications, Media and Information Technology', in P. Nihoul (ed.), *Telecommunications and Broadcasting Networks under EC Law: The Protection Afforded to Consumers and Undertakings in the Information Society* (Bundesanzeiger: Köln, 2000), pp. 286–309.

Sauter, W. and Vos, E., 'Harmonisation under Community Law: The Comitology Issue', in C. Harlow and P. Craig (eds.), *Lawmaking in the European Union* (The Hague: Kluwer Law International, 1998).

Scannel, P. and Cardiff, D., *A Social History of British Broadcasting: Volume 1 1922–1939* (London: Basil Blackwell, 1991).

Scheuer, A. and Strothmann, P., *Media Supervision on the Threshold of the 21st Century: What are the Requirements of Broadcasting, Telecommunications and Concentration Regulation?* (Strasbourg: European Audiovisual Observatory, 2001).

Schiller, H., *Information Inequality* (New York, Routledge, 1996).

Schuman, G., *Regulation of Advertising in the New Television without Frontiers Directive: Background Paper for the Plenary EPRA/2001/08*, 26–8 September 2001.

Shelanski, H., 'The Policy Limits of Markets: Antitrust Law as Mass Media Regulation', *Law and Economics Workshop Paper 7* (Berkeley: University of California, 2003).

Shoemaker, P., and Cohen, A., *News Around The World* (New York: Routledge, 2006).

Shore, C. and Wright, S. (eds.), *Anthropology of Policy* (London: Routledge, 1997).

Slot, P. J., 'Harmonization', *European Law Review* 21 (1997), 378.

Smith, A., *The Shadow in the Cave* (London: Allen & Unwin, 1973).

Smith, F. and Woods, L., 'The GATS and Audiovisual Sector', *Communications Law Review* 9(1) (2004), 15–21.

Smythe, D. W., 'Communications Blindspot of Western Marxism', *Canadian Journal of Political and Social Theory*, 1 (1977), 120–7.

Sorauf, F., 'The Conceptual Muddle', in C. J. Friedrich (ed.), *The Public Interest* (New York: Atherton Press, 1962).

Steiner, J., 'Drawing the Line: Uses and Abuses of Article 30 EEC', *Common Market Law Review* 29 (1992), 749.

Steiner, J. Woods, L. and Twigg-Flesner, C., *EU Law*, 9th edn (Oxford: Oxford University Press, 2006).

Swaine, E. T., 'Subsidiarity and Self-Interest, Federalism at the European Court of Justice', *Harvard International Law Journal* 41 (2001), 1.

Thompson, J. B., *The Media and Modernity: A Social Theory of the Media* (Cambridge; Polity Press, 1995).

Ideology and Modern Culture: Critical Social Theory in the Era of Mass Communication (Cambridge: Cambridge University Press, 1992).

Tigchelaar, N., 'State Aid to Public Broadcasting Revisited: An Overview of the Commission's Practice', *European State Aid Law Quarterly* 2 (2003), 169–81.

Timms, D., 'Sky: We'd Pay the Same again for TV Football', *Media Guardian*, www.mediaguardian.co.uk 7 December 2005.

Toft, T., *Sport and Competition Law*, Comp/C.2/TT/hvds D, 2005.

Tongue Report, appended to the European Parliament Resolution on The Role of Public Service Television in the Multi-Media Society, 19 September, A4-0243/96, 1996.

Tracey, M., *The Decline and Fall of Public Service Broadcasting* (Oxford: Oxford University Press, 1998).

Tridimas, T. and Nebbia, P. (eds.), *European Union Law for the Twenty-first Century: Rethinking the New Legal Order*, vol. 2 (Oxford: Hart Publishing, 2004).

Turner, B. S., 'Outline of a Theory of Citizenship', *Sociology*, 24(2) (1990), 189–217.

Ungerer, H., 'Competition in the Media Sector – How Long Can the Future be Delayed?', *Info* (2005) 7(5) 52–60.

Valcke, P., 'The Future of Must-carry: From Must-carry to a Concept of Universal Service in the Info-Communications Sector', in *To Have or Not To Have Must-Carry Rules, IRIS Special* (Strasbourg: European Audiovisual Observatory, 2005).

van de Gronden, J. W., 'Rule of Reason and Convergence in Internal Market and Competition Law', in A. Schrauwen (ed.), *Rule of Reason: Rethinking Another Classic of European Legal Doctrine* (Groningen: Europa Law Publishing, 2005), pp. 79–94.

van Velzen Report *on the Commission Communication 'Towards a new Framework for Electronic Communications Infrastructure and Associated Services – The 1999 Communications Review'* (COM (1999) 539 – C5-0141/2000 – 2000/2085 (COS)).

Varney, M., 'European Controls on Member State Promotion and Regulation of Public Service Broadcasting and Broadcasting Standards', *European Public Law* 10(3) (2004), 503–30.

Verhulst, S. G., 'Protection of Minors in the Media', in A. Rossnagel (ed.), *Television and New Media in Europe: Legislation, Liberalisation, Self-Regulation*, Schriftenreihe des Instituts für Europäisches Medienrecht, 22 (Munich and Berlin: Jehle Rehur, 2001), pp. 35–52.

Von Bogdandy, A. and Bast, J., 'The European Union's Vertical Order of Competences: The Current Law and Proposals for its Reform', *Common Market Law Review* 39 (2002), 227–68.

Walden, I., 'European Union Telecommunications Law', in I. Walden and J. Angel (eds.), *Telecommunications Law* (London: Blackstone Press, 2001).

Waldron, J., 'Minority Culture and the Cosmopolitan Alternative', *University of Michigan Journal of Law Reform* 25 (1992), 751.

Wallace, H., 'The European that Came in from the Cold', *International Affairs*, 67(4) (1991), 648–64.

Wallace, H. and Wallace, W., *Policy-Making in the European Union* (Oxford: Oxford University Press, 1996).

Ward, D., *The European Union Democratic Deficit and Public Sphere: An Evaluation of EU Media Policy* (Oxford: IOS Press, 2004).

Ward, S. J. A., *The Invention of Journalism Ethics: The Path to Objectivity and Beyond* (Montreal and Kingston: McGill-Queen's University Press, 2004).

Weatherill, S., 'Better Competence Monitoring', *European Law Review* 30(1) (2005), 23–41.

'Why Harmonise?', in T. Tridimas and P. Nebbia (eds.), *European Union Law for the Twenty-first Century: Rethinking the New Legal Order*, vol. 2 (Oxford: Hart Publishing, 2004).

'Sport as Culture in EC Law', in R. Craufurd Smith (ed.), *Culture and European Union Law* (Oxford: Oxford University Press, 2004).

EC Consumer Law and Policy (London and New York: Longman, 1997).

Webster, F., *The Information Society Reader* (London: Routledge, 2004).

Weiler, J. and Lockhart, N., '"Taking Rights Seriously" Seriously: The European Court and its Fundamental Rights Jurisprudence', *Common Market Law Review* 32 (1995), 51–94 and 579–627.

Wells, M., 'BBC Defends Digital Ratings as MP Criticises "Bribery"', *Guardian*, 8 January 2003.

Wesseling, R., 'The Rule of Reason and Competition Law: Various Rules, Various Reasons', in A. Schrauwen (ed.), *Rule of Reason: Rethinking another Classic of European Legal Doctrine* (Groningen: Europa Law Publishing, 2005), pp. 59–76.

Wichmann, A., 'Electronic Programme Guides: A Comparative Study of the Regulatory Approach Adopted in the United Kingdom and Germany, Part 1',
C.T.L.R. 19(1) (2004), 16–23.

Wiener, A. and Della Sala, V., 'Constitution-making and Citizenship Practice: Bridg-
ing the Democracy Gap in the EU?', *Journal of Common Market Studies*, 35(4)
(1997), 595–614.

Williams, K., *Understanding Media Theory* (London: Arnold, 2002).

Williams, R., *Culture and Society* (Harmondsworth: Penguin, 1958).

Wilson, B. J., Linz, D. and Randall, B., 'Applying Social Science Research to Film
Ratings: A Shift from Offensiveness to Harmful Effects', *Journal of Broadcasting and Electronic Media*, 34 (1990), 443–68.

Winston, B., *Media Technology and Society: A History: From the Telegraph to the
Internet* (London: Routledge, 1998).

Woldt, R., *Perspectives of Public Service Television in Europe* (Düsseldorf: European
Institute for the Media, 1998).

Woods, L., 'The Application of Competition Rules to State Aids for Culture', in
Culture et Marché ERA-Forum, 1 (2005), pp. 37–45.

Free Movement of Goods and Services within the European Community (Aldershot:
Ashgate, 2004).

'Culture in the European Union', in M. van Empel (ed.), *From Paris to Nice: Fifty
Years of Integration in Europe* (Leiden: Kluwer Law International, 2003), pp.
109–29.

Woods, L. and Scheuer, A., 'Advertising Frequency and the Television without
Frontiers Directive', *European Law Review* 29 (2004), 366–84.

Woods, L. and Scholes, J., 'Broadcasting: The Creation of a European Culture or the
Limits of the Internal Market?', *Yearbook of European Law* 18 (1997), 47–82.

Writers Guild of America, west, *Press Release*, 'Entertainment Guilds Call for Industry Code of Conduct or FCC Regulation for Product Integration in Programming and Film – Guilds Issue White Paper Report on the Runaway Use of
Stealth Advertising in Television and Film', 14 November 2005, available at
www.wga.org/subpage_newsevents.aspx?id = 1422

Wyatt, D., 'The Growing Competence of the European Community', *European Business Law Review* 16(3) (2005), 483–8.

INDEX